ISBN 978-1-333-68219-4
PIBN 10528494

This book is a reproduction of an important historical work. Forgotten Books uses
state-of-the-art technology to digitally reconstruct the work, preserving the original format
whilst repairing imperfections present in the aged copy. In rare cases, an imperfection in
the original, such as a blemish or missing page, may be replicated in our edition. We do,
however, repair the vast majority of imperfections successfully; any imperfections that
remain are intentionally left to preserve the state of such historical works.

1 MONTH OF
FREE
READING

at
www.ForgottenBooks.com

By purchasing this book you are eligible for one month membership to ForgottenBooks.com, giving you unlimited access to our entire collection of over 1,000,000 titles via our web site and mobile apps.

To claim your free month visit:
www.forgottenbooks.com/free528494

English
Français
Deutsche
Italiano
Español
Português

www.forgottenbooks.com

Mythology Photography **Fiction**
Fishing Christianity **Art** Cooking
Essays Buddhism Freemasonry
Medicine **Biology** Music **Ancient
Egypt** Evolution Carpentry Physics
Dance Geology **Mathematics** Fitness
Shakespeare **Folklore** Yoga Marketing
Confidence Immortality Biographies
Poetry **Psychology** Witchcraft
Electronics Chemistry History **Law**
Accounting **Philosophy** Anthropology
Alchemy Drama Quantum Mechanics
Atheism Sexual Health **Ancient History**
Entrepreneurship Languages Sport
Paleontology Needlework Islam
Metaphysics Investment Archaeology
Parenting Statistics Criminology
Motivational

HISTORY

OF

C A S T I N E ,

PENOBSCOT, AND BROOKSVILLE,

MAINE;

INCLUDING THE ANCIENT SETTLEMENT

OF

𝔓entagöet ;

BY

GEORGE AUGUSTUS WHEELER, A. M., M. D.

———•◦•———

" *One of those old Towns—with a History.*"—HOLMES.

———•◦•———

BANGOR:
BURR & ROBINSON.
1875.

as to excellence, are due solely to the character of the original negatives, and not at all to the heliotype process. The wood-cut of the Normal School House was kindly loaned by the State authorities. The wood-cuts of the Forts were made by an *amateur* engraver of this town, and are his first attempts. I am, with regret, obliged to omit the valuable and well-executed Plan of the Cemetery, prepared by Mr. Alfred Adams, of this town. The scale upon which it was necessarily drawn is so large that when reduced to the proper size for a book, the references are illegible. I am in hopes, however, that the citizens of the town will have it furnished to them in a more suitable form for reference, than it would have had in this volume.

To the friends who have assisted me in the prosecution of this work, I take the present opportunity of acknowledging my indebtedness. I have received favors from too many individuals, to specify them *all* by name; but it affords me great pleasure to acknowledge my special indebtedness to Mr. Alexander W. Longfellow, of the U. S. Coast Survey, for the many facilities he has furnished me in this undertaking; to Honorable Joseph Williamson, of Belfast, for his almost unexampled generosity in furnishing me with many valuable documents and references, relating to the period of the French occupation of this territory—the fruit of many years of labor on his part, and intended for his own use; to Mr. G. H. Snelling, and Honorable J. Wingate Thornton, of Boston; and Mr. Hosea B. Wardwell, of Penobscot, for many old documents preserved in their families; and to Messrs. Joseph L. Stevens, M. D., Samuel Adams, Honorable Charles J. Abbott, George H. and William H. Witherle, Samuel T. Noyes, Charles J. Whiting, Reverend Alfred E. Ives, and Philip J. Hooke, of this town, for their suggestions and aid.

It is also proper that I should, in this connection, acknowledge to the public the great obligations that I have been under to my brother,—the late William A. Wheeler, of the Boston Public Library. It is in no slight degree due to his kindly interest that I have been led to persevere in my somewhat laborious employment, and his assistance and advice have been at all times freely extended to me—as they were, indeed, to all who sought them. Had he lived, this volume would have received, in its revision as it went through the press, the benefit of his experience and conscientious care. The task had but just been commenced when his earthly career was terminated.

In preparing this History, I have had somewhat in view the benefit such a work would be to the rising generation of this town. I trust the perusal of its pages may tend to increase the already well known affection of its children for the place of their nativity, or adoption. Although not myself "to the manor born," my interest in the town in which I have taken up my abode, can hardly be surpassed.

To the citizens of Castine, therefore, without whose liberality this book might never have been published, to whom I am indebted for many acts of kindness, and around whose beautiful town cluster so many ancient and interesting associations, I offer this volume as a token of gratitude and respect.

CASTINE, MAINE, January 20, 1875.

G. A. W.

LIST OF AUTHORITIES CONSULTED.

Acadie—Murdock's.
Acadie—Whipple's.
Account of Capture of Castine—Sherbrook.
Account of Centennial Celebration at Bangor, Maine.
Ancient Dominions of Maine—Sewall.
Annals of Warren—Eaton.
America; or Description of New World—Ogilby.
Belknap's Biography.
British Plutarch.
Boston Journal, November, 1850.
Biographical Sketches of Loyalists of the American Revolution—Sabine.
Castine Newspapers, Files of
Champlain's Voyages.
Courts and Lawyers of Maine—Willis.
Collections of Maine Historical Society.
Collections of Mass. Historical Society.
Da Costa's Mount Desert.
Drake's Book of the Indians.
Drake's Dictionary of American Biog.
Dwight's Travels.
Early Settlement of Acadia by the Dutch—De Peyster.
Farmer's Almanac, 1795—Robert B. Thomas.
Field Book of the Revolution-Lossing.
Field Book of the War of 1812-Lossing.
Geological Survey of Maine—Jackson.
History—Botta's.
History of Camden—Eaton.
History of Hancock Lodge, F. & A. M. Webster.
History of Maine—Sullivan.
History of Maine—Williamson.
History of Mass.—Hutchinson.
History of the Navy—Peterson.
History of Newbury—Coffin.

History of New England—Coolidge and Mansfield.
History (Geographical) of Nova Scotia. London, 1749.
History of Plymouth Colony-Bradford.
History of Portland—Willis.
History of Thomaston, So. Thomaston, and Rockland—Eaton.
History of Virginia—Smith.
Historical Magazine.
Incidents in the Life of Samuel A. Whitney.
Journal of the Revolutionary War—Thatcher.
Journal of the Siege of Penobscot—Calef.
La Hontan's Voyages.
Life and Writings of Washington—Appendix 3—Sparks.
Maine Register, 1874.
Memorials of English and French Commissaries, concerning the Limits of Nova Scotia or Acadia.
New France—CharleVoix.
Niles's Weekly Register, 1814-15.
Pennsylvania Journal, 1775.
Providence Patriot, 1815.
Remarks upon a Copper Plate—Read before the Am. Antiq. Soc. by Charles Folsom, Esq.
Reports of Adjutant General of Maine, 1861, 1866.
Statistical Views of Maine—Greenleaf.
State Papers—Hutchinson.
The Dutch at North Pole and in Maine, De Peyster.
The Neutral French.
Winthrop's Journal.
Wisdom and Policy of the French—London, 1704.

IN MANUSCRIPT.

[In State Department at Boston.]

Governor Pownal's Speech.
Letter to Governor Hancock, 1784, by Mr. Cobb.
Letter to the Executive, 1811, by Judge Parker.

Documents collected in France, by B. Perley Poore.
Massachusetts Letter Book.
Massachusetts Records, Vols. 1 to 17.
Penobscot Expedit'n, Vol. in regard to

vi

William Hutchins's Narrative of the Siege of Penobscot, &c.

Lawrence's Orderly Book.

Perham's Letter from Colonel Brewer.

Account of Burton's escape from Fort George.

New Ireland—original paper.

Topographical Sketch of Castine—Wm. Ballard.

[*Miscellaneous.*]

Church Records of First Parish.

Church Records of First Trinitarian Church.

Custom House Records.

District School Records.

Redhead's Journal of the Siege of Penobscot.

History of Methodism in Castine.

Peters' Field Notes of Survey of Penobscot.

Records of Castine Light Infantry.

Reports of School Committees.

Town Records.

Sundry Letters and Memoranda.

CONTENTS.

PART I.

PENTAGÖET.

CHAP. I. EARLY EXPLORATIONS AND SETTLEMENTS.
CHAP. II. OCCUPATION BY THE FRENCH.
CHAP. III. BARON CASTIN AND FAMILY.
CHAP. IV. FRENCH OCCUPATION FROM 1671 TO 1759.
CHAP. V. WAR OF REVOLUTION—AMERICAN EXPEDITION.
CHAP. VI. WAR OF REVOLUTION—AMERICAN DEFEAT.

PART II.

CASTINE, PENOBSCOT AND BROOKSVILLE.

CHAP. I. TOPOGRAPHY, NATURAL HISTORY, CLIMATOLOGY, &C.
CHAP. II. MUNICIPAL HISTORY OF PENOBSCOT.
CHAP. III. MUNICIPAL HISTORY OF CASTINE.
CHAP. IV. GENERAL AND SOCIAL HISTORY OF CASTINE.
CHAP. V. ECCLESIASTICAL HISTORY.
CHAP. VI. EDUCATIONAL HISTORY OF CASTINE.
CHAP. VII. MILITARY HISTORY—SINCE INCORPORATION OF PENOBSCOT.
CHAP. VIII. COMMERCIAL HISTORY OF CASTINE.
CHAP. IX. ANCIENT BUILDINGS, FORTS, BATTERIES, &C.
CHAP. X. BIOGRAPHICAL SKETCHES.
CHAP. XI. MUNICIPAL HISTORY OF BROOKSVILLE.
CHAP. XII. PRESENT AND FUTURE OF THE THREE TOWNS.

PART III.

DOCUMENTARY.

SECTION I. DOCUMENTS RELATING TO THE ANTE-REVOLUTIONARY PERIOD.
SEC. II. DOCUMENTS RELATING TO THE REVOLUTIONARY PERIOD.
SEC. III. DOCUMENTS RELATING TO THE MUNICIPAL PERIOD.
SEC. IV. APPENDIX.

LIST OF ILLUSTRATIONS.

View of Castine from High Head...........................Frontispiece.

Map of the old Forts and Batteries.............................Page 42.

Map of Castine, Brooksville, and Penobscot........................ " 54.

Castine Village from Normal School House........................ " 84.

Eastern Normal School House.................................. " 148.

Supposed Plan of Fort Pentagöet............................. " 187.

Plan of Fort George.. " 188.

Outline of Battery Griffith.................................. " 191.

Landing Place of the Americans, 1779........................ " 192.

Facsimile of the "Castine Coins"............................ " 194.

Facsimile of the "Copper Plate"............................ " 196.

Portrait of William Hutchings.............................. " 203.

Portrait of Hon. William Abbott............................ " 212.

Portrait of Deacon Samuel Adams............................ " 232.

x

ADDITIONS AND CORRECTIONS.

Page 14, line 15, from bottom, for 'Agoucy' read 'Agoncy.'

Page 19, line 1, from bottom, (also on Pages 37, 40, and 43) for 'Hutchins' read 'Hutchings.'

Page 35, line 10, from top, for 'Ones' read 'One's.'

Page 43, line 3, from bottom, for 'awaited the signal to retreat' read 're- mained until a retreat was ordered.'

Page 55, line 17, from bottom, for 'Alemogin' read 'Algemogin.'

Page 60, line 8, from bottom, for 'were' read 'was.'

Page 74, line 15, from top, for 'town' read 'village.'

Page 92, line 14, from top, for 'Jothan' read 'Jotham.'

Page 99, line 7, from bottom, for 'Sopher's' read 'Soper's.'

Page 103, line 2, from top, for 'phthisis pulmonalis (consumption)' read 'Phthisis Pulmonalis (Consumption).'

Page 103, line 4, for 'Stephens' read 'Stevens.' (Also on Page 143, line 5, from bottom.)

Page 107, several lines, and page 108, line 1, for 'doctor' read 'Doctor.'

Page 107, line 21, from bottom, for 'appoited' read 'appointed.'

Page 108, line 17, from bottom, for 'and Doctor' read 'and of Doctor.'

Page 144, line 15, from top, for 'at' read 'a.'

Page 152, line 10, from top, for 'County' read 'Country.'

Page 166, line 7, from bottom, for 'Samuel' read 'Seth.'

Page 196, line 9, from top, for 'Damæ' read 'Dominæ.'

Page 202, line 16, from top, for 'November 30, 1831,' read 'August 5, 1833.'

Page 204, line 6, from bottom, for 'union,' read 'Union.'

Page 306, line 18, from bottom, for 'constiution' read 'constitution.'

Page 369, lines 1, 2, and 3, from top, under " Co.," for " C " read B."

Page 373, line 11, from bottom, under " Regt.," for " 11th " read " 18th."

NOTE.—The Portrait of Doctor Joseph L. Stevens has been heliotyped, and it was expected up to the present moment that it would appear in this book. It is fully as good as the other illustrations, but on account of their dissatisfaction with it—or for some other reason—the parties who offered to furnish it, now decline to do so. The author still hopes for its insertion—in which case it will be found on Page 222.

PART I.
PENTAGÖET.

"One's heart felt sorrow that it had ever been destroyed."

Pownal.

PENTAGÖET.

CHAPTER I.

SITUATION AND TERRITORIAL LIMITS.—ABORIGINAL IN-
HABITANTS.—ADVENT OF EUROPEANS.—EARLY EX-
PLORATIONS.—MEANING OF THE NAMES APPLIED TO
LOCALITIES.—SETTLEMENT BY PLYMOUTH COLONY.—
PILLAGED BY THE FRENCH.—ATTACK BY AULNEY.

Ancient Pentagöet, situated upon the eastern side of
Penobscot bay and river, may be said to have embraced
the territory now comprised in the three towns of Penobscot, Brooksville and Castine. It composed a part of the
ancient land of the Etchemins, and was occupied, before
the advent of Europeans, by the numerous and powerful
tribe of Tarratines,—as the Penobscot Indians were then
called.

The Tarratines are described as of elegant stature and
of agreeable form. They are said to have been as tall as
the Europeans, and much better proportioned. After the
arrival of the Europeans, they, like all other Indian tribes,
adopted the vices more than they did the virtues of the
white men. They have generally, however, been represented as chaste, constant in marriage, and as much more
peaceable than the other tribes. It has been said of them,
" that no other eastern tribe had treated the English with
so much forbearance and honor," and this too, though their
sympathies and predilections must doubtless have been for
the French. On more than one occasion during the period
of the Indian troubles in New England, they expressed
themselves earnestly for peace, and in at least one war
against them, our own people must have been the first
aggressors. Owing to the labors and teachings of Father
Lauvergat—who was a missionary to them about the year
1721—and of other priests, they were converted to the

3

Catholic faith. They became ultimately the wards of the State, and were limited, territorially, to the islands at Old-town and in the river above, about the year 1796. Note-worthy among their chieftains was Madockawando, both on account of his disposition and personal character, and on account of the influence he exerted over other sachems, and more especially for having been the father-in-law of the Baron de St. Castin. All historians agree, that, though brave, he was peaceably inclined, and that the prisoners under his keeping were remarkably well treated. He assisted Pontneuf at the capture of Casco Fort, in May, 1690. He was also in the attack upon Wells, in 1692. In 1694, he went with Villieu to the attack at Oyster river, Piscataqua, accompanied by two hundred and fifty Indians. They killed or captured nearly one hundred prisoners, and burned twenty houses. In 1736, an attempt was made to prove, by a deed to which his signature was appended, that he was not a sachem of the Penobscots. The weight of evidence is, however, the other way. He died in 1697, and was succeeded by Wenamouet, or Wenaggonet. Orono, who is represented as being a man of very exemplary char-acter, and who is reputed to have been a son of the Baron de St. Castin, was also at one time a sachem of the tribe. The town of Orono, in Penobscot County, com-memorates his name.

The eastern section of Maine, was one of the first por-tions of the continent visited by the early explorers. Penobscot bay and river will be found quite particularly, though very curiously, delineated upon all the early charts. It went by the various names of Agoucy, Norumbegue, Rio Grande (the Great River), Rio Hermoso (the Beauti-ful River), Rio de las Gamas (Deer River), Rio de Gomez (River of Gomez), and Rio Santa Maria. Its appellation of Penobscot was given on account of its rocky shores—penops, in the Indian dialect signifying rocky, and auk, place. [Williamson 1, p. 512.] The meaning of the term Pentagöet, called by the Dutch Pountegouycet [De Peyster, Dutch in Maine, p. 73], applied originally to the peninsula of Majabagaduce by the French, is not known with abso-lute certainty. Dr. J. H. Trumbull, however, is inclined to the opinion that it means " the entrance of the river." He has no doubt of its being an Indian name handed down through the French. The arm of the sea which runs up into the town of Penobscot, between Brooksville and

Castine, and which divided ancient Pentagöet into two nearly equal parts, and which now goes by the name of Bagaduce river, was in former times called by the name of Matchebiguatus. Although undoubtedly an Indian name, it is somewhat singular that no reference can be found to it earlier than the year 1644, [Winthrop's Journal, Vol. 1, p. 220, note], and that no such name is to be found in any of the English or French documents relating to the Castin family, or to Pentagöet. This name has suffered very singular corruption, unless, as is possible though not very probable, two separate and distinct Indian appellations have been confounded. In 1760, it was called Baggadoose; during the Revolution, Maja-bagaduce and Maja-bigaduce. [Me. Hist. Col., Vol. VI, Art. Castine Coins.] Williamson says in his History of Maine, [Vol. 1, p. 71,] that it was named for a French officer by the name of Major Bigayduce. He says subsequently, however, that it is derived from Marche-bagaduce, an Indian word meaning "No good cove." Eaton says, also, that it means "A bad harbor." [Annals of Warren, p. 20, note.] A tradition exists, amongst some of the Penobscot Indians, that the upsetting of a canoe full of Indians, at some remote period, caused great sorrow and distress, and hence the word is thought by some to signify "a place of sorrow." Jacob McGaw, Esq., of Bangor, has stated that it was said by some of the old Indians, to mean "a river having large coves or bays." A Penobscot Indian told Mr. Alexander W. Longfellow, in the summer of 1872, that it was called by them, Ka-bag-a-duce, the meaning of which is, "your daughter is floated out by the tide." Mr. Longfellow also informs us that he has somewhere seen a reference to an Indian of the Kennebec tribe who was called Bagadusett. Doctor J. H. Trumbull, of Connecticut,—reputed to be the ablest living student of the Indian dialects—says, in a letter to the author:—"That the original name was something like Matsi-abagawadoos-et, (Matsi-anbaga ꝸ atœs-ek, as Râle would have written it) and that it means 'at the bad shelter place,' i. e. where there is no safe harbor, I have scarcely a doubt." Of the various meanings given to this name, the latter is probably the correct one. Yet few who have ever sailed up and down the river, even in canoes, would dream of speaking of it as a river having no good coves, though it was doubtless a bad place for the landing of canoes upon this peninsula, especially in an easterly wind.

Champlain is commonly supposed to have been the first European to have landed (about 1604) upon these shores. If, however, any confidence whatever can be placed in the account of Thevet—who is not considered to be a very trustworthy authority—there must have been a French fishing or trading station, prior to the year 1556, in this vicinity, if not within the limits of what was called Pentagöet. [Me. Hist. Col. (Doc. Hist.),Vol. 1, pp. 416 to 419.]

1605. The river and bay were again explored, in the year 1605, by James Rozier, the companion of Weymouth, in honor of whom the cape at the southwestern extremity of the town of Brooksville, received its name. [Me. Hist. Col., Vol. V, p. 384, note.] The Indian name of this cape was Mose-ka-chick, signifying a moose's rump. There is an interesting legend connected with this name. The tale is, that as an Indian was pursuing a moose over the peninsula upon which Castine is situated, it came to the shore, and jumping in, swam across to the other side. The dogs of the Indian were unable to follow the game, but the Indian himself pursued it in a canoe, and succeeded in killing it upon the opposite shore. Upon his return he scattered the entrails of the animal in the water, where they may be seen—in the shape of certain rocks strung along at intervals—even to this day. [Mr. A. W. Longfellow, U. S. Coast Survey.]

1613. In the year 1613, "a new project was formed in France, to get possession of Pentagöet, a river which lies thirty leagues S. W. from St. Croix: with this view a colony duly furnished with missionaries was transported thither." This colony is, however, believed to have settled at Mount Desert. [Geog. Hist. of Nova Scotia, London, 1749, p. 53.] This year Captain Argall, of Virginia, was cast ashore here while on a fishing cruise. He did not remain any length of time. The first French fort was probably erected here about this time. [Ogilby, America, p. 137.]

1614. In the year 1614, Captain John Smith explored this coast, and refers to the French traders being in this vicinity. [Smith's Journal pp. 213-215.]

1626. The first permanent settlement of much consequence, however, was made here in the year 1626, by Isaac Allerton, under direction of the Plymouth Colony of Massachusetts, who established here a trading house for the purpose of bartering for furs with the Indians. This trading house, like all others of that period, was built for defense, and was probably surrounded by a stockade. The Plymouth Colony retained undisturbed possession of it until the year 1632, when it was pillaged by the French.

1632. Early in June of this year, a French vessel, piloted by a wily and treacherous Scotchman, and commanded by a Frenchman from Nova Scotia, named Rosillon, visited the place. The captain pretended he had put into the harbor in distress, and requested permission to repair his vessel and refresh his crew. The crew, finding that the commander of the station was, with most of his men, on a trip to the westward after goods, first examined the arms of the fort to see if they were loaded, and then, seizing their swords and muskets, compelled the surrender of the few remaining keepers of the trading house. They forced them, moreover, to deliver up their goods and help put them on board the vessel. After taking property to the amount of £500, they, upon leaving, said :—" Tell your Master to remember the Isle of Rè," alluding to the brilliant successes of the French at the Isle of Rè, in France, in 1627. [De Peyster, Dutch in Maine, p. 50—also, Williamson's Hist. of Me., Vol. 1, p. 249.]

1635. In the year 1635, Charles de Menou d'Aulney de Charnissy, who was a subordinate officer under General Razillai, the Governor of Acadia, attacked the trading house and drove off its occupants. The Plymouth Colony soon attempted to regain possession, and Captain Girling, of the *Hope*, a ship hired at Ipswich, Massachusetts, accompanied by Miles Standish, attacked the place, but did not force a surrender, although it was only occupied by eighteen men. Had Captain Girling listened to the advice of Standish, and not commenced his attack until he got close in, he might have succeeded. He actually, however, used up all his powder before he got sufficiently near to do any harm. [Bradford's Hist. of Plymouth Col., p. 333.] From this time until the year 1654, the French held undisputed possession of the place.

CHAPTER II.

QUARREL BETWEEN AULNEY AND LA TOUR.—SEVERE
EARTHQUAKE.—LA TOUR'S ATTACK· UPON AULNEY'S
MEN AT MILL.—ATTACK UPON FARM-HOUSE.—WAN-
NERTON KILLED.—AULNEY'S DEATH.—LA TOUR'S
MARRIAGE TO AULNEY'S WIDOW.—LA TOUR'S COM-
MAND OF THE FORT.—CAPTURE BY THE ENGLISH.—
CROMWELL'S PATENT TO LA TOUR.—PENTAGöET SUR-
RENDERED TO THE FRENCH.

1635. General Razillai, commander of Acadia, gave the
subordinate command of all the country to the eastward of
the river St. Croix, to Charles St. Estienne de La Tour,
and of all the country to the westward of that river—
as far as the French claimed—to Monsieur Charles de
Menou d'Aulney. Pentagöet, therefore, came under the
control of Aulney.* After the death of Razillai, which
occurred this same year, Aulney and La Tour quarrelled
in regard to the supreme command in Acadia, which each
claimed. This quarrel lasted many years, and during its
continuance, a bitter contest was waged, with varying success, between these two leaders and their respective adhe-
rents. ˙ La Tour applied for assistance to the government
of Massachusetts. The rulers of that commonwealth gave
their consent to his hiring ships and men to carry on his
contest. He accordingly hired four vessels, and with eighty
men attacked Aulney at St. Croix, who fled to Penobscot.

1638. With the exception of the "Great Earthquake,"
which happened June 1, 1638,—and the motion of which
was felt for twenty days,—nothing of any importance occurred here until 1643.

1643. In this year La Tour attempted the capture of
the place. Although the commander-in-chief of the vessels hired at Boston could not be persuaded to make any
assault upon Aulney, yet thirty of the New England men
went voluntarily with La Tour's men and drove some of
Aulney's force from a mill where they had fortified themselves. Three of Aulney's men were killed in this conflict,

*Commonly, though less correctly, written D'Aulney.

and three of La Tour's men were wounded. [Mass. Hist. Soc. Coll., Vol. 5, 2d Sec., p. 483.] They set the mill on fire, and burned some standing corn. They received a fire from Aulney, however, as they went on board their vessels. [Winthrop's Journal, p. 307.]

1644. In the summer following, La Tour, hearing that the fort was weakly manned and in want of victuals, dispatched Mr. Wannerton, of Piscataqua, and some other English gentlemen who were with him at the time, together with about twenty of his own men, to take Penobscot. They went to a farm house of Aulney's, situated about six miles from the fort.* Wannerton and two of his men knocked at the door of the house. One of the inmates opened the door, when another at once shot Wannerton dead, while a third shot one of Wannerton's companions in the shoulder, but was himself immediately shot dead in return. The rest of the company now came in, took possession of the house, and made the two men who remained, prisoners. After killing all the cattle, they burned the house, and at once embarked for Boston.

On the eighth day of October, articles of peace were concluded between Aulney and John Endicott, Governor of New England. Notwithstanding this treaty, La Tour was allowed to hire vessels to carry supplies to his fort at St. Croix. This gave offense to Aulney, who became troublesome, and seized upon all the vessels he could, that attempted to trade with La Tour.

1651. Aulney retained quiet possession of his fort from this time until his death, which took place in the year 1651. The history of this long-continued and bitter quarrel ends much like a romance, La Tour having married the widow of his foe within one year after the death of the latter. Aulney is said to have been the first to teach the Indians in this region the use of fire-arms. The French settlers at this time were very ignorant and depraved, and were also, excessive bigots in their religion. The government of the place was simply a military despotism. Under such auspices no great progress in the growth of the place could be looked for. After the death of Aulney, La Tour exercised authority over the place for about two years. He was here in person but seldom, however, his principal residence being at St. John, N. B.

*This farm house was probably situated at the head of Northern Bay, near what was subsequently called the Winslow farm. It was between the shore and where Mr. Perkins' store now stands.–See Hutchins's Narrative in Part III.

1654. Pentagöet was taken, in the year 1654, by the English, acting under orders from Cromwell. They retained undisturbed possession for thirteen years. The place was, however, still occupied by the French settlers.

1656. In the year 1656, Cromwell issued a patent to Stephen de La Tour (son of Charles St. Estienne), Sir Thomas Temple, and William Crowne, giving to them the territory called Acadia, which included Penobscot. Subsequently Temple and Crowne purchased all his right and title to the territory from La Tour.

1662. In the year 1662, Colonel Temple left, having surrendered the fort to Captain Thomas Bredion. The latter dismissed Edward Naylor, who had charge of "Negew," in Penobscot, and Lieutenant Gardner, in charge of the fort, together with all the officers and soldiers. [Naylor's Deposition, Part III.]

1667. As a result of the war between England and France, the Province of Nova Scotia was, by the treaty of Breda, surrendered to the French, July 31, 1667.

1668. During the month of February, 1668, another article was added to this treaty, ceding the whole of Acadia to the French, and specifying "Pentagöet," or Penobscot, by name.

1670. The place was not, however, actually given up to them until the year 1670, when Captain Richard Walker made a formal surrender of it to Monsieur Hubert d'Andigny, Chevalier de Grandfontaine. [Part III, Deed of Surrender.]

By the instructions of the French king, and according to the provisions of the treaty, the inhabitants were left entirely free to remain, or to leave and take away all their property. Grandfontaine was instructed to make this place his head-quarters, and to put it in a complete state of defense. Also, to promote business and traffic along the coast, especially the fisheries and preparing of furs. Strangers were obliged to have a special permit from the king, in order to do business here, though the English who were here were allowed to remain, upon taking an oath of allegiance to the French crown. Nearly all the soldiers desired to settle here. The Lieutenant of Grandfontaine, at this time was the Sieur de Marson. [French Documents, Part III.]

CHAPTER III.

ARRIVAL OF THE BARON CASTIN.—HIS PREVIOUS LIFE.
HIS CHARACTER.—DESCRIPTION OF HIS RESIDENCE.—
HIS MARRIAGE TO MADOCKAWANDO'S DAUGHTER.—
HIS FAMILY.—DESCRIPTION OF MADAME CASTIN.—
HIS SUBMISSION TO THE ENGLISH.—DEPARTURE FOR
FRANCE.—ACCOUNT OF HIS SONS, ANSELM AND
JOSEPH DABADIS.—DEPARTURE OF ANSELM FOR
FRANCE.—DEATH OF THE BARON.—LATEST ACCOUNT
OF THE FAMILY.

> *   *   *   *   One whose bearded cheek
> And white and wrinkled brow bespeak
>   A wanderer from the shores of France.
> A few long locks of scattering snow
> Beneath a battered morion flow,
> And from the rivets of his vest,
> Which girds in steel his ample breast,
>   The slanted sunbeams glance.
> In the harsh outlines of his face
> Passion and sin have left their trace;
> Yet, save worn brow and thin grey hair,
> No signs of weary age are there.
>   His step is firm, his eye is keen,
> Nor years in broil and battle spent,
> Nor toil, nor wounds, nor pain, had bent
>   The lordly frame of old Castine.
>   *Whittier.—Mogg Megone.*

1667. About the time of the treaty of Breda, Baron Jean Vincent de St. Castin,* came from Quebec to Penobscot. The Baron Castin was born at Oléron, France,—a town situated near the borders of the Pyrenees. He is represented as a man of good abilities, very daring and enterprising, of very fascinating address and manners, and as possessing a competent education. He was liberal and kindly in his feelings, but a devout Catholic in his religion. He probably possessed a fair knowledge of the military arts of that period. He was at one time a colonel in the king's body guard. He was afterwards commander of a regiment called the "Carignan Salières." About the year 1665, he and his troops were ordered to Quebec. At the close of the war (1667), they were discharged from the army. It is reasonable to suppose that he would feel chagrined and incensed at his dismissal. However this may be, it is certain that he determined to remain in this country, and

---

*He is called, in one of the French letters, the Sieur de Badie, Baron de St. Castin.

to take up his abode among the Indians. Probably the grant from the king, of a considerable quantity of land, had something to do with his choice. [Wisdom and Policy of the French, London, 1704, p. 86.] He accordingly settled on this peninsula, where he erected a safe and commodious residence. His house is generally thought to have been situated near the site of Aulney's fort, and to have been not far from where the house of Mr. George H. Webb now stands, on Perkins Street. It was a long, low, irregular building, constructed partly of wood and partly of stone, and had rather a grotesque appearance. [The Neutral French.] The windows were small and quite high, so that no one could look in from the outside. The fort surrounding it, contained twelve guns, a well, a chapel with a bell, and several out-buildings; and a garden, containing quite a number of fruit trees, was attached to it. This orchard was, according to the traditions of the place, situated on the upper side of the present street, and opposite the fort. There is now no trace of it, but some of our octogenarians well remember seeing it in their younger days. According to a pretty trustworthy account, some of the young trees from this orchard were transplanted to Sedgwick, and apples were gathered from one of them as late as the fall of 1873. They are on the farm of Levi Gray. The entire grounds were encompassed by a palisade. [Part III, Deed of Surrender of Fort Pentagöet.]

The character attributed to Castin, differs according to the various prepossessions of those describing him. He was generally held in high esteem by the French, by whom he is said to have been a man of sound understanding, and quite "solicitous of honor." His relations, however, with the Governor, Monsieur Perrot, were not very amicable, and, at one time, the latter detained him seventy days upon the charge of a "weakness he had for some females." By the Indians, over whom he had great control, he was considered in the light of a tutelar divinity. He was feared as well as hated by the English, who accused him of inciting the savages against them, and of providing them with arms and ammunition. They made several attempts to induce him to desert the French cause, and, at one time, Mr. Palmer, a judge at New York, offered him a grant of all the lands he claimed as his, upon his becoming a *British* subject. He always, however, refused to recognize the English, and thereby preserved the possession of the place to the French. His letters show him to have been a very cautious man, and unwilling to avouch anything he might not be able to sustain. He was also a man of means, having come into an inheritance in France, about the year 1686, of 5000 livres a year. There is no doubt but that he was at one time quite licentious; but he afterwards reformed, and about the year 1687—or 1688—he was married to a daughter of Madockawando, a sagamore of the Tarratines. [French Documents, Part III.] La Hontan (said to have been his personal friend), asserts that he never had any other wife, "showing the savages," as he says, "that God is not pleased with inconstant men." [La Hontan's Biog., Vol. I, p. 223.] By most authorities, however, he is declared to have had three or four wives. [Williamson; Sullivan; also Hutchinson papers, p. 563.] According to an entry in the register of the Parish of St. Jean Baptiste, at Port Royal, a son and a daughter of Sieur Vincent de St. Castin, by the Dame *Mathilde* of the Parish of St. Famille, were each married the same day, October 31, 1707. In the same register is to be found the record of the marriage, on the fourth of December of the same year, of another daughter of the Baron's by the Dame *Marie Pidiaskie*. Notwithstanding the records of the above mentioned register, it is highly probable that the daughter of Madockawando was the only one to whom he was *legally* married, i. e., by the rights of the Catholic church. Were it otherwise, it is highly improbable that his son Anselm, would have made any claim upon the estates and property of his father, in France.* He may, of course, have contracted a second marriage after the death of his first wife.

If we may credit the accounts of the poet and the novelist—the latter of whom claims truth as the basis of her remarks—the daughter of Madockawando must have been a very lovely woman. She is described as being of a very light color, and is said to have possessed:—

> "A form of beauty undefined,
> A loveliness without a name,
> Not of degree, but more of kind;
> Nor bold nor shy, nor short nor tall,
> But a new mingling of them all.
> Yes, beautiful beyond belief,
> Transfigured and transfused, he sees
> The lady of the Pyrenees,
> The daughter of the Indian Chief."
> [*Longfellow.—The Baron Castin, of St. Castin.*]

*In Catholic countries, like France, no marriages were legal except such as were performed by the Catholic priests.

Besides several *reputed* sons, Castin had two acknowledged sons, Anselm and Joseph Dabadis. He had also
two daughters, married, as has already been said, with rich
dowries, to Frenchmen. Father L'Auvergat, in a letter to
Father de La Chasse, dated Panouamske, July 8, 1728,
speaks of an unmarried son, and of "all the sons being
continually drunk and insolent." [Historical Magazine,
Vol. 2, 3d Series, No. 3, p. 126.] The "Robardie" mentioned in Williamson's History of Maine, was probably
Joseph Dabadis, a son of the Baron.

1692. In 1692, the Governor of New England attempted the forcible abduction of Castin. The English having
previously captured two Frenchmen, named James Peter
Pau and St. Aubin, with their families, and brought them
to Boston, the Governor sent them, with two deserters
from the French army, to this place, with instructions to
seize Castin and take him to Boston. He also detained
their wives and children as pledges for their faithful per-
formance of this command. They, however, disclosed the
whole matter, and gave up the two deserters. Sieur Villebon, the French Governor, gave them 554 livres as a
reward for their fidelity, and in order to relieve their neces-
sities. He also assisted them in recovering their wives and
children. [French Documents, Part III.]

1693. In 1693, the Baron and his family gave in their
adhesion to the English.

1701. In 1701, Baron Castin left for France, taking
with him two or three thousand crowns in "good dry gold."
It is probable that he never returned to America, although
it is not unlikely that he intended to do so. It appears
from the French letters, that he went to France to give
an account of his conduct in regard to trading with
the English, his justification for which was the necessity
that he was under, he being unable to obtain the goods he
needed, either at Newfoundland or at Port Royal. He
also requested a grant of land upon the river de la Pointe
au Hestre, and stated that he had a design of establishing
a fishery at Molue, and of removing the Indians there.

Anselm, the elder son of the Baron Castin, commonly,
though erroneously, spoken of as "Castin the Younger,"
was, of course, a half-breed. He was a chief sachem of
the Tarratines, and also held a commission from the French
king, as 2d Lieutenant of the navy, with the pay and
emoluments of the same. He had an elegant French uni-

form, but usually dressed after the mode of the Indians. He is said to have been mild, generous, humane, and magnanimous in his disposition; to have possessed foresight and good sense; to have been a cautious, sensible man, and a good talker. In the expedition against Port Royal (1707), he was sent, with others, from Annapolis, with dispatches to Governor Vaudreuil, in Canada. He spent a few days with his family here,—Levingstone, who accompanied him, receiving from him every mark of hospitality and attention. They then proceeded up the Penobscot river. When they reached the Island of Lett,* an Indian, who had recently joined them, attempted to kill Levingstone with a hatchet, and would have succeeded had not the noble-minded Anselm thrust himself between them, and rescued him at the risk of his own life.

In the year 1721, on account of his having been with a party of Indians that had lately appeared in array at Arrowsic Island, some eastern soldiers, under general orders to seize such Indians as were in arms, captured and sent him to Boston. They could nôt try him for rebellion or treachery before the Superior Court in Suffolk, as that would be putting him on trial in one county for an offense committed in another, which would have been contrary to law. He was, therefore, examined by a Committee. He professed the highest respect and friendship for the English; said that he had lately returned from abroad on purpose to prevent his tribe from doing mischief; solemnly promised to try to keep them in a state of peace, and was at last discharged. His arrest, imprisonment and examination, were alike unjustifiable and cruel.

In 1722, he visited Béarn, in France, to obtain possession of his father's property, honors, and seignorial rights, of which he had been deprived, under the pretense of his illegitimacy, by the "first chicanier† of Europe, and Lieutenant General of the town of Oléron, in Béarn, who for long years enjoys this property."‡ This, too, in spite of the fact that he had the certificates of the missionaries and other evidences of the legality of his claim. [French Documents, Part III.] Whether he ever succeeded in getting possession of his rightful property is not known. He must have returned from France, as Father L'Auvergat speaks of both the sons as being in this country in 1728, and

*Probably Orphan's Island, now the town of Verona.
†Tricky lawyer.
‡The Baron Castin must, therefore, have been dead several years.

Murdoch mentions his being in Acadia, in 1731. He left one son and two daughters. The latter are said to have been married to highly respectable men.

Of Joseph Dabadis de St. Castin, or "Castin the Younger," but little is known. He is represented by Father L'Auvergat—who, however, was prejudiced against both him and his brother—as being frequently drunk and disorderly, but as having signalized himself in contests with the English. He was captured on one occasion, and had his vessel, and an English lad whom he had purchased of the Indians, taken from him. The account of this capture is contained in the following letter, written by him to Lieutenant Governor Dummer:

" PENTAGÖET, 23d July, 1725.

SIR:—I have the honor to acquaint you that the 9th of this present month, as j rode at anchor in a small harbour about three miles distant from Nesket, having with me but one jndian and one Englishman whom j had redeemed from the salvages, as well as my vessel, j was attacked by an English vessel, the commander of which called himself Lieutenant of the King's ship, and told me also his name, which j cannot remember.

Seeing myself thus attackt and not finding myself able to defend myself, j withdrew into the wood, forsaking my vessel. The commander of the vessel called me back promising me with an oath not to wrong me at all, saying that he was a merchant who had no design but to trade and was not fitted out for war, specially, when there was a talk of peace, and presently set up a flag of truce, and even gave me two safe conducts by writing, both which j have unhappily lost in the fight. Thus thinking myself safe enough, j came back on board my vessel, with my jndian and my Englishman, whom j brought to show that j had no thoughts of fighting, and that j had redeemed him from the jndians as well as the vessel. But as j was going to put on my clothes to dress myself more handsomely the commander who was come in my vessel with several of his people would not permit me to do it, telling me j was no more master of anything. He only granted me after many remonstrances to set me ashore.

But after j came down and they held forth to me a bag full of bisket that was given to me as they said as a payment for my Englishman. They did catch hold of me and the jndian who accompanied me, j got rid of him who

was going to seize upon me, but my jndian not being able
to do the same, j betook myself to my arms—and after
several volleys j killed the man who kept him, and got him
safe with me. This is the second time that j have been
thus treacherously used, which proceedings j do not suppose that you approve of being against the laws of Nations.
Therefore j hope that you will do me the justice, or that at
least you will cause me to be re-imbursed of the loss j have
sustained.

Namely:—

For the vessel that costed me 80 French pistoles; For
the Englishman 10 pistoles; 51 pounds of beaver that were
in the vessell with 20 otters, 3 coats that have costed me
together 20 pistoles; 56 pounds of shot that costed me
twenty pence a pound; 2 pounds of powder at 4 livres a
pound; 20 pounds of tobacco at 20 pence a pound; a pair
of scales 8 livres; Tow cloth blankets each 23 livres; Tow
bear skins 8 livres apiece; 4 skins of sea wolf 8 livres for
the four; 3 axes 15 livres for both; 2 kettles, 30 livres for
both, and several other matters, which they would not
grant me, so much as my cup. The retaken Englishman
knoweth the truth of all this, his name is Samuel Trusk of
the town of Salem near to Marblehead.

j have the honor to be
Sir
Your most humble & most
obedient Servant JOSEPH.
DABADIS DE ST. CASTIN."

[Hist. Magazine, Vol. 2., 3d Ser., No. 3, p. 125.]

The Samuel Trask mentioned above, had been purchased
by Castin from the Indians, who held him as a captive—
under the following circumstances:—a season of great
scarcity occurred, which drove the Indians to the cranberry beds for subsistence. On one occasion, while they
were gathering cranberries, a flock of wild geese alighted
near by, and Trask's success in capturing the birds so commended him to Castin's favor, that he "redeemed" him.
After being taken from Castin, Trask was transferred to a
vessel commanded by the celebrated Captain Kidd,—with
whom he remained for some time. [Williamson's Hist. of
Me., Vol. 2, p. 144; also Sewall's Ancient Dominions of
Me., p. 251.] In the office of the Secretary of the Commonwealth of Massachusetts are letters referring to Indian
affairs, written by Joseph Dabadis St. Castin, as lately as

1754. No trace is to be found of any of the family since that time. Inquiries made a few years ago, in the south of France, by Augustus C. Hamlin, M. D., of the mayors of the Provinces of Pau and Oléron, go to show that no trace of the family can now be found there. In all probability, all the records—and possibly the family itself—were destroyed by the Revolution.

CHAPTER IV.

Occupation of Pentagöet by Grandfontaine.—By Monsieur de Chambly.—Attack by Corsairs.— Capture by the Dutch.—Baron Castin in Possession.—Castin's House Pillaged by Andros.— Phipps takes Possession.—Sieur Villieu in Command.—Phipps obtains a Title from Madocka-wando.—Conference between Commissioners and Indians.—Torture of Thomas Gyles.—Caldin Trades at Pentagöet.—House of Anselm Castin Plundered by the English.—Church's Expedition.—Visit of Captain Cox.—Governor Pownal's Visit and Description of the Place.—The New Settlement of Maja-bagaduce.—Some of the Early Settlers.

1671. Monsieur le Grandfontaine held possession of, and resided at, Pentagöet for about four years—during a part of which time the Baron Castin was his Lieutenant. In the year 1671, in a letter to the Minister at Paris, he mentions the fact of the arrival of the French vessel *l' Oranger*, having on board sixty passengers—among whom were four girls and one woman. They were on their way to Port Royal. This is the earliest mention of any vessel bringing passengers here. In this same letter he remarks that he has bought a ketch from Colonel Temple, for the purpose of carrying the inhabitants and provisions to Port Royal. He says, also, that he must send to New England for a carpenter to construct a small vessel for him. He incidentally remarks *that the air here is very good*. A census of Acadia, taken this year, gives the population at this place as consisting of thirty-one souls—six civilians and twenty-five soldiers.

1673. In the year 1673, Grandfontaine was succeeded by Monsieur de Chambly. The white population at this time was the same as at the last date. The next year an attack was made upon the fort by pirates.

1674. It seems that an Englishman, named John Rhoades, gained access to the fort in disguise, and remained there four days. In a short time he returned and attacked the place with the crew of a Flemish Corsair—numbering two hundred men. This vessel was " *The Flying Horse*," from Curaçoa, under the command of Captain Jurriaen Aernouts, who had a commission from his Highness, the Prince of Orange. [De Peyster, Dutch in Maine, p. 76.] The garrison were taken completely by surprise, but the soldiers defended themselves bravely for the space of an hour, until Chambly received a musket shot in the body, and his Ensign was wounded, when they surrendered. The pirates pillaged the fort, took away all the guns, and carried Chambly and Marson to St. John's river. The former was held for ransom at the price of a thousand beaver skins. Chambly was somewhat blamed by the French king for his negligence in the matter. This act was disavowed by the English, but the leader had an English pilot from Boston, and the English there were thought to have encouraged the affair. [French Documents, Part III.—See, also, Murdock's Acadie.] According to Williamson, the attack was made by a Dutch man-of-war. [Hist. of Maine, Vol. 1, p. 579; also, Part III, Governor Leverett's letter.]

1676. Two years subsequently--in the spring of 1676— the Dutch sent a veritable man-of-war, which attacked and captured the fortification here. Several vessels were soon sent from Boston, and the Dutch were very shortly after driven from the peninsula. [Williamson's Hist. of Me., Vol. I, p. 581; I. Hutchinson's Hist., pp. 280, 353.] For the next ten years the French remained in quiet possession, and Castin was probably in command for the greater part of the time ; occupying himself in bartering for furs with the Indians, and, as sachem of the Tarratines, influencing and in a measure controlling their conduct with each other and with the English.

1685. In 1685, the French Governor, Monsieur Perrot, borrowed money from Baron Castin, and purchased two fishing vessels. As none of the French inhabitants would man them, however, he was obliged to employ English fishermen. The enterprise failed, owing to the dishonesty of the fishermen, who stole the fish and sent them to Boston. [French Documents, Part III.]

1686. In the year 1686, Palmer and West, commissioners appointed by the Governor of Sagadahock, laid claim to the country as far east as the St. Croix river. Not being aware of this fact, a shipmaster of Piscataqua landed a cargo of wines here, thinking the place was under French rule—as, in reality, it was. Because, however, the duties had not been paid at Pemaquid, Palmer and West sent Thomas Sharpe here in command of a vessel, to seize the cargo. This greatly offended both the French and the New England people, but a restoration of the wines was ordered by the English Court, and the trouble was smoothed over. [Williamson's Hist. of Me., Vol. I, p. 583.] Palmer forbade Castin's interference in this matter of the wines. He also forbade his threatening the subjects of the English king, "among others, those who dwell on the island of Martinique."* He also informed him that he would not be allowed to remain if he aided the Indians. The great trade in beaver skins at this time was proving injurious to the fisheries. [French Doc., Part III.]

1687. In the year 1687, Castin· was notified by the Government of New England that he must surrender the fort at Pentagöet. He did not, however, comply with this demand. He was this year engaged in constructing a mill for the Commonalty of Port Royal. He asked to have thirty soldiers sent to him, in order to be able to sustain himself against the English, and offered, if the assistance was granted, to make a settlement here of four hundred Indians. Castin complained strongly against Monsieur Perrot, because he retailed brandy by the half pint, and would not allow any of his domestics to do it for him.

1688. In the year 1688, sometime in the month of March or April, Sir Edmond Andros, Governor of New England, arrived in the frigate *Rose*, commanded by Captain George, and anchored opposite the fort and dwelling of Castin. Captain George sent his Lieutenant ashore to converse with the Baron.† The latter soon retired to the woods with all his people, and left his house shut up. Governor Andros and the others then landed and went into the house. They found there, in what appeared to be the common room of the family, a small altar and several pictures and ornaments, all of which they left uninjured. They took away from his house, however, all his arms, powder, shot, iron kettles, some trucking cloth, and his chairs. Verbal notice was sent to him by an Indian, that, if he would ask for his goods at Pemaquid, and come under obedience to the King of England, they would be restored

*Query.—Can it mean *Matinicus?*

†It was probably at this time that Andros carried to Madockawando the presents referred to in the letter of Mons. Pasquine, dated December 14, 1688. See Part III.

to him.   Andros, finding the fort had been originally built of stone and turf, and was now quite a ruin, concluded to abandon rather than to repair it.   Castin was justly incensed at this outrage, and would undoubtedly have retaliated, had not the government of Massachusetts disavowed all responsibility in the matter, and adopted pacific measures. [Murdock.]   The English, who were trading here this year, were driven away, and three or four small vessels carrying English goods, were sent back.   About this time a fly-boat* belonging to Castin, was captured by the pirates, on her return from Quebec. [French Documents, Part III.]

1689.   About the year 1689 or 1690, one Thomas Gyles, who had been a prisoner to the Indians for several years, attempted to escape, but was retaken.   He was carried to the heights of Maja-bagaduce, where he was subjected to torture.   His nose and ears were cut off and forced into his mouth, and he was compelled to swallow them.   He was then burned at the stake, while his savage captors indulged themselves in a war-dance.   [Sewall's Ancient Dom. of Me., p. 204.]   A census of Acadia, taken this year, shows that there were here, in addition to the Indians, only four persons, viz.,—a priest, a man and his wife, and one boy under fifteen years of age.

1690.   In May 1690, Sir William Phipps was sent, by order of the General Court of Massachusetts, to subdue the Province of Nova Scotia.   He met with but slight resistance, and took formal possession of all the coast, from Port Royal to Penobscot.   He visited several of the French settlements, and among them this.   [Williamson's Hist. of Me., Vol. I, p. 596.]

1693.   In the year 1693, Castin, foreseeing, in all probability, that the English supremacy would eventually be established upon this part of the coast, gave in his adhesion to the English Crown.   ▪The English possession of the place at this time could, however, have been merely a nominal one, as we find a French officer, Sieur Villieu, in command soon after.   The inhabitants at this time, were— Castin, aged 57, his wife and one child; Jean Renaud, aged 38, his wife (Indian) and four children; Des Lauries, aged 40, his wife, named Jeanne Granger, and three children; making a total of fourteen.   [French Documents, in Mass. Archives.]

*A flat-bottomed Dutch Vessel.

1694. To confirm his title to the place, Governor Phipps obtained, this year (1694), a deed from Madockawando, covering the lands granted to Beauchamp and Leverett, in the year 1629, by the Council of Plymouth. Somewhere about .this time, one Denis Hyenan, a Dutchman, sent to Pemaquid on business for Governor Slaughter, reached *Penobsquid*, as this place was then called by the Dutch. Having been induced to come ashore, he was seized and sent to Canada, where he was kept a prisoner two years. [De Peyster, Appendix to Dutch in Maine, p. 11.]

1696. In the year 1696, Castin went out into the bay with a flotilla of canoes and two hundred Indian warriors, to join the French under Iberville, in their attack on Pemaquid. [Sewall's Ancient Dominion, p. 213.]

1697. On the eleventh day of September, 1697, by the treaty of Ryswick, peace was - concluded between the English and French. On the fourteenth of October following, a conference was held at this place, between Major Converse and Captain Alden, Commissioners from Massachusetts, and six sachems—attended by a large concourse of Indians. The latter, though mourning for Madockawando, who had but recently died, sang the songs and smoked the pipe of peace. The Commissioners insisted upon the release of all the prisoners and the banishment of the Catholic missionaries. The Indians consented to the release of the prisoners, but said that " the good missionaries must not be driven away."

1698. During the year 1698, one Caldin (or Alden), is mentioned as trading at Pentagöet. He bought furs of, and sold goods to, a son-in-law of Baron Castin, and three other Frenchmen, who resided here. He paid three livres —equivalent to from forty-eight to sixty cents of our money —for every fourteen ounces of beaver, and fifty-five sous— equivalent to about eighty cents of our money—for winter beaver. The inhabitants at this time, were unwilling to dispose of their furs to the French, on account of the facilities they had for trading with the English. Complaint is made that the priest who was here at this time, *traded* more openly than his predecessors.

1700. In the year 1700, complaint is made that Castin sold furs to the English in Boston, and took his pay in English goods—which hindered the sale of French goods. It is also said that on account of the controlling influence of Castin and the missionary, the Indians had this year refused to receive presents from the French. The missionary declared, however, that the Indians refused to receive the customary presents because Monsieur Villieu, the Governor, wanted at the same time to sell them brandy, which they did not want to buy,—"foreseeing the excess into which they fall when intoxicated." [French Documents, Part III.]

1703. Up to the time of his departure for France, in 1701, the abode of Castin remained unmolested. Two years after his departure, however, some English settlers, who resided at the westward, visited the house of Anselm Castin, under the guise of friendship, and, in retaliation for some misdemeanors of the Indians, plundered it of all its valuables. Anselm complained and expostulated, but possessed too good judgment to retaliate.

1704. In the year 1704, *Queen Anne's* war, as it was called, was being carried on between the English settlers and the Indians, the latter instigated and abetted by the French. In May of this year, Colonel Benjamin Church commanded an expedition made along the eastern coast. As he came up the bay he captured many French and Indians, among the latter of whom were the Baron Castin's daughter and her children. She stated that her husband had gone to France to visit her father. Church went as far as the Bay of Fundy, and again visited Penobscot upon his return. [Williamson's Hist. of Me.]

From this time until the war of the Revolution, the peninsula of Bagaduce remained in a condition of comparative quiet—notwithstanding the several Indian wars which kept the whole Province of Maine in a tumult. The Penobscot Indians, although not entirely quiet, behaved, on the whole, much better than the neighboring tribes. During this whole period of seventy years, there is a great gap in the history of the place. The only things to be found, relating to it, are an account of a second severe earthquake, which happened on the eighteenth of November, 1755; the visits to this place, of Captain Cox and of Governor Pownal, and brief accounts of the earlier settlers.

1757. In the year 1757, one Captain Cox came here in a small vessel and killed two Indians, whom he *scalped.* He carried off with him two canoes, a quantity of oil, some fish, and some sea-fowl feathers. [Williamson's Hist. of Me., Vol. 2, p. 326.]

1759. Governor Pownal came over here from Fort Point, in 1759, and gives the following description of the place at that time:—"About noon left Wasumkeag point, and went in sloop Massachusetts to Pentaget, with Captain Cargill and twenty men.—Found the old abandoned French Fort and some abandoned settlements. Went ashore into the fort. Hoisted the· King's colors there and drank the King's health." In another place he says:—"To the east (of Long Island), is another Bay, called by the French Pentagöet, or Pentooskeag, where I saw the ruins of a French settlement, which from the seite and nature of the houses, and the remains of fields and orchards, had been once a pleasant habitation: Ones' heart felt sorrow that it had ever been destroyed." [Maine Hist. Col.—Gov. Pownal's Voyage, p. 385, and Note.]

1760. In the Governor's Address, January 2, 1760, he says that there are a great many families stand ready to go down to Penobscot, and as every other obstacle is removed, "you will take care that no uncertainty to the titles of the grants they may have, may be any objection to settlements which will be so greatly beneficial to the strength of the Province."

1767—1774 The first information to be found in regard to any settlers here, subsequent to the abandonment referred to by Governor Pownal, is in the year 1767, when Samuel Averill settled upon the northwest side of Northern Bay, and Jacob Perkins near him. In 1769, Finley McCullam settled upon the east side of Northern Bay, and in the year 1773, Daniel Brown settled also on the eastern side. In 1774, Joseph Willson settled at the head of Northern Bay. [Peter's Field notes for first survey of Penobscot.—Man.] There were undoubtedly other settlers here at this time, but their names are not known.

1775. In the Pennsylvania Journal, of August 23d, 1775, the following passage occurs:—"About the same time five sloops that had been sent by General Gage for wood, were taken by the inhabitants of Major Baggadoose, a small, new settlement, not far from Fort Pownal; and as there was some reason to fear that the Fort which stood at the head of Penobscot Bay (Fort Pownal), might be taken by the King's troops, and made use of against the country, the people in that neighborhood dismantled it, burnt the blockhouse, and all the wooden work, to the ground.—The prisoners taken at Machias and Major Baggadoose, about forty in number, were on their way to Cambridge, when the gentleman who brings this account, came away."— This is the last reference to this place that we have been able to find, prior to the War of the Revolution.

CHAPTER V.

Commencement of Revolutionary War.—English Charts of the Coast.—McLean Establishes a Military Post.—Description of the Fort.—Americans make Preparation for an Expedition.— Description of the American Fleet.—State of Affairs with the English.—American Attack. Defense by the British.

1776. During the war of the Revolution, the British became aware that they were suffering severely from the operations of the American cruisers and privateers—who possessed all the harbors in the eastern waters. According to the most generally received opinion, the Americans had a much more intimate knowledge of the various channels and harbors along the coast than did the English, and were thus enabled, with comparative impunity, to inflict much damage upon the commerce of the latter. The facts, though, in regard to our present maps of the coast, would seem to indicate exactly the opposite. There are in the U. S. Coast Survey Office, and in possession of some individuals, ten lithographic maps of the several parts of the Coast of Maine. From the original ten of these charts, all the present maps in use are derived. There is, also, in possession of one of the officers of the Coast Survey, a copper-plate map of this harbor and Penobscot bay. This copper-plate map was published by J. P. Desbarres, by order of an Act of Parliament, April 27; 1776. It has recently been found that the lithographic map of Penobscot bay, is a copy of this copper-plate map.* As this map was published only seventy days prior to the Declaration of Independence, it was not very likely to be in possession of the Americans until after the war. It was doubtless published, at the date mentioned, in anticipation of the approaching conflict, and copies were probably furnished to the entire English navy. So far, therefore, from the English

*Mr. Samuel T. Noyes, of this town, made the discovery by copying the lithographic map upon tracing paper, and applying this copy over the copperplate map. They were found to correspond quite accurately—enough so to show, without doubt, that the former was copied from the latter.

having but a slight acquaintance with this part of the coast, they must, on the contrary, have had much more accurate charts of it than the Americans possessed at that time.*

1779. Whatever may have been their knowledge of the coast, the English determined, on account of the military importance of this country to the Americans, and also for its importance in supplying them with wood, lumber, masts, fish, etc., to establish a military post at this place. Accordingly, in the year 1779, General Francis McLean† embarked at Halifax, with about seven hundred men, composed of detachments of the seventy-fourth and eighty-second Regiments, in a fleet of some seven or eight sail, and arrived at this place, June the seventeenth.‡ [Calef's Journal, Part III.] They landed, without opposition, in front of Joseph Perkins's house—which stood on what is now the southeastern corner of Main and Water streets. Although they landed without opposition, they acted as if they expected an attack from a concealed foe. [Hutchins's Narrative, Part III.] They did not remain on shore this day, but returned to their vessels. The next day they came on shore, and encamped on the open land to the eastward of where the present fort stands. The time from this date to the eighteenth day of July, was occupied in clearing up the ground, felling trees, and building a fort upon the high ground in the central part of the peninsula—and also a battery near the shore—together with storehouses, barracks, etc. The fort was intended to be square, with a bastion at each angle, and to be sufficiently large in area to contain a block-house in the center, with rooms in it for the officers' quarters, and barracks for the soldiers. It was also the intention to surround it with a wide and deep moat.

The Americans becoming alarmed at the possession by the English of a military post upon the eastern frontier, the General Court of Massachusetts, in the latter part of

---

*It is stated by officers of the Coast Survey, that the English must have been fully twenty years in making their surveys for these maps of the coast of Maine. They are quite minute, and valuable as showing the location of houses and lands. The map of Penobscot bay shows every house, probably, that was upon this peninsula at that time. A very important fact to be derived from this map is, that the Variation of the compass at this place, was at that time, only 9 deg. W., whereas, it is now 15 deg. 30 min. W.

†The name is given as *Allan* McLean, in Drake's American Biography.

‡Williamson says they landed June the twelfth, and gives the number of soldiers as nine hundred.

June, without consultation with the continental authorities, ordered the State Board of War to engage such armed vessels as could be procured, and to be prepared to have them sail on an expedition against the British at Penobscot, at the earliest possible moment. The Board of War were authorized to charter or impress the requisite number of private armed vessels; to promise the owners a fair compensation for all losses, of whatever kind; and to allow the seamen the same pay and rations as those in the Continental service. Generals Cushing and Thompson, Brigadiers of Militia in Lincoln and Cumberland Counties, were each ordered to furnish six hundred men for this expedition, and Brigadier General Frost was ordered to send three hundred men from the York County Militia. They took with them the following supplies and munitions of war, namely;—nine tons of flour and bread; ten tons of rice, and the same quantity of salt beef; twelve hundred gallons of rum and molasses, *in equal quantities;* five hundred stands of arms; fifty thousand musket cartridges, with balls; two 18-prs., with two hundred rounds of cartridges; three 9-prs., with three hundred rounds of cartridges; four field pieces; six barrels of gunpowder, and the necessary quantity of axes, spades, tents, and camp furniture. The fleet consisted of nineteen armed vessels, and twenty-four transports—carrying three hundred and forty-four guns. It has been described as " the most beautiful that ever floated in eastern waters." The vessels composing the fleet were the following:—

Frigate *Warren*, 32 guns, (18 and 12 prs.,) Com. Saltonstall. Ships *Monmouth*, 24 guns; *Vengeance*, 24 guns; *General Putnam*, 22 guns; *Sally*, 22 guns; *Hampden*, (Captain Titus Salter,) 20 guns; *Hector*, 20 guns; *Hunter*, 18 guns; *Black Prince*, 18 guns; *Sky Rocket*, 16 guns. Brigs *Active*, (Captain Hallet,) 16 guns; *Defiance*, 16, (6-prs.); *Hazard*, 16 guns; *Nancy*, 16 guns; *Diligence*, (Captain Brown,) 14 guns; *Tyrannicide*, 14 guns. Sloops *Providence*, 14 guns; *Spring Bird*, 12 guns; *Rover*, 10 guns.

The *Black Prince* was owned by Captain Williams and others, and cost £1000. The *Hector* was owned by Jonathan Pert and others, and cost £1000. The *Hunter* was owned by Samuel Silsbee, and others, and also cost £1000. The *General Putnam* was impressed. The estimated cost of the latter was £900. There were on board the fleet, in addition to the seamen, some three or four hundred soldiers and marines—and about one thousand more were expected. Moses Little, of Newbury, Massachusetts, was appointed to command the naval force, but he felt obliged to decline, on account of ill health, and the command was therefore given to Dudley* Saltonstall, of New Haven, Connecticut. [Coffin's History of Newbury.] Saltonstall was a man of good abilities, and had seen something of naval warfare. He possessed, however, an exceedingly obstinate disposition, and was rather overbearing in his manner. Solomon Lovell, of Weymouth, a Brigadier General of the Suffolk Militia, had control of the land forces. He was a man of undaunted courage, but had never before had command of troops in actual service. General Peleg Wadsworth was the second in command. The charge of the ordnance was given to Lieutenant Colonel Paul Revere, famous for his "midnight ride." Although twelve hundred of the militia had been ordered, yet they had less than one thousand soldiers. If they exceeded the enemy somewhat in number, yet they were entirely undisciplined—never having even paraded together more than once—and were, consequently, not likely to be very reliable in an engagement. The whole force was very quickly in readiness, and upon the twenty-fifth day of July the fleet made its appearance in this harbor.

Intelligence of this expedition was received by General McLean, July 18th,† and was fully confirmed a few days later. McLean changed his intention of making a regularly constructed fortress, and prepared, in a more expeditious manner, to erect one suitable merely for the present emergency. His troops were kept vigorously at work by night and day. Provisions, at this time, were very scarce, and the inhabitants were almost destitute of arms, as well as of food. A meeting was held, to determine on defence or submission, and Colonel Brewer, of Penobscot, and Captain Smith, of Marsh Bay, were appointed a committee to treat with the General. They did so, and received the assurance that, if the inhabitants would be peaceable, and attend quietly to their own affairs, they should not be disturbed in their person or property. They were compelled,

---

*Drake, in his American Biography, calls him *Gurdon;* and Calef writes " G. Saltonstall." Williamson, in his history of Maine, calls him *Richard.* The order to take the command of the fleet is, however, addressed to *Dudley* Saltonstall.

†Seven days before its arrival. Williamson says that the English received this information only *four* days before the arrival of the fleet.

however, to take an oath, either of allegiance or of neutrality. Six hundred and fifty-one persons came in and took an oath of the above nature. The fort, at this time, was ill prepared to resist an enemy. The northerly side of it was but four feet high, and the easterly and westerly ends were laid up sloping, and resembled somewhat a stone wall. From the back side to the front there was simply a depression, and the ground was not broken. The ditch was in no part over three feet in depth. So low were the walls that a soldier was heard to say that he "could jump over them with a musket in each hand." No platform had been laid, or artillery mounted. There was one 6-gun battery at Dyce's Point, and a small one begun somewhere on Cape Rozier. One hundred of the inhabitants, under the leadership of Mr. John Perkins, came in—some voluntarily, and others because compelled—and in three days' time, cleared the land of all the wood in front of the fort. Mr. William Hutchins, then a boy of fourteen, was one of this number, and helped to haul the first log into the south bastion. One hundred and eighty men were also sent on shore from the men-of-war, to assist in preparing the defences. A messenger was dispatched to Halifax for aid. On Saturday, July 24th, a fleet was seen standing up the bay, and Captain Mowatt, in command of the English men-of-war, determined to detain the sloops *Albany*, *North* and *Nautilus*—which had been ordered for other service. The other vessels of the fleet had departed some time previously. The three sloops dropped down the harbor, and moored, in close line of battle, across the entrance, between the rocks at Dyce's Head and the point of Nautilus or Banks' Island—often, at that time, called Cross Island. On shore, some cannons were soon mounted, and the troops were in garrison the next morning. At three o'clock p. m., of the twenty-fifth, the American fleet made its appearance, and a brisk cannonade was kept up for about two hours. The Americans, also, made an attempt to land, but without success, owing to the high wind. The next day, July 26th, the English sloops moved further up into the harbor, and another cannonading took place, lasting two hours and a quarter, with but slight damage to either side. The Americans again attempted to make a landing upon the point, but were repulsed. At six p. m., however, they made a landing on Nautilus Island,

with two hundred men, dislodged a party of twenty
marines, and took possession of four 4-prs.—two of which
were not mounted. On the twenty-seventh there was
some cannonading, and at three p. m., a boat, in passing
from the American vessels to Nautilus Island, was struck
by a random shot from the fort, and sunk.

The morning of the twenty-eighth of July, was calm
and foggy. At three o'clock a. m., the American vessels
were in line up and down the bay—just beyond musket shot
of the enemy. Two hundred of the marines and two
hundred of the militia were ordered into the boats. Mowatt's
position at this time controlled the mouth of the harbor,
and prevented a landing on the southern and eastern sides
of the peninsula; and a trench had been cut across the isthmus at the northward, which completely severed the neck
from the main land, and prevented a hostile approach from
that direction. [Williamson, Vol. 2, p. 473.] A landing
could only be effected on the westerly side—which was
at most places very precipitous. The boats landed, therefore, upon this side, at a point about one-third of the way
between Dyce's Head and the high bluff at the northwestern extremity of the peninsula.* The English troops, posted
upon the heights, opened a brisk fire upon the boats just as
they reached the shore, and a shower of musketry from the
cliffs, was sent into the faces of the troops as they attempted
an ascent. It is stated by an American officer—present at
the time—that balls from the English vessels passed over
their heads; but as the latter had moved further up the harbor, it would seem almost incredible that their light metal
(6 prs.) could have thrown so far. The ascent at the place
of landing being found altogether impracticable, the troops
divided into three parties. The right and left wings sought
more practicable places for ascent, while the center kept up
an incessant fire of musketry, to distract the attention of the
foe. The right pressed hard upon the British left, and succeeded in capturing a small battery. The left, however,
closing in rather too quickly upon the enemy, gave them a
chance to escape, and they retreated, leaving thirty killed,

*This bluff is now called Block-house Point. At the place where they
landed is a large granite boulder, commonly known as the "white rock," or
as "Trask's rock." A fifer boy by the name of Trask, was behind this rock playing the fife while his comrades made the ascent. This Trask, some fifty-five
years ago, visited this place, and pointed out to several citizens, the exact spot
where the landing was made. Previously to Trask's visit, it was called
"Hinckley's rock," after a Captain who is said to have climbed upon it to
cheer on his men, and to have been shot on the rock.

wounded and taken.   The Americans lost in this attack,
according to the British account, one hundred men out of
four hundred.   [Calef's Journal, Part III.]   According to
General Lovell's statement, however, the loss was only fifty.
[Mass. Letter Book, No. 57, p. 305.]   The loss was most
severely felt by the marines, who ascended the steeper and
more difficult part upon the left.   The engagement, though
a very brilliant one, was short, lasting only about twenty
minutes.   After the capture of the battery, the ships were
enabled to move in nearer to the shore.   Williamson says,
[Hist. of Me., Vol. 2, p. 473,] that the place where the ascent
was made, was up a steep precipice two hundred feet in
height.   As the highest point of land on the peninsula is
only two hundred and seventeen feet, this statement, of
course, is incorrect.   It seems from the several accounts,
that the marines suffered the most.   Now, according to military usages, the left of the line would be given to them.
Upon the right, a comparatively easy ascent could have been
made.   Nowhere, however, upon the left of their landing
place, could an ascent have been made, except by climbing
a very precipitous bank some thirty or forty feet in height.
After making this ascent, the ground, though covered with
boulders. and still rising, would present no great difficulties.
There is no doubt whatever, but that this was a very daring assault, and had the American troops eventually succeeded in taking possession of the fort, this attack would
have been one of the most brilliant achievements of the
war.   Their final defeat, however, obliterated all recollection of their former bravery.*   Some hours later upon
this day, cannonading took place between the British vessels and the battery on Nautilus Island ; but, finding their
6 prs. were of but little service against the heavier guns of
the battery, Captain Mowatt deemed it advisable to move
still further up the harbor.†   Sir John Moore,—who was
killed at Corunna, Spain, June 16th, 1809, and in com-
memoration of whose burial the ode commencing, "Not a
drum was heard, nor a funeral note," was composed—was
at that time a Lieutenant and Paymaster in H. B. M's 82d
Regiment, and was present on picket when this attack was

---

*They are reported to have buried their dead upon the level ground just
above Trask's rock.   The presumption in favor of their burial being in that
place, is very strong; but the surface of this region has become so changed
by time, that those now living, who once knew, are unable to designate the
exact spot.

†For more particular accounts of this attack, see Calef's Journal, in Part III,
and Williamson's Hist. of Maine, Vol. 2, pp. 470 to 473.

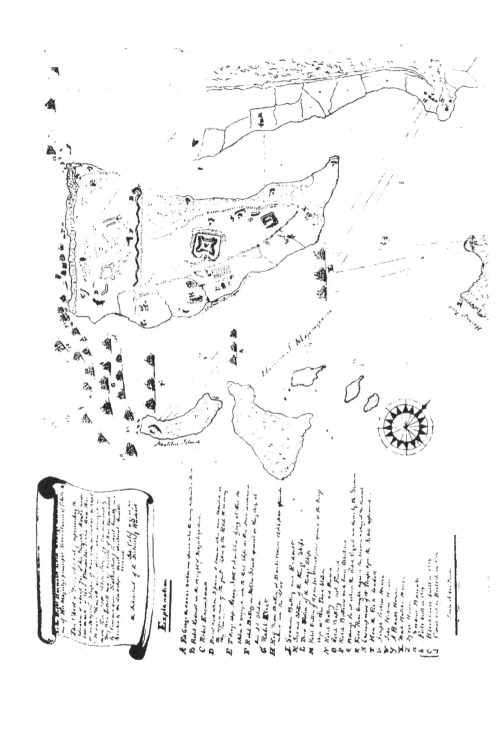

made.* [British Plutarch, p. 243.] Captain, afterwards Sir James Henry Craig, was also present and held some command at the time of this siege. [Drake's Dict. of American Biography.]

On the 31st, a detachment of militia and marines, under command of General Wadsworth, landed at the westward of the half-moon battery (situated at the left of the main fort), and attacked the enemy's picket. They found five of the enemy dead, and took fourteen prisoners, but were themselves soon repulsed with considerable loss. Upon the third of August, they erected a battery on the main land north of the peninsula, in the field behind where Captain Joseph Wescott's house now stands, between it and the shore. Three days later, the British erected a battery directly opposite, on what is now known as Hatch's Point. On the seventh, as a boat was crossing from Nautilus Island to Henry's Point (then called Hainey's plantation) where the Americans had a picket, the boats from the *Nautilus* succeeded in capturing her, but the crew made out to escape and join the picket.

Immediately after the engagement of the 28th ult., a council of war of the American land and naval forces, was called. The officers of the land forces were in favor of demanding an immediate surrender, but Commodore Saltonstall, and some of his officers, were opposed to it. It was next proposed to storm the fort, but the marines had already suffered so much, that the Commodore refused to disembark any more, and even threatened to recall those already on shore. Their force being thought insufficient to capture the place, special messengers were sent to Boston, in *whaleboats*, for assistance. The time, up to August 13th, was occupied by Commodore Saltonstall, in manœuvering about the entrance of the harbor, and in frequent cannonading, while General Lovell gradually advanced, by zigzag intrenchments, to within seven hundred yards of the fort, besides erecting the batteries already mentioned, and several others. This lapse of time gave the British every advantage, and General McLean improved the time by perfecting his fortifications, erecting new defences, and mounting cannon.

Upon the eleventh of August, two hundred men, under the command of Brown and Bronville, took post near the half-moon battery, and awaited the signal to retreat. A

---

* Mr. Hutchins declared that he knew him well, and that he went by the name of "Skipper Moore."—So it is stated to us.

party of the enemy, concealed behind a barn, fired upon
them when they left. The next day it was decided by
the Americans to make a combined attack with the entire
force, both of land and sea, and upon the thirteenth,
General Lovell, at the head of two hundred men, took
the *rear* of Fort George. [Deposition of Samuel McCobb,
in Vol. on Pen. Exp. in Sec. of State's Office, Boston.]
It was too late. The same day he received intelligence
by one of his vessels which had been reconnoitering, that
a British fleet was standing up the bay. A retreat was at
once ordered.

About this time, Captain Little, of the American sloop
of war *Winthrop*, captured a sloop in the bay, from the
crew of which he learned the position of an armed brig
of the British, which, having previously taken the sloop,
had sent her out after coasters. Captain Little determined to take this brig by surprise. The *Winthrop*,
accordingly, bore down in the night, having forty men—
dressed in white frocks, in order to distinguish friend
from foe—in readiness to jump aboard the brig. When
close by, she was hailed by the enemy—who supposed her
to be a prize of the sloop—who cried out, " You will run
aboard." " I am coming aboard," answered Captain Little,
and immediately Lieutenant (afterwards Commodore) Edward Preble, with fourteen men, sprang aboard. The
rest missed their opportunity—owing to the speed of the
vessel. Captain Little called to Preble, " Will you have
more men?" The latter, with great presence of mind,
loudly answered, " No ; we have more than we want; we
stand in each other's way." The greater part of the
enemy's crew leaped overboard, and swam to the shore.
Lieutenant Preble made the officers of the brig prisoners
in their beds, assuring them that resistance was in vain.
The troops upon the shore fired upon them, and they
experienced a heavy cannonade from the battery. Notwithstanding this, they succeeded in getting the brig safely
out of the harbor, and to Boston. [Peterson's Hist. of
Navy, pp. 175, 176.]

CHAPTER VI.

ARRIVAL OF BRITISH FLEET.—DESTRUCTION OF AMERI-
CAN FLEET.—CAUSE OF FAILURE OF THE EXPE-
DITION.—SUBSEQUENT BRITISH OCCUPATION OF THE
PLACE.—CONDITION OF THE INHABITANTS.—ANEC-
DOTE OF ATWOOD FALES.—OF WALDO DICKE.—AC-
COUNT OF THE ESCAPE FROM FORT GEORGE, OF WADS-
WORTH AND BURTON.

1779. Aug. 14th. During the night of the thirteenth
of August, the Americans silently removed their cannon
from the peninsula, and embarked in their vessels.
Early on the morning of the next day, they spiked and
dismounted their cannon on Nautilus Island and, going on
board a brig, made haste to join their fleet. The British
fleet soon appeared in the offing. It consisted of:—The
Raisonnable, Captain Evans, 64 guns, 500 men, Sir
George Collier's F. S.; *Blande*, Captain Berkley, 32 guns,
220 men; *Greyhound*, Captain Dickson, 28 guns, 200
men; *Galatea*, Captain Read, 24 guns, 180 men; *Camilla*,
Captain Collins, 24 guns, 180 men; *Virginia*, Captain
Ord, 18 guns, 150 men; *Otter*, Captain—, 14 guns, 100 men.
Making in all, seven vessels, carrying two hundred and four
guns, and fifteen hundred and thirty men. This number,
added to the three sloops-of-war already in the harbor,
made such a vastly superior force, that it would have been
folly to attempt any resistance. Nothing was left, therefore, for the Americans, but to retreat. Commodore
Saltonstall arranged his fleet across the bay, in the form
of a crescent, for the purpose of checking the advance of
the enemy sufficiently to enable the land forces on board
the transports to make good their escape. Sir George
Collier, however, feeling such entire confidence in the
very great superiority of his fleet, advanced at once, without hesitation, and, pouring in a broad-side, caused the
American vessels to crowd on all sail, and attempt an
indiscriminate flight. The *Hunter* and *Hampden*, in
attempting to escape by way of the passage between Long
Island and Belfast, were cut off and taken. The former
vessel was run on shore with all her sails standing, but

her crew succeeded in reaching the land. The *Defiance* ran into an inlet near by, and was fired by her crew. The *Sky Rocket* was blown up near Fort Point ledge, and the *Active* was burned off Brigadier's Island. The others escaped further up the river, but were all set on fire and blown up by their crews, to prevent them from falling into the hands of the enemy.

Thus this expedition, notwithstanding the bravery of the first attack, ended both disastrously and disgracefully to the Americans. A comparatively small garrison, with only three sloops-of-war, held out successfully for twenty-one days, against a vastly superior force. The whole blame, undoubtedly, falls upon Commodore Saltonstall, who was popularly charged with having bêen "bought by British gold." He was tried, subsequently, for cowardice, by a Court Martial, and cashiered. The following petition, signed and sent to him by the Lieutenants and Masters of the several vessels of the fleet, shows plainly what his subordinate officers thought : —

"Tuesday A. M., July 27th, 1779.

Your petitioners, strongly impressed with the importance of the Expedition, and earnestly desiring to render to our country all the service in our power, would represent to your honor that the most speedy exertions should be used to accomplish the design we came upon. We think delays, in the present case, are extremely dangerous —as our enemies are duly fortifying and strengthening themselves, and are stimulated so to do, being in daily expectation of a reinforcement. We do not mean to advise, or censure your past conduct, but intend only to express our desire of improving the present opportunity to go immediately into the harbor, and attack the enemy's ships. However, we humbly submit our sentiments to the better judgment of those in superior command. We, therefore, wait your orders, whether in answer to our petition, or otherwise. And, as in duty bound, will ever pray." [Pen. Expedition, in State Archives, Mass.] Even the British commander did not hesitate to call him a coward, and said that he should have surrendered the very first day, if such a demand had been made. Ignorance, on his part, of the condition of the British defences, cannot be urged as an excuse ; for Colonel Brewer, who had inspected them the previous day, visited him, and gave him an exact account of them.

Upon Brewer's urging him to make another attack, Saltonstall coarsely replied :—" You seem to be d–d knowing about the matter! I am not going to risk my shipping in that d–d hole!" The British retained possession of the place until after peace was declared. They evacuated it in December, 1783.

The English, during their occupation of the place at this time, treated the inhabitants, upon the whole, in as conciliatory a manner as could be expected. This was done, doubtless, partly from policy, but partly, also, in view of the fact that many of the inhabitants were at heart tories. This assertion is rendered probable by the following passage, which occurs in an order to General Lovell, dated at the Council Chamber, July 2d, 1779 :— " And as there is good reason to believe that some of the principal men at Majorbagaduce requested the enemy to come there and take possession, you will be particularly careful that none of them escape, but to secure them, that they may receive the 'just reward for their evil doings." Notwithstanding the friendliness of many of the citizens, a great deal of discrimination was used, and none of them were allowed within the fort, except Mr. Nathan Phillips, Mr. Cunningham and his family and driver, Mr. Dyce and family, and Mr. Finley McCullum,. who were all employed in His Majesty's service. The inhabitants were obliged to bring in all their guns—for which they were paid at the rate of three dollars each. They were forbidden to leave the peninsula, without permission, and were compelled to labor upon the defences. Provisions, at this time, were very scarce among them, and, as they had no guns, they were obliged to depend upon the rations issued to them by the English Commissary. This compelled a majority of them to labor in the English service, as none others could draw rations. The English, also, from time to time, issued orders to them to bring in wood, lumber and vegetables. [See MacZachlar's Order, Part III.] Orders were, on the other hand, issued to the troops, strictly prohibiting any digging of potatoes, or other vegetables belonging to the inhabitants, or plundering of any kind. Marauding and setting fire to the houses, of the inhabitants were also forbidden, by *special* orders. All strangers, upon their arrival in town were ordered to report to Doctor Calef.* Those not com-

* A Surgeon and an *acting* chaplain.

plying, were to be fined or *corporeally* punished. This
order was sent to all the neighboring towns. The inhabitants were also commanded to be always in readiness for
military service, and to be mustered and inspected once a
week. At one time, small change became so scarce, that
the British commander ordered all silver dollars to be cut
into five pieces, and each piece to pass current for one shilling. This practice, however, gave such an opportunity
for fraud, that it was soon found necessary to call them in,
and rescind the order.

1780. On October 27th, 1780, there was a total eclipse
of the sun, visible here, but not total farther west.
Observations were made at Long Island, by Reverend
Samuel Williams, Hollisean Professor of Mathematics, at
Harvard College. The British officer in command here
refused to allow his party to land upon this peninsula, and
only allowed them until the 28th to remain in the bay.
This was, perhaps, the earliest observation of the kind
made in this country. The winter of this year was probably the coldest ever known in this vicinity. The cold
was so intense, and for so long a period, that the bay was
frozen over from here to Camden, and Lieutenant Burton
came all the way from that place on the ice. He was in
search of a man by the name of Libby, who was imprisoned here at the time. After obtaining his release, Burton returned with him in the same manner.

The following episodes of events occurring during the
British occupation, are of interest, and may appropriately
be inserted in this place.

In the year 1779, while the American force was attempting the capture of the place, one Atwood Fales, of
Thomaston, who belonged to Lovell's force, while going
out one morning for a pail of water, was twice fired upon
by a whole company—numbering some sixty men—of the
English at once, with no detriment to himself, but to the
immense astonishment of the assailants, who thencefor-
ward considered him invulnerable. [Eaton's Hist. Thom.
S. Thom. and Rockland, p.152.]

In the year 1780, Waldo Dicke, of Warren, with some
other tories, captured a sloop at Maple Juice Cove, near
Rockland, and succeeded in getting her safely here.
General Campbell, who had succeeded McLean in command of the post, was not, however, particularly well
pleased, either with the manner in which the exploit was

performed, or with the parties engaged therein. He accordingly offered her back at a very moderate ransom,* and the tories found they had had a great deal òf labor to very little purpose. [Hist. of Thom. &c., pp. 144–145.]

An account of the celebrated and really remarkable escape of General Wadsworth and Major Burton, from their imprisonment in Fort George, will be a fitting termination to our history of this period.†

In the month of February, 1780, General Campbell, the commander of the garrison, learning that General Peleg Wadsworth was at his home in Thomaston, without any troops except a guard of six soldiers, determined to make him a prisoner. He accordingly sent a force of twenty-five soldiers, under the charge of Lieutenant Stockton, for this purpose. After a sharp contest, in which several of the British soldiers were killed and wounded, and in which General Wadsworth was himself severely wounded, they succeeded in making him a prisoner. On their arrival at the British post, the capture of General Wadsworth was soon announced, and the shore was thronged with spectators to see the man, who, through the preceding year, had disappointed all the designs of the British in that quarter; and loud shouts were heard from the rabble, which covered the shore; but when he arrived at the fort, and was conducted into the officers' guard-room, he was treated with politeness. General Campbell sent his compliments to him, and a surgeon to dress his wounds, assuring him that his situation should be made comfortable. He was furnished with books, allowed to receive visitors, and at the hour of dining, he was invited to the table of the commandant, where he met with all the principal officers of the garrison, and from whom he received particular attention and politeness. General Wadsworth soon made application for a flag of truce, by which means he could transmit a letter to the Governor of Massachusetts, and another to Mrs. Wadsworth. This was granted him, upon condition that the letter to the Governor should be inspected. The flag was intrusted to Lieutenant Stockton, and on his return, the General was relieved from all anxiety respecting his wife and family. At the end of five weeks, his wound being nearly healed, he requested of General Campbell, the customary privilege

* His offer was not accepted.

† This account is taken from Thacher's Journal of the Revolutionary War.

of a parole, and was told in reply, that his case had been reported to the commanding officer at New York, and that no alteration could be made until orders were received from that quarter. In about two months, Mrs. Wadsworth and Miss Fenno arrived. About the same time, orders were received from the commanding General, at New York, which were concealed from General Wadsworth. He finally learned that he was not to be paroled or exchanged, but was to be sent to England, as a rebel of too much consequence to be at liberty. Not long afterwards, Major Benjamin Burton, a brave and worthy man, who had served under General Wadsworth the preceding summer, was taken and brought into the fort, and lodged in the same room with the General. He had been informed that both himself and the General were to be sent, immediately after the return of a privateer, now out on a cruise, either to New York or Halifax, and thence to England.

The prisoners immediately resolved to make a desperate attempt to escape. They were confined in a grated room in the officers' barracks, within the fort. The walls of this fortress, exclusive of the ditch surrounding it, were twenty feet high, with fraising on the top, and *chevaux de frise* at the bottom. Two sentinels were always in the entry, and the door, the upper part of which was of glass, might be opened by these watchmen, whenever they thought proper, and was actually opened at seasons of peculiar darkness and silence. At the exterior doors of the entries, sentries were also stationed, as were others in the body of the fort, and at the quarters of General Campbell. At the guard-house a strong guard was daily mounted. Several sentinels were stationed on the walls of the fort, and a complete line occupied them by night. Without the ditch, glacis, and abatis, another complete set of soldiers patrolled through the night. The gate of the fort was shut at sunset, and a picket-guard was placed on, or near, the isthmus leading from the fort to the main land. The room in which they were confined was ceiled with boards. One of these they determined to cut off, so as to make a hole large enough to pass through, and then to creep along till they should come to the next, or middle entry—lowering themselves down into this by a blanket. If they should not be discovered, the passage to the walls of the fort was easy. In the evening, after the sentinels had seen the prisoners retire to bed, General Wadsworth got up, and, standing in a chair, attempted to cut with his knife the intended opening, but soon found it impracticable. The next day, by giving their waiter (Barnabas Cunningham), a dollar, they procured a gimlet. With this instrument they proceeded cautiously, and as silently as possible, to perforate the board, and in order to conceal every appearance from their servants and from the officers, they carefully covered the gimlet holes with chewed bread. At the end of three weeks, their labors were so far completed that it only remained to cut with a knife the parts which were left to hold the piece in its place. When their preparations were finished, they learned that the privateer, in which they were to embark, was daily expected.

In the evening of the eighteenth of June, a very severe storm of rain came on, with great darkness, and almost incessant lightning.

This the prisoners considered as the propitious moment. Having extinguished their lights, they began to cut the corners of the board, and in less than an hour, the intended opening was completed. The noise, which the operation occasioned, was drowned by the rain falling on the roof. Major Burton first ascended to the ceiling, and pressed himself through the opening. General Wadsworth next, having put the corner of his blanket through the hole, and made it fast by a strong wooden skewer, attempted to make his way through, by standing on a chair below, but it was with extreme difficulty—owing to his wounded arm— that he at length succeeded in doing so, and reached the middle entry. From this he passed through the door, which he found open, and made his way to the wall of the fort, encountering the greatest difficulty before he could ascend to the top. He had now to creep along the top of the fort, between the sentry boxes, at the very moment when the relief was shifting sentinels; but the falling of heavy rain kept the sentinels within their boxes, and favored his escape. Having now fastened his blanket round a picket at the top, he let himself down through the *chevaux de frise*, to the ground, and, in a manner astonishing to himself, made his way into an open field. Here he was obliged to grope his way among rocks, stumps and brush, in the darkness of the night, till he reached the cove. Happily, the tide had ebbed, thus enabling him to cross the water—which was about one half a mile in breadth, and not more than three feet deep.

About two o'clock in the morning, General Wadsworth found himself a mile and a half from the fort, and proceeded on, through thick wood and brush, to the Penobscot river. After passing some distance along the shore, being seven miles from the fort, to his unspeakable joy, he saw his friend Burton advancing towards him. Major Burton had been obliged to encounter, in his course, equal difficulties with his companion—having come face to face with a sentinel, when leaving the fort, whose observation he eluded by falling flat upon the ground. Such were the incredible perils and obstructions which they surmounted, that their escape may be considered almost miraculous. It was now necessary that they should cross the Penobscot river, and very fortunately they discovered a canoe, with oars on the shore, suited to their purpose. While on the river, they discovered a barge, with a party of British from the fort, in pursuit of them. By taking an oblique course, and plying their oars to the utmost, they happily eluded the eyes of their pursuers, and arrived safely on the western shore. After having wandered in the wilderness for several days and nights, exposed to extreme fatigue and cold, and with no other food than a little dry bread and meat, which they had brought in their pockets from the fort, they reached the settlements on the river St. George, and no further difficulties attended their return to their respective families.*

* For full particulars in regard to Burton's escape, see manuscript narrative, by William D. Williamson, in Archives of Maine Hist. Society. Dr. Joseph L. Stevens, of this town, has also a copy of the same.

PART II.
PENOBSCOT, CASTINE AND BROOKSVILLE.

"Far eastward o'er the lovely bay,
Penobscot's clustered wigwams lay;
And gently from that Indian town
The Verdant hillside slopes adown
To where the sparkling waters play
Upon the yellow sands below."

Whittier—Mogg Megone.

8

MAP OF
CASTINE.
BROOKSVILLE & PENOBSCOT
HANCOCK COUNTY
MAINE
Scale of Miles

CHAPTER I.
TOPOGRAPHICAL AND DESCRIPTIVE.

BOUNDARIES. — DIVISIONS. — AREAS. — NATURAL SCEN-
ERY. — SOIL. — CROPS. — GEOLOGY. — MINERALOGY. —
FLORA.—FAUNA.—CLIMATOLOGY.

The territory which includes the three towns of Penobscot, Castine and Brooksville, is situated upon the eastern
side of Penobscot river and bay, about twenty-five miles
from the mouth of the bay, and thirty-six miles below the
head of navigation. The distance, in an air line, from Portland, is about ninety miles, and from Washington, six
hundred and seventy miles. It is bounded on the north
by the town of Orland, on the east by Surry and Bluehill,
and upon the south by Sedgwick, Algemogin* Reach and
Penobscot bay. The latitude, at Dyce's Head, is 44°
22' 57" N., and the longitude 68° 48' 49" W. This territory is intersected by an arm of the sea, called the Bagaduce river, which, expanding in its upper part into
two bays—called, respectively, the Northern and Southern bays—and connected by a stream with a large sheet
of fresh water, called Walker's Pond†, makes a wide
sweep, and comes again to within about a half-mile of
the waters of the ocean at Alemogin, or Eggemoggin,
Reach. The former town of Penobscot was divided into
three nearly equal parts. That portion upon which the
town of Castine is now situated, is a peninsula extending
southwardly into the waters of Penobscot bay. That
portion of this peninsula upon which is the village of Castine, was formerly itself a smaller peninsula, but is now—
by reason of the canal, made by the British in 1814— in
reality an island, bearing some resemblance in its shape to
a boot, the toe of which points to the northeast. Its area is
about 2,600 acres. The town of Brooksville is also a
peninsula, the lower part of which, like that of Castine,
is almost an island; two large coves, called Lawrence's Bay,

*Usually written Eggemoggin. The word we have used is the oldest, and
probably the most correct.

† The Indian name of this pond is said to signify, " The beautiful water
place." It being Winne-agwam-auk, contracted into Winnewag.

and Orcutt's Harbor, forming indentations which approach within a half-mile of each other. The southwestern extremity of Castine is known as Dyce's Head, and the southwestern portion of Brooksville as Cape Rozier. The remaining portion of the territory, northward, forms the present town of Penobscot. The town embraced, before Castine was set off, an area of 38,410 acres. Castine, at the time of its incorporation, comprised an area of 18,100 acres, to which, subsequently, about 5,000 acres were added from Penobscot. Brooksville, at the time of its incorporation, took from Castine about one-half, and from Penobscot about one-fourth of its territory, and also received a small portion from Sedgwick.

NATURAL SCENERY.

The natural scenery of this region, though not so grand as that of mountainous districts, nor so sublime as that of many places lying more exposed to the ocean, is, nevertheless, both variegated and beautiful. The hills, dales and ponds of Penobscot and Brooksville; the bays and isles of Brooksville and Castine ; and the view of Penobscot river and bay, from all these towns, afford scenes, the picturesqueness of which can hardly be surpassed. Penobscot possesses two ponds, called, respectively, Pierce's and North Bay Pond. In addition to these, about one-half of Toddy Pond bounds the town upon the northeast. Brooksville contains six ponds, all,—except Walker's— of less size than those just mentioned, but of equal beauty. Castine has no natural pond, but it boasts the possession of a harbor " in which the navies of the world might ride at ease," and which contains many beautiful islands. Of these, Nautilus Island, containing about thirty acres of land, comes within the jurisdiction of Brooksville—being connected with that town by a bar. Holbrook Island, further to the southwest, containing about fifty acres, is a part of the municipality of Castine. In addition to these, are the two "Nigger*" Islands, Hospital or Noddle Island, —opposite the village—and some seven or eight small rocky islets.

* Is it not possible that the name of these islands is derived from the "Negew," over which Edward Naylor had command, in 1662? There is no satisfactory tradition to account for the name of these islands.

SOILS AND CROPS.

The soil of this region is, generally speaking, a sandy loan, devoid of much humus. As a whole, it has few claims to being considered a profitable farming locality, though it is as much so, perhaps, as similar situations upon the seashore.* There are some fine farms, and excellent pastures, as well as timber lands, in Penobscot and in Brooksville, and the gardens and orchards in the village of Castine are quite productive. The principal crops are grass, rye, oats and potatoes. Of late years, the cultivation of the cranberry has received considerable attention in Castine, and bids fair to become, eventually, a paying crop.

GEOLOGICAL FORMATION.—MINERALS.

The Geological formation consists of talcose, micaceous and plumbaginous slate, slate and trap rocks, gneiss, mica schist and granite. [Jackson' Geological Report.] The only minerals occurring here, that we are aware of, are quartz, mica, and copper and iron pyrites—which are found in considerable abundance in Brooksville. A very good quality of clay is found here in abundance, and along the shores are to be found many extensive deposits of clam shells—no oyster shells have, however, been observed amongst them. These, and other shells, are frequently found collected into petrifactions, and the impressions left by them in the mud, in past ages, are often now seen in the rocks.

FLORA.

The Flora of this region is, in general, similar to that of the rest of the eastern coast of Maine. The description in this place is confined solely to the trees found here. A list of the other plants found here is given in the Appendix.

The woods upon the peninsula of Castine, have been pretty thoroughly decimated by the axe. In Brooksville and Penobscot, there is still a large quantity left. Among the Forest Trees commonly found may be mentioned the Beech, Birch, Alder, Cedar, Juniper, (or Hackmatack,) Oak, Hemlock, Spruce and Willow. Those which are much less commonly to be met with are the Ash, Cherry, Elm, Horse Chesnut, Maple, Fir and Pine. Those which

* Monsieur Talon compared it—in 1670—to Port Royal, and the region about the river St. John.

may be considered as *rare*, are the Hornbeam, Wild Plum, and Poplar. The above constitute the principal trees known, with certainty, to be found at the present time, or which are thought to have grown here in olden times.

FAUNA.

A description of the Fauna of this region must necessarily, in a book of this kind, be of a very general nature, and expressed in general terms. Amongst mammalia, the only animal of a ferocious nature ever met with, in this vicinity is the Wildcat. This animal was so abundant in former times. that bounties were offered for the destruction of it. Although much less common at present, it is still to be found, in the winter season, in our woods. Bears were probably met with here, in early times, but no reference to them has been found, and none have been seen of late years. Of the Deer family, the only kind now met with is the common Red Deer, though the Moose is known to have been formerly a denizen of our woods. The only one of the Dog family known in this region, at the present day, is the red, and possibly the silver gray Fox. The other animals valuable for their *fur*, that are (or were) found here, are the Beaver, Ermine*, Marten, Mink, Weasel, Rabbit, Squirrel, Skunk and Woodchuck. Of still smaller animals, the Hedgehog, Rat, domestic and field Mouse, and Moles, are all that are known to exist in this region.

The list of Birds is much larger. Of the small land birds the Black-bird, the Blue-bird, Blue Jay, Bobolink, Crow, Cherry-bird, Humming-bird, King-bird, Martin, Night-hawk, Oriole, Owl, Robin, Sparrow, *bank*, *barn*, and *chimney* Swallows, Woodpecker and Yellow-bird, please the eye by their variegated plumage, or gratify the ear with their melody. Amongst aquatic birds, the Black Duck, Brant, Brown Coot, Curlew, Dipper, Wild Goose, Heron, King-fisher, Petrel, Plover, Sandpiper, Sheldrake, and the various species of Loons and Gulls are frequently to be seen. Of birds of prey the Brown Hawk, Hen-Hawk, Fish-Hawk, and Brown and Bald Eagles are common. The only *game* birds—besides the aquatic— ever met with here are the Partridge (or quails) the wild Pigeon, and occasionally, the Woodcock.

*The author saw one in the winter of 1871.

In the class of Fishes, the Cod, Cunner, Cusk, Haddock, Hake, Tom Cod, Common Eel, Conger Eel, Lamprey Eel, Flounder, Pollock, Lumpfish, Skate, Sculpin, Squid, Alewife, Smelt, Mackerel, and Salmon are abundant. Amongst Aquatic Mammals (classed here with fishes, for convenience simply), Seals are often found in the harbor, but are very shy, and Whales and Porpoises are once in a great while seen. The Horse Mackerel and the Shark are occasionally, though very rarely, found in our waters. The only fresh water fish found about here is the Brook Trout.

In the class of Reptiles, the only kinds found here are the Speckled Frog, the Bull Frog, the Lizard, Toad, and black, green and striped Snakes.

In the class of Crustaceans and Mollusks, Muscles, Clams, Lobsters, Crabs and Snails are to be found in abundance. Razor Shell Fish are becoming rare here, but are occasionally found. Scallops are quite abundant, and the particular variety found here is thought to be rare elsewhere.

In the class of Radiates, Sea-cucumbers, Sea Urchins, Dollar-fishes, and Star-fishes, the Sea-Anemone and Jelly-fishes abound.

The classes of Insects and of small Marine Animals are altogether too large to admit even of enumeration in this connection.

CLIMATE.

The climate of this region is very much milder than might be supposed from its latitude, and from the general severity of the seasons in New England. Its place, in the winter season, on an isothermal chart, would be, at least, on a level with Boston, if not still further south. In the summer, the heat of the land is so tempered by the breezes from the sea, that its temperature corresponds to that of places very much farther north. Extremely severe weather is, of course, occasionally experienced here ; but, on the whole, it will compare favorably, as regards temperature, with any other locality in the State. A continuous journal of the weather was kept in Castine, by Honorable Job Nelson, from January 1st, 1810, to January 1st, 1850—a period of forty years. From this journal we are enabled to give, not only a valuable resumé of the average temperature of each month during that time, but also many other extracts not devoid of interest. The following is Judge Nelson's summary :—

Average Monthly Temperature from January, 1810 to 1850.

Jannary,	21°.41	July,	64°.82
February,	22.54	August,	64.66
March,	30.38	September,	58.39
April,	41.43	October,	48.41
May,	50.27	November,	38.07
June,	59.42	December,	25.56

The *yearly* average for the forty years, is 43°.78. The *highest* temperature recorded, was on August 1st, 1814, when the mercury stood at 93°. The *lowest* recorded temperature was on January 30th, 1813, when the mercury stood at .—13°. The *average* highest temperature of any month was in July, 1825. The average for this month was 68°.66. The *average* lowest temperature of any month was in January, 1844. The average for this month was 12°.17 The greatest variation in the temperature was on January 20th, 1810, when in *eight* hours the mercury fell forty-four degrees. This was the celebrated " cold Friday." The earliest recorded occurrence of frost* was on September 26th, 1816. The earliest fall of snow occurred on September 30th, 1823. The *severest* snowstorms occurred on the following dates :—In 1829, on March 6th. " More snow on the ground than ever known before," is the language of the journal. In 1831, on March 30th. In 1834, May 15th. In 1835, March 21st. In 1840, December 22d, and 23d. In 1841, March 7th, and 13th, and April 13th. In 1842, March 26th, and November 24th. In 1843, March 28th, and November 10th. In 1844, March 4th, and 30th. In 1845, March 15th, and April 13th.

The earliest date at which potatoes have been planted, was on April 28th, in 1814. The earliest arrival of birds, frogs and migratory fishes were as follows :—

Of Frogs, as early as April 14th, in 1824.
 " Blackbirds, " " " 29th, in 1820.
 " Martins, " " " 9th, in 1827.
 " Robins, " " March 16th, in 1825.
 " Salmon, " " April 25th, in 1820.
 " Smelts, " " March 26th, in 1828.

*By this, Judge Nelson undoubtedly means of a " black " or blighting frost.

Since the incorporation of Castine, Penobscot bay has been frozen over, so as to permit a passage to Belfast upon the ice, some four or five times only. The first three times in which this event occurred were the three consecutive years of 1815, '16 and '17·

Two shocks of earthquake have been felt here since the year 1787. The first was on May 22d, 1817, and the other on Aug. 27th, 1829. November 7th, 1819, was a very dark day. At this time, fowls went to roost at midday, and superstitious people thought the "day of doom" had come*. The night of November 17th, 1835, is recorded as being very uncommonly light; from what cause is not stated.

The record of the winds, in Judge Nelson's journal, is very incomplete. Reckoning from the data given, however, it may be said, of this period of time, that the rain storms nearly all came from the southeast, the snow storms from the northeast, and that nearly all the gales, unaccompanied by rain or snow, came from the northwest. When the wind blew from the southwest, it was almost invariably fair weather.

This journal gives no account of fogs. Their not infrequent occurrence, probably, in Judge Nelson's opinion, rendering any statement in regard to them unnecessary. Although fogs are of common occurrence here in the summer season, when southerly winds are prevailing, yet it is believed to be the fact, that they are of less frequent occurrence, less dense, and more apt to be dispelled by the rays of the sun, than is the case at the neighboring seaports to the east of us.

Doctor Joseph L. Stevens, of Castine, has also kept a record of the weather from 1821 to 1871—a period of fifty years. As this record has not been kept in a *tabular* form, it is not possible to give more than the relative character of each year, together with a few miscellaneous facts of interest. The following is a summary, by years, given in Doctor Stevens' journal :—

1832.—Was a wet and and cold year.

1833.—Ditto. A remarkable shower of meteors was witnessed by him on the night of Nov. 13.

1834.—Was warm and fruitful.

1835.—Ditto.

*This was not, however, the "dark day" celebrated in the annals of New England. The latter occurred May 19th, 1780.

1836.—Very dry, and very cool. Short hay crop.

1837.—Cool. No corn, but wheat abundant.

1838.—Summer warm, and year fruitful.

1839.—Summer extremely wet.

1840.—Summer warm and fruitful. A very healthy season.

1841.—Summer very dry. Very few storms this year.

1842.—No epidemic, except that of Scarlatina, from which there were six deaths.

1843.—Year fruitful. Grass abundant. No epidemics.

1844.—Apples and fruit in abundance. The potato rot makes its first appearance here.

1845.—Excessive fall of rain. Complete failure of the potato crop. Healthy here, but sickly in the neighboring towns.

1846.—Summer very warm. Epidemic of Scarlatina. More deaths here, from all causes, than ever before known.

1848.—Very rainy year. Summer cool. No epidemic, but more deaths than last year.

1849.—Warm and dry. Healthy.

1850.—Spring *very* wet. Summer temperate. Autumn pleasant. No epidemics.

1851.—Winter very cold. A very healthy year.

1852.—Summer cool. Apples abundant. No epidemic except Influenza.

1853.—A very mild, but a very windy year. Many disasters at sea. No epidemics.

1854.—Summer very dry. A great many snow storms in winter. " Healthiest year I ever knew."

1856.—No epidemics, except sore throats.

1857.—Year unusually cold and wet. Very healthy.

1858.—Year cool and wet. No epidemics.

1859.—A great quantity of snow in December.

1861.—No epidemics, and unusually few deaths.

1862.—Scarlatina and Typhoid fever. Apples and fruit abundant.

1863.—Very few storms. Short hay crop. A few cases of Diphtheria—otherwise, healthy.

1864.—A very dry and fair summer. Healthy here, but not in Brooksville.

1867.—Cool and wet. Dull and healthy.

1868.—Wet and foggy. No epidemics.

1869.—Cold summer. No epidemics.

1871.—Year very mild. Crops and business good. Many disasters at sea. Healthy.

The earliest date at which wild geese have been noticed on their passage north, was on March 4th, in 1871. The earliest date of blooming of trees, and certain plants, was as follows:—

Apple trees were in bloom, May 25th, in 1814.
Cherry trees were in bloom, May 15th, in 1825.
Lilac trees   "   " .   " 30th, in 1826.
Plum trees   "   "   " 20th, in 1825.
Peonies   "   "   " 24th, in 1826.
White Roses   "   "   July 4th, in 1826.
Strawberries   "   "   April 30th, in 1833.
Tulips,   "   May 24th, in 1826.
Violets,   "   "   April 9th, 1825.

The earliest date on which the grass in his garden was mowed, was on June 9th, in 1831. The earliest date at which blueberries and garden vegetables were obtained by him, as follows:—

Blueberries were ripe on July 20th, in 1826.
Cucumbers were fit for use, July 16th, in 1826.
Green Corn was fit for use, June 9th, in 1831.
Green Peas were fit for use, July 13th, in 1822.*
New Potatoes were fit for use, July 18th, in 1826.

All attempts to foretell the character of the summer by that of any of the previous months, are, of course, futile. It would seem, however, from this record of Doctor Stevens, that there has been, for the period of time which it embraces, a remarkably close correspondence between the character of the month of March, and that of the season following. A cold March has been almost invariably followed by a cold summer, and a warm or wet March, by a warm or wet summer. Whether this is merely an accidental coincidence, or is due to some climatic law not yet understood, remains for further observations to determine.

*Green Peas and new Potatoes are often to be had here as early as July 4th.

CHAPTER II.
MUNICIPAL HISTORY OF PENOBSCOT.

PLANTATION No. 3. — NEW IRELAND. — EARLY SET-
TLERS. — FIRST SURVEY OF TOWN. — ABSTRACT OF
TOWN RECORDS. — CASTINE SET OFF. — HIGHWAYS. —
SCHOOLS.

(PRIOR TO THE INCORPORATION OF CASTINE.)

1762. The town of Penobscot was Number Three, in
the first class of townships granted by the Provincial
General Court, in 1762. In accordance with the terms of
these grants, the proprietors were bound, themselves,
their heirs and assigns, in a bond of fifty pounds, to lay
out no township more than six miles in extent on the
bank of the Penobscot, or on the sea coast; to present to
the General Court, by the thirty-first of the ensuing July,
plans of the survey; to settle each township with sixty
protestant families within six years; and to build an equal
number of dwelling houses, at least eighteen feet square;
to fit for tillage three hundred acres of land, erect a meeting-house, and settle a minister. One lot in each township was to be reserved for the parsonage, one for the first
settled minister, one for Harvard College, and another for
the use of schools. These grants were not, however, presented to the Legislature for confirmation, until the year
1785.

1780. About the year 1780 or 1781, an attempt was
made by the British Government to colonize the country
between the Penobscot and St. Croix, under the name of
New Ireland. Thomas Oliver, a former Lieutenant Governor of Massachusetts, a resident of Cambridge, and a
graduate of Harvard College, was proposed as the first
Chief Magistrate. Daniel Leonard, a prominent loyalist,
afterwards a judge in Bermuda, was to be the Chief Justice. The plan was abandoned, in consequence of the
doubts of the Attorney General of England, as to the
right to the soil. New Brunswick and Nova Scotia, therefore " became the asylum of thousands of the former cit-

izens of New England, who otherwise would have settled
New Ireland, and rendered Castine what Shelburne in
Nova Scotia once was, and what St. Johns and Halifax
now are."* There was an association formed to promote
this settlement, under the title of the "Associated
Refugees." [Letter from Lord George Germain, to Sir
Henry Clinton, in Appendix 3, to Spark's Life and Writings of Washington, Vol. VIII, p. 519.] Whether any
actual settlements, under the auspices of this association,
ever took place, is not known; but as the British force
did not leave until two or three years subsequently, and
as there were certainly some settlers here in 1775, it is not
at all unlikely that such was the case. This is rendered
still more probable by the discovery among the papers of
the late Mr. Jeremiah Wardwell, of the following;—

"NOTIFICATION:

1784. These are to notify and require all persons at
and near Majorbagaduce, in the unincorporated towns,
that have been inimical to the United States of America,
during the last war with Great Britain, to depart out of
the Commonwealth of Massachusetts on or before the
thirteenth day of September next, or they will gain the
Displeasure of the Subscribers and many others of the
Citizens of the Commonwealth, that have suffered by the
War.   August 11th, 1784.

N. B.   All those that are well disposed to the United
States are desired to meet at the Fort on Bagaduce, on the
said thirteenth day of September, to Consult what measures to take, in case the above Requisition is not complied
with."

(Signed)   JOHN MOOR.
[All the other names missing.]

1785. In the year 1785, the legislature passed an Act,
allowing to the several settlers convenient lots of one
hundred acres each, so surveyed as to include their
improvements, and divided the rest—after reserving twelve
hundred acres in each town for public uses—amongst the
original grantees and their representatives. [Resolve of
General Court, in regard to Plantation No. 3, Nov. 17th,
1786.]   This year, eight or ten families came hither from
Fort Pownal, and some of those who had left during the

* From an account of New Ireland, in a paper read by the Hon. Joseph
Williamson, before the Maine Historical Society.

period of the Revolutionary War, returned. [Williamson, Hist. of Me., Vol. II, p. 534.] Messrs. Philip, Leonard, and Charles Jarvis, had a considerable interest in the lands embraced by this Plantation, and were prominent agents for the settlers, in obtaining a confirmation of their title. About this time, the earliest survey of the town was made by John Peters, Esq., subsequently of Bluehill.*

1787. By Act of the General Court of Massachusetts, the town of Penobscot was incorporated on February 23d, 1787. The first meeting of the town was held at the house of Colonel Johannot, on Wednesday, April 18th. At this meeting, Mr. Joseph Hibbert was chosen Moderator; John Lee, Clerk; and Captain Joseph Perkins, Jeremiah Wardwell, Oliver Parker, Joseph Hibbert, and Captain Joseph Young, were chosen Selectmen; and Mr. John Perkins, Town Treasurer. At a meeting of the town, held the May following, Messrs. John Lee, Oliver Parker, Joseph Young, Jeremiah Wardwell, and Joseph Perkins, were chosen a Committee, to make an adjustment with the former proprietors of Plantation No. 3. The following were the instructions given to the Committee:—

"The Report of the Great and Grand Court of the Commonwealth, of November 17th, 1786, confirming the lands to the Proprietors and Settlers of this township, being of the utmost importance, the Proprietors by it are enjoined to allot and meet out one hundred acres of land to each Settler who settled and made improvements before the first of January, 1784. We are fully confident that the design of Government, in passing the aforesaid Resolve, was to do us justice; yet we fear that it will be attended with much difficulty to meet out the lands to such settlers, in such a manner as to secure to them the full benefit intended them by the said Resolve. Therefore we request you, our Committee, chosen to make an adjustment with the said proprietors, to attend fully to the following instructions. You will, as soon as possible, make out a statement of the claims of all the settlers who are entitled to land upon the principle of said Resolve, in the most explicit manner possible, in doing which you will pay particular attention to the true intent and meaning of the said Resolve, a copy of this State of Claims to lay in some one place, to be open to the inspection of any person who

* The original field notes and map of this survey are in possession of the Hon. C. J. Abbot, of this town.

is a settler in this town, who wishes to examine the same. By this statement of the Claims of each settler (when completed) upon the principle of said Resolve, containing each person's claim, with the names of the settler under whom he holds—with the bounds and the date of settlement, you will know what quantity of land will of right belong to the settlers,—therefore from this statement you will be able to determine what will do each settler justice. When the Proprietors' Committee attend to meet out the land to the settlers as required by said Resolve, you will represent to them how desirous the Inhabitants of the town are to have an amicable adjustment of every matter, respecting the Lands, with them—to effect which they are determined not to be wanting on their part, and as we wish for nothing but what the said Resolve has confirmed to us, and as the Proprietors cannot reasonably wish for any advantage that the said Resolve has not given them, it is hoped and expected that they will cordially agree to make an adjustment upon such terms as will be for the mutual interest and advantage of both Proprietors and Settlers."

1788. At the Annual meeting of the town in 1788, the former board of Selectmen were re-elected, and in December following, George Thatcher Esq., was elected as the first representative to the General Court. The Committee appointed to confer with the former Proprietors of the township, reported as follows :—

" On the arrival of Leonard Jarvis, Esq., agent of, and one of the principal proprietors of, this town, we had a conference with him upon the subject of an adjustment. Mr. Jarvis observed that he came to mete out the land to the settlers agreeable to the resolve of the General Court. We assured him the inhabitants of the town were glad to see him, and that they were exceedingly desirous to have an amicable settlement with the proprietors, and that they wished for nothing more than was confirmed to them by the Grand Court. We, in obedience to our instructions, stated the manner in which we supposed each settler would have justice done him. That such settlers as were so situated as to render it very inconsistent, if not impossible, to have the hundred acres which the proprietors were enjoined to grant, allot and mete out to them, in one lot, should have such deficiency made up to them elsewhere, to this proportion, founded strictly, as we conceived, upon the resolve of Court. Mr. Jarvis replied that he would, by no means, agree to what, he pretended, was never meant by the Court, though the letter of the resolve of Court is fully in our favor. In reasoning upon this subject, we found that he put such illiberal constructions upon the resolve of Court, that it was impossible for us to make any adjustment with him upon the principle of justice, or consistent with our duty. Nay, Mr. Jarvis plainly intimated that he should not pay any regard to the Town, as a Town, or to their Committee, but that he would proceed to mete out the land to the settlers in such a manner as he should think was agreeable to the meaning of the Court. How far he has attended to the resolve of Court, while upon this business, it is not for us to determine. Though we think it our duty upon this occasion to observe that, notwithstanding the great esteem we have for Mr. Jarvis, which occasions us great pain, when we declare our surprise that he should infringe upon the privileges of this town, by ordering a road to be run out, when by law the Selectmen, for the time being, or such other as they should appoint, have the sole power to lay out or alter roads within the limits described in our Incorporation Act.

Finding that an adjustment could not be made with the proprietors, we conceived it our duty to furnish Mr. Jarvis with a memorandum of each settlers' claim, without date or signature, a copy of which is now laid before the Town."

1789.   Three town-meetings were held during the year 1789. At the first, held March 25th, Captain Joseph Perkins, Peletiah Leach, Joseph Hibbert, Captain Oliver Parker and Mr. John Wasson, were chosen Selectmen. The town voted that "the sum of £300 be raised for the building a Meeting-House for the public worship of God." A vote was also passed that in future the town-meetings be held at the house of Mr. Joseph Binney. At a meeting held on April 21st, the town voted to build a meeting-house sixty-five feet in length by fifty feet in breadth. Captain Daniel Wardwell, Giles Johnson, Oliver Parker, John Willson and John Wasson, were chosen a committee to superintend the erection of the building, and to act as a Board of Trustees. At this meeting Mr. Gabriel Johannot was elected as Representative to the General Court. At a meeting held on the first day of September following, the town voted not to make any additional appropriation for the meeting-house, but to have the pews classified and sold at public auction, and to use the money thus obtained, in completing the building.

1790. Fifty persons were *warned* from the town in the year 1790.* This year Messrs. Oliver Parker, Joseph Hibbert, Captain Daniel Wardwell, Captain Seth Blodgett, and Doctor Oliver Mann, were chosen Selectmen.

1791. In the year 1791, the town made its first appropriation for a public school. This year, Messrs. John Perkins, Elijah Littlefield, David Hawes, David Willson and Pelatiah Leach, were chosen Selectmen. Isaac Parker, Esq., was elected Representative to the General Court.† At a meeting held September 12th, a committee of eleven citizens was appointed to wait upon Mr. Leonard Jarvis, Agent for the former proprietors of Plantation No. 3, and determine upon terms of settlement with them.

1792. At the annual meeting, in March, 1792, Captain Oliver Parker, Doctor Oliver Mann, and Messrs. John Wasson, John Willson and Sparks Perkins, were chosen Selectmen. The town at this meeting voted " against a separation of Government." Whether this meant against a separation of the District of Maine from the Commonwealth of Massachusetts, or against a division of the town, can only be inferred. It was probably the former, as no petition for any separation accompanied the warrant for the meeting. At a meeting held in November, the town passed a vote against a removal of the Courts to any other place in the county, or to any different location in this town. It was also voted that, in the future, the town-meetings should be held in the meeting-house on the peninsula.

1793. At the annual meeting held in 1793, Messrs. Jeremiah Wardwell, Pelatiah Leach, John Wasson, Doctor Oliver Mann and John Willson, were elected Selectmen. At this meeting, the town voted to raise no money for the support of preaching, or for schools. This vote was afterwards reconsidered, and thirty pounds was appropriated for preaching. At a subsequent meeting, held May 8th, the sum of fifty pounds was appropriated for the support of schools. At this latter meeting, Isaac Parker, Esq., was chosen Representative to the General Court. At a meeting held June 20th, the town voted an appropriation of three pounds for the erection of some *stocks*,—to be placed near the Court House, on the peninsula.

*In regard to this matter of "warnings" from town, see chapter 3d.

†Williamson [Hist. of Me., Vol. 2, p. 534], erroneously says that Mr. Parker was the *first* Representative of Penobscot to the General Court.

1794. At the annual meeting in 1794, the last board of Selectmen were re-elected.   The town, at this meeting, voted an appropriation of twenty pounds, to purchase a supply of ammunition.

1795. At the annual meeting of the town, in 1795, Captain Thatcher Avery, Mr. Joseph Binney, and Mr. Thomas Wasson, were elected as Selectmen.

Mr. Mark Hatch, and others in the second or lower parish, having petitioned the General Court, to be set off as a separate town, a meeting of the inhabitants of the first parish was called, in reference thereto, on December the 21st.   The following votes were passed :—

1. That the first parish will show cause to the General Court why the second parish ought not to be separated and become a distinct town.

2. That Captain Jeremiah Wardwell, Mr. Pelatiah Leach, Captain Thatcher Avery, Isaac Parker, Esq., Captain Joseph Perkins and Captain John Perkins, be a committee to agree upon lines, and terms of separation.   This committee reported, at a meeting held December 31st, "that in consideration of the length of highways in an unrepaired state which would be in the upper part of the town, the committee for the petitioners had offered to pay two hundred dollars in two annual payments.   The committee on the other side, then proposed four hundred dollars,— when, for the sake of harmony and accommodation, it was offered to divide and give three hundred,—which the committee would agree to give with the consent of the town." The town, however, refused to accept the terms offered, and sent Mr. Pelatiah Freeman to the General Court to oppose a separation.   No further allusion to the separation appears in the town or parish records.

The municipal history of Penobscot, thus far, is equally as much that of the towns of Castine and Brooksville. Matters relating to the establishment of religious preaching and schools, will be found incorporated with the chapters upon the ecclesiastical and educational history of Castine.

(SUBSEQUENT TO THE INCORPORATION OF CASTINE.)

1796. At the annual meeting of the town, held April 4, 1796, Captain Thatcher Avery, Mr. Joseph Binney, and Mr. Thomas Wasson, were elected Selectmen.   At this meeting, Captain Jeremiah Wardwell, Pelatiah Freeman,

John Wasson, Captain Thatcher Avery and Pelatiah Leach, were chosen a committee to confer with a similar committee, on the part of the town of Castine, in regard to the settlement of the accounts between the two towns. Their report was that of the joint committee, and will be found in the next chapter. At a meeting held May 13th, Messrs. Joseph Binney, Daniel Wardwell, Jr., John Snowman, Jotham Stover, Samuel Wasson, Samuel Russell, Ralph Devereux, and Captain Jeremiah Wardwell, were chosen a committee to divide the town into eight school districts, and to apportion the scholars and money to each district.

As the municipal history of Penobscot, subsequently to this time, contains almost nothing of general interest, and so very little even of what might be deemed of *local* interest, a further adherence to the records of the town-meetings seems unnecessary. In fact, from this date down to the time of the late civil war, the chief business of the town at its annual meetings, seems to have been that of laying out, accepting, or altering, new roads, and of increasing or changing the number of school districts.

The length and number of the roads in Penobscot, is probably greater than that of any other town in the county— of no larger territorial extent—and the expense attending them has been great. A full account of the road-making and of the appropriations for this purpose, though it might possess some value, would not be very interesting, and does not come within the scope of this work. It will be sufficient to say, in general terms, that from the date of incorporation to the present time, the appropriations for highways have been about double those for schools. The appropriations for schools, from the date of incorporation to the year 1850, inclusive, amounted to the sum of twenty-one thousand six hundred and sixteen dollars. This is an average of three hundred and sixty-six dollars per annum.

Our inability to obtain possession of any of the district records, as well as the limited time we were able to bestow upon the perusal of the town records, prevents our giving as full an account of the SCHOOL HISTORY of this town as we could desire. We can, therefore, mention only such facts in regard to this, and other matters, as have come to our knowledge.

1808. In 1808, the town voted by a very large majority, against a separation of the District of Maine from the Commonwealth of Massachusetts.

1812.   In the year 1812, the sum of one hundred and ninety dollars was added to the town's appropriation for schools.   This amount accrued from the sale of lumber from the school-lot.

1825.   In the year 1825, the town paid Mr. William Hutchins five dollars for the draft of a plan for a new school-house.

1826.   In 1826, a portion of the school lot was sold for the sum of one hundred and forty-five dollars and eighty-seven cents; and the minister's lot was sold for three hundred and fifty-seven dollars and fifty-five cents.

1836.   In the year 1836, the school fund amounted to eight hundred and thirty-five dollars and ten cents.   This year the town voted to accept a town-house, forty feet long by thirty wide, built by Mr. William Grindle, at a cost of four hundred and sixty-six dollars.

1839—1845.   In the year 1838, the school fund had increased to eight hundred and forty-eight dollars and two cents.   In the year 1840, the town voted to allow the districts to choose their own school agents.   In 1845, the school fund had lessened somewhat, and now amounted to seven hundred and twenty-four dollars and seventy-nine cents.

The military history of the town, will be found fully treated of in connection with the same period in the history of Castine.

CHAPTER III.
THE MUNICIPAL HISTORY OF CASTINE.

INCORPORATION OF TOWN.—WARNINGS FROM TOWN.—
REPORT OF COMMITTEE OF CONFERENCE.—SETTLE-
MENT OF FIRST PASTOR.—CEMETERY PURCHASED.—
EFFECT OF THE EMBARGO.—RESOLUTIONS IN REGARD
TO IT.—PETITION TO THE PRESIDENT OF THE UNITED
STATES.—COMMITTEE OF PUBLIC SAFETY.—FEELING
IN REGARD TO THE WAR OF 1812.—TITLE TO COM-
MON.—HEARSE PURCHASED.—TOWN MAKES A STAND
AGAINST INTEMPERANCE.—BOARD OF HEALTH CHOS-
EN.—POOR FARM.—FIRE ENGINE PURCHASED.—TOMB
PRESENTED TO THE TOWN.—TOWN LIBRARY ESTAB-
LISHED.—COPY OF STUART'S PORTRAIT OF WASH-
INGTON PRESENTED TO THE TOWN.—LOCK-UP VOTED.—
BY-LAWS ADOPTED.—BOUNTIES VOTED TO SOLDIERS.

1796. By an act passed by the Commonwealth of
Massachusetts, the town of Penobscot was, upon the
tenth day of February, 1796, divided into two separate
towns. One portion retained the name of Penobscot.
The southerly portion of the old town was incorporated
by the name of Castine, in memory of the noted man
whose life was so intimately connected with the history of
Pentagöet.

The first meeting of the town was held on the fourth
day of April following. The warrants for this meeting
were posted at Captain Joseph Young's house, on Cape
Rozier; at Mr. Jacob Orcutt's, near Buck's Harbor; and
at the door of Mr. Daniel Johnston's store, on the peninsula. At this meeting, Oliver Parker was chosen Moderator; Thomas Phillips, Town Clerk; Captain Joseph Perkins, Captain Joseph Young, and Mr. David Willson,
were chosen Selectmen and Assessors; and John Lee, Esq.,
Town Treasurer. The law, at that time, required voters
to be twenty-one years of age, to have lived in town one
year, and to have "a freehold estate within said town of
the annual income of three Pounds, or any estate to the

value of sixty Pounds." The law also authorized towns
to expel from their limits, upon fifteen days notice, all
persons, that might be deemed necessary, who had not
been sufficiently long in town to acquire a residence.
This law, which to us seems so arbitrary and unjust, was
doubtless enacted to enable towns to protect themselves
against shiftless and worthless persons, who might otherwise become a public charge. It has happened in many
towns, however, that persons thus *warned* have subsequently become the most esteemed citizens. One of the
first acts of this town was, in accordance with this law
and the custom of the time, to warn from town one
Miriam Freethy, and, a few weeks later, five other
individuals. These are the only cases in which this law
was ever applied here. The population of the town, at
this date, was 178. At this meeting, Isaac Parker, Esq.,
John Lee, Esq., Captain Mark ·Hatch, Mr. David Howe,
and Captain John Perkins, were chosen a committee on
the part of the town, to confer with a similar committee,
appointed by the town of Penobscot, in relation to the
settlement of the accounts between the two towns, and
were given full power to adjust the same. On May the
tenth, a second town-meeting was called, and the town
districted for schools. On September the twenty-fourth,
at a legal town-meeting, it was voted to extend an invitation to the Reverend Micah Stone, to be settled as Pastor
of the town, and that " the sum of four hundred dollars,
as agreed by the town, be given him as a yearly salary;
also, that the sum of eight hundred dollars be given him,
upon his settlement as our Pastor." This vote, however,
never went into effect. Upon the twenty-fifth of October,
the town assembled to hear the report of the committee
of conference for adjusting the accounts with the town of
Penobscot. The committee reported as follows:—

" First, your Committee determined that the apportion-
ment of property and debts which belonged to the whole
as parts of the town of Penobscot, should be made according to the ratio adopted in the Act incorporating the town
of Castine,—that is to say; that Castine should be respon-
sible for three-fifths of the amount of debts subsisting
against the old town of Penobscot, and should be entitled
to the same proportion of the property belonging to said
town—the remaining two-fifths belonging to the present
town of Penobscot.

They find the amount of property belonging to the towns to be one thousand one hundred and eighty-five dollars; consisting of, the meeting-house on the peninsula, the Town Pound, a note of hand signed by Sparks Perkins, and sundry window sashes.* * * * The Committee agreed that the town of Castine should take the meeting-house on the peninsula, at the price estimated by them. They likewise agreed that Castine should assume the whole of the debts due to the inhabitants of that town, and be credited for the surplus beyond their due proportion of debt—being one hundred and thirty-two dollars and fifty-six cents.

*   *   *   *   *   *   *   *

The Committee have likewise agreed that the land appropriated to the uses of Township Number Three, for supporting schools, minister's lot, and the lot for the use of the ministry, shall be equally divided between said towns of Castine and Penobscot, and they have drawn a Petition to the General Court, to have this agreement carried into effect. They have likewise agreed upon a division of the roads which are to be put into repair, according to the Act of the General Court incorporating · Castine.

*   *   *   *   *   *

Castine takes upon itself to put in repair, according to said Act, the road from Lymburner's Ferry to Sedgwick; likewise, the road from 'the peninsula by David Willson and Joseph Hibbert, up to the line of Plantation Number Two; also, the westerly part of the cross road leading from the last mentioned road to Pelatiah Freeman's, as far in the same road as Samuel Farnham's house."

The consideration of this report was laid over to another meeting. At a meeting held the November following, this report was accepted by the town. At this meeting, the town elected its first School Committee, consisting of six members. It also, this year elected Isaac Parker, Esq., as its *first* Representative to the General Court of Massachusetts. As, at the time of the incorporation of the town, Penobscot was the shire town of Hancock County, and as all the County buildings were situated upon this peninsula, Castine was, by the Act aforesaid, declared to be the County seat.

1797. About the time of the incorporation of the town, the question in regard to a separation of the District of Maine from the Commonwealth of Massachusetts, began to be quite generally discussed, and an attempt was soon made to bring it about. The question was submitted to the towns of the Commonwealth in 1797, and the vote of Castine was found to be in a very decided majority against it. The General Court of Massachusetts this year passed a Resolve, dividing the Minister's Lot, etc., equally between the two towns.

1798. The only measure occurring the next year, entitled to notice in this place, was the invitation extended to Reverend William Mason, to become the pastor of the town, at a salary of three hundred and fifty dollars per annum, for three years. He was also to receive eight hundred dollars, upon his settlement over the town. He was ordained upon the second Wednesday of October.

1799. In April, 1799, Mr. Barnabas Higgins was chosen town sexton.

1800. In August, 1800, Water street was laid out. There having been some talk in regard to removing the County seat from Castine, the town, by a formal vote, protested against any change of location.

1801—1807. In 1801, Job Nelson Esq., was chosen Representative to the General Court. He was succeeded in 1803 by Doctor Oliver Mann, who was annually re-elected, until the year 1806, when he was succeeded by Captain Otis Little. He was, however, again elected in the year 1807. In the year 1804, in accordance with resolves of the General Court, Commissioners were sent here to settle, finally, the differences between the proprietors and settlers, in what was formerly Township No. 3. The proprietors received in Township No. 7* an equivalent for the lands taken by settlers in No. 3. The number of acres settled in the latter township, *prior to the year* 1784, was stated in their report at sixteen thousand one hundred and eighty-one acres and fifty-eight rods.

1807. In the year 1807, the town voted to purchase for a cemetery, one acre of land from Captain Mark Hatch, for the sum of thirty dollars—one-half of which Captain Hatch remitted. The town agreed to fence the land, and hang a gate near the *windmill.* It also agreed to give Captain Hatch his choice of a burial lot. The town this year

*Now the city of Ellsworth.

voted a second time, against a separation of the District from the Commonwealth.

About this time, the English began to exercise what was claimed by their government as the RIGHT OF SEARCH. According to this doctrine, the English navy claimed a right to detain and search all neutral vessels, and to impress all British subjects found therein. This practice bore particularly hard upon the American marine, since the difficulty of determining, in all cases, the respective nationality of English and American sailors led to a total disregard of the rights of the latter. The only way to repress this outrageous proceeding of the English government was, either to put a stop to all mercantile communication between the two countries, or openly to declare war. Congress, whether wisely or unwisely is even now a debatable question, chose the former alternative. An embargo was, accordingly, declared upon the twenty-second of December of this year. The seaboard States were all violently opposed to this measure, and none more so than the Commonwealth of Massachusetts. The citizens of this town, depending for their prosperity upon maritime pursuits, looked upon the prospect of a long embargo with gloomy forebodings. Their sentiments and fears upon this subject, only a few months after the passage of the embargo laws, are aptly described by a youthful poet of the times.*

> " See the bold sailor from the ocean torn,
> His element, sink friendless and forlorn!
> His suffering spouse the tear of anguish shed,
> His starving children cry aloud for bread!
> On the rough billows of misfortune tost,
> Resources fail, and all his hopes are lost;
> To foreign climes for that relief he flies,
> His native land ungratefully denies.
> * * * * *
> The farmer, since supporting trade is fled,
> Leaves the rude joke, and cheerless hangs his head;
> Misfortunes fall, an unremitting shower,
> Debts follow debts, on taxes, taxes pour.
> See in his stores his hoarded produce rot,
> Or Sheriff's sales his produce bring to naught;
> Disheartening cares in thronging myriads flow,
> Till down he sinks, to poverty and woe."

Having experienced, in a measure, some of the miseries so vividly portrayed in the above quotation, it was not unnatural that this town should, like many others in New England, attempt to exercise some influence over the National Councils.

*Written by William Cullen Bryant, when only fourteen years of age.

11

1808. Accordingly, in the year 1808, the town voted that the Selectmen transmit, under their hands, to the President, the following petition :—

" To the President of the United States:

The inhabitants of the Town of Castine, in Town-meeting legally assembled, respectfully represent: —

That, habituated to commercial pursuits, and drawing their support and wealth from the ocean and from foreign countries, the laws laying an embargo are peculiarly distressing to them. Although they have doubted the expediency of these laws, and even their constitutionality—when imposed for an unlimited time,—yet they have hitherto waited with patience, in the hope that our difficulties with the great powers of Europe might be so adjusted, that it would be consistent with the policy of our Government to remove the embargo. That this distressing measure has had any favorable influence on our foreign relations, does not at present appear ; but that your petitioners have endured heavy losses, their idle ships and perishing commodities unfortunately bear positive testimony.

The events now taking place in Spain, so glorious to that nation, and so propitious to the LIBERTY and happiness of mankind, open to your petitioners the prospect of a ready market for their surplus produce, and at the same time afford them an opportunity, which they would eagerly seize, of repaying an ancient obligation.

They, therefore, pray your Excellency that the Embargo may be in whole or in part suspended, according to the powers vested in you by the Congress of the United States ; and, if any doubt exist as to the competency of those powers, that Congress may be convened to take the subject into their consideration."

1809. In the year 1809, Captain Otis Little was, a second time, elected Representative to the General Court, This year, a bounty of twelve and a half cents *per capita*. was offered by the town, for all *crows* killed within its limits. At a town-meeting held January thirtieth, Mason Shaw, Otis Little, Job Nelson, John Perkins, Moses S. Judkins, and Captain Mark Hatch, were chosen a Committee of Public Safety. At this same meeting, the town voted that: " the thanks of this meeting be given to Captain Samuel A. Whitney, for his manly and patriotic conduct in withdrawing his guns from the cutter, in the service of the United States, to enforce the Embargo laws." This vote plainly shows that the doctrine of " State Rights " must have had advocates in this section of the country, even at that early day. On what other ground could it be called patriotic, to throw impediments in the way of the execution of National laws?

1812. On June 18th, 1812, war was declared between Great Britain and the United States. Party spirit ran high at this time, and the people of this town, in common with the majority of those in the District of Maine, were even more opposed to the war than they had been to the embargo. One of the resolutions, passed about this time, shows the state of feeling then prevalent.—" We consider the sea our FARM, and our ships our STOREHOUSES, and that our rights therein ought not to be diminished or destroyed."

The town, at its different meetings this year, passed resolutions in favor of the liberty of speech and of the press, and in regard to the duty of the people to raise their voice against the wrong-doing of the government. Also, against the embargo, non-intercourse and non-importation laws, and against a declaration of war with Great Britain. Also, deprecating any alliance with France; against *voluntary* enlistments—but in favor of resisting actual invasion; and against the conduct of the Senate, " *de-facto*," of Massachusetts, in refusing to submit the choice of electors for President and Vice-President, to the people at large. A second Committee of Public Safety were chosen, consisting of Captain Joseph Perkins, William Abbott, Esq., Mason Shaw, Esq., Captain Elisha Dyer, and Job Nelson, Esq. The town also, at this meeting, voted that " the thanks of this meeting be presented to the gentlemen composing the former Committee of Safety, for their patriotic conduct in sending to the Governor for arms and ammunition, and that their doings be approved of." It was also voted that the Committee of Public Safety be instructed to deliver the arms, that might be furnished the town by direction of the government, to such applicants as they should judge expedient for the best protection and safety of the town. Also, that they should take the applicant's receipt therefor, that they should be returned, in good order, on demand.

In addition to the excitement in regard to national affairs, the people of this town were considerably agitated in regard to the proposed removal of the Courts. The Representative to the General Court was instructed to use all legal measures to oppose such a removal, and a committee was appointed to draw up a remonstrance against the measure, and to forward copies thereof, to the Selectmen of the several towns of the county.

1813. The feeling against the war continuing to exist in all its intensity, the town, at its annual meeting in 1813, passed a resolution that,—"the Representative of this town be instructed to use his influence with the Legislature, that they may assert the just rights of this Commonwealth; put an end to the calamities which we now endure; restore to us the inestimable blessings of peace and commerce; and secure on a permanent basis that liberty purchased by the blood of our ancestors." At a subsequent meeting, held October 27th, it was voted:—"That Job Nelson, William Abbott, and Thomas E. Hale, Esqrs., be a committee to prepare an address to the General Court, expressive of our feelings and sentiments relative to the alarming consequences which are likely to follow from the further prosecution of the war, and from several unconstitutional clauses in the late act of the government of the United States, laying an embargo—particularly in restricting the coasting trade from one port to another in the same State— and that they make their report at the adjournment of this meeting." The town this year passed a vote of thanks to Major Otis Little, for his faithful services as their Representative to the General Court of the Commonwealth. It also appears upon the records for this year, that the Firewards were provided, at the expense of the town, with suitable badges of their office.

1814—1815. In the year 1814, the town offered a bounty of two dollars, for each wild-cat killed during the year. The town this year voted to have a bridge built across the narrows at Captain F. Bakeman's Mill Pond. The building of this bridge was set up at auction, and Jonathan L. Stevens bid it off at the sum of two hundred and twenty dollars. Mr. Thomas Adams represented the town this year at the General Court. The town was occupied by the British, during a portion of the years 1814 and 1815, but no allusion to this event appears in the Municipal records. In the latter year, a title was, for the first time, obtained to the Common.

1816. In 1816, Thomas E. Hale was chosen Representative to the General Court. The town at this meeting voted: " That the thanks of this town be given to Deacon

David Willson, for his long and faithful services as a Selectman; he having served in that office for *nineteen* years successively, and now at this meeting declines a re-election." The town this year voted a *third* time against a separation of the District of Maine from the Commonwealth of Massachusetts.

1817. In 1817, the first hearse was purchased, and the first stove for warming the meeting-house. The Common was this year levelled and otherwise improved.

The town also passed a vote in favor of having Cape Rozier set off to Sedgwick. Instead of that, however, by an act of the General Court, the town of Brooksville was incorporated—taking all that portion of Castine east of the Bagaduce River, (below Northern Bay,) except the islands not connected to the mainland by a bar. At the same time, about one-fourth part of Penobscot was annexed to Castine.

1819. In the year 1819, the town was for the *fourth* time called to vote upon the question of the separation of the District from the Commonwealth. This time it voted, by a small majority, in favor of such a separation, and William Abbott, Esq., was chosen a delegate to attend a Convention to be held in Portland, for the purpose of framing a Constitution for a new State. Samuel Upton was chosen Representative to the General Court.

1820. On the fifteenth of March, 1820, the District of Maine was, by act of Congress, divorced from the Commonwealth of Massachusetts, and admitted into the Union as an independent State.

1822. In the year 1822, William Abbott, Esq., was elected as the Representative of the town to the State Legislature. Mr. Abbott was not only the first Representative chosen by the town to the Legislature of Maine, but was also the only one chosen by this town alone—as this office has since been filled by the joint votes of several towns. About this time, some of the inhabitants of a portion of Penobscot petitioned to be annexed to Castine. This town, however, voted against receiving them, and instructed its Representative to oppose it in the Legislature.

1823. The next year—1823—coasting down Main street was forbidden, by vote of the town. The boys were, doubtless, as obedient to this mandate of the town as boys are apt to be, in regard to requirements which militate against their supposed rights. The town this year voted to purchase a hearse-house. Whether the hearse had been allowed to remain exposed to the weather all this time, or had been stored in some barn, the records do not state.

1829. In the year 1829, the town made its first stand against intemperance, by refusing to license the sale of liquors.

1831. In 1831, a committee was appointed to remonstrate against a removal of the Courts.

1832. During the summer of 1832, the cholera was prevailing in this country, and the excitement incident thereto extended to this town. Joseph Bryant, Esq., Joseph L. Stevens, M. D., Hezekiah Williams, Esq., Joshua Carpenter, John H. Jarvis, Joshua Hooper, and Nathaniel Willson, were chosen as a Board of Health, and one hundred dollars was appropriated to their use. They established a quarantine for vessels, inspected every house in town, and compelled the removal of all nuisances and filth. The measures taken were effectual, as no cholera cases occurred here, although the disease made its appearance in some of the other sea-board towns.

1833. In the year 1833, the town voted to purchase a Poor Farm. This farm was located in Brooksville, on what was formerly called Hainey's Plantation. It was bought of Major Hodsden, for the sum of fifteen hundred dollars. It contained one hundred and eighty-seven acres of land ; yielded from twenty to thirty tons of hay ; had on it a large quantity of young wood ; was well watered, and contained a mill privilege, and a house and barn. The house was thirty feet wide, by thirty-six feet in length. It was a story and a half high, and had four rooms on the lower floor—all finished and painted. The second story was unfinished. There was a cellar under the whole house, and a good well on the premises.* This year the town again refused to license the sale of liquor. From this time to the outbreak of the War of the Rebellion, the town records contain very little of interest.

1836—1840. In 1836, the town again voted against the removal of the Courts—though this time without producing any beneficial effect. The Courts were removed to Ellsworth, in 1838. In 1840, the town purchased the

*This farm has been sold by the town within a few years, and the town poor are now boarded.

Court House, of Charles J. Abbott, Esq., for the sum of three hundred dollars. It has ever since been used as a town-house.

1845. In the year 1845, money was appropriated for the purchase of the Bagaduce fire engine. This appears to be the earliest appropriation of money, made by the town, for the purchase of a fire engine, although there was such an engine in town at a much earlier date.

1848. In 1848, the town passed its first code of By-Laws, and, for the first time, elected some policemen—six in number.

1849. In 1849, the town voted "that ten per cent of the highway tax be annually appropriated to the purchase and setting out of ornamental trees.

1852. In the year 1852, the Common was fenced. This year the following letter—donating a Tomb—was received by the Selectmen:—

"BANGOR, October 14th, 1852.
To the Selectmen of the town of Castine.

Gentlemen: Being the owner of a tomb in the cemetery at Castine, I propose to give it to the town, to be used by them as a receiving tomb. If they accept the gift, it is my wish that it be always in the care of the Selectmen of the town, and that once a year—say in the month of May—it should be cleaned of all the dead bodies which may have been deposited there.

With a lively recollection of the many favors bestowed on me while I was a citizen of your town, and with my wishes for the welfare and happiness of its inhabitants, I remain,

Respectfully, Your Obedient Servant,
JOSEPH BRYANT."

The town, at its first meeting thereafter, formally accepted the gift of this tomb.

1853. The next year,—1853—the town voted to have plank sidewalks upon *every street* in the town.

1855. In the year 1855, the town Library was established. The books left by the Social Library Association formed the nucleus of this library. The town voted:— "To raise a sum equal to one dollar on each poll assessed the last year, one-half to be collected the present year, and one-half the next year, to be expended in establishing a public library." Is voted also—" that a committee of five persons be appointed by the Moderator, to make the rules

and regulations for governing said library." Charles J.
Abbott, William H. Witherle, Roland H. Bridgham, Samuel Adams, and Joseph L. Stevens, were appointed as this
committee. Mr. Frederic A. Hooke was chosen Treasurer,
and Charles J. Abbott, Hezekiah Williams, Joseph L.
Stevens, Charles A. Cate, and J. Haskell Noyes, were
chosen Superintendents of the library. A book-case was
also purchased this year.

1856. In 1856, a copy of Stuart's portrait of Washington was presented to the town by the artist—Miss E. M.
Judkins.

1857. In 1857, the town voted to have a lock-up, for
the temporary incarceration of offenders against the public weal.

1858—1859. In 1858, the town voted in favor of a
State prohibitory liquor law. In 1859, it passed resolutions in favor of building a railroad to the Aroostook.

1861. In the year 1861, the town adopted the code of
By-Laws now in operation, and elected twelve men as
watchmen. From this time until the close of 1865, was
the period of the Civil War. Nothing of importance, however, occurs in the records, in reference to this event,
except the votes concerning the passage of appropriations
for bounties, etc. In July, 1861, the sum of twelve hundred dollars was appropriated towards furnishing supplies
to the families of volunteers, and William H. Witherle,
Roland H. Bridgham, Charles J. Abbott, Samuel Adams,
and George H. Emerson, were chosen to disburse the
same.

1862. In 1862, the sum of fourteen hundred dollars
was appropriated, to pay one hundred dollar bounties
with ; also the twenty dollar bounties. The troops raised
here were also furnished with two days' rations, upon
leaving town.

1863. In the year 1863, the sum of two thousand dollars was appropriated for aid to the families of volunteers.
Drafted men were also paid one hundred dollars, and volunteers two hundred dollars, as a town bounty.

CASTINE FROM NORMAL SCHOOL HOUSE.

CHAPTER IV.

GENERAL AND SOCIAL HISTORY OF CASTINE.

EARLY CONDITION AND CIRCUMSTANCES OF THE CITI-
ZENS.—WELCOME TO HON. ISAAC PARKER.—BENONI
THOMAS. — THEATRE ROYAL. — CELEBRATION OF
QUEEN'S BIRTHDAY.—ILLUMINATION OF THE TOWN
ANNIVERSARIES.—MOURNING FOR GENERAL WASH-
INGTON.—HOUSE WARMINGS.—ASSOCIATIONS OF DIF-
FERENT KINDS.—TAVERNS AND BOARDING HOUSES.
NEWSPAPERS. — MAILS.—SHIPWRECKS, AND CAP-
TURES OF VESSELS.—DEATHS BY DROWNING AND
OTHER CASUALTIES.—FIRES AND FIRE COMPANIES.—
. . . . . . AND MORTALITY.—COURT TIMES AND
. . . .—TRADITIONS AND ANECDOTES.

The social condition and circumstances of the inhabitants
of Castine, in by-gone days, can only be inferred from our
general knowledge of the times, and from the few facts and
occurrences that have been preserved. Separated and
almost isolated as they are by the surrounding water, from
nearly all the neighboring towns, the citizens of this place
are, and have always been, in a great measure obliged to
find their sources of amusement at home. Such was especially the case in early times, when the relative importance
of the place was so very much greater than at present, and
there was no inducement to go elsewhere, and especially
when, indeed, the wealth and fashion of this
section of country centered here. We learn accordingly,
as far back as the date of the incorporation of the town,
that balls, parties, theatrical exhibitions, and celebrations
of various kinds, were of common occurrence.

12

CAST NE FROM NORMAL SCHOOL HOUSE.

CHAPTER IV.

GENERAL AND SOCIAL HISTORY OF CASTINE.

EARLY CONDITION AND CIRCUMSTANCES OF THE CITI-
ZENS.—WELCOME TO HON. ISAAC PARKER.—BENONI
THOMAS. — THEATRE ROYAL. — CELEBRATION OF
QUEEN'S BIRTHDAY.—ILLUMINATION OF THE TOWN.
ANNIVERSARIES.—MOURNING FOR GENERAL WASH-
INGTON.—HOUSE WARMINGS.—ASSOCIATIONS OF DIF-
FERENT KINDS.—TAVERNS AND BOARDING HOUSES.
NEWSPAPERS. — MAILS. — SHIPWRECKS, AND CAP-
TURES OF VESSELS.—DEATHS BY DROWNING AND
OTHER CASUALTIES.—FIRES AND FIRE COMPANIES.—
DISEASES AND MORTALITY. — COURT TIMES AND
TRIALS.—EPITAPHS.—TRADITIONS AND ANECDOTES.

The social condition and circumstances of the inhabitants
of Castine, in by-gone days, can only be inferred from our
general knowledge of the times, and from the few facts and
occurrences that have been preserved. Separated and
almost isolated as they are by the surrounding water, from
nearly all the neighboring towns, the citizens of this place
are, and have always been, in a great measure, obliged to
find their sources of amusement at home. Such was especially the case in early times, when the relative importance
of the place was so very much greater than at present, that
there was no inducement to go elsewhere for amusement;
when, indeed, the wealth and fashion of the whole eastern
section of country centered here. We find, accordingly,
as far back as the date of the incorporation of the town,
that balls, parties, theatrical exhibitions, and celebrations
of various kinds, were of common occurrence.

12

AMUSEMENTS AND FESTIVITIES.

The earliest event, of any social significance, of which there is any record, was a WELCOME given to Honorable Isaac Parker, on his return from the General Cour in 1797. It consisted of a public supper, at which were present several distinguished officers from abroad, as well as the officers and members of the Castine Artillery Company, who appeared in uniform. The occasion was enlivened by speeches and toasts, accompanied by the amount of *noĭse*, in the shape of the beating of drums and firing of cannon, that is usually considered necessary at such times. In 1810, there was an Exhibition at Mason's Hall, of a very distinguished personage of the time, one *Benoni Thomas*, an adult, who was said to be only two feet and eight inches in height.

On the second of January, 1815, the first play was given at the " Theatre Royal." This Theatre was held in Mr. Hooke's *barn*, which was fitted up for the occasion. This barn was afterwards removed off the Neck, and now composes a portion of Mr. Thomas Hatch's barn. The actors upon this occasion, belonged to the English garrison—at that time occupying the town—and the scenery, decorations, dresses, etc., were brought hither from Halifax. The garrison relieved the tedium of barrack life, by giving dramatic performances once a fortnight. The following lines, written by Doctor Mackesy, Surgeon of H. B. M.'s 62d Regiment, will give some idea of the actors, as well as of the performances :—

Occasional Epilogue to the Comedy of the Poor Gentleman.

"The scene is closed, and Worthington* at rest
From weary care that filled his anxious breast,
His cottage raised in western wilds once more,
But quits Saint Lawrence for Penobscot's shore.
Here social views his little band inspire,
To breathe responsive to Appollo's lyre ;
In tragic strains or Thalia's sprightly art,
Aim to enlarge and humanize the heart;
With mimic woes the feeling bosom warm,
Or merry satire calm the wintry storm.
The drama's past, we close the sportive page ;
More varied duties now our thoughts engage.
Emily,† this night so blessed in love and riches,

*Worthington (the Poor Gentleman)—Lieut. Gastin, Royal Artillery.
†Emily Worthington—Major William Hull, 62d Regt. (Major of Brigade).

At morning's dawn draws on her boots and breeches;
Then Amazon-like extends the martial line,
Gives out commands and seals the countersign.
The proud Lucretia,* though so nobly bred,
Oft bleeds and blisters at the Galen's head;
And gay Sir Charles,† forgetting Emily's loss,
Attends all duties under Corporal Foss.‡
Frederick,§ no grave magistrate surpasses,
In ministering oaths and writing passes.
While Old Harrowby's‖ Voice the Vale alarms,
With 'Attention! ! Steady! ! Shoulder Arms!'
And warlike aims the Cornet's¶ soul inflame;
He shuts up shop, and treads the paths of fame.
At Sir Robert's** nod the firm Ramparts rise,
The Bastions range—the Vengeful Bullet flies.
Anxious to please, each member of the corps,
Shall do his best to cheer this dreary shore; •
More thankful still when, tried by candor's laws,
The Poor Gentleman's efforts merit your applause."

Two weeks after the above mentioned comedy was acted, the Queen's birthday was celebrated by the military.

On the twenty-eighth of April following, the departure of the British forces from this place, was celebrated by an illumination of the town, which was, doubtless, as brilliant as the lack of gas or coal oil would permit. The houses, most of them, were illuminated by candles stuck into potatoes for candlesticks.

At a somewhat later period, House Warmings came into vogue. These were suppers given by the first occupants of newly built houses—usually ending with music and dancing.

The Anniversaries of our National Independence were generally celebrated in former times by military parades, and a general effervescence of military spirit among the people,—too often accompanied by an outpouring of spirits of another kind! After the disbandment of the military companies, the day, so far as we can learn, has not been celebrated here until quite recent times. •

*The Honorable Miss Lucretia Mactab—Surgeon J. Mackesy, 62d Regt.
†Sir Charles Cropland—Ensign J. Tummers, 62d Regt.
‡Corporal Foss—Lieut. J. Broodrick, 29th Regt.
§Frederick—Major Irvins, 62d Regt.
‖Farmer Harrowby—Lieut. Col. Ximines, 62d Regt.
¶Cornet Ollapod—Adjutant J. Veazie, 29th Regt.
**Sir Robert Bramble—Captain Bonnycastle, Royal Engineers.
[Stephen—Lieut. B. Wild, 29th Regt. Dame Harrowby—Lieut. J. Dennis, 62d Regt. Mary—Lieut. W. Hewatt, 62d Regt.]

July 17th, 1797, the anniversary of the day when our Treaties with France were abrogated by act of Congress, was celebrated by the discharge of cannon, and a parade of the artillery.   After these exercises were over, the citizens assembled at the meeting-house, where a prayer was offered by Reverend Mr. Mason, and an oration delivered by Mr. Isaac Story.   A collation was served in the evening, at Woodman's "Coffee House."

SERVICES COMMEMORATIVE OF THE DEATH OF GEORGE WASHINGTON.

The twenty-second of February, 1800, was selected by Congress as a day of National Mourning for the death of General Washington.   The citizens of this town were not behindhand in their preparations for the day.   A citizens' meeting was held several weeks previously, and a committee of the most prominent men of the town, chosen to super-intend the arrangements.   We quote the account of the proceedings upon that day, from the *Castine Journal*, of that week.

" The day was announced by the discharge of a cannon, at sunrise, by Lieutenant Lee's Artillery.   At twelve o'clock M., a procession was formed at the Court House, in the following order.

Company of Artillery,
(Music and Standard in mourning.)
Schoolmaster and Scholars,
Youths from fourteen to twenty-one years of age,
Sheriff of the County,
Minister and Orator,
Officers of the Continental Army,
Military Officers (in uniform),
Judges and Justices of the Peace,
Clerk of the Court and Town Clerk,
Selectmen,
Register of Deeds and Representatives,
Physicians,
Hancock Lodge—

properly clothed with jewels, columns, etc., in mourning, the Master and Wardens bearing candlesticks with candles, the Wardens' candles burning, the Master's extinguished. When arrived at the meeting-house, the candlesticks were placed in a triangle on the Pedestal of the Lodge, which

was covered with black and placed in the center of the broad aisle, and continued, two burning and one extinguished, during the solemnities.—
Citizens, two and two.

The procession proceeded with slow and solemn music, from the Court House to North street, down North to Water street, up Water to Main street, up Main to Court street, and thence to the meeting-house;—during the procession, sixteen minute-guns were fired. The Artillery and youths opened to the right and left, the Artillery with arms reversed. The procession moved through, the music playing a Dead March. After entering the meeting-house, the audience being seated, a pertinent and well-adapted prayer was delivered by Reverend William Mason, a funeral anthem was then sung by a choir of singers selected for the purpose ; after which an excellent oration was pronounced by William Wetmore, Esq. The meeting-house exhibited appearances of mourning which were calculated to impress the mind with seriousness and veneration ; the Pulpit covered with black, and the windows and pillars hung in festoons of black."

SOCIETIES.

Besides the foregoing amusements, celebrations and anniversaries, which were, of course, attended by all, old and young, male and female, there have been at different times associations of various kinds—either charitable, literary or social in their character—the membership of which has been more or less limited.

Foremost, in point of time, is Hancock Lodge, No. 4, of Free and Accepted Masons. The charter of this Lodge is dated at Boston, June 9th, 1794, and is signed by John Cutler, Grand Master; Mungo Mackey, Grand Senior Warden ; Samuel Parkman, Grand Junior Warden ; and Samuel Colesworthy, Grand Secretary. David Howe, Esq., was elected as the first Master. The first lodge was opened November 11th, 1794, at the house of the widow Deborah Orr. In September, 1814, the hall was taken possession of by the English, and the lodge met at the house of David Howe. As a result of the Anti-Masonic Crusade—the effects of which were at that time still felt—the charter of the lodge was surrendered about the year 1849 or '50· In the year 1851, the old charter was re-issued by the Grand Lodge of Maine, and Samuel K.

Whiting was elected the first Master of what was, virtually,
a new lodge—although enough of the old members were then
living to constitute its *charter* members.   The new lodge
was fortunate in finding most of the Masonic furniture
of the old, carefully preserved.   Singularly enough, the
Seal of the old lodge was found between the ends of two
timbers of the old schooner *Michigan*, while it was under-
going repairs at Deer Isle, in 1866.*

In the year 1801, the Social Library Association was
formed.   The preamble to the constitution of this Association—probably written by Reverend William Mason—
gives so clear an idea of the object of the Society, that
we insert it entire :—

PREAMBLE.

" It is greatly to be lamented that excellent abilities are
not unfrequently doomed to obscurity, by reason of
poverty ; that the rich purchase almost everything but
books ; and that reading has become so unfashionable an
amusement in what we are pleased to call this enlightened
age and country.   To remedy these evils ; to excite a
fondness for books ; to afford the most rational and profitable amusements ; to prevent idleness and immorality ;
and to promote the diffusion of useful knowledge, piety,
and virtue, at an expense which small pecuniary abilities
can afford, we are induced to associate for the above purpose ; and each agrees to pay for the number of shares
annexed to his name, at five dollars per share."

This Association commenced with thirty-five share-
holders, and a fund of one hundred and seventy-five dollars.   Reverend William Mason was chosen clerk and
librarian.   Mr. Otis Little was chosen treasurer, and Mr.
Doty Little, collector.   Captain Joseph Perkins, Captain
John Perkins, Deacon Mark Hatch, Thomas Cobb, Esq.,
and Doctor Moses Adams, were elected trustees.

The number of books belonging to this Association is
not given ; and, so far as the records show, but few meetings of its members were ever held.   The last records of
the Society are dated June 4th, 1849.   The greater number of the books belonging to it were given to the Castine
Public Library.

*We are indebted for the foregoing account to a very interesting History of
Hancock Lodge, compiled by Mr. David W. Webster, Jr., a citizen of this
town, and a past Master of the Lodge.

Several Societies were organized about the same time, in the year 1828. The Hancock Debating Club comes first. This Club was formed January 9th, for purposes of mutual improvement. No records of it have been preserved. On February 12th, the Hancock Agricultural Society, and the Liberal Temperance Society were formed. The records of neither Society can be found, and have probably been destroyed. The latter Society was the first Temperance Association ever organized here, and was, as its name implies, *liberal* in its prohibitions, compared with more modern associations for a similar object, and its pledge was only binding for one year.* Since the dissolution of the above named Society, there have been several temperance organizations formed here. A company of " Washingtonians " existed here for a long time, and was followed by a Division of the Sons of Temperance. The latter society was succeeded by a Lodge of Good Templars.† All of these associations have done a good work in the cause of temperance, and the latter still continues in a thriving condition.

TAVERNS.

The taverns and stores afforded the same opportunity to many, in former times, that they do now, to obtain the current news of the day through the medium of the weekly papers and the mails. The earliest tavern in this region, to which any reference can be found, was one kept "over the Ferry," in Penobscot, by a Mr. Brewer, in 1795. [R. B. Thomas—Farmer's Almanac, 1795.] The next was the inn kept by the widow Deborah Orr, in 1798. It was situated on the south side of Main street, nearly opposite the house now occupied by Miss Nancy Dodge. In the year 1799, there was one that went by the name of Woodman's Coffee House. The building is now owned and occupied by Mr. Josiah B. Woods. In more recent times, the following taverns have from time to time flourished here. One, called the Lakeman House, situated near the present residence of Captain Joseph Stearns, was kept by the widow Lakeman. The Atlantic House, kept by John Little, was in the building now owned and

*Deacon Samuel Adams, Mr. John Dresser, and Doctor Joseph L. Stevens, were the originators of this Society. The first-named individual was also the first person in Castine to voluntarily give up the sale of intoxicating drinks.

†Rising Virtue Lodge, No. 109.

occupied by Messrs. Alexander J. and Augustus G. Perkins. The Castine House, kept by Benjamin Robinson, is
now the handsome residence of Mr. Alfred Adams, on
Main street. The Bagaduce House, kept by Nathaniel
Hooper, is still owned and occupied by his sons. It is
opposite the Custom House. The Union House (previously the *Lakeman*,) was kept by James Hooper, and
the Jarvis House was kept by a Mr. Leman. The latter
is now the Castine House, kept by Captain Horatio D.
Hodsdon. In addition to these, there was a sailors'
boarding-house, called the " Green Dragon," kept in the
building now used by Mr. Alfred Adams, as a stove store;
and another kept by the widow Perkins, in the house now
occupied by Mr. Jothan Gardner. There were, doubtless,
many other boarding-houses kept during the period when
the Courts were held here; but they seem to have passed
out of the recollection of the inhabitants, with the exception of one kept by Mr. Richard Jaques, in the house
where Mr. William Sawyer now lives. He and his wife
were a very singular couple. He is said to have been of a
peculiarly crusty and taciturn nature, while his wife was
decidedly the reverse. It is related of the latter, that on
one occasion, when she was not feeling very well, she told
her minister that when she died, she " wanted to go to
heaven by way of Boston." This goes to show that there
were people at that time, as now, who considered nothing
as worth having, unless it came by way of the Modern
Athens.

NEWSPAPERS.

Castine was the first town in this eastern section, and
the fourth in Maine, to possess a weekly newspaper. The
one first issued here is said, by Honorable William Willis,
[History of Portland,] to have been called the Castine
Gazette, and to have been established in 1798, by Daniel
S. Waters. " Isaac Story, a young lawyer of promise in
that town, being, he says, " a principal contributor." The
Gazette of Maine was taken in this vicinity by subscribers
as early as 1793; but it is believed to have been the one
published in Portland, and not, as thought by some, the
one referred to by Willis, nor even the one, by the same
name, that was published in Bucksport, in 1808.*

*We have in our possession a bill for subscription to this paper from
Nov. 4th, 1793, to Nov. 4th, 1794. The amount (*not including postage*) was
seven shillings and sixpence. The bill is receipted by John Lee. We have
also a copy of the paper published in Buckstown, in 1808.

In 1799, the Castine Journal and Eastern Advertiser was published here, by Daniel S. Waters. Isaac Story assisted in its editorial management. This paper was well filled with the foreign news of the period, and some attention was given to the general news of the country; but none whatever to local matters. In 1809–10, a paper called The Eagle, was published here, by Samuel Hall. It was similar, in its general character, to the Journal, but was not quite so large. In this paper are to be found advertisements in regard to three fugitive apprentices, for one of whom, a young mulatto boy, *one cent* is generously offered. In 1828, a paper was published here, by Benjamin F. Bond. It was called the Eastern American, and was somewhat larger than any of its predecessors. It was more devoted to politics than either of the others, and more frequent allusion was made in it to local matters. In one number, reference is made to a calf, born on the farm of David Wasson, of Brooksville, which weighed at birth seventy-seven pounds, and which, in less than a month, had increased in weight to one hundred and twenty pounds.

Sometime in the course of this year, an attempt was made to establish a literary paper here, by the name of The Crescent. Only three or four numbers were issued, when the undertaking was abandoned, for want of sufficient patronage. No weekly paper has been published in this place since that time.*

POST-OFFICES AND MAILS.

In former times, when the mail was received at long intervals, and postage was high,† letters were considered of much greater consequence than they are now. They were then anxiously looked for, were read again and again by hosts of friends, and were the topics of conversation for weeks. The earliest reference to a regular mail, is in 1793. At that time, George Russell, of this town, carried the mail on foot, once a week, from here to St. George, and intermediate places. He carried it at first, tied up in a

*In 1872, a monthly paper, called the Castine Gazette, and devoted exclusively to local matters, was published by us, in order to test the feasibility of converting it into a weekly. Only eighteen numbers were issued, when the undertaking was abandoned.

†In 1798, the postage on a letter between here and Boston was twenty-five cents.

yellow handkerchief; but his business increased to such
an extent, that he afterwards used saddle-bags. [Eaton's
Thomaston, So. Thomaston, and Rockland.] In 1799,
there were letter mails once a week, but the regular newspapers were delivered by a special post. The earliest
mail from this place, to the eastern part of the State, was
carried by John Grindell, of Sedgwick, about the year
1795. His contract with Joseph Habersham, Post Master
General U. S. A., has been preserved. According to
the terms of this contract, he was to carry the mail " from
Passamaquoddy, by Machias, Gouldsborough, Sullivan,
Trenton and Bluehill, to Penobscot, in the District of
Maine; and from Penobscot by the same route to Passamaquoddy, once in two weeks, at the rate of eighty-four
dollars and fifty cents for every quarter of a year."
There were no roads at that time, and he carried the mail
in a boat along the shore. The earliest mail to Ellsworth,
that we can learn of, was carried by Abner Lee, of this
town. Mr. Lee at first drove the stage with two horses;
but having, through some misfortune, lost one of them,
he afterwards drove it for several years with a horse and
heifer harnessed together.* The regular mail was first
carried to Bucksport, in 1819, by Benjamin F. Stearns.
David Howe, Esq., was the Post Master here in 1800, and
was the first of whom any record exists. There was no
daily mail to this town, until some time in the month of
February, 1828.

Captures of Vessels.

The news carried each way by the mail or special post,
was not always the cause of rejoicing. Accounts of shipwrecks and captures abroad, together with the occurrence
of fires, diseases, trials, deaths, and other calamities at
home, gave occasion for the exhibition of more serious
feelings. During the troubles with France and England
—from 1799 to 1810—there were many captures made of
vessels hailing from this port. On June 1st, 1799, the
schooner *Polly*, bound from Barbadoes to Wilmington,
was captured by the French, and the crew made prisoners.
The schooner *Lark* was also captured by the French, the
same year, and her deck load destroyed. In 1800, the

*Such is the traditional account here. We have no positive testimony to
this effect.

ship *Hiram*, Captain Samuel Austin Whitney, was captured four times, by the French. In the year 1810, the schooner *Abigail*, Captain John Perkins, was also taken by the cruisers of the same nation. The account of the third capture of the ship *Hiram*, in a book entitled, " Incidents in the Life of Samuel Austin Whitney, [pp. 37 to 41, of Appendix,] is so interesting that we give it entire:—

" On the thirteenth of September, 1800, the Hiram was taken by a French armed vessel. By dint of long persuasion, the Frenchmen were prevailed upon to allow Captain Whitney to stay by his vessel, together with his young brother Henry, an old man, and a boy. They put a prize-master and nine men on board—one of whom was a negro. Captain Whitney had secured his pistols in a crate. When his companions saw him putting out of the way every article that could be used as a weapon, clearing up decks, and making everything tidy, they concluded that ere long they should be called upon to bear a hand ; and in this they were not disappointed.

The prize-master was lying on the hen-coop, dozing ; there was a light wind, and some of the crew chanced to be in the forecastle. Captain Whitney went below, after placing the heavers where he could see them, and took his rusty pistols from the crate. He came on deck, went directly aft, and knocked down the man who was steering. He next grappled the prize-master, lying upon the hen-coop, who proved too stout for him ; and while he was trying to put him overboard, the men below heard the outcry, and ran to the rescue. As the ship rolled at that moment, he pushed the prize-master overboard, and regained his footing just as the crew reached the quarterdeck. He then drew his pistol, saying that he would shoot the first man that came another inch aft, and leveled a blow with his fist at the leader, who ran forward, the rest following,—Captain Whitney at their heels, with a hammer in one hand, and a pistol in the other. They ran forward around the long boat, and so aft, and as often as they turned, he would point the pistol, saying :—' Surrender, and I will use you well ; resist, and I will shoot,' or words to that effect. There was a negro—he might have been the cook ; but I do not recollect about that— who sallied out from the rest of the crew, armed with an axe, which had been overlooked. As they passed around the long boat forward, the negro made a stand to disable

Captain Whitney, as he went by, driving the crew before him ; but a shot from the pistol brought him to the deck, and a well-directed blow with the axe killed him upon the spot.   After this decisive act, the men made only one more turn, and ran into the cabin ; and so terrified were they, that Captain Whitney, who followed them in, seized a chest by the handle, and drew it clear to the deck of the ship.   He afterwards remarked :—' I never could tell how it was done, for it was very heavy.'   Having landed it on deck, the first thing that met his eye was the man he had thrown overboard, who had just regained the deck, and stabbed his brother Henry, with a dirk.   He said to the old man, ' Stop that fellow ;' and himself dealt a blow which so staggered him that he was able to put him into the cabin with the others,—now eight in all.   Poor Henry was in a sad state, faint with loss of blood, and no means of stopping it at hand ; but the Whitney courage never failed him.   His brother took some oakum, and bound it over the place made by the knife, and, carrying him to the forecastle, laid him down beside a lot of bottles.   He stationed the old man at the companion-way, also with several bottles—to be used in case of resistance.   He then ordered the men up, one by one, and they were all put down into the ship's forecastle.

Having secured his prisoners, his next thought was for his young brother, who had gone below, and seemed to be quite comfortable ; but in three days, he was very ill.   On examining the wound, it proved to be very badly gangrened, and Captain Whitney was certain he must lose him ; but all he could, or did do, was to keep the wound wet with brandy, till Henry was convalescent.

Captain Whitney had possession of his ship ten days ; and during that time, and until he was again captured, he passed all the food to the crew through a hole which had been made for a funnel, when, on his previous voyage, he carried passengers forward.   He and the man handled the heavy canvass, so that the ship was under easy way.

About nine o'clock in the morning, his man, then at the helm, discovered a sail, bearing directly for them, but a long distance off.   He called Captain Whitney, who, after watching the stranger some time with his glass, said, ' We will keep on our course ; I have no doubt it is a French Man-of-War.'   When within a mile of her, the captain took the helm, and sent the man below.   They were soon within speaking distance, when he was ordered to send his boat on board ; but he took no notice of the privateer, which had shot ahead, rounded to, and run across the stern of the Hiram quite near, hailing, ' Send your boat on board of us.' After tampering with his pursuers in this way for some time, they fired on him; but he still kept on his course ; they backing, filling, chasing and firing, till finally, the wind dying almost entirely away, they ran so near as to inquire what he meant. He had no colors flying. He replied that he was alone, and could not leave his ship ; and if they wanted anything of him, they must come and see him; at which they asked him to heave back his topsail. He called his man, and hove the ship to, and a boat was sent to him, the French captain, who spoke English, coming himself.

A long discussion ensued between Captain Whitney and the French commander, who, at first, was incredulous at his statement; but, while they were talking, some ot the boat's crew went to the forecastle, and set the prisoners free. The prize-master soon told the whole story, whereupon the French captain exclaimed: ' Sacre, one man take nine ! ' The prize-master entreated them to spare him. It was mortifying enough to be taken, but he did not wish to hear about it. It was a long time before Captain Whitney could persuade them to let him remain by the ship. He urged upon them the unfairness of taking him away, as they might fall in with an English cruiser, and in that case he would be on the spot to claim his property. At last they consented, and to let Henry stop with him; but his man was taken on board of their vessel. He belonged in Newport, and was living at the time Captain Whitney told of these transactions. They put on board the Hiram a lieutenant and eighteen men.

Captain Whitney's first work now was to destroy, or put out of order, all their nautical instruments. His own quadrant he was master of himself, and kept a dead reckoning, so that he knew something of their position. After sailing about a week, the crew grew uneasy, and the officers lost confidence in themselves, and applied to their prisoner to navigate the ship. He told them that he would do so, and gave them his word that he would do all in his power that they should be well treated ! Finally they gave him the command. He shaped his course for Savannah, as nearly as he could, and in a few days had the inexpressible joy of seeing the land, and feeling the land breeze. Said he: 'In twenty-four hours I should have been in, had not the lieutenant called the men aft, and telling them what an everlasting disgrace it would be to him, persuaded them to let him again have command.' Twice they foiled him in this way. Twice he had made his port, and twice they took all hope from him; and when they turned from land the second time, he told them, in pretty strong language, that they might take the ship and go to perdition, for he would have no more to do with them; and then he went below. 'In a day or two after this,' he said 'as I was lying in my berth, I heard a great noise on deck, and as I rolled over, the ship came round within half cable-length of the shore, and not a soul but myself knew where we were. It was Bermuda. I then made up my mind that I would advise a little, and directed them how to shape their course for Guadaloupe, meaning all the time to bring up at Martinique, and in this I was pretty successful.' He continued: 'It was about eight o'clock in the morning, when the lieutenant came below, and told me we had made a large ship, that we must be near Guadaloupe, and before morning, would be in. I laughed to myself, to see how nicely they were caught, but said nothing, till they were so near that there was no chance for escape. I then said to the lieutenant, 'You had better have gone to the United States; you are a prize to the English.' The lieutenant was perfectly dumb for a moment. He saw what must take place; and as they got ready a barge from the ship, he begged of me, when they hailed, to say, 'an American ship.' 'I will,' I replied, 'but I will also add, a prize to the French, which I did, and the reply was, 'We shall be most happy to relieve you.'

He was at Port Royal three months; and the court before which the case was tried gave several dinners without asking him, or even inviting him to the table; and when the salvage was paid, he found the dinners charged also, costing him several hundred dollars! At last he set sail under convoy, and arrived in Savannah some time in 1801."

SHIPWRECKS AND DROWNING.

In a town situated upon the sea-side, whose chief interests and pursuits have always been of a maritime nature, it would be expected that shipwrecks and deaths by drowning would be events of not uncommon occurrence. Disasters to navigation have been, perhaps, as common to the citizens of this community as to others; but deaths by drowning have been comparatively rare occurrences. There is no record to be found of any such accident happening, prior to the year 1794. From that date down to the year 1860, a period of sixty-five years, there have been in all, forty-four persons, residents of Castine, who have thus lost their lives. An average of .62 per annum. Of this number, twenty-four were lost at sea, one at New Orleans, and two in Penobscot Bay, leaving but eighteen who could have been drowned within the limits of this harbor. Of this latter number, in six cases the record of their death does not state where they were drowned. The saddest event of this kind was the loss of the schooner *J. M. Tilden* and crew, on the island of Amherst—one of the Magdalen group— in October, 1867. Eighteen men, in all, perished at this time. The captain, Benjamin Sylvester, and one man, belonged in Deer Isle. The remaining sixteen belonged in this town. One-half of the men were married, and all of them were very worthy young men. Many of them were part owners of the vessel. In addition to the above mentioned cases, the schooner *Samuel Noyes* was wrecked, on the thirteenth day of February, 1848, it being the second day out, on her trip to Cuba, and five men perished on board, from exposure. The captain, Mr. James Hatch, was taken from the wreck, after nine days exposure, and died in Glasgow, Scotland, two days after having had his leg amputated. In 1842, Robert McFarland, of this town, aged twenty-nine years, was murdered, by the natives, on the coast of Africa.

FIRES AND FIRE COMPANIES.

Castine has suffered but few times from fires, and never from any very extensive conflagration. The earliest fire in this vicinity, to which any reference can be found, was that of Mr. Justus Sopher's house, at Penobscot, in 1797. In 1809, the schooner *Commerce*, owned by Messrs. Hooke and Witherle, was destroyed by fire. In 1819, a barn, belonging to T. Avery, Esq., of North Castine, was struck by lightning, and burned. In 1821, occurred the most extensive fire that has ever been known here. The stores of Major Little, Holbrook & Brooks, Witherle & Jarvis, and Joseph Palmer, being entirely consumed, although their contents were for the most part saved. On March 6th, 1828, the rope-walk was burned, and October 7th, 1830, the new one erected in place of it was also destroyed by fire. On August 21st, 1848, the houses of Mr. Otis Little, and of Judge Nelson, were burned. The last serious fire occurred in the year 1857, upon the first of March. At this fire, the store of Hatch & Bridgham, occupied at that time by Mr. James B. Crawford, and Charles J. Abbott, Esq., was entirely consumed.

The first fire engine in town was the Hancock, Number One. When, and by whom, this engine was obtained, is a matter of some doubt. It was not likely that it was purchased by the town, since no appropriation for it appears upon the town records. The only accounts we have of the company belonging to it, are contained in a few scorched leaves—parts of the records of the company— which were found on the wharf, shortly after the burning of the store of Hatch & Bridgham, and in a list of its members for the year 1840. The following extracts from the leaves referred to, will be of interest:—

" Friday, August 13th, 1819. Last evening, after four days continued fog, the wind suddenly changed to northeast, and the clouds seemed to indicate a storm approaching. Between eight and nine o'clock, the thunder and lightning was frequent and heavy, though apparently some distance off. At ten, the storm commenced; the wind veered to southeast, attended with thunder and lightning, heavy and sharp in the extreme; the rain descended in torrents. About twelve o'clock, the wind changed to northwest, and three severe shocks of thunder and lightning were heard, in quick succession, dreadful beyond comparison. A barn, belonging to T. Avery, Esq., was struck at this time, and entirely consumed, with its contents, about fifty tons of hay, farming utensils, etc. It also struck the house of Mr. Avery, and slightly damaged it ; also entered the house of Mrs. Freeman, and split a bedstead, on which were two females. It also struck the Packet sloop *General Washington*, lying at Gray's wharf, and split the mast from the topmast to the deck, taking out almost one-quarter of the mast. The fire seemed at first a considerable distance off, and, it then storming very bad, it was thought best not to start the engine. About three o'clock, morning, the bell sounded the alarm of fire, the storm having abated, and Captain Avery being fearful of the wind coming to the north, in which case his house would be endangered from the burning ruins of the barn, sent for the engine to assist in quenching it. Repaired to the spot with the engine, with all possible dispatch."

* * * * * * * *

"Monday, July 3d, 1820. At four o'clock to-day, repaired to the engine house. Voted to meet at eleven o'clock to-morrow morning, to choose officers, and to partake of some punch, to be provided by the committee. Mr. Fuller came late, and was fined one shilling and sixpence. I. S. COFFIN, Clerk."

"Tuesday, July 4th, 1820. Met this day at Mason's Hall, per adjournment, and partook of some refreshments, provided by the committee. Jonathan L. Stevens was re-chosen captain, and I. S. Coffin, clerk. Messrs. J. H. Jarvis, T. B. Capron, and S. Adams, committee to serve for the year ending May, 1821. I. S. COFFIN, Clerk."

* * * * * * *

"Sunday, January 28th, 1821. Early this morning, the inhabitants of this town were alarmed by the cry of fire. It originated in the counting-room of the store occupied by Holbrook & Brooks, and had made great progress before it was discovered. This building, (viz:— stores occupied by Major O. Little, Holbrook & Brooks, Witherle & Jarvis, and Joseph Palmer) was entirely consumed; the contents principally saved. The store of B. Brooks, on the wharf, caught fire two or three times, but was as often extinguished. The exertions of all, on this occasion, were great in the extreme, and deserve much credit—of which the females are entitled to a good share. Never were people more engaged, or more resolute. The store of David Howe, Esq., distant only fourteen inches from the building on fire, was not even scorched. Sails were suspended from the eaves of this building, and kept constantly wet, to which, in a great degree, should be attributed its salvation. Where all did well, it is hard to select; but the active, the zealous exertions of Messrs. E.

14

M. P. Wells, John Lee, C. K. Tilden, George Coffin, and
Joseph Palmer, were so conspicuous, that we should do
injustice, not to put their names on record. The whole
loss is estimated at seven thousand one hundred and fifty
dollars.   I. S. COFFIN, Clerk."

In the year 1840, the military company, known as the
Hancock Guards, offered their services to the town, as
Engine Men. Their offer was probably not accepted, as a
number of other persons agreed to put the engine in
thorough repair, to keep it in good condition, and to perform all the duties required of Engine Men. The following
is the list of members approved, at that time, by the
Selectmen :—

M. P. Hatch,	Frederick A. Jarvis,
Andrew Brown,	Otis Morey,
John Clark,	Sylvester Simpson,
Nathaniel Hooper,	Charles H. Averill,
Mason H. Wilde,	Joseph W. Stearns,
Joseph B. Brooks,	Elisha D. Perkins,
Benjamin D. Gay,	J. S. Gardner,
James H. Hall,	Joshua Hooper, Jr.,
Francis Vanwycke,	Noah Mead, Jr.,
Levi S. Emerson,	Elbridge G. Bridges,
Daniel Gallighan,	Thomas Sellers,
Thomas Williamson,	Elbridge G. Hall,
James B. Crawford,	Asa Howard.

Josiah B. Woods.

This engine was the only one in town, until the year
1845, when the Bagaduce, Number Two, was purchased.
At what time the fire ladders were bought, and the
boxes made for them, is not known with certainty, since
no reference is made to them in the town.records. It is
not unlikely that they were purchased about the same
time that the Bagaduce Engine was, and were paid for
from the contingent fund.

DISEASE AND MORTALITY.

Castine has always enjoyed a remarkable immunity
from epidemic and infectious diseases. Indeed, it may be
considered a pre-eminently healthy place. The mortality
of the town compares favorably with that of any other in
the State, and is mostly confined to those advanced in life.

The few deaths which occur here are principally from *phthisis pulmonalis* (consumption). Typhoid Fever and Dysentery are almost unknown here as epidemics. Doctor Joseph L. Stephens, who has kept a record of all the deaths in town for more than thirty years, informs us that the proportion of deaths from pulmonary consumption is much below the average, and that the percentage of deaths, from ALL causes, he believes to be below the general average of the country towns in New England—averaging for the last half century, only 1.38 per cent. of the population. To use his own language :—" Dysentery is scarcely known here, there having been but three deaths from it within fifty years. Cholera Infantum usually appears every autumn—deaths averaging from one to five. Of Inflammation of the Lungs, the average is thought to be large. In the number of dangerous chronic diseases are Epilepsy and Insanity. It is feared that in this place they may even be called endemic. Of the former, six cases have been known to exist at once,—varying in duration from one year to forty. Of Insanity, the proportion is large. There are now, from this town, four cases in the asylum at Augusta, and there has been an average of three there, ever since it was first founded. For the first twenty years of the writer's residence here, not one fatal case of Croup is remembered. Since then, a number have occurred, but none within the last five or six years. Of Chronic Rheumatism, we have probably our full share ; but of Acute Rheumatism, (Rheumatic Fever,) the proportion of cases is very small. We think it can be noted as a matter of congratulation, the comparative freedom of the town from Intemperance. Prior to the remarkable temperance reform which commenced about forty-five years ago, there would occur, occasionally, a case of Delirium Tremens. The Washingtonian movement, so called, in aid of this reform, happened soon after. Since then, not a single case, of any severity, has occurred here. During the whole residence of the writer in town, but one fatal case has occurred, and that was complicated with a very serious and painful injury. It must be stated, however, that many cases of disease have been indirectly owing to intemperate habits."

Such being the facts in regard to the health of the town, it is not surprising that but little attention should have been paid here to sanitary matters—except at rare intervals. In the year 1803, owing to some cases of a malignant disease having been brought to town, by a vessel, a quarantine was established for a few weeks. In 1805, there were several cases of Small Pox ; and again in the years 1840 and 1859, a few cases of this disease occurred. About the tenth of September, 1832, owing to the general prevalence of Cholera in this country, some alarm was manifested here ; a quarantine was established, and the whole town cleansed and disinfected.

Notwithstanding the general healthfulness of this community, however, it has never been deprived of the services of those valuable *non-producers*—physicians. There has always been, at least, one reputable doctor here—and during the palmy days of the town, there were three or more at one time. The healthy condition of the people has, however, had the effect of rendering the *fees* of physicians rather larger than in most places of the same size. It may surprise some to learn that the prices charged for each visit by the doctors here as long ago as 1816, were exactly the same as to-day.* Such is the fact, nevertheless. The only difference is, that in old times, the physicians furnished .more medicine than they do to-day. Whether this was to the advantage of their patients or not, we will leave the *homeopathists* to decide.

COURTS AND TRIALS.

At the formation of the County of Hancock, in 1790, Penobscot was made the shire town, and in June of that year, the first term of the Court of Common Pleas was held. The second term was held in September. The Probate Court was also held here. Honorable Oliver Parker, of this town ; Honorable Paul D. Sargent, of Sullivan ; and Honorable William Vinal, of Vinalhaven, were the Judges. As the County buildings were situated upon this peninsula, Castine was made the shire town, at the time of its incorporation, in 1796. By act of the Legislature in 1801, one term of the Supreme Court was held here each year. Castine remained the only shire town of the County until 1814, when Bangor was made a half shire town. Ellsworth was made the shire town, and the courts removed thither, in 1838. Our inability to examine the old Court Records, prevents our giving, as we in-

*Some bills of Drs. Gage and Mann, of that date, are in the author's possession.

tended, a somewhat extended account of the more important trials—civil as well as criminal—and of the parties engaged in them, during the forty-eight years that Penobscot and Castine were the shire towns of the county. From other sources, however, we have been enabled to obtain some imperfect accounts of the several *murders* on account of which individuals have undergone trial before the Supreme Court, at this place. The earliest trial of this kind, of which we are able to obtain any account, occurred in the year 1811, before Judges Parker, Sewall, and Thatcher.

At that time, a man by the name of Ebenezer Ball, who resided on Deer Island, was tried here, for the murder of John Tileston Downes, a deputy sheriff, who was attempting to arrest him, on the charge of passing counterfeit money. He was convicted, and sentenced to be hung. An attempt was made to obtain a pardon from the Executive, but it was unsuccessful, and the sentence was carried into execution on Thursday, October 31st, 1811. [Judge Parker's Letter to Executive, Mass. Archives.] The gibbet was erected in the center of Fort George. A large concourse of citizens followed the criminal, when escorted from the jail to the place of execution, prominent among whom was "old Parson Fisher," of Bluehill, who distributed to the crowd copies of a very pathetic ballad written by himself, for the occasion. The following extracts constitute all of this poetry that we have been able to obtain :—

"The day is come; the solemn hour draws near,
When Oh! poor Ball, you quickly must appear
Before your God and Judge.

*　　*　　*　　*　　*

The people from all quarters come
With intent to see Ball hung.

*　　*　　*　　*　　*

When mounted on the gallows high,
He to a friend did say:
'Pray take my body when I'm dead,
And safely it convey.

Deer Isle :—I pray inter it there;
This is my last request.
This, this is all I have to say;
Oh, leave it there to rest!'

*　　*　　*　　*　　*

Take warning, then, O my dear friends,
Let me advise you all;
Pray shun all vice, and do not die
Like Ebenezer Ball."

In the year 1817, [Williamson's History, Vol. I, p. 501,] an Indian, named Susup, was tried here, for the murder of Captain Knight, a bar-keeper at Bangor. This murder was committed under extreme provocation, and much sympathy was felt for Susup. Judge Mellen, then in the height of his popularity, defended the prisoner. Judge Mellen appeared on this occasion in the full court dress of that period, and gave undoubted indications of his intention to secure the acquittal of his client, if possible. Sometime in the course of the trial, he arose, and informed the Court that Governor Neptune, of the Penobscot tribe of Indians, was present, and desired to be heard. The consent of the Court being obtained, Neptune arose, with great dignity, and standing for a moment with head bowed, but with body erect, with great solemnity commenced the following plea—unsurpassed in eloquence by any of the speeches imputed to the famous Logan:—

" One God make us all! He make white man, and he make Indian. He make some white man good, and some Indian good. He make some white man bad, and some Indian bad. But one God make us all.

You know your people do my Indians great deal wrong. They abuse them very much—yes, they murder them— then they walk right off; nobody touches them. This makes my heart burn. Well then, my Indians say, ' We will go kill your very bad and wicked men.' ' No,' I tell 'em ; ' never do that thing ; we are brothers.' Some time ago, a very bad man about Boston shot an Indian dead. Your people said surely he should die ; but it was not so. In the great prison-house he eats and lives to this day. Certainly he never dies for killing Indian. My brothers say, ' Let that bloody man go free—PEOL SUSUP, TOO.' So we wish. Hope fills the hearts of us all. Peace is good. These, my Indians, love it well. They smile under its shade. The white man and the red man must be always friends. The Great Spirit is our Father. I speak what I feel."

This appeal to the jury was so far successful that Susup was only sentenced to one year's imprisonment, and to be bound over in the sum of five hundred dollars, to keep the peace for two years. John Neptune, and other Indians, were his sureties. Susup's wife and four or five children, a large number of his own tribe, besides several St. Johns and Passamaquoddy Indians, attended this trial.

About this time, though possibly two or three years later, Doctor Moses Adams, of Ellsworth, previously a practicing physician in this town, was tried here, before Judge Mellen, for the murder of his wife. The latter was found dead in the house, her throat having been cut by an axe. Suspicion fell upon the doctor, because he was seen, shortly after the time when the deed was supposed to have been committed, on a road some distance back of the house, walking rapidly, and occasionally turning around and looking towards the house, as if to see whether he was pursued. Judge Mellen, however, in his charge to the jury, called attention to the fact that the day was oppressively warm, the doctor a fast walker, and that nothing was more natural than for him to turn around occasionally, to obtain the benefit of what little breeze might be blowing from that direction. The prisoner was acquitted, for want of sufficient evidence.

On February 3, 1825, one Seth Elliott, of the town of Knox, in Waldo Co., was hung here for the murder of his child, whom he killed in a fit of intoxication. The gallows was erected in the same spot where that used in the execution of Ball, was placed. The particulars of the *trial* we have been unable to obtain, but Doctor Joseph L. Stevens, who was, at the time, the physician appoited to attend the prisoners of the County, informs us that Elliott was confined in the jail for one year previous to his execution, and that during this time he twice attempted suicide. The second time he succeeded in cutting his throat to such an extent as completely to sever the trachea. The wound was however, closed by the doctor, and his life prolonged to the appointed time. The night preceding his execution, the doctor called to bid him farewell. He had just shaken hands with him, and started to leave, when the prisoner recalled him, and inquired from whom he expected payment for his services. "My dear sir," remarked the astonished doctor, "why do you think of this at such a time! I presume the bill will be paid by the County." The prisoner then informed him that he should leave some property, and that he was sure his family would see him remunerated, adding: "The County *ought* to pay it. It is hard for a man to be imprisoned and then hung, and be obliged to pay his doctor's bill for the time, too." It was the duty of the doctor to be present at his execution, and to determine the fact of his death. It was currently reported at the time—

much to the amusement of the good doctor—that the body, after being cut down, was removed to his office, where it was resuscitated by him.

The latest trial of this kind was that of a Mrs. Keefe, who was tried for poisoning her husband. We have been unable to obtain any particulars whatever, in regard to this case, except the mere fact that she was acquitted for lack of evidence.

EPITAPHS.

In the cemetery of the town, are to be found some graves of quite old date, though very few of them contain upon their head-stones any epitaphs of peculiar interest. We insert, however, two or three of the most noteworthy. The first occupant, a British officer named Charles Steward, was interred in 1783. He is said to have killed himself with his own sword, on account of his mortification at being put under arrest by his commanding officer, for having sent a challenge to another officer with whom he had recently quarrelled. In 1849, the following tablet was erected to his memory, chiefly through the exertions of the late Mr. William Witherle and Doctor Joseph L. Stevens:

In memory of
CHARLES STEWARD,
The earliest occupant of
This Mansion of the
Dead, a native of Scotland,
& 1st Lieut. Comm. of his
B. M. 74th Regt. of foot,
or Argyle Highlanders,
Who died in this town while
it was in possession
of the Enemy,
March, A. D. 1783,
and was interred beneath
this stone. Æt. about 40 yrs.
This Tablet was inserted
A. D. 1849.

Captain Skinner's tombstone reads as follows:—

" CAPT. ISAIAH SKINNER,
Died Aug. 11, 1837,
Aged 72 years.

He chose the post of duty in which he could do most good; and filled a long life with skill, fidelity and usefulness. The first to sail a Packet between this and the opposite shore, he daily risked his health and life for the safety of others. Honest without pretension, and firm without rashness ; he was known through the State for his civility as well as care ; for the good fortune with which, in his well managed boat, he *thirty thousand times* braved the perils of our Bay, and for the admirable union of the frankness of a sailor, with the constancy and method of a man of business."

The epitaph on Doctor Mann's tombstone is very expressive. It is as follows :—

" Thousands of journeys, night and day,
I've travelled weary on my way
To heal the sick.
But *now* I'm on a journey never to return."

ANECDOTES AND TRADITIONS.

To relieve the minds of our readers from the serious mood likely to be engendered by a perusal of the foregoing, we will bring this chapter to a close by the narration of some traditional accounts of a somewhat different nature.

There is a tradition extant, that for some time subsequently to the siege of the town, Mr. Joseph Perkins lived in a small house which stood on the site of the store occupied, at present, by Tilden & Co. In the cellar of his house was an old-fashioned stone oven, in which, once a week, it was customary to do the baking. Mrs. Perkins had an Indian woman for a servant. This woman had an infant which she was accustomed every afternoon, after getting it to sleep, to put away in this oven. One day, after thus stowing the baby away, she left the house. Mrs. Perkins—knowing nothing about this habit of the woman— concluded to bake upon that afternoon, and accordingly built a fire under the oven. Of course there was soon on hand a sufficient supply of *roast pappoose!* The cellar has ever since had the reputation of being *haunted.*

15

During the occupation of the town by the British (in 1814—15), a semi-fatuous individual by the name of Hate-evil Corson—popularly known as Haty Co'sn—called one day at head-quarters, and asked permission to see General Gosselin. On being shown into this officer's presence, the following colloquy occurred :—

Corson. "Are you General Gosselin?"

The General. "Yes, I am."

Corson. "Damn the *goose* that hatched you, then!" His business thus concluded, he left the irate presence at once.

This same individual called one cold winter's day at the house of Mr. John Perkins. After standing awhile before the kitchen fire, he, much to the astonishment of those present, deliberately divested himself of his shirt, and going out of doors, proceeded to bury it in the snow. After leaving it there some ten or twelve minutes, he went out and brought it in, and going to the fire-place, held it just far enough above the flames to prevent its catching afire. On being interrogated as to what he meant by such actions, he replied :—"I've always heard that sudden heat and sudden cold would kill the devil, and I want to see if it won't kill *these* —"

He was the same " crazy vagabond" who, at Bangor, one Sunday in church,

"To wake the dozing worshipers,
Conceived a novel notion,
And, possibly, their appetites
He thought to re-awaken,
So laid upon the burning stove
Some sausages and bacon."

CHAPTER V.

ECCLESIASTICAL HISTORY.

EARLY CATHOLIC MISSIONARIES.—FIRST PROTESTANT
MINISTER.—ITINERANT PREACHERS.—APPROPRIATION
OF MONEY BY TOWN.—MEETING-HOUSES BUILT.—
PETITION OF INHABITANTS OF CAPE ROZIER.—COST OF
THE MEETING-HOUSES IN 1792.—TOWN DIVIDED INTO
PARISHES.—REVEREND MR. ABBOTT HIRED.—REVER-
END JONATHAN POWERS CALLED TO FIRST PARISH.—
HIS LETTER OF ACCEPTANCE.—HIS ORDINATION.—
RECORDS OF THE FIRST CHURCH OF PENOBSCOT.—
FIRST PARISH OF CASTINE.—LETTER IN REGARD TO
MINISTER'S LOT.—REVEREND MICAH STONE CALLED.—
REVEREND WILLIAM MASON CALLED.—HIS LETTER
OF ACCEPTANCE.—FIRST CONGREGATIONAL CHURCH
OF CASTINE.—RULES AND REGULATIONS FOR THE
SEXTON.—FIRST TRINITARIAN CHURCH OF CASTINE.—
FIRST METHODIST SOCIETY OF CASTINE.—FIRST BAP-
TIST SOCIETY OF PENOBSCOT. — FIRST METHODIST
SOCIETY OF PENOBSCOT.—FIRST BAPTIST SOCIETY OF
BROOKSVILLE. — FIRST TRINITARIAN SOCIETY OF
BROOKSVILLE.—FIRST METHODIST SOCIETY OF BROOKS-
VILLE.

From an early period, the eastern region of the Penohscot, and especially the peninsula of Castine, has been
noted for its ecclesiastical record. The first English Settlement was made by a company of Puritans, from the
colony so celebrated in the annals of New England.

As early as 1611, a French missionary—Father Biard—
is mentioned as having been here, [Relations des Jesuites.]
and two years later, other missionaries were sent here.
[Geographical Hist. of Nova Scotia, p. 53.] During the
occupation of the place by the French under Aulney, in
the year 1648, a Capuchin priest, by the name of Friar
Leo, erected a chapel here, which was probably the same
edifice referred to in the Deed of Surrender of Fort Penta-

göet, in Part III. During the residence of the Baron de St. Castin, there were several Catholic priests here. Amongst others, Messrs. Chamboult, Guay—who is said to have been "a good priest, and an upright man"—Gaulin, Masse, Thuray and Bigot. [Murdock's Acadie—also Letter from Monsieur de Bronillan to the Minister, in Part III.] Williamson remarks that " no other place in this eastern region was so much the resort of Catholic Missionaries, as the fortress of D' Aulney."

In the year 1761—one year previous to the Act of the General Court making a grant to proprietors of Plantation Number Three—the Reverend Isaac Case is reported as having removed hither from Thomaston. [Eaton's Thomaston, etc., Vol. 2d, under Letter C.] If this account is correct, he was, probably, the first Protestant minister ever at this place, and there must, of course, have been some settlers here, at that time. During the occupation by the British at the time of the Revolution, the only religious services known to have been held here were conducted by John Calef, M. D.—the Chaplain of the English garrison. From that time until after the date of Incorporation, all religious services in this vicinity were conducted by itinerant preachers.

The earliest action of the town of Penobscot, having any reference to the establishment of regular religious services, was in the year 1789. At the March meeting of this year, the town voted, that " the sum of three hundred pounds be raised, for the building a meeting-house, for the public worship of God." At a meeting of the town, held the April following, it was voted to have the meeting-house sixty-five feet long, and fifty wide. Captain Daniel Wardwell, Giles Johnson, Oliver Parker, John Willson, and John Wasson, were chosen as a Building Committee and as Trustees. About this time, certain individuals living upon the peninsula, desirous of having preaching at a more convenient place for themselves than where the meeting-house above referred to was located—at the Narrows—started a subscription paper for a meeting-house on the peninsula. This gave considerable offence, and the town, at its last mentioned meeting, passed the following Resolutions :—

" Resolved, that the town pass a vote of their disapprobation of a subscription for building a Meeting-house on the peninsula, which has been set on foot by certain persons merely for the advancement of their own private interests, with a view of drawing the inhabitants off to their measures, and without consulting the collective views of the town, for the accommodation of its inhabitants at large.

That the town deem the undue and immoral measures which have been adopted by the agents of this subscription, as an high insult offered to its inhabitants at large, and calculated to form a schism in their religious communion, and establish a party spirit.

That the town will not, directly or indirectly, be concerned in or countenance the erecting of said building, or any person who shall officiate and preside in' said Meeting-house.

That the town· will indemnify every subscriber who may have been misled to affix his name to the said Subscription, and who is disposed to be governed by the legal and orderly proccedings of the town, from paying any sum he may have subscribed.

That the town will deem as enemies to its peaceable and orderly government all such individuals who shall obstinately continue to adhere to the said Subscription for building any other Meeting-house than shall, by majority of the inhabitants in Town Meeting assembled, be resolved and selected, and will take every legal measure of procedure, with the law prescribed, against them.

That the inhabitants of this town, in their elective capacities, were not capable of building but one Meeting-house, and giving support to one respectable clergyman.

That the town appoint a Committee, and empower them effectually to take every legal measure against any person or individuals who may daringly attempt an innovation on their privileges, or take any measure to establish a schism in their religious communion, and that they will defray the expenses thereof.

That the Selectmen be a Committee, to proceed as the eleventh article prescribes in said resolve."

The committee appointed to decide upon the land for a meeting-house, and to prescribe the limits of the same, reported: " that to convene the town, we think, according to our best judgment, the same ought to stand on land claimed by Mr. Joseph Binney and Mr. Webber, to convene the same with a suitable common, viz : on the northern side of State street, so called, fronting said street (six rods, running back twenty rods). The said owners agree to part with the said land, at a reasonable rate."*

At a meeting of the town held September the first, of this same year, it was voted not to appropriate more money, but that the pews be sold, to raise money for building and finishing the meeting-house ; that Mr. Oliver Parker, Mr. Matthew Ritchie, and Mr. William Webber, be a committee to superintend the sale of the pews ; that the pews be put into three classes ; that the first class of pews be estimated at six pounds, the second at four pounds and ten shillings, and the third at three pounds ; that the purchasers of pews pay to the committee, cash or other materials, at a certain price, to be determined by said committee ; that the sale of pews commence on Thursday, October 8th, and that the committee post up notices of the time of sale. It was also voted at this meeting that the petition of the inhabitants of Cape Rozier, Buck's Harbor, etc., be accepted. This petition was as follows :—

" To the Selectmen of the Town of Penobscot.

We, the subscribers, inhabitants of Cape Rozier and Buck's Harbor, and others on the southerly side of the river—who may become subscribers in six months from this date, in that quarter of the town—qualified to vote in town-meeting, request of you, gentlemen, to insert an article in your warrant for a Town-meeting, fully to comprehend this our declaration, with the *Proviso* which hereafter followeth. We declare ourselves free and willing to aid and assist the town in building a meeting-house for the Public Worship of God, on the place and in the way and manner that the town has heretofore determined by vote and on record. That our persons and property are free to be taxed in a full proportion to defray the charges thereof,—as also to settle and support a minister whenever the town shall think proper so to do—*provided* the town shall pass a vote, and the same be recorded, that we are at any time and at all times free to petition the General Court to be set off by ourselves or to be connected with a part of the town of Sedgwick ; that this town will not directly or indirectly be any let or hindrance thereto ; also, that when we shall

*The *frame* of this meeting-house was first erected on the rising ground back of where Mr. Joshua Emerson now lives. According to the town records, it must have been subsequently moved a short distance.

obtain a Bill of Incorporation, either as a town or a district, that the town of Penobscot do hold and oblige themselves ready and willing to refund back to us, the subscribers, all the money that we may be taxed for, or that shall really be paid to the Treasurer, for the building and finishing said Meeting-house, and our proportion of the minister's settlement, if any is given,—improvement thereof first deducted. When the subject matters shall be laid before the town we [will] submit to any reasonable amendment that may then appear necessary between party and party."

This petition was signed by David Hawes, Samuel Wasson, Elisha Hopkins, Noah Norton, Thomas Kench, Benjamin Howard, John Bakeman, Jr., Thomas Wasson, John Wasson, John Condon, Edward Howard, Malachi Orcutt, Jacob Orcutt, John Redman, and John Bakeman.

In the year 1790, deeds of the land upon which the meeting-house was erected, were obtained from Joseph Binney and William Webber. In 1791, the town refused to make any further appropriation for the finishing of the meeting-house.

In the year 1792, the town voted that the sum of thirty pounds, lawful money, be appropriated to hire preaching for that year, and that Messrs. Oliver Parker, Matthew Ritchie, and Pelatiah Leach, be a committee to engage a suitable person to preach, and to decide upon the place where the preaching should be held. It was also voted that the town should *not* be divided into parishes. A vote was also passed this year to make the meeting-house which had been built upon the peninsula, (notwithstanding the disapproval of the town in its corporate capacity) the property of the town, by paying—or allowing—the bills against the same. Messrs. David Hawes, Captain Joseph Perkins, Oliver Parker, William Webber, and Pelatiah Leach, were appointed a committee to examine the said bills. Another committee was also chosen to provide the material for furnishing the meeting-house at Webber's, and also to procure a minister. The cost, at this time, of the church at Webber's, amounted to the sum of £205 3s. 2d., and of the one on the peninsula to £371 10s. 2d.

In the year 1793, the town received from Captain John Perkins, a deed of the land on which the meeting-house on the peninsula stands. The town at first voted not to raise any money this year for preaching, but afterwards made an appropriation of thirty pounds. The exact time when the town was divided into parishes, cannot be certainly determined, owing to the loss of several pages of the early records. It was probably, however, about this time, as the town voted this year that the preaching be held one-half the time on the peninsula, and one-half the time at the first narrows. The First Parish included all of the present town of Penobscot and that portion of North Castine, north of the present residence of Captain Joseph Wescott. The remainder of the old town of Penobscot, formed the Second Parish. At this same meeting, it was voted to hire Reverend Mr. Abbott, for three months after his then engagement was ended. At a meeting held some time subsequently, the town voted to pay him fifteen pounds extra, if he chose to preach for a longer time than the committee had engaged him for.

At the annual meeting in 1794, the town voted an appropriation of thirty pounds for the support of preaching. At a meeting of the First Parish, held in September following, it was voted to engage Mr. Jonathan Powers to preach, and a committee of seven were appointed to wait upon him with an invitation.

In April, 1795, the town voted to give Reverend Mr. Powers eighty pounds annually, and when he should be settled as minister over the First Parish, to give him £150 for a settlement. In response to the call of the First Parish, Mr. Powers wrote the following letter of acceptance to the Clerk of the parish, and requested to have it recorded.

"Sensible of my own insufficiency and unworthiness to be an embassador of Christ, and also of my absolute need of Divine strength and grace, which I hope has been measurably granted me, and now renouncing self-dependence and looking to God and relying upon Christ for all ministerial gifts and graces, I freely accept the invitation and call given me by the First Parish in this town, to settle with them as their Gospel Minister, by taking the oversight of them in the Lord. Which call of the parish is agreeable to the votes passed on several days, and upon March second on which they voted the call, second, upon March twenty-third, on which they voted to give me one hundred and fifty pounds for a settlement, and third, upon April sixteenth, on which they voted to give me eighty pounds for a yearly salary.

(Signed)   JONATHAN POWERS.
(Dated) PENOBSCOT, June 17th, 1796."

At a parish meeting held July 13th, 1796, it was decided to have the ordination on the last Thursday of August, and that Reverend Peter Powers, Mr. Merrill, and Mr. Emerson, of Georgetown ; Eaton, of Harpswell; Gilman, and Anderson, of North Yarmouth, be the Ordaining Council. The sum of ten pounds was appropriated to defray the expenses of the Council. The parish also voted to allow Mr. Powers four Sabbaths in each year, in which to visit his friends, and *preach to the poor.*

FIRST CONGREGATIONAL CHURCH OF PENOBSCOT.

On the seventeenth of the previous June, an Ecclesiastical Council having been called for that purpose, a Congregational Church was organized, consisting of fifteen members, a sermon being preached by Reverend Peter Powers. A Confession of Faith, and Covenant, drawn up by the pastor elect, were adopted by the church. These articles are remarkable for their number and fulness, and were sharply Calvinistic. The names of the original church members were as follows :—Caleb Merrill, David Hawes, John Wasson, Samuel Wasson, Thomas Wasson, Jeremiah Stover, Sarah Parker, Rebecca Hawes, Elizabeth Wasson, Mary Wasson, Mary Blake, Olive Stover, Sarah Bowden, Elizabeth Bridges, Olive Basteen.

A church having been organized, and Mr. Powers having accepted the call of the parish, a meeting was held to take measures for his ordination. At this meeting, an active opposition was made to the ordination of Mr. Powers, based on objections to the Articles of Faith adopted by the church. The final vote, in favor of ordaining, was carried by thirty-six against sixteen.

Mr. Powers was ordained and installed August 26th, 1795. Reverend Ezekiel Emerson, of Georgetown, preached the sermon. Notwithstanding the opposition to his ordination, the attendance on the ministry of Mr. Powers was general, including those who had been active in opposition, until the endeavor was made to tax the parish for his support—his " settlement " of one hundred pounds, and his salary of fifty pounds, afterwards increased to eighty, having previously been raised by subscription.*

*So say the church records. It is a matter of fact, though, that the town did, a portion of this time, Vote an appropriation of money " for the support of preaching." There is no evidence, however, in the town records, that this money was paid to Mr. Powers, and there is some degree of uncertainty in regard to the matter.

The vote to raise the tax was carried, also a vote recognizing Mr. Powers as the "town minister,"—which entitled him to the lot of land appropriated to the first settled minister. It proved that "a tax was more dreaded than the preacher's sentiments, though he used often to be faulted for his distinguishing doctrines." The opposition to a town tax for the support of Mr. Powers became so extensive, that this action of the town was reconsidered and reversed in May, 1799. The supporters of Mr. Powers were incorporated into a Parish in 1801, and in the same year, a new house of worship was erected in North Castine, near the present store where the road branches to the east, leading to the Head of the Bay.

Among the items of interest in the church records, is the following. In 1798, "a difficulty arose by reason that several had made profession and joined the church, who had previously been guilty of the sin of"—*immoral practices*, the church generally not knowing the facts, and the individuals "did not know that the church required a confession. But upon trial, it appeared to be the minds of almost all, that a confession should be made for that and other scandalous offences." Accordingly, three complied with the condition, and three of the others were finally, in 1800, excommunicated, for refusing to make public confession of sin *committed before uniting with the church.*

"The members of the church and society were generally separated at a great distance, both by land and water," coming largely from the present townships of Penobscot and Brooksville. They had difficulty in raising the salary and sustaining the ordinances of the gospel. A council, called for that purpose, advised the dismission of Mr. Powers, but the people were unwilling to part with him. He continued with them till 1804, after which his time seems to have been largely spent away in missionary labors. In 1807, he returned home, sick from his exposures and labors, and died November 8th, of the same year, aged forty-five years. A sermon, delivered at his funeral, and an elegy by Reverend Jonathan Fisher, of Bluehill, were printed at Buckstown.

> "Seiz'd with a cold, when laboring in the cause
> Of Great Immanuel, and his holy laws;
> Opprest with feVer, and consumption's force,
> The worthy POWERS has fulfilled his course.

His charge not wealthy; compensation small
In earthly treasure; prest with many a call,
Hard to be answered; he prepares once more,
Should counsel point an honorable door,
To leave his charge—on Missionary ground,
Appointed, enters; quickly there is found
By dire disease; returns enfeebled home,
And waits the summons which must shortly come.

*　　*　　*　　*　　*　　*

*　　*　　* 　　His mortal strength decays,
His tongue no more his scattering thought obeys;
Death's chilly hand benumbs the vital tide,
The pale dark shadows o'er his visage slide,
With the last gasp the portals wide display,
His soul, prepared, slips unobserved away,
Meets her kind convoy, and with rapture flies
On speedy wing beneath the nether skies."

The ministry of Mr. Powers, during his pastorate, was blessed with seasons of revival, and additions to the church—twenty in 1797, thirteen in 1803, and smaller numbers in the other years.

On May 28th, 1809, Reverend Philip Spaulding commenced his labors with the church, as a preacher of the gospel. October 4th, he was invited to be their pastor—which invitation he accepted November 20th. No notice of his ordination appears on the church records, but the date is elsewhere given as November 22d, 1809,—which does not give the needed time between his acceptance and the meeting of a council. Mr. Spaulding's pastorate would seem to have been by no means peaceful. With one brief exception, in 1810, the records of the church, kept by himself, treat of cases of church discipline, and of nothing else. On August 3d, 1813, an Ecclesiastical Council met, to act on the question of dismissing Mr. Spaulding. Among the reasons urged for his dismission, was one reflecting on his deportment, which had created dissatisfaction. He was dismissed August 4th, of this year.

There was no pastor of the church after this date, and the subsequent church meetings seem to have been held in Brooksville. The last items of record are the public excommunication of three members,—the offence of one being " the selling of bull beef,"—and the dismission of three other members to the new Trinitarian Church, organized in Castine, July 26th, 1820—three of the fifteen composing that church. Four other members of the Penobscot church afterwards united with the church in Castine—in all seven.

These constitute a connecting link between the First Church, whose central point and place of meeting was in North Castine, and the present Trinitarian Church. A portion of the remaining members of the First Church were embraced in the Congregational Church at West Brooks-ville; organized January 4th, 1826. The First Church, ceasing its organization as such, has become " two bands " in two of the townships embraced originally in Penobscot.

First Congregational Church and Society of Castine.

The Second Parish had no settled minister while it was a part of [the town of Penobscot, though Mr. Powers, Mr. Abbott, and some itinerant preachers officiated there a portion of the time. By the terms of settlement agreed upon by the joint committee of the two towns of Penob-scot and Castine, the meeting-house on the peninsula became the property of the latter town, and was thereafter known as the meeting-house of the First Parish of Castine. The lands included under the title of " minister's lot and lot for the ministry," were divided at this time. The fol-lowing letter from the agent of the proprietors of Planta-tion Number Three, states these lots at three hundred acres—which would give one hundred and fifty acres to each town.

" CASTINE, September 6th, 1797.

Gentlemen, Selectmen of the
    Town of Castine:

The Resolve of the General Court with respect to Township Number Three, commonly known as Majabig-waduce, makes it a condition that the proprietors of the said township shall reserve three hundred acres of land for the first settled minister in said township. As their agent, I inform you that the land allotted for that pur-pose is lot Number Twenty-nine, back of the *Gore* lot, and lot Number One on Penobscot River, and so much of lot Number Fourteen as will make up the three hundred acres to be laid out contiguous to lot Number Twenty-nine. I do myself the pleasure to give you this information, and shall also send a similar letter to the Selectmen of Penobscot, and I think it will not be amiss to have this letter put upon your town records.

I am, Gentlemen,
Your very humble Servant,
PHILIP JARVIS."

Reverend Micah Stone is believed to have preached here at the time of the incorporation of the town, and in September, 1796, the town gave him a call, and voted him a salary of four hundred dollars, and a " settlement " of eight hundred dollars. The call was not accepted by him, and, accordingly, in the year 1798, an invitation was extended to Reverend William Mason, to become pastor of the town, at a salary of three hundred and fifty dollars per annum, for three years. He also received eight hundred dollars upon his settlement over the town. At the same time, Barnabas Higgins was elected sexton. The following is Mr. Mason's letter of acceptance :—

" CASTINE, August 13th, 1798.

To the Committee of the Congregational Society of Castine:—Gentlemen :

Impressed with a sense of the importance of Christianity, and the high degree of responsibility there is attached to the ministerial office, I have considered your invitation to settle with you as a religious instructor. It has been my endeavor to weigh every circumstance connected with the invitation, with candor and impartiality, and should I hereafter find cause to lament my determination, I think it will not be attended with those painful reflections which naturally result from want of deliberation. I am sensible there are many common difficulties attending the work of the gospel ministry ; but I confess, many of them are removed by your declared willingness to give a liberal support to a gospel minister, and *specially* by your unanimity in calling for your pastor; for it has ever been my determination never to continue in a society where my public performances would be obnoxious to a respectable number. This I should not consider duty, as I could not be useful, and I think duty and usefulness are generally

connected.   After all, there are difficulties; but I do not
expect to be free from them while in this vale of tears;
they are the lot of humanity.   Trusting in God, the doctrines of whose Gospel I have endeavored, and shall still
endeavor, to preach,—that he will afford me his assistance
and protection,—I have concluded to accept your invitation to settle with you as a gospel minister, and do at this
time inform you of my acceptance ;—with this *proviso:*
that a reasonable time annually be reserved for visiting my
friends.   I do not mention any particular time, because,
on account of the passing being chiefly by water, it is
uncertain what time would be necessary to pass and
repass ; probably, however, I should not wish, in general,
to spend more than two Sabbaths with my friends.   Wishing for your temporal, but particularly for your spiritual
prosperity ; that you may be endued with the Christian
graces, and be built up in the holy faith of the gospel of
Jesus Christ, I subscribe myself your Christian friend,

WILLIAM MASON."

From the old records of the First Parish, which we have
been fortunate in obtaining, we give such extracts as will
be likely to be of general interest.   The records commence
with the church covenant—which is short, and does not
differ much from those now in use in many churches.
The following are the names of the original signers to this
covenant:—Honorable Oliver Parker, Captain John Perkins, Captain Mark Hatch, Captain Joseph Perkins, Mr.
Barnabas Higgins, Captain Stover Perkins, Mr. Benjamin
Lunt, Mr. David Willson, Mr. Moses Gay, Mr. Abraham
Perkins, widow Martha Perkins, Phebe Perkins, (1st),
Abigail Hatch, Phebe Perkins, (2d), Lydia Perkins,
Esther Lunt, Miriam Willson.

Agreeably to the vote of the town, an Ecclesiastical Council, composed of Reverend Messrs. Alden Bradford, of
Wiscasset ; Jonathan Huss, of Warren ; and Daniel
Stone, of Augusta ; with delegates, convened on the
ninth of October, 1798.   The next day, the church was
formed, and, the necessary business being attended to,
Reverend William Mason was ordained as the first minister
in Castine.   The first meeting of the church was held
October 24th, and it was voted that the pastor be the permanent Moderator of the church.   Honorable Oliver Par-

ker and Captain Mark Hatch were unanimously elected deacons. In regard to the admission of members to the church, it was voted that the names of persons proposing to join should be, under ordinary circumstances, proposed two Sabbaths previously. It was also voted: "that we will baptize the children of those who live regular lives, though, through a sense of unworthiness, they may not come to the communion." At this meeting, Captain Mark Hatch was requested to procure suitable "vessels" for the use of the church.

At a church meeting held March 12th, 1799, it was agreed that the first communion be held on the second Sunday of April ensuing, and that the sacrament be afterwards administered on the second Sunday of every other month. A lecture was to be given the Thursday preceding the sacrament, at two o'clock in the afternoon.

A church meeting was held November 14th, 1799, for the purpose of choosing a deacon in the place of Oliver Parker, who declined service.

"After addressing the throne of grace, proceeded to a choice, and Mr. David Willson was unanimously chosen. After disagreeing on several subjects, not suitable for record, adjourned."

On August 17th, 1800, the pastor and two delegates attended the ordination of Reverend James Boyd, of Bangor. In December of this year, it was voted to dispense with the communion service until the following April, "on account of the great inconvenience of attending from the general inclemency of the winter season."

On October 8th, 1801, a church meeting was held, to attend to some difficulty between Oliver Parker, Esq., and some of the other members of the church. Mr. Parker's complaint was, that several of the members of the church had signed a petition, preferred to the General Court, for the removal from office of the justices of the Court of Common Pleas and General Sessions—of which he was one. The charges were:—

1. That they had "neglected to cause records of the proceedings of said Court to be kept, as the law requires, whereby the property of the good citizens of said County is insecure and precarious."

2. That they had permitted an action, in which neither plaintiff nor defendant were citizens of the State, "to be entered in said Court, the writ not having been

proved according to law, and had rendered judgment on said action, for a large sum, contrary to law."

3. That they had, " after a conviction of theft, in said Court, rendered judgment that said convict should be discharged, without inflicting the punishment which the law in such cases directs."

4. That they had " defrauded the said County by making out and laying fraudulent estimates before the Legislature, by which many large sums have been obtained to be granted, as for the necessary charges of the County, when in fact, such sums were not wanted for the uses stated in such estimates, and had not been applied for the purposes therein set forth."

5. That they had " applied the money assessed upon and paid by the citizens of said County, to the payment of illegal charges of officers, judicial and executive, in said County, and to other uses not authorized by law."

6. That they had " taken and received from the County Treasurer, and applied to their own private use, large sums of money, to which by law they had no right."

This petition was signed by nearly all the prominent men of the town, including most of the church members.

After hearing the complaint of Mr. Parker, the meeting adjourned to Thursday, the 29th inst. Upon that day, the subject was again brought before the members of the church, and, " after much discourse, by which a reconciliation was so far effected, though the business was not fully settled," it was agreed to take no action unless Mr. Parker should again urge the matter. For a period of twelve years, nothing of any importance occurred in connection with this society, so far as the records show. In July, 1813, the pastor and two delegates attended an Ecclesiastical Council held in Penobscot, for the purpose of considering the question of dissolving the connection between the pastor and church, in that town. In June, 1814, the pastor and Mr. Doty Little, attended an Ecclesiastical Council held at Camden, to decide in regard to the dismissal from the ministry, of Reverend Mr. Cochran. At a church meeting called September 15, 1828, in response to a request of Mr. Doty Little, who desired to transfer his connection to another church, it was voted —" That the pastor be a committee to notify Mr. Little, that as his standing now was, his request could not consistently be granted." At a subsequent meeting, held September the 18th, a letter was presented by Mr. Little, himself, which was of such a character " as to *fully* satisfy the church," and his request for a transfer was granted. Upon May 5, 1833, the records of the church had the following entry made in them:— " This day the sacrament of the Lord's Supper was administered, and Mr. Moses Gay officiated as deacon, filling the place which, for thirty-three years, had been filled by Deacon David Willson, who departed this life April 29th, last passed." The early records of this church are not continued after July 28th, of this year.

During the thirty-five years over which these records extend, there were baptized one hundred and ninety-four persons, of whom one hundred and eleven were males and eighty-three females. The baptisms included all ages. During this time there were two hundred and sixty marriages solemnized here by Reverend Mr. Mason. The following are the names of the members who joined the church after its organization:—

Thomas E. Hale, Jacob Orcutt, Doty Little, John Darby, Jonathan Hatch, William Abbott, David Coffin, Mary Perkins, Hannah Fay, Agatha Hale, Mercy Little, Lucy Mann, Elisabeth Judkins, Abigail Mason, Rebecca Abbott, widow Mary Crawford, Susan D. Shaw, Phebe Gay, and Temperance Johnston.

Reverend Mr. Mason dissolved his connection with the First Parish, in 1834. He preached his farewell sermon on Sunday afternoon, April 27th. His text was from 2d Cor. 13, VII:—" Now I do pray to God that ye do no evil ; not that we should appear approved, but that ye should do that which is honest, though we be as reprobates."

He was succeeded by Reverend Samuel Devens, who preached his first sermon, June 8, 1834, taking for his text, Psalm 107, v. 8. Mr. Devens, was followed by Reverend William D. Wiswell, who first preached here December 24, 1835. In February, 1838, Reverend John B. Wight, was pastor. He was the last settled preacher to the old society, though Mr. Wiswell preached here, occasionally, subsequently to this time,—alternating between this place and Ellsworth.

The First Parish, after this time, had no worship in town, until the year 1867, when, by the exertions of the Maine State Missionary of the American Unitarian Association, the religious society was revived, and in the year 1868, Reverend George F. Clark was settled as the minis-

17

ter over it. He was succeeded in 1870, by Reverend Henry L. Myrick, who resigned his charge in 1873. The society still exists in a prosperous condition, under the pastoral care of Reverend John W. Winkley.

As the First Parish was, at the time of the incorporation of the town, the only parish in Castine, the duties of the sexton were prescribed by the town. The town agreed to pay him twenty-five dollars annually, and he was to receive by subscription thirty-five dollars. The following were the

Rules and Regulations for the Sexton.

"1. The Meeting-House shall be kept clean by sweeping the floors, dusting the seats, and sweeping down the cobwebs and dust from the windows.

2. The Sexton shall see that the door is shut when necessary, and take care that the dogs make no disturbance.

3. When any child is to be baptized, he shall see that water is prepared.

4. He shall ring the bell every Sunday morning at nine o'clock and half-past ten—the second bell to be tolled till the minister gets into meeting. He shall also ring the bell on Fast, Thanksgiving, Lecture, and Town Meeting days, at the hours usual on such days.

5. He shall attend to the customary business of sextons at funerals, for which he is to be paid a reasonable sum by the persons who employ him.

6. He is to ring the bell every day in the week, (except Sunday,) at one o'clock p. m., and at nine o'clock in the evening."

The meeting-house was not completed for many years after its occupation, and was not warmed in winter until the year 1817. It would be interesting to know the total amount expended upon this building up to the present time ; but the accounts are imperfect, and some of them missing, so that it is impossible to tell with any exactness.

Second Congregational, or First Trinitarian Church.*

The Trinitarian Church was organized, by an Ecclesiastical Council called for that purpose, July 26th, 1820.

The Council was called by Thomas Adams, Thomas E.

*This sketch, and that of the First Church of Penobscot, were furnished by Reverend Alfred E. Ives, of this town.

Hale, and Bradford Harlow, " to form them and others in
the place into a church, should they see fit," and met first,
for that purpose, on July the fourth. These individuals
had united, the year before, with the church in Bluehill.*
The Council, after duly considering the communications
laid before them, and learning the general state of things,
invited Reverend Mr. Mason, and others of his church, to
a conference, with reference to some arrangement that
should be satisfactory, by which they could " unite in one
body for religious worship, and the enjoyment of Christian
ordinances." The invitation was accepted ; there was a
free and friendly conference, " it being agreed on all
hands that a union was exceedingly desirable." On a
comparison of views, however, the parties were found to
differ so materially, that the Council " could not see it
expedient to advise a union ; " but not wishing to be
hasty, and " to give time for the removal, if possible, of
existing difficulties," they adjourned to July the twenty-
sixth. The condition of things remaining unchanged, the
church was organized upon that day.†

The three individuals calling the Council, three belonging to the old First Church in Penobscot, and nine others
—fifteen in all—constituted the church, as first organized,
namely :—Mark Hatch, Thomas E. Hale, Thomas Adams,
Bradford Harlow, Amos Bowden, Avis Hatch, Cynthia
Holbrook, Jane Adams, Nancy Fuller, Mary W. Foster,
Abigail Hatch, Eunice Parker, Phebe P. Stevens, Rebecca
Fickey, and Lois Myrick. Four others from the Penobscot church afterwards united with this—these seven
forming a bond of connection with the church whose
house of worship, and a part of whose membership, were
in the present limits of Castine.

*In a printed pamphlet, entitled " Correspondence between the Committee
of the Trinitarian Society and the Committee of the First Society in Castine,
on the subject of a union of said Societies, &c.," it is stated [p. 23,] that
these individuals were members of Mr. Mason's Society. This was true;
but only one (Mr. Hale,) was a member of his church. Mr. Hale received no
dismissal from the church of the First Society, and consequently his being
received into the church at Bluehill, caused, at that time, considerable ani-
madversion. At the present time—when the lines of division are so widely
drawn—nothing would be thought of it.

†It is proper to state, in this connection, that Reverend Mr. Mason, and the
members of his church, objected strongly to what they considered the *irreg-
ularity* of these proceedings, and claimed that the Council had no jurisdiction. No objection was ever made against the moral character of Mr. Mason,
or of any member of his church; and the formation of the new Society was
made solely on account of the different views entertained in regard to certain
matters of Faith—chiefly " respecting the doctrine of the Trinity and the
doctrine of Election."

For eight years after its organization, the church had no settled pastor.   On May 12th, 1828, Mr. John Crosby, of Andover Seminary, was invited to become their minister with a salary of six hundred dollars, and, in addition, a "settlement" of one hundred and fifty dollars.   Mr. Crosby accepted the invitation, and was ordained and installed on June 11th, of the same year.   The ordination sermon was by Reverend Mighill Blood, of Bucksport The church at this time consisted of thirty members.

About two years after his ordination, his health failing, Mr. Crosby was obliged to be absent, most of the time, till February 26, 1832, when he sent in his resignation.   He was dismissed by Council, on May 3d, of the same year. He afterwards visited the West Indies, for his health, and died at Barbadoes, May 26, 1833, aged thirty years.

On the twenty-third of May, 1832, an invitation to become their pastor, was extended to Reverend Wooster Parker, of Bangor Seminary, with a salary of five hundred dollars.   Mr. Parker accepted the invitation, and was ordained and installed September 20, 1832, Reverend Doctor Pond, of Bangor Theological Seminary, preaching the sermon.   Mr. Parker continued here for about three and a half years, when, at his own request, he was dismissed, January 18, 1836.   During the pastorate of Mr. Parker, forty-one were received into the church,—thirty-two by profession.   The whole membership at this time, was about forty-five.

On the twenty-fourth of May, 1837, Reverend Baruch B. Beckwith, was installed as pastor, the sermon on the occasion being preached by Reverend Mighill Blood, of Bucksport.   Mr. Beckwith received a salary of six hundred dollars.   After laboring with the church for about five years, the ill health of his wife making a change of climate desirable, Mr. Beckwith asked for a dismission.   His pastoral labors ceased, June 20, 1842.   His formal dismission occurred February 13, 1844.   During Mr. Beckwith's pastorate, thirty-eight were admitted to the church, thirty on profession of faith.   Mr. Beckwith, after leaving Castine, became pastor of the church in Gouverneur, N. Y., retaining his pastoral charge there, till a short time before his death, which occurred July 4, 1870, at the age of forty-five years.   From 1833 to 1839, inclusive, fifty-one were received into the church on profession of faith; from that date to the close of 1844, forty-two were received on profession.

On the fifth of November, 1845, Reverend Daniel Sewall was installed pastor of the church, the sermon on the occasion, being preached by Reverend Stephen Thurston, of Searsport. His salary was five hundred dollars per annum. Mr. Sewall's pastorate continued for about seven and a half years, he being dismissed April 5, 1853. During the period of his pastoral charge, fourteen were received into the church, including five by letter. Mr. Sewall died at Augusta, April 21, 1866, aged fifty-seven years. The whole membership of the church in 1854, was seventy-five.

January 1, 1855, Reverend Alfred E. Ives was invited to become pastor of the church. Mr. Ives was installed by Council, June 20, 1855, Reverend Doctor Shepard, of Bangor Seminary, preaching the sermon. The yearly salary was eight hundred dollars. The pastorate of Mr. Ives still continues, the twentieth year now commencing. Up to this time, during his ministry, eighty have been added to the church.*

On August 27, 1838, Sewall Watson and Samuel Adams were elected deacons of the church. On June 11, 1841, Francis Vanwyck was chosen to succeed Deacon Watson, who had removed from the place. Deacon Vanwyck having also removed, in December, 1843, Mark P. Hatch was chosen deacon. Deacon Adams has been Superintendent of the Sabbath School for thirty-six years.

The church, at its organization, having no meeting-house, occupied the Court House for public worship. It continued to do so for about nine years. In 1829, a church building was erected on Main street, which was dedicated on the sixth of October of that year, at which time the Hancock and Waldo County Conference held their session here. A narrow room, in the front of the building—back of the singing gallery—was occupied for conference and prayer meetings.

In the year 1848, the church was enlarged, making an addition of eighteen slips, in the audience room.

The last Sabbath service in the church, in its old form,

*Mr. Ives has always been earnest in promoting the *educational* and *moral interests* of the town, and his long residence here has caused him to be greatly beloved by all our citizens. As his name does not appear in our Biographical Sketches, it is proper to remark, in this connection, that he is well known for his literary attainments, and has received favorable notice in Allibone's Dictionary of British and American Authors. He was graduated at Yale College, in 1837.

was on July 21, 1867. The edifice was reconstructed, the
work commencing the same week. The building was
raised nine feet, with an excavation adding three more
feet, giving room for a basement of brick, and for a large,
airy, dry, and well ventilated vestry, ladies' room, kitchen,
etc. The old edifice was thoroughly rebuilt. A new spire,
of about one hundred and twenty feet in height, was added,
which, in proportion, grace and beauty, is perhaps, not surpassed by any in the State. A new chancel was added,
and an orchestra ; new windows of stained glass ; the seats
remodeled and newly arranged ; the walls handsomely
frescoed ; the whole carpeted and the seats all uniformly
cushioned ; the pulpit and its furniture, chandelier and
lamps, all new. The rooms below, also, are furnished complete, and—except the kitchen—carpeted. A new, finely
toned bell, of about one thousand six hundred pounds
weight, was presented by N. Wilson Brooks, Esq., of
Detroit, Michigan. The cost of re-building, including
everything, was about twelve thousand dollars. The building, within and without, has no sign of its former self, and
is commended by all for its convenience and comeliness,
being an ornament to the village. The house was re-dedicated February 3, 1868, the sermon by the pastor.*

THE FIRST METHODIST SOCIETY OF CASTINE.†

The First Methodist sermon in Castine village, was
preached about the year 1800, by Reverend Joshua Taylor.
According to traditionary accounts, Mr. Taylor, instead of
being received and treated as a minister of the gospel, was
sent away after being " shamefully handled."‡ This will
not occasion surprise to any one conversant with the general
state of intolerance common to all of the more powerful
sects, even at so late a date as that. The Methodist *heresy*

---

*On November 30, 1872, at noon, this edifice was discovered to be on fire.
The fire had been started for Sunday, and the cold-air boxes closed. The
wind blew a gale at the time, and the fire in the furnace burned so fiercely as
to ignite the lathing and studding, through the plaster forming one side of the
cold air duct. The weather was intensely cold and the difficulty of handling
the hose and of getting at the fire was very great. By the earnest exertions
of all, it was at last extinguished. The damage to the building was repaired
at an expense of one thousand two hundred dollars, but had the fire succeeded
in getting headway, the greater portion of the village must have been destroyed.

†From a manuscript " History of Methodism in Castine Village," furnished
the author by Reverend James A. Morelin.

‡It is said he was " rode on a rail" over the line into Penobscot. He is reported to have been considerably injured, and was taken home and his wounds
dressed by a grandfather of Mr. Hosea Wardwell.

was no more to be tolerated here, it was thought, than that of the Quakers or Baptists had been in other parts of New England. Notwithstanding the opposition to the new form of worship and belief—perhaps, somewhat in consequence thereof—a small class was formed, but was not long sustained, for want of teachers. In 1834, Reverend Mark Trafton was stationed on the North Castine circuit. He preached an occasional lecture in the village, and organized a class of five members. Reverend Messrs. Moore, Palmer and Gerry, succeeded Trafton on the North Castine circuit, and occasionally visited and preached to this class. But little accession, though, was made to their number until the year 1841. In 1840, Reverend Theodore Hill, who was stationed on that circuit, commenced preaching on the Sabbath at the village. His first sermon was preached from the embankment of Fort George. His next, was in the ship-yard. In the meantime the little class of eight or ten, " began to cry to God," says Mr. Hill, " and as our faith increased, ' we began to see a small cloud gathering over this dark spot' where there had been no revival for a number of years." The result of Mr. Hill's labors was a revival, and at the close of the year, the class numbered about thirty. Mr. Hill was stationed on the North Castine circuit for two years, holding regular services, one-half the time, at the Court House in this village.

In 1842, agreeably to a petition from this village, the Maine Annual Conference reported Castine village as a separate station, and Reverend Charles Munger was appointed as the regular pastor for the ensuing year. The appointment was very fortunate in its results. The congregation was invited to occupy the meeting-house of the First Society, which was at that time unoccupied. Mr. Munger served here a second year, during which the society was under the necessity of returning to the Court House as a place of worship. He received three hundred dollars per annum. The Methodist chapel was built in the year 1844, chiefly—if not entirely—by Mr. John Jarvis. It cost about two thousand dollars. The successors of Mr. Munger were :—

Abner Hillman,	1843–4.	Obediah Huse,	1849.
David Higgins,	1845–6.	Cyrus Scammon,	1850.
George Pratt,	1847.	John Atwell,	1851–2.
Phineas Higgins,	1848.	Charles B. Dunn,	1853.

William J. Robinson, 1854–5.   George D. Strout,   1862.
W. J. Wilson,   1856.   W. T. Jewell,   1864–5–6.
John N. Marsh,   1857.   Josiah Fletcher,   1867.
L. D. Wardwell,   1858–9.   B. B. Byrne,   1868–9–70.
M. D. Matthews,   1860–61.   J. A. Morelin,   1871–3.

METHODIST EPISCOPAL CHURCH OF PENOBSCOT.[*]

The first Methodist preacher in Penobscot was Joshua Hall, who preached there in the year 1795. In the succeeding year, Reverend E. Hull preached there. The number of Methodists in town at that time was ninety-three. The Penobscot circuit was formed in the year 1798, by Peter Jayne, a deacon in the M. E. church, who preached with great success. In 1799, Reuben Hubbard was appointed to this circuit by the New England Conference, and, under the presiding eldership of Joshua Taylor, regulated the circuit, and established the church on a firm basis. The church had a healthy and vigorous growth, but the year 1819 was the most remarkable for its rapid increase of members, under the preaching of John S. Ayer. The following year, seventy persons were added to the church. It is recorded that at a prayer-meeting held at the house of William Hutchings, Jr., nine persons were instantly converted, and all the others present "convicted." "The shouts of the converts in praise of God, and the cries of the others for mercy, occasioned so great a noise that the shouts and cries could scarcely be distinguished from each other." In 1834, the Methodists complained that "in Castine we were some troubled with Universalism, some members withdrawing from our society, having embraced that pernicious doctrine." In 1841 and 1842, under the preaching of Theodore Hill, large numbers were added to the church. In 1871, the membership was one hundred and seventy-one, and the value of the church property was five thousand seven hundred dollars. There are three churches belonging to the denomination in this place. One was erected at North Penobscot, in 1837, and dedicated in December of the same year. One was erected in 1858, at the Head of the Bay, and was dedicated January, 1859. The third was erected in 1864, upon the *Doshen* shore.[†]

[*]From the Records of the Methodist Episcopal Church of Penobscot, abridged by Mr. Hosea B. Wardwell.

[†]This name is applied to the western shore of Penobscot, between Hardscrabble and the Castine line. The derivation of the word is uncertain. There are several traditions concerning it, but none are satisfactory.

The following are the names of the ministers, so far as known, with the date of their ministry: Joshua Hall, 1795; E. Hull, 1796; P. Merritt, and E. Mudge, 1797; Peter Jayne, 1798; J. Merrick, 1799; J. Gore, 1800; J. Baker, 1801; A. Metcalf, 1802; P. Munger, 1803; W. Goodhue, 1804; Levi Washer, 1805; E. Fairbanks, 1806; Daniel Ricker, 1807; D. Kilburn, 1808; D. Stimpson, 1809; B. Jones, 1810; J. Wilkinson, 1811; J. Emerson, 1812; Thomas F. Norris, 1813; John S. Ayer, 1819; John Briggs, and H. Nickerson, 1821; Samuel Baker, and David Richards, 1822; Thomas Smith, and William Douglass, 1823-4; John Lewis, 1825; James Jaquis, 1826-28; David Stinson, 1829; Jesse Stone, 1830-31; Benj. D. Eastman, 1832; Abel Allton, 1833; Mark Trafton, 1834; Joseph C. Aspenwall, 1835; J. Batchelor, 1836; Asahel Moore, 1837; Moses Palmer, 1838; Joseph Gerry, 1839; Theodore Hill, 1840-42, '54 and '55; J. W. True, 1842; Mace R. Clough, and Benjamin Lufkin, 1843; Asa Green, 1844; E. H. Small, 1845, '48 and '49; John Taggart, 1846; Mr. Chase, 1847; B. B. Byrne, 1850; R. S. Dixon, 1851; C. B. Roberts, 1856-57; Samuel S. Lang, 1858-59; E. Bryant, 1860; Joseph King, 1861-62; William Read, 1863; A. Plummer, 1864; C. L. Plummer, 1865-66; F. P. Caldwell, 1867-68; Students from Bangor Theological Seminary, 1869; O. R. Wilson, 1870-71; Fred. A. Bragdon, 1872-73.

FIRST BAPTIST SOCIETY OF BROOKSVILLE.

This Society was organized while Brooksville was a part of Castine, and was known at that time as the First Baptist Society of Castine. It was probably formed about the year 1813, as certificates of membership to it, at that date, are now on file in the Town Clerk's office at Castine. Israel Redman, and Benjamin Rea, were the Parish Committee at that time. We have been unable to obtain any further information in regard to this Society.

CONGREGATIONAL SOCIETIES OF BROOKSVILLE.

The First Congregational Society was organized in West Brooksville, January 4th, 1826. It was an off shoot from the First Church of Penobscot, of which a portion of

18

its first members originally constituted a part. This
Society has had, we believe, a steady and wholesome
growth, notwithstanding the formation of a Second Society
in South Brooksville.*

*We have been unable to obtain any further particulars in regard to the
other religious societies in this town and in Penobscot.

CHAPTER VI.

EDUCATIONAL HISTORY OF CASTINE.

LAW IN REGARD TO EDUCATION.—ESTABLISHMENT OF
PUBLIC SCHOOLS.—ESTABLISHMENT OF SCHOOL DIS-
TRICTS.—FIRST SCHOOL COMMITTEES.—RE-DISTRICT-
ING OF SCHOOLS.—SCHOOL FUND.—SCHOOL APPROPRI-
ATIONS.—DISTRICT MEETINGS.—ATTEMPT TO ESTAB-
LISH AN ACADEMY.—PRIVATE SCHOOLS.—STATE NOR-
MAL SCHOOL.—SCHOOL STATISTICS.—SCHOOL TEACH-
ERS.—SCHOOL REPORTS.—HIGH SCHOOL DIPLOMAS.

Education and religion in olden times, went hand in
hand. The commonwealth of Massachusetts from the earliest period of its history made strong efforts to promote
the general education of its citizens; believing the truth of
the adage, that " knowledge is power" as well as that
" education is the pillar of a State." In bestowing tracts
of land upon proprietors, it invariably required that a lot
should be set apart for educational purposes, and also, as
mentioned in the preceding chapter, one for the ministry
and for the first settled minister. In addition to this it was
required by law, as early as 1693, that every town of fifty
householders that failed in employing a schoolmaster, constantly, should be fined. In all towns embracing one
hundred householders, the teacher was required to be
capable of teaching the sciences and learned languages.

This town early displayed an unusual interest in the
subject of education, and, taking the entire period of its
corporate existence, has probably not been surpassed in
zeal by any town in the State.

As early as May, 1796, a special town meeting was called
to take action in regard to the establishment of public
schools. The town was divided into four school districts.
North Castine constituted one district; Castine village
made the second; Cape Rozier the third; and the remainder, of what is now Brooksville, constituted the fourth, and
was called the Buck's Harbor district. The school house
in the first named district was located " in the crotch of

the road, between the bridge and Scott's house." That
for the village, or Peninsula district, as it was called, was
located upon the " common lot." The location of the
school houses in the Buck's Harbor and Cape Rozier districts, was left to the residents in those districts to determine for themselves. The first school committee consisted
of six persons, viz. :—Captain Ephraim Blake, Mr. Ebenezer Leland, Mr. Jacob Orcutt, Captain John Perkins,
Captain Mark Hatch, and Captain Stover Perkins. The
town appropriated, this year, the sum of two hundred
dollars for the support of the schools. This sum, though
apparently small, was in reality an assessment of one dollar
and twelve and one-half cents upon every individual in
town ; about what the the average percentage has been in
the most prosperous years. Of this sum, the Northern district received seventeen dollars and fifteen cents ; Buck's
Harbor district, twenty-one dollars and seventeen cents ;
the Cape district, twenty-eight dollars and fifty-seven cents ;
and the Peninsula district, one hundred and thirty-three
dollars and sixteen cents. The old citizens of the town,
apparently believed that the public schools needed considerable inspection and supervision, for we find in 1813, when
the number of scholars was only seventy, that *twelve* persons were elected members of the school committee. At
its annual meeting this year, the town found it necessary to
direct the school committee " to employ school masters and
mistresses, and to appropriate the money raised for schools
to the best advantage." Whether these instructions were
rendered necessary in consequence of the unusual number
of members upon the committee may, perhaps, admit of a
doubt.

In 1817, the town voted :   " That the money raised for
the support of schools, etc., be divided in proportion to the
number of scholars in each school district." Also, " that
the money belonging to any school districts in which a
private school or schools are kept, be applied to the support of those private schools, in proportion to the number
of scholars taught in them, under the authority of the
school committee." The town, moreover, instructed the
school committee to return to the Assessors the number and
names of scholars in each district, between the ages of three
and sixteen years, in order to ascertain correctly the respective proportions of the school money to which each district was entitled.

In 1818, the school committee were instructed to district the town anew, but this, for some reason, not having been attended to, the town at its next annual meeting, voted that the Selectmen should proportion the number of scholars to each district, and alter the districts if necessary. The action of the Selectmen not, however, being satisfactory, the town voted the next year, "that Jonathan Hatch, Thatcher Avery, John Wilson, Joshua Hooper and Richard Hawes, be a committee to divide the part of the town situated off the peninsula, into school districts, in such a manner as they shall think proper." The town in 1821, acting upon the suggestion of this committee, divided the portion of the town off the peninsula into two districts. This year, for the first time, school agents were elected by the town. In 1828, a new school district was made out of the two off the peninsula, and the districts were named and numbered as follows :—

The Peninsula district was called No. 1.
The Middle (new) district was called No. 2.
The Northeast   "   "   "   " 3.
The Northwest   "   "   "   " 4.*

In 1834, the town passed a vote : " That the Board of Trustees of the Castine School Fund, consist of five persons, viz. : Thomas Adams, Charles J. Abbott, Samuel Adams, Hezekiah Williams, and Frederic Webber." This school fund originated from the sale of the land belonging to the "ministerial and school lot."

In 1836, the school committee, for the first time, made a report to the town of the condition of the schools. The subsequent year it was voted : " That the town will receive from the State its proportion of United States moneys, and, after deducting twelve hundred dollars, for paying town debts, the balance to be loaned by the Selectmen, at six per cent. per annum, the interest to be paid semi-annually, and appropriated to the support of schools." Unfortunately, however, the interest in education at this time began to wane, and the citizens accordingly, at their next annual meeting, foregoing the certainty of future benefit for the sake of present gain, reconsidered the above vote, and voted, instead, to pay out this money, *per capita*, to the people.

In the year 1845, the town voted :—" That the interest of the Ministerial and School fund, as it existed on the

*The districts are thus designated at the present day.

first day of January last, be used for the support of schools annually, and that sufficient security be obtained for the principal." The ministerial fund had vested in the First Congregational Society. This vote of the town was resisted by those interested in the Society, and, after a resort to the Legislature, without success, for an act to divert the fund, the attempt to have it appropriated for schools was abandoned.

The appropriations made by the town for the support of its schools, have always depended somewhat, of course, upon the state of its financial prosperity; but quite a steady correspondence exists between the amounts appropriated each year, and the population of the town at the time. Thus from 1796, to 1804, the annual appropriations were pretty uniformly two hundred dollars. From 1806 to 1810, there were between five and six hundred dollars. In 1811, the appropriation was eight hundred and fifty dollars. In 1812, it was twelve hundred. From that time until 1815, it decreased gradually to five hundred. From 1815 to 1833, it was between one thousand and one thousand five hundred. From 1834 to 1844, it fell off gradually to between six and eight hundred dollars. From 1845 to 1856, it was between one thousand and one thousand seven hundred. From 1857 to 1864, it ranged from two thousand to two thousand five hundred. The whole amount of money appropriated by the town, for the support of its schools, *exclusive* of that raised by the several districts, and of that derived from the " ministerial and school fund," amounted, in 1864, to about seventy-two thousand dollars. This is an *average* of over eight hundred dollars per annum—the average of the entire population for that length of time being about one thousand.

DISTRICT MEETINGS.

The first account we have of a school-house in the Northern district, was in 1804, when a meeting was held, to see if the inhabitants of that district would build a school-house, and determine where it should be located. The matter was not decided at this meeting, but the next year the district voted an appropriation of one hundred and eighty dollars, to defray the expense of building one. Where the school-house was situated, is nowhere stated. It could not have been the first one off the peninsula, as there was one in 1796 situated, as before mentioned, " in the crotch of the road." We are unable to ascertain at what time the school-houses in the Northeastern and Northwestern districts were built, or the cost of the same, as the records of these districts are not to be found.

School-meetings were called in the Buck's Harbor district in 1800, and again in 1806, to decide where the school should be kept. As only the *warrants* for these meetings have been preserved, it is not possible to state when the school-house was built, or where it was located.

In the Cape district, a school-meeting was called—as shown by the *warrant*—to choose a committee to build a school-house, and to select a master for the school. In the year 1817, there were two school-meetings held in this district. At the second meeting, the following votes were passed:—1. To build a school-house between David Dyer's and John Bakeman's—at a cost not exceeding three hundred dollars. 2. To build another school house near John Redman's—the cost not to exceed one hundred. 3. To reconsider the vote in regard to petitioning the town to divide the district. 4. That any material needed in building should be a lawful tender, *if ready when wanted.*

The first school-house in the Peninsula district was located on the " common lot." The exact time when it was built, its dimensions, etc., we have been unable to ascertain. On April 5th, 1802, this district voted to build a school-house two stories in height, thirty-six feet long by thirty feet wide, with a cupola on top ; the back thereof to be " on the northwesterly line of the common, square with the southwesterly side of the meeting-house." The sum of seven hundred dollars was appropriated, to defray the cost of erecting the same, and it was voted to allow the use of one story for an Academy. Captain John Perkins, Captain Mark Hatch, and Captain Joseph Perkins, were chosen a committee to superintend the erection of the building. At a meeting held July the fifth, it was voted to reconsider so much of the previous vote as related to having the building two stories high. Messrs. Otis Little, Thomas Stevens, and Moses Gay, were chosen a committee to draw up a plan for the building. As there has never been any Academy in this town, the cause of the above votes requires explanation.

It appears that in the year 1797, the General Court of

Massachusetts, by an act passed February twenty-seventh, offered one half-township of the public lands to such applicants, for a charter for an Academy, in each county, as should secure for it, by private subscription, funds to the amount of three thousand dollars. About the time of the passage of these votes by the district, there being no incorporated Academy in Hancock County, several towns attempted to establish one—and this town, as well as others. A paper was circulated here, and subscriptions made to more than the required amount. The above vote was taken by the inhabitants of the Village district, and the following petition was sent to the Legislature of Massachusetts:—

" To the honorable, the Senate and the House of Representatives of the Commonwealth of Massachusetts, in General Court assembled, at Boston, January, 1803.

Humbly shew your petitioners, that the inhabitants of Castine, in the County of Hancock, and its vicinity, conceiving that an Academy in the said town of Castine would be of great public utility in promoting piety, religion, and morality, and for the education of youth in the languages, liberal arts and sciences, have subscribed three thousand eight hundred and thirty dollars, for the purpose of erecting and supporting the same, as will appear by the subscription paper accompanying this petition*; *provided*, the General Court will endow said Academy with an half-township of land, six miles square, of the unappropriated lands in the District of Maine.

We would humbly beg leave to represent to your honors, that we conceive great benefit would result to the county at large from the said Academy being established at Castine. At least, this place has as many advantages as any town in the county; and many more than the towns in general. - It is free of access both by land and water, at all seasons of the year; and the peninsula on which it is proposed to erect the building, is one of the most healthy spots in the United States. Such is the population of the place, that probably within a quarter of a mile, good accommodations may be found for as many students as will ever be at the Academy; and we will venture to say [they] can be supplied at as cheap a rate as at any place in the county. The place is generally supplied with an abundance of fresh provisions of different kinds; and

*This list has not been preserved in the files of town papers.

there is a constant intercourse with Boston, so that whatever is necessary to be obtained from thence, may be easily and cheaply obtained. For these, and various other reasons, which it would be easy, were it necessary, to set before your honors, we flatter ourselves the prayer of our petition will be granted. Impressed with this idea, and believing that such characters as are best qualified for trustees, could not so well be known to your honors as to those among whom they live, the subscribers aforesaid, at a full meeting, unanimously agreed to mention a number of gentlemen, out of which number, should the prayer of this petition be granted, they pray your honors the trustees may be appointed.

Wherefore the subscribers and others have appointed your petitioners a committee to pray your honors, that an Academy may be established in said Castine, by the name of CASTINE ACADEMY, and that one half-township of land may be granted for supporting the same, and trustees incorporated for managing the prudential affairs of said Academy, with the privileges, powers, and authority usually vested in such corporations; and as in duty bound will ever pray." [Signed by the committee in the original, but no names given in the copy on file.] Doctor Oliver Mann was the Representative to the General Court this year, and did his utmost to induce that body to locate the Academy in this town. The following copy of a letter to him from the committee who drew up and forwarded the above mentioned petition, will show still more clearly the efforts that were made by the citizens of this town:—

"Sir: We have the pleasure to inform you that the business of the Academy you have so much at heart, now looks with a pleasing appearance, as you will see by the petition and subscription paper which we now inclose you, to present to the Honorable Court. By a vote of the petitioners, we are appointed a committee to write to you, and forward the petition, &c. It was thought best by them, at a full meeting, to nominate and recommend such persons for trustees as the petitioners were fully acquainted with—and in order to assist you in the nomination, as the names might not readily occur to you at the time. We have in the petition mentioned some of the advantages that Castine possesses over the other towns; but we think there are a number of others which it will be better for you to mention, than to have a very long petition.   There is one thing which we suppose will be very much urged by the opposition, to wit ; that scholars cannot be boarded as cheap as at the other towns that have applied for the grant.   This we think you can oppose with the greatest propriety, as it is a fact that the advantages Castine possesses will enable the inhabitants to board the scholars as cheap as, if not cheaper than, any town in the county. There is another thing you can mention from your knowledge of the petitioners, to wit: that they are all able to pay the sums set against their names, and that no names are put there for a mere show.   There was some deficiency in the form of the old subscription paper, and it was therefore, at this meeting, proposed to draw a new one.   The names are all upon it but yours—when you add that with the sum you subscribed on the old one, it will make just the sum mentioned in the petition, as you will observe.   Not doubting but you will pay every attention to the business, we remain,

Your friends and humble Servants."

Notwithstanding the exertions that were made to have the Academy located in this village, the town of Bluehill must either have possessed better claims, or have urged them more persistently upon the attention of the General Court, for the Academy in that town was incorporated at this session of the Court.   In consequence of the failure to establish an Academy here, the district this year voted to reconsider their vote of 1802.

In the year 1811, a lot of land, one hundred by fifty feet, running northwest from " Center " street, was deeded to the district, by Messrs. Joseph and John Perkins.   A meeting of the district was called this year, to decide whether the school-house should be altered, or a new one built.   Probably but little, if anything, was done to the building, as a district meeting was again called in 1815, to decide the same question.   What was decided upon at this latter meeting, we do not know ; but in 1823, a school-house was built, by Mr. Edward Lawrence, for which the district paid him three hundred and forty-one dollars.   In 1840, the district voted to sell the land and buildings on the Northeast side of Center (or Green) street ; and they were accordingly purchased by Jonathan Hatch, for one hundred and fifty dollars.   In 1841, the district voted to raise the roof of the Northwestern school-house, and to reduce the wages of female teachers to two dollars and seventy-five cents a week. On April 5th, 1847, Messrs. Charles J. Abbott, William Witherle, Charles Rogers, John Dresser, and Benjamin D. Gay, were chosen a committee to procure a site for a new school-house, and to make arrangements for building the same. Upon the twenty-fourth of this month, Messrs. Charles J. Abbott, Stover P. Hatch, Samuel Adams, William Jarvis, and Josiah B. Woods, were chosen a committee, to superintend the erection of the building. An appropriation of six hundred dollars, was also voted. On a subsequent meeting, held May 8th, the committee elected on the fifth of April was excused from further service, and the building committee was instructed to purchase a lot, but was restricted to the sum of one hundred dollars. At a meeting held December 22d, it was decided, if the consent of the town could be obtained, to alter the town-house, so as to make it suitable for a school-house. On March 27th, 1848, the district voted to discharge their building committee, and Messrs. Josiah B. Woods, Charles Rogers, and Charles J. Abbott, were chosen in place of those discharged. At this meeting, it was voted that this committee superintend the fitting up of the town-house into a school-house, and cause the necessary repairs to be made upon the Western school-house. The appropriation voted at a previous meeting was reduced to four hundred dollars, and was to be spent in making the above named repairs. On March 26th, 1849, by vote of the district, the agent sold to Mr. George Vose the lot of land (then occupied by him) adjoining the Western school-house, for the sum of thirty dollars. On March 7th, 1851, it was voted: " that the school agent be authorized to pay Mr. Hunt six hundred dollars, for teaching the high school the ensuing year." Mr. Hunt was to employ an assistant in the school, at his own expense, and to have the privilege of receiving scholars from other towns into his school, *provided* this did not interfere with the privileges of scholars in the district. On March 8th, 1853, Messrs. Charles Rogers, Joseph L. Stephens, and William Witherle, were chosen a committee to procure a suitable lot of land upon which to erect a school-house; to fix upon a plan of the same, and to estimate the expense. At a subsequent meeting, this committee reported that they had bargained with Jotham S. Gardner for the land, for the sum of two hundred and fifty dollars. They recommended the building of a double house, and set the estimated expense of the same at about two thousand eight hundred dollars. Their report was accepted, and the amount above specified was voted. Messrs. Stover P. Hatch, Charles Rogers, Ithiel Lawrence, Charles J. Abbott, and Charles K. Tilden, were chosen a building committee. The committee was authorized to borrow the amount of money that had been appropriated, and was instructed to have the school-house completed within eight months. In the year 1856, the sum of two hundred and fifty dollars was appropriated for philosophical apparatus, and the agent authorized to procure the same. In 1857, the district voted to relinquish the right of occupying the town-house as at school-house. On March 19th, 1859, the district voted to build a school-house two stories in height, near the site of the Intermediate school-house. It also voted to raise the money by loan—to be paid in ten annual installments. Messrs. Samuel Adams, Jr., Stover P. Hatch, Ithiel Lawrence, Stephen W. Webster, and Charles J. Abbott, were chosen a building committee. The sum of four thousand dollars was appropriated, and the committee was instructed to dispose of the Intermediate school-house. At a meeting of the district, held September 24th, it was voted to have a cupola upon the building ; also, to accept the report of the committee upon the completion of the " Abbott " school-house. In the year 1861, the district decided that the Apprentice school should be commenced in November, and be continued as long as it was found profitable. The district also voted at this meeting that the High school-house should hereafter be known as the " Adams " school-house. On September 1st, 1863, the district voted to allow one of the school-houses to be used for five years, for a State Normal School, and to have it suitably altered for this purpose. Messrs. Charles J. Abbott, Samuel Adams, and William H. Witherle, were chosen a committee to make an offer to the State, of one of the buildings, and to make all necessary preparations for the transfer. This committee thereupon, very shortly after, made the following offer to the commissioners appointed by the State :—

" The undersigned a committee of the citizens of Castine, pursuant to votes at a public meeting of said citizens, and of the inhabitants of School District Number One in

Castine, qualified to vote in school-district affairs, at a legal meeting of said district, hereby offer to the State of Maine, under the Act of March 25th, 1863, for the establishment of Normal Schools, the Abbott school house in Castine, for the use of a Normal School, for five years. This school-house is of two stories, with a basement, and is fifty-eight feet by thirty-four, giving school-rooms forty-five feet by thirty-two, and was built in 1859, in the best manner. The citizens will furnish double desks and fixed chairs—of Boston manufacture—and settees for two hundred scholars. They will, if necessary, have one of the school-rooms fitted with sliding doors, so as to be used for two recitation rooms; and the attic, which is fifty-eight by fourteen feet, shall be finished off, and properly furnished, lighted, and ventilated, for a recitation room. Two rooms suitable for apparatus and library rooms are connected with the school-rooms. Suitable clothes room accommodation shall be provided. A Philosophical Apparatus belonging to the High school, and the Public Library, of seven or eight hundred volumes, may be used by the Normal School. Board at a rate not exceeding two dollars and a half a week, can be obtained by the Normal School scholars.*"

The third article of the warrant for the district meeting, on April 9th, 1864, read as follows:—" To see if the district will divide the Primary school into two independent schools, with a teacher for each. The schools to be called the First and Second Primary schools. Each to be kept for two terms in a year. The first to have an assistant; to commence as soon as possible, and to continue thirteen weeks. The second to commence in August, and continue seventeen weeks. Each to be taught by a female." The other articles of the warrant were :—To see if the district would vote to have three terms of the Intermediate and Select schools—all the terms to be taught by females ; to employ a master for a Free school for both sexes, to commence in December, and to continue sixteen weeks ; to choose a committee of three, to classify the scholars, and transfer them, as found needed, from school to school.

*In the Spring of 1873, the State relinquished the use of this building, the new Normal School-house having been completed. The district did not, however, cease to extend its patronage to this institution, but gave it a loan of all the furniture then in use in it. In addition to this, Deacon Samuel Adams presented it with a handsome bell, and Mr. John Jarvis with a very superior clock. The town had previously deeded to the State the land on which the building stands.

Upon the third article being called for consideration, the following petition was presented:—

" The undersigned, Ladies of School District Number One, in Castine, deeply interested in the cause of education, respectfully beg leave, in their own behalf, in behalf of the children, and of the present and future welfare of society, to express to the meeting to be holden in said district, on the ninth instant, their most earnest desire that *no change* should take place in the present admirable system of our schools, and that they be maintained, *without interruption*, on their present footing." This petition was signed by almost every female in the district. Probably induced thereto more by their fears of what *might* happen, than by anything expressed in the warrant itself. This petition was respectfully laid on the table, and all the articles were adopted. Messrs. Josiah B. Woods, Alfred F. Adams, and Joshua Hooper, were chosen a committee to classify the scholars.

PRIVATE SCHOOLS.

There have been, from time to time, ever since the incorporation of the town, if not before, schools kept here by teachers who were not employed to act in this capacity by the town authorities. As no record of these schools was required by the town, our sources of information in regard to them are necessarily very meager. The Misses Almira A., and Sarah H. Hawes, taught private schools for thirty or forty years. They were very successful in their teaching, and usually had full schools. Nearly all of the present adult population of the town have, at some time, been under their tuition. A number of other persons have also, from time to time, taught private schools, to the satisfaction of their patrons, but we are unable to obtain any particulars as to their schools, and none of them have taught for so long a time as the ladies mentioned.

EASTERN STATE NORMAL SCHOOL.

This school was opened in the Abbott school-house, September 7th, 1867. The opening exercises were conducted by Reverend Doctor Ballard, State Superintendent of Schools, who delivered the keys of the building to Mr. G. T. Fletcher, of Augusta, the Principal of the school. Appropriate remarks were made by citizens of the town, and by others present. A class of thirteen was admitted to the school. The school increasing in size, Mrs. Fletcher was appointed assistant teacher at the beginning of the second term.

The exercises at the close of the year were very interesting. Governor Chamberlain and Council, and many friends of education were present. Mrs. Fletcher having declined to serve longer, at the beginning of the second year—in August, 1868—Mrs. Julia E. Sweet, of Boston, was appointed assistant. Mr. John W. Dresser, of this town, who had kindly given his services for two terms, adding much to the interest and profit of the school, was appointed teacher of music. At the commencement of the winter term, Miss Anna P. Cate, of Castine, was added to the corps of teachers, and at the commencement of the Spring term, Miss Helen B. Coffin, was transferred from the Normal school at Farmington to this, and Miss Lucy V. Little, of this town, was employed temporarily.

' The close of the Spring term of 1869, marked an era in the progress of the school, by the graduation of its first class, of eight pupils. Governor Chamberlain and Council were present, and all expressed the feeling that the two years of trial had established the school on a firm basis. The Fall term of this year opened with an attendance of fifty-one pupils. At the commencement of the Winter term, Miss Eliza A. Lufkin, of this town, a graduate of the school, was appointed assistant, in place of Miss Sweet, who had resigned.

At the beginning of the Spring term of 1870, Miss Mary E. Hughes, of Pennsylvania, was added to the corps of teachers. At the close of this term, the second class—of twenty-six—was graduated. The Fall term opened with an attendance of one hundred and nineteen pupils. Miss Cate having resigned her position, Miss Ellen G. Fisher, of Massachusetts, was appointed to fill the vacancy. Mr. Park S. Warren, teacher of the High school, was appointed teacher of Music, in the place of Mr. Dresser, who had resigned.

The Spring term of 1871, opened with an attendance of one hundred and forty pupils, and closed with the graduation of the third class—consisting of twenty. At the close of the Fall term, Miss Fisher resigned her position for one in Boston, and Miss Clara Bartley, of Cambridge, Massachusetts, was elected to fill the vacancy. At different times during these years, Doctor George A. Wheeler, of Castine, and Doctors George B. Stevens, and Calvin Cutter, of Massachusetts, favored the school with lectures on Physiology, and Doctor N. T. True, of Maine, with lectures on Geology.

The Spring term of 1872 closed with the graduation of a class of fifteen. The town having presented to the State a fine lot of land, at a cost of about one thousand dollars, an appropriation of twenty thousand was made by the Legislature, to build a new Normal school-house. Plans drawn by Mr. Alfred F. Adams, of this town, having been accepted, the contract for the building was awarded to Messrs. Foster & Dutton, of Bethel. The ground was broken in May of this year, but, the season being unfavorable, the house was not completed until January, 1873. The school was moved into the new house in February, but, on account of the severe weather, and bad travelling, the dedicatory exercises were post-poned until the close of the term in May. The closing examination of the year took place on Wednesday, May 22d, and on the same evening the house was dedicated. Governor Perham and Council, the Board of Trustees, members of the Press, friends of education and of the pupils, and citizens, made an audience of five hundred people in Normal Hall, and there was still room for a hundred more. The exercises were very interesting. Speeches were made by the Governor and members of the Council, and by other officials, by citizens, and people from other States, and other parts of our own State ; and, in behalf of the school, by the Principal. The Normal choir, and the Lawrance Cornet Band, of Castine, furnished excellent music. On the succeeding day, the fifth class graduated, with honor to themselves and the school. The new building is an ornament to the town, and is in many respects one of the best school-houses in the State. It has ample accommodations for two hundred pupils.*

School Statistics.

The average annual number of scholars in each district, from 1813 to 1845, was, omitting fractions, as follows :—

* We are indebted to Mr. Fletcher, the Principal of the school, for the material for the foregoing account.

EASTERN NORMAL SCHOOL HOUSE, CASTINE, ME.

In District Number One, two hundred and eighty-seven.
"   "   "   Two, fifty-one.
"   "   "   Three, forty-three.
"   "   "   Four, thirty.

The following are the names of all the teachers mentioned in the records of the several districts, or which we have been enabled to obtain, from other sources, and the decade in which their names occur. The exact dates it is impossible, in most cases, to ascertain. The records are very defective, and consequently many names are, without doubt, omitted from this list which would otherwise appear.

The teachers in District Number One were:—From 1820 to 1830.—Hannah D. Gay, Cynthia Holbrook, Miss C. S. Jellison, Joseph Lull, Susan Stevens, and E. M. Porter Wells. From 1830 to 1840.—Emeline Perkins, Andrew Pingree, Nancy Vose, Sarah Vose, Nancy Watson. From 1840 to 1850.—Mr. Abbott, Mr. George Adams, Mr. Collins, Rev. Mr. Farwell, Sarah H. Hawes, Frances Hosmer, Abigail Mead, Richard Potter. Mehitable Rogers, and Mr. Savage. From 1850 to 1860.—L. H. Hatch, Mary E. Field, L. Hunt, Georgie Lane, Charlotte Y. Little, Lizzie H. Morse, Hannah M. Perry, Ellis Peterson, Bertha Rogers, Hannah D. Robbins, Emeline C. Sawyer, Cornelia Upham, Susan R. Upham, L. D. Wardwell, David W. Webster, Jr., Zadoc Witham, and Miss H. A. Wood. From 1860 to 1865.—Fannie J. Gardner, Miss Condon, Anna P. Cate, Marietta Hatch, Ellis Peterson, Miss A. G. Porter, Miss E. E. Sawyer, and Miss A. Wilder.

In District Number Two:—

From 1820 to 1830.—Miss Abigail Hatch. From 1830 to 1840.—William F. Nelson, Alexander Perkins, Miss Wright. From 1840 to 1850.—J. W. Hutchins, Fannie Little, and David W. Webster, Jr. From 1850 to 1860. Phœbe Ellis, Fannie Little, Hester Lull, G. S. Hill, Reverend William J. Robinson, Hosea B. Wardwell, Laura Webber, Clara Wescott, Sarah N. Wescott, Irene Witham, and Zadoc Witham. From 1860 to 1865.—Lucy Hatch, Sarah Hooke, Mary Lufkin, Mary J. Robbins, Hannah Robbins, Reverend Mr. Wardwell, and David W. Webster, Jr.

In District Number Three:—

From 1820 to 1830.—Sarah Hayden, and William B.

Webber.   From 1850 to 1865.—George E. Brown, Mary
E. Dodge, Edwin Ginn, Clara A. Littlefield, Hosea B.
Wardwell, David W. Webster, Jr., Sarah M. Wescott, and
Zadoc Witham.

In District Number Four:—

A school is said to have been taught in this district two
years before the incorporation of the town, by a Mrs.
Parker, in her dwelling-house.   The following winter it
was taught by a Mr. Downes.   In 1801, the school was
taught by an Englishman named Bowlin.   He is said to
have been an escaped convict, and to have been carried
back to England by the British, when they left here in 1815,
and to have been afterwards hung.   It is further said of
him, that his mode of punishing unruly scholars, was to
cause them to sit down on a " peaked brick."   From 1806
to 1820.—Mr. Rowlinson, and Reverend Mr. Ricker, taught
in this district.   From 1820 to 1830.—Andrew Steele. —
From 1830 to 1840.—Harriet Devereux, Sarah H. Hawes,
Charles Hutchings, Harrison Hutchings, Ursula Lawrence,
Miss Minot, Louisa Rogers, Betsey Steele, Angelina Steele,
Lucretia Stone, Theodosia M. Wescott, Robert Wardwell,
Jeremiah Wardwell, and Zadoc Witham.   1840 to 1850.—
Nehemiah Basset, Clara Basset, Franklin Chatman, Harriet
Dresser, Lucy Osmore, Miriam Patten, Nathan Patterson,
Hannah Perry, Sarah Trott, Betsey Turner, Jeremiah
Wardwell, Zadoc Witham, Samuel Wasson, Sarah Wescott,
Lucy J. Wescott, and Clara White.   From 1850 to 1865.
Rufus Cole, Lizzie Dodge, Henry Folsom, Harrison Ginn,
Amanda Hatch, Amelia Harriman, Caroline Higgins, Ellen
S. Hutchings, Harrison Hutchings, Ruby King, Abby
Oakes, Louisa Perkins, Mary J. Robbins, Sarah Rowell,
Louisa Springfield, S. D. Staples, Rebecca Trott, Austin
Wardwell, Eliakim Wardwell, Evan Wardwell, Mary E.
Wardwell, David W. Webster, Jr., and Zadoc Witham.

Owing to the loss of so many of the school returns, it is
impossible to estimate, with any exactness, the average
wages, for each term, of the teachers, in the different districts.   All that it is possible to state is that the *average* of
the districts off the peninsula has been somewhat below
fifty dollars a term, and of district Number One, somewhat
below seventy-five dollars.

SCHOOL REPORTS.

The first report of any school committee was in 1836. It was very short; gave no particulars in regard to the schools; contained no recommendations, and simply reported the schools as in a very prosperous condition.

In the next report, in 1841, the committee complain of a great want of attendance, and lack of punctuality on the part of the scholars. They recommend *fewer* studies; a greater uniformity of books; more frequent visiting by parents and others; an improvement of the school houses; and that the school on the peninsula be kept for forty-two weeks in the year, by a male teacher. They also recommend, we regret to say, that the *wages* of *all* the teachers be reduced. This report is signed: B. B. Beckwith, *for the committee.*

The superintending school committee in their report for 1856, recommend the introduction, into all the schools, of Tower's series of Grammars, and also recommend a change in the Readers. " Believing that an interest in the subject of education may be awakened by the printing and cirenlation of the Annual School Reports among the families of this town," they recommend that subsequent committees be authorized, at their discretion, to have the report thus printed and circulated. Joseph L. Stevens signs for this committee.

The report for 1857, is printed. In this report the Primary school is declared to be altogether too large for one teacher, numbering, as it did, one hundred and three scholars. In his remarks the writer says: " We are more and more impressed with the importance of having a teacher of thorough training and ample qualifications, placed in charge of this school. Perhaps there is no one in the series requiring in the teacher, for the best success, such an unusual combination of qualities as does the Primary. Here it is that systematic effort is first made to awaken in the young mind its slumbering capacities; here, that it is first taught to act and think; and here it is that character is most impressible." The Apprentice school is well spoken of in this report, though it, like the other schools, is said to have suffered from unsteady attendance. It is stated in this report that there were two principal objects sought to be accomplished in the establishment of this school. One, " the efficient instruction in the essential branches of practical education of those who could attend school only for some weeks of the winter season. This could be done only in a school especially designed for them." The other object was "that the High school might reach the condition of a *high* school." In his remarks in regard to the High school, the writer speaks in the highest terms of the ability and devotion of the teacher, Mr. Ellis Peterson. This school is declared to afford ." better advantages of education than can be enjoyed in most of the Boarding-schools and Academies in the County." The closing paragraphs of this report refer to the " Labor question." They are full of sound sense, and would be especially applicable at the present day, the drift of them being that Labor to compete successfully with Capital, *must* be educated.

In their report for 1858, the committee state that the condition of the schools off the peninsula is not what it ought to be. They fail, however, to give the reason why such is the case. The report speaks commendably of all the village schools. It states also, that the grading of the schools on the peninsula was, this year completed.* They were divided into four schools, called the Primary, Intermediate, Select and High. For transfer from the Primary to the Intermediate school, the scholar was required to be able to read fluently in Sargent's First Reader, and to pass a satisfactory examination in Emerson's Arithmetic, and in the addition and multiplication tables. For transfer to the Select school, the scholar must have passed through Mitchell's Primary Geography, Colburn's Arithmetic—as far as section 7, page 79—and through the simple rules of common Arithmetic. For transfer to the High school, Colburn's Arithmetic must have been finished; also, Mitchell's Common School Geography, Tower's Elements of Grammar, Quackenbos's History of the United States, and Greenleaf's Introduction to the Common School Arithmetic, as far as decimal fractions. Sargent's Readers, and Worcester's Spelling Book, were introduced into the schools this year, the old books having been in use for twelve years. The committee recommend the fixing up of the Western school house for an Apprentice school, and the erection of a new building for the Primary and Intermediate schools.

*The grading principle began to be acted on in our schools in 1840. Joseph L. SteVens, Hezekiah Williams, and Charles J. Abbott, being the school committee who inaugurated it, and from whom we obtain our information.

This latter suggestion they urge strongly, not only on account of the interests of the schools themselves, but also as a means of counteracting, somewhat, the great depression of business which was being felt by the laboring classes of the town.

The report for 1860, shows a very commendable improvement in all the schools. The committee are very decidedly in favor of strict discipline in school. The report concludes by expressing the obligation the people of District Number One were under, to Mr. John W. Dresser, for the gratuitous instruction in music, given by him for many months, to the members of the High and Select schools. The last three reports are signed, *for the committees*, by Mr. Charles J. Abbott.

The report for the year 1862, is printed. In it the committee remark that the schools, taken as a whole, have been more successful than in any former year, the result of the steady liberal support yielded them. The report dwells much upon the importance of educating the children, rather than allowing them to *educate themselves*. This report is signed, *for the committee*, by Mr. David W. Webster, Jr.

In the year 1864, Diplomas were, for the first time, given to those who graduated from the High school. These diplomas were upon parchment, and read as follows:—

Diploma
of Castine High School.
Awarded

To..

Who has attended the Castine High School for more than four years; has been distinguished for Constant Attendance, Exemplary Deportment, and Diligent and Thorough Study; and who is believed to be entitled by Culture and Scholarship, to this Diploma.

} School Committee
of
Castine.

Teacher...

Castine, ...186

A large class of young gentlemen and ladies was graduated this year. A few classes have, we believe, received
diplomas since then, but of late years no graduations have
taken place.*

From the foregoing rather incomplete account of the
attention paid to educational matters in this town, it is
plainly to be seen, that the citizens of Castine, have a
right to feel a pride in the past history of their public
schools. It is equally to be seen that these schools have at
no time been free from imperfections. Perfection can no
more be looked for in the future than in the past, but it is
hoped that this record of what was done for the cause of
education by our forefathers, may incite all to increased
zeal in the matter of a common education provided by the
people for the people.

*Until this year (1874), when a class of seven or eight were publicly grad-
uated. It is to be hoped that in future, each year will see a class ready for
graduation.

CHAPTER VII.

MILITARY HISTORY.

(Subsequent to Incorporation of Penobscot.)

IMPORTANCE OF CASTINE AS A MILITARY POST.—MILITIA AND REGULARS HERE IN 1787 TO 1812.—WAR OF 1812. — BRITISH EXPEDITION. — BRITISH OCCUPATION. — BRITISH GARRISON EVACUATED. — FORT GEORGE RE-OCCUPIED BY THE AMERICANS.—ROSTER OF CASTINE ARTILLERY COMPANY.—HANCOCK GUARDS.—TROOPS SENT TO THE AROOSTOOK.—CASTINE LIGHT INFANTRY.—IT VOLUNTEERS FOR SERVICE IN 1861.—SERVICES RENDERED BY THE THREE TOWNS IN THE WAR OF THE REBELLION.

Probably no place in the State of Maine has passed through so many changes, as the peninsula of Castine. Indians, French, Flemish pirates, Dutch, English, and Americans, have each occupied it. France held possession of it for almost the entire seventeenth century. No less than five naval engagements have taken place in its harbor. To use the language of another: " it has never been without a garrison from 1630 to 1783, and has always been dealt with by the nations in whose possession it has been as a place of great importance." General De Peyster remarks : " This is one of the most remarkable points all along our coasts; which, under any other government than our own, would have long since been transformed into a naval and military fortress of the first class." [Dutch at North Pole, and Dutch in Maine, p. 49.] Such was the military character of the place before its incorporation ; and although since that time, the foot of the invader has pressed its soil but once, yet even its later military history will be found not devoid of interest.

As early as 1787, there was a company of the 1st Regiment, 2d Brigade, 8th Division of Massachusetts Militia here—of which Mr. Jeremiah Wardwell was Captain. On July 10th. 1799, a recruiting office for the 15th U. S. Regiment was opened here. The recruiting officer was Captain John Blake. Eli Forbes was made the Captain of a company, Doctor Oliver Mann a Surgeon in the regiment, and Thomas Stevens a Lieutenant in Captain Hunnewell's company. On November 1st, forty men left town, to join their regiment. These men were all *regulars*, but we find it stated in the Castine Journal of this date, that an artillery company, of which Lieutenant Lee had command, paraded here upon that day. This company formed, probably, a part of the State militia. During the first six months of the year 1800, this company was in mourning for General Washington. In 1810, a meeting of the regiment to which it belonged was called, in Castine, to elect a Colonel, to take the place of Joseph Lee, who had resigned.

In the year 1804, Jeremiah Wardwell, of Penobscot, was in command of some regiment, possibly of the one above mentioned. The following letter proves this fact, and also shows that they were called into service, though it is not certain that they ever left town :

" Col. J. Wardwell, Sir :

It appears that an insurrection has broken out in the settlement west of Belfast, and the insurgents threaten to burn the town of Belfast, and it appears necessary that the militia should be put in readiness to march at the shortest notice.

You are hereby ordered to examine the town stocks of ammunition within the limits of your regiment, and have them filled up immediately, and have fifty men equipped and ready to march, if they should be called for.

I am, Sir, your most obedient and humble Servant,

JOHN CROSBY, B. General.

HAMPDEN, June 29, 1804."

The only time, since the municipal period of the town commenced, that it has been in possession of a foreign foe, was during what is generally known as the War of

1812. The long continued impressment of American seamen by the British—which was upheld by them—together with numberless insults to our flag, and the superior policy of Napoleon, in abandoning the right to search neutral vessels; all these things combined to compel the United States, on June 18th, of that year, to declare War against Great Britain. Active hostilities did not commence for more than a year, but the note of preparation began at once to be heard. Sometime in the year 1813, a detachment of regular troops, belonging to the brigade of General Blake, was stationed in town. [Williamson, Vol. 2, p. 632.]* In April, 1814, there were at this place nineteen men belonging to Captain Fillebrown's company, of the 40th Infantry, viz: one 3d Lieutenant, one Sergeant, two Corporals, and fifteen privates. On May 16th, a detachment of the same company, commanded by Lieutenant Andrew Lewis, was added. On the thirty-first of July, the detachment, which had been converted into one of artillery, consisted of one 2d Lieutenant, one Sergeant, and six privates. The ordnance consisted of one 24-pounder, twelve hand-spikes, nine muskets, and six bayonets. [Monthly returns of 40th Regt.] This year a body of men from two British armed vessels entered, in the night, the fort at Thomaston, spiked the guns, destroyed the buildings and ammunition, set fire to one vessel, and towed off two others. This daring exploit created such general alarm, that the militia of the State were ordered out to act as a coast guard, and a draft was made upon the militia at Bangor and vicinity, in order to increase the force at this garrison. [Williamson, Vol. 2, p. 642.] An expedition was planned by the English, at Halifax, against Penobscot and Machias. The fleet consisted of the following vessels:

Three 74s—The *Dragon*, *Spencer* and *Bulwark;* two frigates—the *Burhante* and *Tenedos;* two sloops—the *Sylph* and *Peruvian;* one schooner—the *Pictu;* one large tender, and ten transports. Upon these, three thousand five hundred men embarked, besides the usual camp followers. They consisted of the 29th, 62d, 98th, two rifle companies of the 60th, and a detachment of the Royal Artillery, regiments. The 29th Regiment was called the

*There had been, as mentioned before, an artillery company in this town for several years. We are uncertain whether these were the same troops referred to by Williamson, but we think not.

Boston Regiment, it being the same that perpetrated the *Boston Massacre*. One man who was a private at the time of the massacre, was here with the regiment at this time. [Niles' Weekly Register, Vol. 7, p. 280.] The troops had composed a part of Wellington's army, and many of them were said to be Germans. [Ibid. Vol. 7, p. 51.] Lieutenant General Sir John C. Sherbrooke had the chief, and Major General Gerard Gosselin the immediate command of the land forces, and Edward Griffith, Rear Admiral of the White, had the command of the naval squadron. The fleet sailed from Halifax on the twenty-sixth of August, and arrived at the Back Cove on Thursday, September 1st. They seized at once upon a revenue cutter, and upon all the shipping in the harbor. [Eaton's Thomaston, So. Thomaston and Rockland.] So formidable an appearance did this fleet offer, that our troops, which were in garrison at the lower fort—Fort Porter*—without waiting to go through the form of a surrender, immediately discharged their cannon, blew up the magazine, and fled up the bay. The English at once took peaceable possession of the place. In the course of the day, they landed the greater part of their troops, took possession of Fort George, seized the Court House and Custom House—which were used as barracks for the soldiery—erected numerous batteries and a block-house, and took some of the best and most commodious houses for the abode of the officers. They also had a detachment at the old church in North Castine, and occupied Mr. Hooke's barn as a hospital. Captains Gell and Coker, and Lieutenants Sands and Evans, with their servants, quartered in the dwelling house of Mr. Otis Little. They were not aware, however, that a hundred muskets, and an abundance of ammunition were concealed under the hay-mow, in the barn. These munitions of war were the property of the town and State, and were not brought out from their hiding-places until after peace was proclaimed.

When the fleet sailed up the harbor, the whole population turned out to witness the sight, though not without feelings of dismay. The inhabitants on the Brooksville side ascended the high hill in the northern part of the town and

---

*This fort mounted at the time, four 24-pounders. It was evidently untenable against a force of any magnitude, being open to an attack from the rear. [Ballard's man. Sketch of Castine.] According to the account in Nile's Register, [Vol. 7, p. 51.] there were *twenty-four* 32-*pounders*, four of which were destined for the new fort at Portland.

waited, with intense anxiety, to obtain a view of the expected conflict. Making this place the head-quarters of their forces, the British soon began to send out foraging parties through the region round about and even across the bay. In a very short time also, they sent detachments up the river and succeeded in capturing the towns of Hampden, Bangor, Frankfort, and Bucksport. They brought back from their incursion, some eighteen or twenty horses, a large number of oxen, sheep, etc., and six vessels. These vessels were the *Bangor Packet*, the schooner *Oliver Spear*, the *Hancock*,—which was retaken—the *Lucy*,—which was lost—the *Polly*,—which was ransomed—and the "beautiful boat" *Cato*. Making but four vessels actually brought into this harbor. The *Liverpool Trader*, belonging to Mr. Joseph Perkins, was burned. They burned and destroyed many other vessels, and required bonds from the several towns to deliver up at Castine, within about a month, all the remainder that were uninjured. Upon the first and fifth of September, General Sherbrooke and Admiral Griffith issued proclamations to the effect that, if the people would remain quietly at their homes and continue to pursue their usual avocations, would surrender all their arms, and would refrain from communicating intelligence to the Americans, they should have protection and safety ensured to them. Also, that the municipal laws and civil magistrates would be supported, and that all citizens who would furnish the troops with provisions, should receive pay for the same. There were frequent changes of the British forces and vessels, occurring during the year, but there were seldom less than fourteen or fifteen sail of this squadron in the harbor. The English repaired Fort George, occupied it with a garrison, and mounted some sixty cannon there. They also enlarged the trench, said to have been made by Mowatt, in 1779, so as to form a canal ten or twelve feet in width and eighty rods in length. This canal was dug fully as much to prevent desertions as to guard against a surprise. Desertions were becoming of daily occurrence, and still took place after this canal was dug. Two deserters were captured, tried, sentenced, and shot. One was shot while attempting to cross the canal. The English about this time made Castine a port of entry, and appointed William Newton, Collector of the Customs. The property of Mr. Hooke, the former Collector—who had succeeded in escaping with all the public papers—was confiscated.   All the vessels belonging here previous to the surrender of the place were, however, returned to their owners, and were allowed a clearance and free intercourse with New Brunswick, and other British Provinces.   [Niles' Register, Vol. 7, p. 110.]   Upon the twelfth of September, General Sherbrooke and Admiral Griffith, with about one-half the forces, left for Machias.   Rear Admiral Milne and Gerard Gosselin were left in command of the naval and land forces.   All intercourse between the eastern and western sides of the Penobscot was prevented, as much as possible, by both the British and the United States authorities.   The following order was issued by the Post Office Department at Washington :—

GENERAL POST OFFICE, September 26, 1814.

Sundry Post-offices in the District of Maine, being possessed by, or under the control of, the public enemy, and it being possible that others may be in the same situation, it is hereby ordered, that the Post Master (at the nearest safe Post-office to those offices so possessed or controlled by the enemy) detain, open and account for the mails addressed to them, in the same manner as if addressed to his own office.   Whenever it shall become safe to forward mails to such Post-offices, the letters and papers remaining undelivered, are to be remailed and forwarded immediately to their places of destination, either by special express, at the expense of this office, or by the regular carrier.

(Signed.)   R. J. MEIGS, JR.,
                    POSTMASTER GENERAL.

From the above order it would appear probable that all letters for Castine were, at this time, left either at Belfast, or at Prospect.

On November the third, a small fleet of merchant vessels arrived here from Eastport, under convoy of the war-brig *Fantine*.   One unarmed schooner, lately the American privateer " *Snap Dragon*," having on board some British Marines, was hailed by a boat from Waldoboro'—Captain Cook—was fired upon and had two men killed and two wounded.   The boat then returned to port.   Sometime in January, 1815, a transport from Halifax, with a re-inforcement of two hundred and fifty soldiers for the garrison at this place, was chased ashore, not far from here, by three American privateers, and lost. The troops, however, got safely to land and marched to town. [Niles' Register, Vol. 8, p. 108.]

During the whole time of the British occupation, no attempt was made on the part of either the State or United States authorities to regain possession of the place. The question was discussed in the Senate of the commonwealth, but it was decided that any attempt to recover the place, even should it succeed, would involve too much bloodshed. The National government would probably have attempted the expulsion of the enemy from the place, had it not been for the refusal of Governor Strong, of Massachusetts, to assist. However cogent may have been the reasons on the part of the Governor, his indisposition to make any attempt to regain the place, caused him to be very unpopular, not only in portions of his own State, but pretty generally throughout the country. He was dubbed "the HERO of Castine," and according to the *National Advocate*, it was proposed by the inhabitants of the District of Maine, to present him with a sword " as a mark of their estimation of his *patriotic* and gallant defence of Castine, and the prompt and efficient protection he afforded that District when invaded by the enemy." The sword was to be constructed of the best *white pine*, and to be ornamented with appropriate emblems! [Niles' Register, Vol. 7, p. 280, and Vol. 8, Supplement, p. 187.] During this time our citizens had, naturally, to endure very many inconveniences and annoyances, especially from officers like Barrie, Captain of the *Dragon*, a rough sailor, who " was a total stranger to literature, to every generous sentiment, and even to good breeding." Notwithstanding these inconveniences, however, there was much, in the rapid growth of business—in the social amenities observed by some high-minded and generous-dispositioned officers, both of superior and inferior rank—and in the amusements afforded by the mere presence of so large a number of people, as was at that time here, to render the period one of some considerable gayety. No regret was experienced, however, by the majority, when at length—April 15, 1815—the garrison was evacuated, and the town resumed its usual intercourse with its neighbors.

After Fort George was evacuated by the British, our

forces took possession, and a company was sent here to garrison it.   About the year 1818, a Board of Engineers was appointed by the United States Government, to survey the Coast of Maine, with a view to fortifying it.   This Board reported in favor of abandoning Castine, and fortifying Bucksport Narrows.   Accordingly, in March, 1819, the garrison was evacuated by our troops.   Captain Leonard, and Lieutenant McIntyre, were the officers in command here at the time, and Doctor William Ballard, the Surgeon.

There was in Penobscot, at this time, and had probably been for some years, a company of militia.   About this time it was commanded by Captain Eben Hutchings.   We have been unable to ascertain any further particulars in regard to it.

The organization of the Artillery company—mentioned in the first part of this chapter—was kept up for quite a number of years after the evacuation of the town by the British.*   This company mustered in Brooksville, September 18, 1834, under the command of Captain Eben P. Parker, and the members were paid fifty cents each for their services on that day.   The following is the roster of the company at that time :

Captain Eben P. Parker,	Otis Morey,
Edward Lawrence,	William F. Nelson,
William Jarvis,	Thomas A. Murch,
William Averill,	Reuben Turner,
Rufus P. Parker,	James Turner,
Otis Hatch,	John Bridges,
Daniel Moore,	Miles Gardner,
Stephen Witham,	Robert Stockbridge,
John Blake, Jr.,	Isaac Stockbridge,
Robert C. Straw,	Benjamin Wilson,
Darius Lawrence,	Zimri Bryant,
Ithiel Lawrence,	Eldridge Bridges,
John Wilson,	John B. Wilson,
David C. Wilson,	James Foster,
Jotham Gardner,	Jonathan L. Moor,

Robert Moor.

How long the organization of this company was kept up, is uncertain ; but the military spirit of the community

*Captain Charles Rogers, the present Postmaster at Castine, was at one time in command of this company, but is unable to give the date in which he held that office.

was preserved and fostered by the formation, about this time, of a company of Light Infantry, by the name of the HANCOCK GUARDS.

They constituted Company " D " of the First Regiment, First Brigade, Third Division of the State Militia. No account of this company is to be found prior to the year 1839, and the opinion of former members is that it was formed that year. On February 17th, of this year, the State, fearing an invasion, on account of the difficulties with England, in regard to the settlement of the Northeastern Boundary question, ordered all the Militia to the Northeastern frontier. Twenty-one members of Company D went to Aroostook County, and performed military duty for some two months—though they saw no enemy.* This calling out of the State Militia is popularly known as the " Aroostook War," and has to this day, rather unfairly, we think, been the source of much amusement and raillery, at the expense of those who participated in it. It certainly required no small degree of courage, to brave the deep snows and excessive cold of an unbroken wilderness, in the most Northern portion of the United States, for the express purpose of meeting, as they supposed, an armed foe. The men who could cheerfully do this, would, without doubt, have acquitted themselves honorably in actual battle, had occasion required. The expenses of this Company cost the town· the sum of three hundred and ninety-six dollars and thirty-seven cents, which amount was, however, reimbursed by the State. The following bill and vouchers show to whom this money was paid, and for what purposes

" Dr.   THE STATE OF MAINE,

TO THE TOWN OF CASTINE.

Upon Requisition of 17th February, 1839.

1839.

Feb. 17th.	For	am't of		H. Rowell's	bill,	$32.72
" 19th.	"	"	"	Witherle & Jarvis's	"	34.92
" "	"	"	"	William Chamberlain's	"	52.64
"	"	"	"	Adams & Gay's	"	35.60
" "	"	"	"	J. Hooper, Jr's,	"	.55

*The names of those members of Company D, who went to the Aroostook, will be found in Part III.

Feb. 17th.   For am't of Richard Hawes's   bill,   4.00
"   21st.   "   "   " H. M. & J. J. Hyde's "   16.09
"   22d.   "   "   " Pond & Johnson's   "   19.50
     "   "   "   " Joseph Bryant's   "   20.65
     "   "   "   " Joshua Norwood's   "   24.00
"   23d.   "   "   " John A. Avery's   "   15.38
"   —   "   "   " Fayette Buker's   "   20.02
March 11th. "   "   " D. Montgomery's   "   68.00

Upon Requisition of 9th of March, 1839.

March 13. For amount of Charles Rogers' bill,19,68]$363.75
"   "   interest upon $363.75 to Feb 13,
             1840—11 mos., $20.00
          " commissions to Selectmen upon
             purchases, &c., .05 per cent,   18.18
                                                _____
                                                $401.93

Contra Cr.

By amount of sales of camp utensils, &c., returned, $5.56
                                                    _____
                                                    $396.37

The undersigned, a majority of the Selectmen of the
town of Castine, hereby certify that the expenditures
charged in the foregoing account, were made for the purpose of furnishing a detachment of the Militia belonging
to said town, which were ordered into actual service by
the authority of the State, in February and March last,
with transportation, supplies of provisions, camp equipage,
and camp utensils, as provided by law; and that the
account is just and true, according to our best knowledge
and belief.

C. J. ABBOTT,   ) Selectmen of
CHARLES ROGERS,   ) Castine.

From the accompanying account, certificates, and vouchers, it appears 'the number of men for which transportation was furnished' was eighteen, and with Captain Wing,
nineteen.   One man and a one-horse team to Milford
from Castine, forty-seven miles; one man and a two-horse
team to Houlton, from Castine, one hundred and sixty
miles.   The name of the Commanding Officer—late Captain—now Lieutenant Colonel Wing.

The number of men for which supplies were furnished, was eighteen, and with Capt. Wing, nineteen.

Supplies commenced February 21st, 1839, and those furnished were consumed mostly by the tenth of March.

The camp utensils will be found in the several vouchers —chiefly in the bills of H. Rowell, R. Hawes, and Adams & Gay—and those returned in the memoranda of William Chamberlain, auctioneer.

Upon Requisition of 9th of March, 1839, three soldiers, accompanied by Mr. Charles Rogers, one of the Selectmen, went to Bangor. Mr. Rogers paid for their board while there, in preference to purchasing rations, etc., and the charge appears in his bill.

I hereby certify that the camp utensils, supplies, services, &c., charged in the several bills in the foregoing account, under Requisition of 17th February, 1839, were actually furnished for myself and eighteen men from said Castine, of the Hancock Guards under my command, and that Fayette Buker, with his one-horse team, and David Montgomery, with his two-horse team, attended said troops with said camp utensils, supplies, &c., to wit: Fayette Buker from Castine to Milford, forty-seven miles; and David Montgomery from Castine to Houlton, one hundred and sixty miles, and that the certificate marked A, signed by William Chamberlain, contains a true list of the camp utensils returned.

> CHAS. H. WING, Capt. of D Co., L. Inft.,
> 1st Regt., 1st Brig., 3d Division.

We hereby certify that the disbursements for necessary supplies of transportation, provisions, camp equipage, and camp utensils, charged in the foregoing account, were actually made, and are agreeable to the provisions of law, and that said account is just and true.

(Signed,)

> C. J. ABBOTT,   } Selectmen of
> CHARLES ROGERS, }   Castine.

(Dated) January 20th, 1840."

The next reference to this company is to a meeting of it in 1840, when they offered to do duty for the town as

22

Engine Men.   The following letter was sent to the Selectmen of the town:

"At a meeting of the HANCOCK GUARDS, on Monday, the
fourth inst , a question was laid before said H. Guards, by
Captain O. Hatch, ' whether or no the said H. Guards
would volunteer themselves to do the duty of Engine
Men, for the town of Castine?' The above question was
tried by a vote of said H. Guards, and decided in the
affirmative.   And said H. Guards, therefore, volunteer
themselves to do the duty of Engine Men.   By so doing,
they do not wish to injure any one, but have only the
public good in view.   We, the subscribers, were chosen to
lay the above proceedings before the Board of Selectmen.

D. S. O. WILLSON, ｜ Committee for
OTIS HATCH,   ｜ H. Guards."

No further reference to this company is to be found, but
it is most likely that its organization was not long kept up.

On July 17th, 1858, forty-eight citizens—including a
number of the prominent men of the town—petitioned the
Governor and Council for authority to be organized into a
military company, by the name of the CASTINE LIGHT
INFANTRY.   On September 22d, an order was issued by
the Governor, granting the petitions and assigning them,
under the designation of Company " B," to the first Regiment, first Brigade, and seventh Division of the State
Militia.   On August 3d, a temporary organization was
formed, and upon August 12th, a requisition was made
upon the Arsenal-keeper at Portland, for arms and equip-
ments.   On the thirty-first of the month, the company
joined the Encampment at Belfast, and were the recip-
ients of much praise, as well as of a beautiful bouquet,
presented to them by the ladies of Belfast.   At a meeting
of the company held October 20th, Adjutant General
Webster presided, and the company was legally organized
by the election and commission of the following officers,
viz:—Samuel K. Devereux, Captain; Charles W. Tilden,
First Lieutenant; Stephen W. Webster, Second Lieutenant; Alfred F. Adams, Third Lieutenant; John B. Wilson,
Fourth Lieutenant.   The fourth of July, 1859, was celebrated by the first appearance of this company in uniform.
We quote the proceedings ·of that day from the records of
the company.

" After marching through many of the principal streets, received a pretty thorough drill upon the common, where many of our ' noble women' were assembled for the purpose of presenting us with a *beautiful silk banner.* Miss Helen S. Bridgham, from whose hands we received the same, made a very inspiring and appropriate speech, to which Mr. John M. Dennett, our faithful Standard Bearer, replied in a few well chosen and happy remarks. After receiving our banner, we proceeded to the Universalist church where we were favored with an oration by Reverend Mr. Ives, of the Congregational church, which was truly worthy its author. We dined at our armory, and after dinner, listened to a number of excellent toasts from friends who were invited to partake with us. Concluded the celebration by a social dance and a good time generally, at our armory, in the evening." On the twenty-eighth of the same month, this company attended the Centennial Celebration at Fort Point. October 4th, 1859, they attended a Muster at Bangor. On October 20th, they celebrated the anniversary of their organization by a march to North Castine, where they were received by their friends, and entertained with a collation at the house of Mr. Emerson. On June 18th, 1860, the company assembled for the purpose of target shooting. The first prize at this contest, a SILVER CUP, was awarded to James C. Collins, who made the best average shots. The second prize, a large SILVER SPOON, was awarded to William M. Lawrence. The third prize, "a nicely marked and valuable TIN CUP, manufactured by Messrs. B. & B.—was, after due consideration, *solemnly* awarded to Lieutenant J. B. Wilson." July the fourth, of this year, the company spent in Belfast, as the guests of the " City Grays." The last record of this company is dated April 26th, 1861, and was written only a short time before it left town to join the army. When the first call for troops was made, at the breaking out of the War of the Rebellion in 1861, this company *volunteered* its services, and was the *first* company to *start* for the rendezvous of the Second Regiment. Soon after leaving the State, Captain Devereux received an appointment as Collector of Customs at this port, and consequently resigned his commission in the army, and Lieutenant Tilden was promoted to fill the vacancy thus occasioned.* The last record in the jour-

*Captain DeVereux receiVed his appointment as Collector, and left the Regiment while at Willetts' Point, N. Y., *en route* for Washington, D. C.

nal of this company, was left unfinished, but its subsequent history, during the war, forms no unworthy portion of that of the Second Maine Regiment, and is to be found in the records of that regiment. For further information in regard to its particular members, the reader is referred to the Roll of Honor, in Part III.

The towns whose history is being narrated, were all three intensely patriotic, and their efforts to sustain the authority of the government and the supremacy of the Union, place them in the front rank of the towns of this State. This unhappy contest is, however, of too recent occurrence to require, in this place, any lengthy account of all that was done by the towns referred to, either in their corporate capacity, or by their individual citizens. The following statistics, though, will show that no *unfair* claim of supe-riority is made over many towns of the State, and will afford a fitting close to the military history of these towns. They are taken from the published reports of the Adjutant General of Maine.

TOWN CREDITS.—(INCLUDING CALL OF '63.)

Brooksville, - -	130 men.
Castine,	157 men.
Penobscot,	158 men.
Total,	445 men.

TOWN AID TO FAMILIES, FROM 1862 TO 1866.

Town.	Number of Families.	Number of Persons.	Amount Allowed.
Brooksville,	92	203	$3,621.90
Castine,	187	432	7,345.67
Penobscot,	73	223	3,172.88
Total,	352	858	$14,140.45

TOWN BOUNTIES, UP TO 1865, INCLUSIVE.

Brooksville, - - ·	$22,086.00
Castine, - - - -	15,834.07
Penobscot, ($23,782.00, reimbursed by State, to the amount of $600,)	23,182.00
Total,	$61,102.07

AMOUNT OF MONEY DONATED BY CITIZENS, &C.

	Brooksville.	Castine.	Penobscot.*	Total.
U. S. Sanitary Commission,	$300	$400		$700
U. S. Christian Commission,	200	200		400
To soldiers in Maine Camps,	400	300		700
To General Hospitals,	100	100		200
To Regt. Hospitals and Individuals,	200	300		500
To New York, Philadelphia, Boston, and other places,	250	100		350
	$1,450	$1,400		$2,850

*Amount not given in Adjutant General's Report.

CHAPTER VIII.

COMMERCIAL HISTORY OF CASTINE.

Natural Advantages, and Early Trade.—A Bill
of Sale, etc., in 1779.—Provisions in 1781.—The
Value of Labor in 1783.—Business Men of the
Town, from 1799 to 1814.—Business During the
British Occupation, 1814-15.—Duties on Goods.
Smuggling.—Application of Certain Merchants
to Congress for Relief. — Report of Congres-
sional Committee. — Price Current in 1828.—
Customs and Revenue. — Navigation. — Corpora-
tions and Manufactures. — Town Valuation.—
The Seasons of Greatest Prosperity of the
Town, and Causes of its Decline.

At a very early date the French voyagers found the
region of Pentagöet an excellent location for fishing, and
for trading with the Indians. The Plymouth Colony
recognized the commercial importance of the place, and
carried on here a prosperous trade with the natives, for a
period of nine years. Its importance as a trading post, even
more than its advantages for military purposes, induced its
capture by the French under Aulney. The Baron de St.
Castin was also, doubtless, influenced by the natural advantages afforded for trade, to make this his residence. The
fisheries are described as abundant in 1670, though the
privilege of fishing was only granted by the English upon
the payment of a duty of twenty-five crowns—equivalent
to about thirty dollars—upon each boat. In the year 1698
one Caldin (or Alden,) traded here—bought furs of and
sold goods to a son-in-law of Castin, and others. The price
of beaver skins at this time was from fifteen to fifty cents,
according to the quality. During the period of the Revolutionary war there was, in all probability, no business carried on here but farming and fishing—except such as would
necessarily follow a military occupation of the place. The
following bill of sale, of that period, may prove not uninteresting:

"MAJORBAGUADUCE, January 21, 1779.

Received of Mr. Jeremiah Wardwell, the sum of two hundred pounds, Lawful money, in full for one-half part of my Jebacco Boat, that I bought of Capt. Mark Hatch, with her Rigging, Sails, Anchors, and all other appurtenances belonging to the same, which I warrant and defend from all persons whatsoever, as witness my hand.

NATHAN PHILLIPS.

Witness, AARON BANKS.

N. B. If you are a mind to sell the boat, please to sell my part with yours."

A considerable portion of the clothing worn at this time was purchased at Halifax, and the following bill will give some idea of the cost of different articles of apparel:

"July, 1779.

To cash paid Grant & Clearing for 2 ps. Linen and ps. Calaminca,	£15	11s.	2d.
To cash paid for 3 White Cloaks,	3	16	6
To do. do. 3 Hats,	2	9	0
To do. to Mr. Schwartz for 2 Suits Cloth, trimmings, &c.,	13	1	8½"

The cost of living, in 1781, can be seen from the following list of the prices of a few staple commodities:

Pork per lb., 6½ cts.
Pease " quart, 3 "
Butter " lh., 16½ "
Flour " 112 lbs., $5.33 "

At what time the first store was opened in this vicinity, it is impossible to ascertain. It was probably some years prior to the incorporation of Castine, and very likely even before the incorporation of Penobscot. Daniel Low had a tannery here as early as 1784. The following copy of an account will give some idea of the value of labor, &c., at this period:

"MAJORBIGWADUCE, December 4, 1783.

Findly McCullum to Jeremiah Wardwell, Dr.
To Cutting timber and hauling and building a Hovel and covering; and fix for tying Cattle, 30. Halifax Currency £1. 10s. 0d.

To building a yard for hay 10,	£0.	10s.	0d.
To butchering two oxen	0	5	0
To fetching home your cows and calves from the Head of the Bay,	0	5	0
Jan. 5th, 1784. To butchering a Cow ¾,	0	3	4
To fetching one load of hay by water 10,	0	10	0
16th. To cash sent to Brown to bear against the Proprietors 4-6,	0	4	6
To hauling hay and tending cattle and sheep,	3	15	0
To one load ¾ of hay 40,	3	10	0
May. To shearing of your sheep, 4,	0	4	0
1785. To wintering 3, year-olds, 20,	3	0	0
May 24. To shearing sheep, 4,	0	4	0
To 400 of hay ¾,	0	13	4
1793. To one more boat and sails, 3-15,	3	15	0
May 8th. To an order from Woodman, 49,	2	9	0

£20. 18s. 2d.

Credit to Findley McCullum, Majorbagaduce, 1784.

By 5 bushels of wheat, 7, 8,	1£	15s.	0d.
By 6 bushels ¼ of Rye, 5,	1	11	3
Sept., by 1 cow, 80,	4	0	0
By two lambs sold, 10,	1	0	0
Oct. 10, by one calf, 20,	1	0	0
Dec. 26, 1788, by three sheep, 20,	1	10	0

12£ 00s. 3d."

In the year 1799, David Howe, Otis Little, David Johnston, George Haliburton, and James Crawford, sold miscellaneous goods, and the first named is known to have had considerable trade with the Indians; Holbrook & Martin had a hat store; Isaac Stockbridge carried on the sail making business; William Wetmore practiced law, and Oliver Mann was the first settled physician—although Doctor William Crawford had practiced in this region during the ante-municipal period.

In the year 1800, Doctor Moses Adams commenced practice here, and William Abbott, Esq., opened a law office near Woodman's tavern.

In 1802, Mr. Richard Hawes commenced trade here. There were also, at this time seven warehouses here; a tannery, kept by Mr. Freeman; a rope-walk, by Mr. Samuel Whitney, and several saw and grist mills.

In 1809, Doctor J. Thurston settled in town. This year Mr. Bradshaw Hall commenced the pump and block making business ; Mr. Noah Mead had a hardware store ; Mr. William Allison, a chair manufactory ; Enis Barr opened a sail loft; and Messrs. Judkins & Adams, William Witherle, and Samuel Adams, were in trade here.

In the year 1810, Messrs. Doty Little, Daniel Johnston, Samuel Littlefield, Jonathan L. Stevens, John Brooks, John A. Smith, David Howe, Hosmer & Moor, Otis Little, Bradford Harlow, Judkins & Adams, Witherle & Jarvis, Andrew & David Allison, Hooper & Fuller, Joseph Cleaveland, Stevens, Rowell & Co., and James Crawford—seventeen in all—were in trade here. [See advertisements in Castine "*Eagle*," 1810.] Brick making was also carried on quite extensively this year, by Mr. Mark Hatch; and there was a tannery here, owned by Mr. John Wadlin. The business at this time was principally in West India goods, rum, fish and groceries.

During the British occupation of the town—in 1814 and '15—large, and almost daily importations of English goods were made here. One vessel, captured on her way to this port by a barge commanded by Major Noah Miller, of Lincolnville, carried a cargo invoiced at forty thousand dollars. Another, captured on her way hither from Halifax, had a cargo valued at twenty thousand pounds. The schooner *Betsey & Jane*, taken on her way here from St. John, had dry goods valued at one hundred and fifty thousand dollars. Another schooner, taken on her way from Halifax, carried one hundred and forty cases of dry goods, twenty barrels of sugar, and some glass and hardware. A brig, bound from here to Jamaica, with fish and lumber, was also taken. [Niles' Register.] Provisions and lumber were brought here to market and exchanged, at high prices, for European and Colonial produce. A great trade was carried on with all the surrounding country—as far up the river as Bangor, and to the eastward as far as the Union river—but more particularly with the inhabitants upon the western side of the Penobscot. The town at this time was overflowing with people, and there was a daily stage between here and Hallowell. [Providence Patriot, Jan. 28th,

1815.] Foreign goods and merchandise at this time were
abundant and cheap, but live stock was in great demand,
and high. The Custom-house was seized by the British,
and duties levied by them on all imports and exports. Insurance upon vessels from Halifax was, at this time, twenty
per cent. The duties on rum were thirty-eight cents on a
gallon, and on brandy and gin, forty-three cents. Molasses
retailed for seventy-five cents per gallon. Fresh beef sold
for from five to six dollars per hundred-weight. Flour was
the same in price as at Boston. Merchantable boards
were worth ten dollars per thousand. Calicoes are said to
have sold for one dollar per yard. As the English would
receive nothing but *specie*—except provisions and lumber—
so great an amount of it was brought hither that quite a
number of banks, in different parts of the State, were
obliged, in consequence of it, to suspend payments. The
duties on dry goods, required at this time from the residents
of the place, were two and one-half per cent. From non-
residents five per cent. was demanded. As duties were also
demanded by the American authorities, upon these same
goods when they were landed at other points, the natural
consequence was that a vast amount of smuggling was carried on between this and the neighboring towns. In the
winter time dry goods were carried across the river, at
different places on the ice. This was generally done at
night, although occasionally one would be found venture-
some enough to attempt it in broad day-light. There are
some now living who assisted in these exciting midnight
adventures, and many others who have listened to the
recital of them at the paternal fireside.

 After the departure of the British forces, the Collector
of Customs, upon his return to this place, conceived it to
be his duty to collect the duties upon all the imported goods
he could find in the town. Some of the merchants positively refused to pay these duties, but many of them furnished
bonds. The Supreme Court of the United States sustaining the action of those who refused payment, the individuals
who had paid, or were under bonds to pay, petitioned Congress for relief. The matter was referred to the Committee
of Ways and Means, which on January 15th, 1824, reported
as follows:—

 "The Committee of Ways and Means, to whom was
referred the several petitions of Joshua Aubin, Nathaniel.
W. Appleton, and C. H. Appleton, John Tappan, William

Whitehead, James Crawford, Daniel Johnston, Otis Little, David Howe, Thatcher Avery, Ebenezer Hodsdon, John Lee, Benjamin Haseltine, Samuel Adams, and James Graham,

REPORT.

That the claim of these petitioners depends upon the facts and circumstances connected with what are commonly called the Castine cases; and, from the documents referred to the Committee, are substantially as follows:—

During the late war between the United States and Great Britain, the town and harbor of Castine, in the collection district of Penobscot, were occupied by the forces of the enemy, from the first of September, 1814, until the twenty-seventh of April, 1815, and were in the entire and exclusive control, and under the jurisdiction of the said enemy.

On the first of September, 1814, the Collector of the Customs for the district of Penobscot, removed, with the papers of his office, to Hampton, [Hampden] on the western side of Penobscot river, and there continued to transact the business of the Custom-house, until after peace was restored between the United States and Great Britain. Immediately after the capture of Castine, the British government there established a Custom-house, or excise-house, and appointed a Collector of the Customs, who from that time until the twenty-fourth of April, 1815, continued to receive entries of vessels and merchandise, conformably to the laws and regulations in the province of Nova Scotia. During this period many merchants residing at Castine imported goods, and entered them with said British Collector, paying duties thereon to the British government; and a part of said goods, on the return of peace, remained in Castine. The United States Collector, after the peace, but before the actual evacuation of Castine, established his office upon, or near the British lines, and required that all goods, of foreign growth or manufacture, which had been imported during the hostile occupation, and were still there, should be entered as if then originally imported into the United States in a foreign vessel, and threatened to seize and detain the goods, unless the owners or consignees, would immediately pay, or secure to the United States, duties thereon as aforesaid. To avoid the great loss and injury which would have been sustained by a seizure and detention of said goods, the owners or consignees thereof, entered the same with said Collector, and gave bonds for the duties, including the additional duty for importation in a foreign vessel. At the time said bonds became due, some of the persons who had given them paid the same, trusting to the Government of the United States for restitution, while others refused to pay, and suits were commenced against them in the district courts of Massachusetts and Maine, for the recovery of the same, which suits were discontinued by order of the Secretary of the Treasury, in consequence of the unanimous opinion of the Justices of the Supreme Court of the United States in the case of United States *vs.* Rice, that the act of the Collector exacting said bonds was illegal, the goods not being liable for the duties to the United States.

The petitioners are of the number of those who actually paid the duties to the Government before the suit against Rice, and before the decision of the Supreme Court, pronouncing their illegality.

The Committee further report that this subject was brought before Congress in the year 1820, upon the application of Jonathan L. Stevens, and others, situated similarly with the petitioners in many respects, and on the eleventh of April of that year, an act was passed for their relief, and authorizing a refunditure of the duties, provided it should be proved to the satisfaction of the Secretary of the Treasury, that the persons named in the law were residents of Castine or Bucksport, or were purchasers from residents, of the goods on which the duties have been imposed.

The Committee do not perceive that the residence of the importer, or owner of the goods, can vary the law applicable to the cases. The decision of the Supreme Court is, that duties could not be legally exacted upon any part of these goods by the United States, and it is presumed that those persons who voluntarily submitted to the authority of the custom-house officers, should not be placed in a worse situation, than others who refused to comply with the requisitions of the Collector.

The Committee do not pretend to ascertain the principle upon which a previous Congress has decided, but believing all the cases to be governed by the same rule of law, they submit to the House the papers and documents they have been able to collect, and that the subject may be fairly considered, they report a bill." [House Reports, 18th Congress, 1st Session.]

In 1828, the first professional dentist took up his abode in town. The following list of the prices of various commodities, that year, will prove not uninteresting at the present time :

PRICE CURRENT, IN 1828.

Beans, per bushel,	- -	$1.25
Butter, per pound,		.12
Cheese, " "		.08
Coffee, " "		.14
Flour, " barrel,	-	5.25
Corn, " bushel,		.38
Oats, " bushel,	-	.50
Lard, " pound,		.10
Molasses, per gallon,	- - - -	.28
Spirits, " "	- -	from 35 to 1.20
Sugar, " pound,	- - -	.12
Tea, " "		.50

About the year 1831 or 1832, a new rope-walk, in place of that recently destroyed by fire, was erected by Mr. John Dresser. It was put up, at first, near the shore, but was afterwards removed to its present location.

CUSTOMS AND REVENUE.

A Custom House for the collection of revenue, was first established, under the authority of the United States, on July 31, 1789. The collection district included Thomaston, Frankfort, Sedgwick, and Deer Isle. The Collector was required to reside here. Mr. John Lee was Collector in 1793, and was, probably, the first one appointed at this place, under the United States government. Whether there was ever, prior to this time, any collection of revenue made here under authority of the Colonial or any foreign government, is not known; but it is extremely improbable that such was the case. The place was made a Port of Entry in 1814. During the occupation by the British in the latter part of that year, a Custom House was established by them, and Willliam Newton was appointed Collector. In 1833, the United States bought of the Castine Bank Corporation, the portion of the County building previously owned and used by the Bank. In 1846, the County Commissioners refusing to make the necessary repairs—on account of the Courts being no longer held in this town—a bill was reported in Congress, appropriating one thousand and one hundred dollars for the purchase of a Custom-house. Accordingly, in 1848, the remainder of the building, of which the United States already owned one-fourth, was bought of the County Commissioners. The present Custom-House and Post-Office was erected in 1870. The first revenue cutter stationed here for the enforcement of the laws, and the prevention of smuggling, is said to have been the sloop *Wealth*, which was here about the year 1800.

NAVIGATON.

The first vessel built here, since the incorporation of the town, is believed to have been the schooner *Nancy*, owned by Hudson Bishop and Oliver Mann. She received a license as a coaster, from the Custom-house, in 1793. In the year 1799 there were sailing from this port, and owned here, wholly or in great part,—three ships, one brig, ten schooners and two sloops—a total of sixteen vessels—not including coasters, of which there were several. The ports to which they sailed were Liverpool, Barbadoes, Dominica, Antigua, Martinique, and Grenada. The amount of tonnage taxed here in 1801, was one thousand six hundred and eighty-five and one-half. We have not been able to ascertain the name of the *first* packet to run between this place and Belfast, but there was one in 1811, that plied between these two places, that was called the *Sally*. The first steamboat ever known in these waters was the "*Maine*," commanded by Captain Daniel Lunt, which run between Bath and Eastport, touching at this place. She made her first trip May 22, 1824. On August 20, 1842, the steam frigate *Missouri*, arrived in this harbor, and remained sometime on exhibition. About the year 1827, the steamer *Hancock* was built here by Noyes and Chamberlain. She was built very differently from modern steamboats, and had no boiler. Her steam apparatus was constructed on what is called, we believe, the "Babcock" principle. Her machinery was put into her in Boston, and on her trip down the harbor she gave out, and had to be towed back to the city. Her machinery was afterwards changed. From 1830 to 1850, ship building flourished here. A great many ships and brigs, of large size, were built here, by the Adamses, Witherles, and others. Messrs. Brooks, Lawrence, and Noyes were the principal contractors and masterbuilders. The growth of navigation, not only up and down the Penobscot, but also to this place, rendered the establishment of a light-house at the entrance of this harbor, a necessity. Accordingly, in the year 1828, the DICE'S HEAD LIGHT-HOUSE was built on the north side of the entrance to the harbor.* It was originally built of wood, and was very shabbily constructed. It became so much in need of repairs, and so unsafe, that in 1858 it was torn down, and another one built in (or near) its place. The present building is a stone tower, sheathed with wood and painted white, attached to a dwelling of wood, one story and a half, painted brown. The light is a *fixed white*, visible at a distance of seventeen nautical miles. The height of the tower, from the base to the *focal plane*, is forty-two feet. The height of the *light* above the level of the sea is one hundred and thirty feet. The compass range of visibility is East by North, by Eastward to North. The lens apparatus is of the fourth order.

CORPORATIONS AND MANUFACTURES.

About the year 1809, the FORT POINT FERRY COMPANY was incorporated. Mr. Elisha Leighton was the President; William Abbott, Esq., the Agent; and Thomas Adams one of the Directors of the company. The names of the other Directors are not known, but they are believed to have been, mostly, citizens of this town. An attempt was made by this company to convey passengers and teams across the river in a flat boat, carrying a sail, but it resulted in a failure, and horse-power was afterwards used.

In 1810, the CASTINE MECHANIC ASSOCIATION was incorporated for the purpose of the manufacture of the screw auger. At that time this was the only place in the world where this kind of auger was manufactured. The Meads having purchased the patent right some two years before, attempted to carry on the business alone, but after a trial of one year the above named association was formed.

*Named, probably, after the first settler in that part of the town. Calef spelled the word Dyce.

In 1816, the CASTINE BANK was established, with a capital of ten thousand dollars. Daniel Johnston, Esq., was President; John Brooks, Cashier; and Samuel Austin Whitney one of the Directors. Who the other officers of the bank were, has not been ascertained. The bank closed up its affairs and relinquished its charter somewhere about the year 1830.

In the year 1828, the PENOBSCOT STEAMBOAT NAVIGATION COMPANY was incorporated. It is believed to have been for this company that the steamboat *Hancock*, referred to in a preceding page, was built. The company met with rather poor success, and did not have a very long life.

About the year 1835, a company was organized for the purpose of carrying on a STEAM FLOUR MILL. The building was erected, three large boilers were introduced, and two run of stone. For some reason, however, the enterprise did not prove a success.

About this time, the firm of Hatch & Mead carried on a CHAIN MANUFACTORY, for the making of cables for vessels. This business proved sufficiently remunerative and was continued many years.

In the year 1849, two corporations were established in Brooksville, both having citizens of Castine amongst the number of their stockholders. The first was the BROOKSVILLE MANUFACTURING COMPANY. The stock was divided into one hundred and seventy shares, and the amount of capital invested was five thousand and seventy dollars. The second, was the SOUTH BAY MEADOW DAM COMPANY. It had a capital stock of one thousand two hundred and fifty dollars, which was divided into seventy-seven shares.

In the year 1867, the CASTINE BRICK COMPANY was incorporated. It had a capital stock of twenty thousand dollars, which was divided into one hundred and ninety-two shares. The following were its officers at that time — Seth K. Devereux, President; Frederic A. Hooke, Treasurer; Seth K. Devereux, William H. Witherle, Samuel K. Whiting, Charles W. Tilden, Mark P. Hatch, and Frederic A. Hooke, Directors. This company still continues in a flourishing condition, and its business is, we are informed, steadily increasing.

VALUATION OF THE TOWN.

The property of the town is shown by the following statistics obtained from the tax lists. As these lists were made out somewhat differently in early than in later times, an exact comparison between the different kinds of property owned at different times, is a matter of considerable difficulty; but the total valuation at the end of each decade, will give the general rate of growth of the town.

In 1797, the valuation of the town was as follows:—Polls, 156; Real Estate, $2,477; Personal Estate, $2,594; Income from professions, etc., $539; unimproved lands, $129; Total number of acres, 4,890; Total valuation, $5,739. In 1810, the total valuation was $26,187. In 1820, $28,686. In 1830, $371,560. In 1840, $393,380. In 1850, $597,390. In 1860, the number of Polls was 269, and the total valuation was $812,840. As this valuation was excessive, it was afterwards reduced, and in 1870, the Polls numbering 258, it was $461,343.

In the decade from 1800 to 1810, Brooksville constituted a part of Castine; and this fact must be borne in mind in reading the statistics of the property owned here in those years. The following description of the property in town, will give an idea of what constituted the wealth of that period, and also of the marked increase in the prosperity of the community.

DESCRIPTION OF PROPERTY, ETC., YEARS 1800, 1810.

	Number or	Value.
Polls,	184	240
Dwellings, -	70	96
Shops,	16	21
Tanneries,	1	1
Ware-houses, -	7	‡
Grist-mills,* -	6	1
Barns, -	31	37
Rope-walks, -	1	‡
Saw-mills, -	3	4
Other buildings, - -	12	‡
Wharfage, superficial feet of †- -	30,560	‡

*One of these mills was, probably, the windmill erected by Mr. Mark Hatch, one was off the neck, and the remainder in what is now Brooksville.

†James Crawford owned six thousand feet, John Perkins, five thousand feet, and Joseph Perkins, eight thousand feet.

‡Not given.

24

Vessels, tonnage of - -	1,490	*
Plate (silver and gold) oz. of†	199	*
Improved land, acres of	423	778
Hay, tons of - -	295	*
Horses, -	19	70
Oxen, -	62	161
Cows and steers,	155	644
Swine, - - - -	88	215
Money at Interest (in excess of amount due) [1801]	$3,150	13,700

The amount of money at interest, in 1801, was in the hands of the following named individuals :—

John Collins,	had $600	in excess of his liabilities.
George Haliburton,	" 200	" " "
Joseph Perkins,	" 600	" " "
Stover Perkins,	" 1500	"
Joshua Woodman,	" 100	"
Richard Hawes,	" 150	"

$3,150

The amount at interest in 1810, was in possession of the following named :—

Mark Hatch,	had $500,	in excess of liabilities.
Hezekiah Rowell,	" 1000	" " "
Joseph Perkins,	" 2400	" " "
John Perkins,	" 5000	" "
Robert Perkins,	" 4000	" "
Isaiah Skinner,	" 200	" "
Sylvanus Upham,	" 100	" " ..
Benjamin Willson,	" 300	" "
Josiah Willson,	" 200	" "

$13,700

A perusal of the preceding pages will convince any one that the most rapid improvement in the condition of the inhabitants, occurred during the first forty years. The

*Not given.

†John Perkins and Warren Hall owned eighteen ounces each, and Samuel A. Whitney twenty ounces. These three owned at that time one-fourth of all the plate in town.

sessions of the Court at this place during that period, as a natural consequence, caused a large number of people to congregate here twice a year. Most of these came from motives of curiosity or pleasure, but many because their attendance at court was necessary. This temporary increase to the population of the town, had, of course, a very favorable effect upon the business interests of the place. The occupation of the town, by the English, in 1814–15, however harrowing it may have been to the patriotic feelings of the citizens, helped to fill their purses, and gave an impetus to business that was felt long after the departure of the enemy. In somewhat later times, the general interest in ship-building, which was felt throughout New England, was experienced here. The fitting out of vessels for the cod and mackerel fisheries, upon the Grand Banks, was also carried on here very extensively.

Although Castine was, in times past, a peculiarly thriving town, its commercial and business career has not been altogether uniform; and within the last twenty-five years, it has seen the greater portion of its business go to other places. The causes of its decline in prosperity have been several.

The first shock it received was from the passage of the Embargo Laws in 1807–12. This was a serious infliction upon the business of the town, although it was partially made up, subsequently, by the advantages afforded by the British occupation.

The next, and by far the most serious, injury occurred in consequence of the removal of the Courts to Ellsworth, in 1838. From this blow, the town has never fairly recovered. The decline in ship-building, and, still more recently, the repeal of the Act granting a bounty to fishermen, were also severe injuries.

The loss to navigation caused by the late civil war—which is said to have taken from town shipping to the value of one hundred thousand dollars—and the inability of our merchants—for lack of a near market—to compete successfully with the merchants of Cape Ann, engaged in the fishing business, in consequence of which the pursuit of that business from this port has been entirely given up, have almost completed the commercial ruin of the place.

CHAPTER IX.

WALKS AND DRIVES, ANCIENT BUILDINGS, FORTS, RELICS, ETC.

WALKS AND DRIVES.—OLD FRENCH FORT.—FORT
GEORGE. — BATTERY FURIEUSE. — BATTERY PENOB-
SCOT. — OLD WINDMILL. — EAST POINT BATTERY. —
WESCOTT'S BATTERY. — BATTERY GOSSELIN. — BAT-
TERY SHERBROOKE. — BATTERY GRIFFITH. — SITE OF
THE BLOCK HOUSE.—FORT MADISON.—OTHER BAT-
TERIES.—TRASK'S ROCK.—OLD CANNON.—OLD MAN-
SIONS.—"CASTINE COINS."—COPPER PLATE.—"COT-
TON'S HEAD."—OTHER RELICS.

There are, unfortunately, but few roads in the town of
Castine. Starting from the Neck by the only road that
leads from it, going down a long hill to the canal that
severs it from the main land, and ascending the opposite
hill, the tourist will come to the "crotch of the roads"
where, in 1796—eighty years ago—stood the little old-fashioned school-house of that period. Taking the right hand
—or stage-road, he will pass along in full view of the Bagaduce river, for a distance of two miles, when he will come
to the crossing place of the Brooksville and Castine Ferry.*

Continuing for about a mile farther—catching, as he pro-
ceeds, occasional views of the same water where it is com-
pressed by the hills into the " Narrows"—he will arrive at
the North Castine Post Office. At this place the road to
Penobscot leads off upon the right. Keeping directly on,
the next mile of his course will take him away from all
view of the water; but the road passing, as it does, through
a more woody country, offers a temporary relief to the eye,
which is not unwelcome. After passing through the grove,
he will arrive at a hill, upon the descent of which he will
obtain a view of the Penobscot river, and will perceive, upon

. *This ferry is supported by the two towns jointly. The ferryman also having what tolls he may receive.

the opposite side, the fine hotel and the light-house at Fort Point. He has now very nearly reached the boundary of the present town, and, turning to the left, he will follow the telegraph or shore road down the Penobscot river, until he again reaches the stage-road upon which he started. In passing along the shore road he will be in constant view of the Penobscot river, and, in addition to the numerous vessels sailing up or down the river, he will be able to discern in succession upon the opposite shore the towns of Prospect, Stockton, Searsport, and Belfast, and the beautiful island known as Brigadier's or Sears' Island. This route is known as the "ten mile square."

If our tourist chooses, he can, instead of returning, follow the road up the river over *Hardscrabble* Mountain, to the town of Orland—or, by turning off at the North Castine Post-office, he can go to the head of Northern Bay in the town of Penobscot. This latter trip, while giving him a view of the water nearly equal to either of the others, will take him over a rough and hilly road. While in Penobscot, he can, however, visit without much trouble Northern Bay pond—about one mile north of the bay—or, by taking the road to Bluehill, can see the Southern Bay and Pierce's pond—which latter, if in the proper season, he will find covered with the beautiful white pond lily (*Nymphea odorata*). From this point he can proceed to Bluehill Mountain, which is nine hundred and fifty feet in height, and which has been visible all the way from Castine, or he can return through the town of Brooksville, and cross the ferry to North Castine.

Visitors to Brooksville, however, generally go from Castine by water. To those fond of yachting, this is by far the best way, as the river and harbor have the merit of being unusually safe for boats of all descriptions. Sudden squalls, such as are often fatally experienced near high mountains, are extremely rare here. The principal places of interest in this town, are the high hill (Tapley's) in the northern part of the town, about a mile from West Brooksville;—the high hill on Cape Rozier called Bakeman's Mountain; Walker's pond,—a large pond in the eastern part of the town; Buck's Harbor, the Granite Quarries, and Orcutt's Harbor, in the southern part. These are all places well worth the trouble of visiting by any one possessing a fondness for natural scenery.

A village which contains not a single street from all parts

of which a pleasant view of the harbor cannot easily be obtained, requires no mention of its particular walks or drives, when all are alike pleasant. The peninsula of Castine has, however, so many points of historic interest, as well as of natural beauty, that it deserves a somewhat extended and more special notice.

FORTS, BATTERIES, ETC.

By far the most important point in the village, is the site of the remains of an old fort—commonly called Castin's Fort, from having been occupied by him. This fort was built by the French, as early, probably, as 1626, and possibly some years earlier. It is generally supposed to have been built by Aulney; but the latter did not in all probability build a fort, but occupied the one formerly in possession of the Plymouth Colony. Without doubt, it is one of the oldest forts in the country. Its ruins are to be distinctly seen in the southern part of the village. At the time of its surrender to Grandfontaine—which was three years after Castin's arrival here—the fort contained four bastions, each of which measured, from the salient angle to the verge of the terrace inside, sixteen feet. The terraces were about eight feet from the curtains. It contained a guard-house ten by fifteen paces in extent; a house of the same dimensions, containing three rooms; a chapel, occupying ground four by six paces; a magazine ten by thirty-six paces; and another building of like dimensions with the magazine. Outside of the fort was a shed for housing cattle, and an orchard. Under a portion of the magazine was a small *cellar*, and in this cellar a *well*. [French Documents—Part III.] To inclose the dimensions specified above, the fort must have contained, at least, fifteen thousand three hundred square feet—calling a pace equivalent to two and one-half feet. As all the embankments to be seen in what is called Castin's fort, are only about twenty-eight and a half by forty-three and a half paces in extent, (seven thousand seven hundred and seventy-six square feet) they could not possibly have comprised the whole fort. Indeed, the whole of the present lot which incloses them is not large enough to contain all the buildings— *with the requisite space around them.* The ruins now to be seen, constitute, therefore, but a small portion of the original fort. They are, in fact, the remains of the magazine alone, and the embankments are the remains of its *founda-tions*. The discovery, not many years ago, of an old well, almost in the center of the supposed fort, proves this con-clusion to be a correct one. This well contained powder-horns, arrow heads, hatchets, and other implements of a war-like nature.*

The site of this fort was probably a favorite place of re-sort for the Indians, long before the advent of Europeans. This is inferred from the existence here of a vast shell de-posit—from which have been extracted pieces of flint, In-dian pipes, etc.

SUPPOSED PLAN OF FORT PENTAGÖET,—1670.

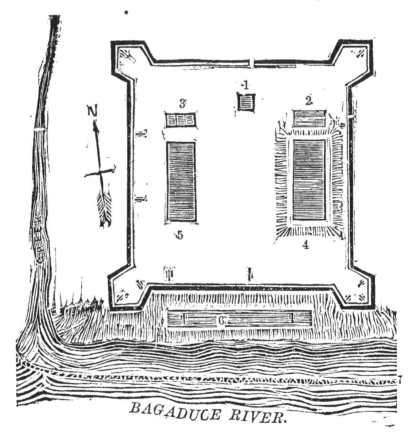

REFERENCES.—No. 1. Chapel. No. 2. Guard-house. No. 3. Officers' Quarters, containing three rooms. No. 4. Magazine—with its embankment, and with well in center. No. 5. Store-house. No. 6. Platform overlooking the sea—on which two guns were mounted. No. 7. Row of Palisades in the river.

*The annoyance caused by so many Visitors to this well, as also its danger-ous condition, has been the occasion of its being closed up.

PLAN OF FORT GEORGE,—1814.

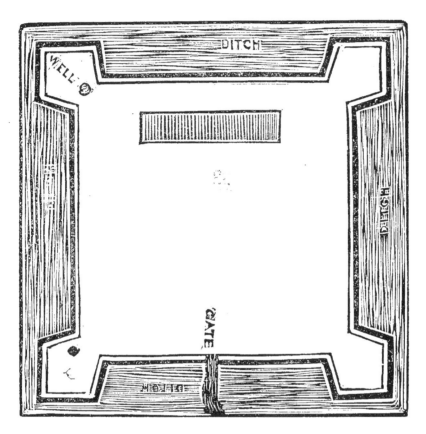

Next in importance to the fort just described, is one situated nearly north from it, upon the high land in the center of the peninsula. It was built by the British in June, 1779, and was named Fort George in honor of his Majesty George III. The fort is tetragonal in form, with a bastion at each of the four angles, corresponding very nearly with the four cardinal points of the compass. The curtains between each bastion face, of course, northwest, northeast, southeast and southwest. The northeast and southwest curtains are each two hundred and thirty feet in length— within the area of the fort. The northwest and southeast curtains are two hundred and twenty-five feet in length. In the southeast curtain is the gateway, fifteen feet wide, facing the town. The moat or ditch is dug down to the ledge—the dirt thrown up to form the ramparts. On account of this ledge, it was impossible, without the expenditure of much time and labor, to dig the ditch deeper. In the west bastion was the well; in the south, the magazine. From the bottom of the ditch to the top of the ramparts, was twenty feet. The ramparts were six feet wide on the top, level, and guarded by fraising and palisades. The latter were made with large cedar stakes but a few inches apart, one end inserted in the ramparts a few feet from the top, the other, sharply pointed, extended horizontally half way across the ditch—rendering an assault difficult and dangerous. The bastion containing the magazine, was fully occupied by it. The entrances to it were made of arched passages of brick and mortar, over which were layers of logs—the whole covered with earth. A row of barracks was built parallel to the northwest curtain. After the British left, in 1815, the American government took possession of and garrisoned it. The fort was repaired and strengthened, and new barracks were erected—the foundations of which are still visible. This was the fort in which Wadsworth and Burton were confined, and from which they made their escape. It was in this fort that the gibbet was erected upon which Ball, and, subsequently, Elliot, were executed. The fort is now,—minus the buildings and munitions of war, substantially the same as when the British garrison left it,—having suffered comparatively little injury, either from climatic causes, or from acts of vandalism. A fine view in all directions can be obtained from its ramparts, and it serves, accordingly, the place of an observatory to the citizens.

At the distance of five hundred and ninety yards south by east from Fort George, and a little over one hundred yards northeast of the old French fort, is the site of Battery Furieuse—which was erected by the British, in 1779, to play against the battery held by the Americans, on Nautilus Island. This battery was the one mentioned in Calef's Journal, as the " half-moon battery, near Banks' house." Mr. Rea's barn, on the corner of Court and Broadway Streets, is said to cover the site.

Battery Penobscot, erected by the British, in the same year as the last named, is seven hundred and twenty yards east by north from Fort George. It is near the southwest entrance to the cemetery, and not far from the site of the old *windmill*, which was built, according to traditional accounts, by Captain Mark Hatch, about the time of the first settlement of the town. The miller's name was Higgins; and, according to the old rhyme, he must have had a deal of trouble with it:—

> " On Hatch's hill
> There stands a mill;
> Old Higgins he doth tend it.
> EVery time he grinds a grist
> He has to stop and mend it."

This battery was rectangular in shape, considerably larger than the last mentioned, and its remains are plainly discernible. It was called the Sea-men's Battery, by the English.

At the extremity of Hatch's point, not far from the sand-bar, is another battery, which was erected by the English, as a defence against the battery erected by the Americans, on the opposite side of the Cove. It was called the East Point Battery. It was built in the shape of a square redoubt. The site of it is rather difficult to find.

A little less than half-way between this battery and Fort George is another—a nameless battery. At the right of the road leading from the peninsula, a short distance to the right of the bridge, is also another. Both of these last mentioned batteries were made by the British, in 1779.

A little south of the last mentioned battery, in the alders, is a stone work called the " Dutch oven," the origin of which is popularly attributed to the Dutch, who captured the fort here, in 1676. It is, however, positively known to have been one of the baking places of the British, in 1779, and was, perhaps, thus named by them.

On the main land, opposite Hatch's point, is another, called Wescott's Battery, built by the Americans, in 1779.

On the left of the road leading off the peninsula, at the brow of the hill, about four hundred and sixty yards northeast by east from Fort George, is Battery Gosselin— named in honor of the English General commanding the garrison in 1815. One hundred and sixty-eight yards north of Fort George are the ruins of Battery Sherbrooke, a semi-circular battery, one hundred and fifty feet in extent, enclosing a redoubt about one hundred and fifty feet inside, which measures forty-six feet. This battery was named in honor of the general who had the supreme command of all the land forces of the English at this place, in

1814. The two last named are small batteries, but are in good preservation, and easily to be found.

A little more westerly, and about six hundred and sixteen yards from Fort George, not far from the dwellings of Messrs. Sawyer and Bevan, is a large redoubt, named Battery Griffith, in honor of Rear Admiral Griffith, who commanded the English naval force here, in 1814–15. The dimensions of this battery are forty-seven feet front, by ninety feet on the sides. It is in shape an irregular quadrilateral—like the accompanying figure.

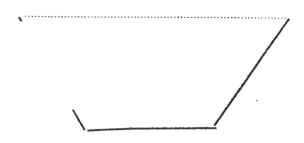

It enclosed barracks, the foundations of which measure, at present, sixteen by thirty feet. This battery commands the back Cove.* It is in a good state of preservation.

Not far from the high bluff at the northern extremity of the peninsula, at the top of a steep hill, is the site of the Block House, erected in 1814. Only the foundation can be discerned. Northeast of the site of the Block House, at the very extremity of the bluff, are the remains of another small battery ; and nearly northwest from the same spot, and near the western extremity of the bluff, those of another, named the West Point Battery. These two batteries and the Block House were built by the British. The Block House was, doubtless, built as much for an observatory as for the protection it would afford. It was twenty feet square on the ground floor, the second story projected over the first, and " above this was an area protected by continuing the sides of the building four feet higher, as a parapet." [Dr. Wm. Ballard, U. S. A.— Manuscript Sketch of Castine.]

In the field at the lower end of Perkins Street, opposite the house of Mrs. Sylvester, is the largest battery of all. It was erected about 1811, by the Americans, in anticipa-

*This Cove ought to be called Wadsworth Bay, in honor of the gallant officer who crossed it, when he made his escape from Fort George.

tion of a war with England. It was called, in honor of the President of the United States, Fort Madison. It was first occupied by a company of the 40th Infantry. It was afterwards occupied by a small detachment of the British, in 1814–15, and it was probably from them that it received its designation of Fort Castine. This name has often caused it to be confounded with the old French fort, which is commonly called Castin's fort. This fort, for such it now is, was rebuilt during the late civil war, and garrisoned by a company of United States troops. It is a square fort, somewhat similar to Fort George, though considerably smaller. It contains a magazine, and, in the last war, mounted five guns—two 24-pounders *en barbette*, and three 32-pound *embrasures*. This fort is generally called, now, the United States Fort, but was, at one time, called Fort Porter. In the rear of this fort, the English erected, in 1779, a small battery, which was taken from them by the Americans, when they landed. It is behind the barn of Mrs. Sylvester's house, but cannot now be distinguished.

The above mentioned comprise all the forts and batteries known to have been built within the limits of the present town of Castine. The British, in 1779, built a small square redoubt, upon the height of Nautilus Island, which is still visible. This battery was the one first captured by the Americans. The latter erected one soon after, upon Hainey's plantation—what is now known as Henry's Point—in Brooksville. It has been partially destroyed, by the crumbling of the bank. There was another small battery erected upon Cape Rozier, but the site of it is not known. [See map, on page 42, for location of these batteries.]

About two-thirds of the way from the Light-house to the Block House Point, was the landing-place of the Americans, under General Lovell. A large white rock— the only *white* one, of any considerable size, upon the shore—marks the spot where the ascent was made. It was behind this rock that Trask, the young fifer, sat, while his comrades were engaged in the ascent. [See view on opposite page.]

But few of the old guns or implements of warfare, used in former engagements, remain. The greater part of them have been taken away either by the State or National

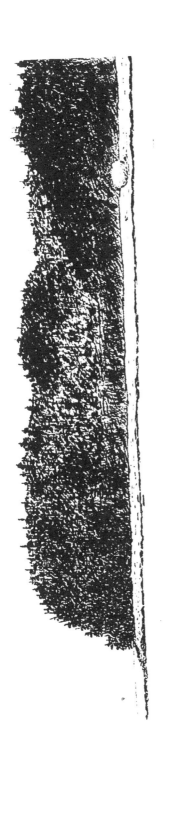

authorities. At the foot of Main Street is a cannon, that formerly belonged to the old ship *Canova;* and in front of Fort George is one of the 24-pounders used here in 1814 ; and there are also two similar ones near the United States Fort. There were—some thirty years ago—two or three mates to these. They are said to have been taken from town by a party of young men from Belfast, who came over here a night or two before the Fourth of July, and carried them off in a scow. They are supposed to be still in Belfast.

OLD MANSIONS.

Nearly all of the old houses built here, about the time of the incorporation of the town, have, like their occupants, passed away. The oldest house in town is believed to be that of the late Doctor Bridgham, though its exact age is unknown. The red house, on Perkins Street, between Main and Pleasant Streets, is also quite an old house ; has probably stood more than ninety years. As it fronts to the south, there is supposed to have been, at the time it was built, a roadway there, running parallel to the present course of Pleasant Street; but this is undoubtedly an error, as the oldest inhabitants have no recollection of such a street. This house was formerly owned and occupied by Doctor Calef, and afterwards by Doctor Mann. The long house on Main Street, commonly known as the " Mullett House," is also quite an old building, and was one of those occupied by the British, in 1812. The residence of Mr. Samuel K. Whiting, near the common, was also one of those occupied by the British. Until within a year or two, there was a pane of glass in one of the windows of this house, which had upon it, scratched with a diamond, by Lieutenant Elliott, of the British force, a representation of the British flag, with the " stars and stripes " underneath, upside down, and the words, " Yankee doodle upset." The pane has been broken, but the design has been preserved. The Unitarian meeting-house is the oldest church building in this vicinity. It was built in 1790. The interior has been remodeled, however, and the old galleries removed. The large house on Perkins Street, near the corner of Pleasant, called the " Cobb " House ; the " Ellis " House, on Water Street, nearly opposite the upper ship-yard ; and the " Hooke" house, on the same street, are all old buildings, and betoken by their size and shape, and the terraced grounds in front of them, the prosperity of their former owners.

RELICS.

Among the most interesting relics of the town are the somewhat celebrated " Castine Coins."*

A lengthy account of the discovery of these coins, and of the coins themselves, has been given by Mr. Joseph Williamson, in the sixth volume of the Maine Historical Collections. The following account is, however, mainly that of Doctor Joseph L. Stevens, who visited the spot at the time and obtained the facts from the party who found them. It is so interesting that we do not hesitate to insert it entire:

" Late in November, 1840, a respectable farmer, Captain Stephen Grindle, of Penobscot, and his son, Samuel P. Grindle, now of this town, while hauling wood from the side of a rocky hill to the shore, distant about twenty rods, found a silver coin. It was a French *crown*. The path is impassable by wheels, requiring the wood to be ' snaked out'—as the rustic term is. This, of course, made a furrow, in which the coin was found, new and bright as though recently issued from the mint—although two hundred years old. This led to further search, and about twenty more were found. Night coming on, with severe cold, followed by snow, prevented any further discovery until the next spring. On searching then, another crown was found on top of a large rock, covered with moss, and by the side of this rock the bulk of the money was found. In April, 1841, the writer, in company with some friends, visited the spot. It had been quite thoroughly dug over, but several French half-crowns were found by our party, without much searching, several feet from the rock, which on its lower side, shelved downwards towards the path. On going to the house, we examined all that had not been disposed of, and each of us purchased a number of them. The writer selected, as nearly as he could, a specimen of each, nineteen in number. There must have been in all nearly, if not quite, two thousand pieces, but a large proportion of them were only small fractions of crowns and dollars. The French money largely predominated; next, the old

*These coins are now in possession of Doctor Joseph L. Stevens, but we are glad to learn that it is his intention to present them, eventually, to the Maine Historical Society.

GOLD

OLD SILVER COINS FOUND NEAR CASTINE.

Spanish " cob" dollars*. These last were irregular in shape, and much worn, yet of full weight, as compared with present standards. The dates on these were mostly illegible, but the pillars, emblems of Spanish sovereignty, were quite evident. There were quite a number of Belgic and Portuguese coins. The most interesting of all were the Massachusetts pine-tree shillings and sixpences, all of date 1652, and in number about twenty-five or thirty. I saw but *two* English coins, shillings—worn nearly smooth. One, now in my possession, is of the reign of Carolus I. or II., and the other, owned by a lady in town, is of the reign of Jacobus I. As the latter monarch died in 1625, it must have been coined prior to that date, and is, probably, the oldest of the whole collection. My theory was, at the time, that they were left accidentally by the Baron de St. Castin, when driven from here by the English, under Colonel Church, very near to the close of the seventeenth century. They probably followed the course of the river up to its head and source in Walker's pond. From the south side of this pond the carrying place is only half a mile to the waters of the ocean in Eggemoggin Reach. From thence to the French settlements in Acadia, there could be no difficulty."†

In connection with the above, it may be stated that a *gold* coin was found in 1863, on the beach below the French fort. It was a " demi Louis d'or" of date 1642. The inscription on one side was,—"LVD. XIII D.G. FR.ET NAV. REX," and on the other, " REGN. VINC. IMP. CHRS." It was in good preservation, and but little worn. Its value, in gold, is two dollars seventeen cents and five mills. There cannot be much doubt but that this coin was lost there by some one of the Castin family, or by some French settler, in the time of the residence here of Monsieur d'Aulney.

In the year 1863, a piece of sheet-copper, ten inches long by eight wide, was found in the ground near the United States Fort, by Mr. William H. Weeks. He, not

*These dollars were also called " cross-money" from the cross on them. In Mexico, they were called "windmill and cross-money." They do not seem to have been made by a machine, but seem like lumps of bullion flattened and impressed by means of a hammer. They were originally made for dollars and are what old writers called " pieces of eight." [Castine Coins, Vol. VI, Me. Hist. Col.]

†Castin left here in 1701. Church did not visit the place until 1704. This money was, possibly, left there by some of the Castin family, when they departed for Canada, some time during the latter year, or it might have been left there by the Baron Castin, when he took to the woods, at the time of the Visit of Governor Andros, in 1688.

noticing anything peculiar about it, cut off a piece to mend his boat with. This fragment was recovered, however, and has been fastened to the plate. The letters upon the plate, as shown by the illustration on the opposite page, are evidently abbreviations of the following inscription :

1648, 8 Junii, Frater Leo Parisiensis, in Capucinorum Missione, posui hoc fundamentum in honorem nostræ Damæ Sanctæ Spei. Of which this is the translation:—

"1648, JAN. 8. I, FRIAR LEO, OF PARIS, CAPUCHIN MISSIONARY, LAID THIS FOUNDATION IN HONOR OF OUR LADY OF HOLY HOPE." This translation was first made by Mr. George H. Witherle, and his reading of it has since been confirmed by antiquarian scholars. In regard to this Friar Leo, nothing has ever been discovered. [Remarks on Inscription &c., in Proceedings of Am. Ant. Soc., April, 1864.] This plate was evidently placed in the foundation of some Catholic chapel, and, probably, of the one erected in Aulney's time, in the old French fort. How the plate came to be where it was found, will always remain a mystery. In all probability it was carried there by some one ignorant of its value. There is no great reason for believing that there were two chapels here at nearly the same time, and the only chapel we have any documentary evidence of, was in the fort which *tradition* places some distance away from where the plate was found. We have shown elsewhere the grounds for believing that the so-called French fort is really a portion of that fort. This plate is now in the possession of Mr. George H. Witherle.

Amongst the "ancient relics" of the town, some mention must be made of a unique piece of home-made statuary, called "Cotton's Head." It is not the head of an individual of that name, but was sculptured by Mr. Isaac Cotton. He was a stone-mason by trade, and was engaged by the town authorities, somewhere about the year 1820, to furnish a stone post for the corner of Main and Water Streets. He chiselled out a round stone, and surmounted it with the before mentioned idolatrous looking head. It stood on the corner for many years, but the post being at length broken, the head was cut off, and affixed to a square stone, which was set up in the same place. Having, after a while, got broken off again, it came into the possession of Messrs. Witherle & Co., and is now on exhibition at their store.

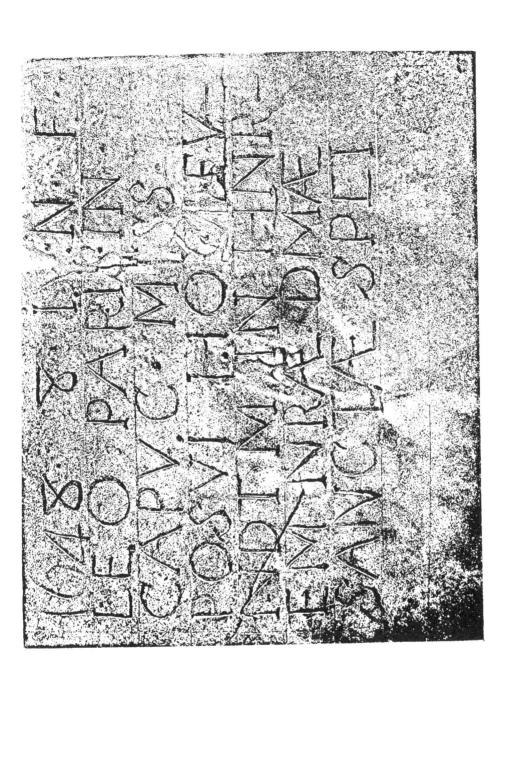

CHAPTER X.

BIOGRAPHICAL SKETCHES OF THE EARLY SETTLERS, PRO-
FESSIONAL MEN, EDITORS, ETC., AND OF MEN PROMI-
NENT IN NATION, STATE, OR TOWN.

A complete genealogical table of the former inhabitants, ·
even of the town of Castine, would involve the unremit-
ting labor of several years; would necessarily, under any
circumstances, be more or less imperfect and incomplete;
and would, morever, be of no great interest to the majority
of our readers. On the other hand, no history of a town
is complete, that does not give some special account of its
founders and note-worthy citizens.

In this chapter, an attempt is made to observe a just
mean, and to give such sketches—longer or shorter, according to the information afforded—as is desirable and
practicable, of those citizens who resided here during the
war of the Revolution, and of the individuals subsequently prominent in the theological, legal, and medical professions, or who were distinguished in literary, mercantile,
or political circles. If the names of any prominent citizens of former times do not appear in this chapter, it is
because the parties who might have furnished the required
information, have failed to do so, or in a few instances,
because no trace of the descendants of such persons could
be found.

EARLY SETTLERS.

At the time of the English occupation in 1779, Messrs.
Aaron Banks, John Jacob Dyce, Mark Hatch, John Perkins, and Joseph Perkins, lived upon the peninsula of
Castine; Mr. William Wescott resided on the mainland,
just north of the present village. Mr. Archibald Hainey
occupied the point of land opposite the village—in Brooksville—where the Misses Henry now reside; and Mr. John
Bakeman lived upon Cape Rozier.

BAKEMAN, JOHN.

Mr. John Bakeman was born in Holland, in 1731. He married Christiana Smart, who was born in 1744, and who died in Brooksville, August 4, 1818—aged seventy-four years. Mr. Bakeman died, in the part of Castine which is now Brooksville, on October 29, 1800—aged sixty-nine years.

The subject of this sketch was a cousin to Martin Van Buren. He had two brothers. One of them settled in New York, and spelled his name Bateman. The other, a clergyman, named Garret, came to Penobscot, but remained here only a short time. He returned to Holland, and was never after heard from. Mr. Bakeman came to this place at the same time as his brother Garret, purchased a tract of land on Cape Rozier, erected some mills, and engaged in ship-building. Mr. Bakeman's wife was a Tory, and it is a family tradition that, trusting in her sympathy for the English cause, General McLean, at the commencement of the siege, intrusted to her care a large quantity of gold, which was honorably returned to him after the siege was raised, notwithstanding that Mr. Bakeman espoused the cause of the Federalists, and that his house was used as a hospital for the wounded Americans. After the contest had ceased, some English soldiers were sent over to seize Mr. Bakeman, but he, having timely warning, had escaped in a boat. A few days later, the English seized his stock of cattle, about twenty in number, and over one hundred sheep. One of his daughters, at that time a little girl of some seven or eight years of age, often declared that she distinctly remembered hearing the soldiers say, while dressing the animals, " Won't we live fat now, all the way to Halifax ! "

Mr. Bakeman went to Bath, Maine, where his family soon joined him. He engaged in making salt from sea-water, at a place near Bath, called New Meadows. When peace was declared, he returned to Castine, but did not find even the foundation of his house remaining. The English had taken it down, and removed it to Castine village, and it was there rebuilt and occupied by Doctor Calef.

Mr. Bakeman was a Justice of the Peace, and was much respected for his sound judgment, and the judiciousness of the advice he gave in all matters relating either to

individual or town interests. His death occurred so suddenly from hemorrhage, that he was unable to give any
information in regard to his property. His family had but
little doubt but that he had gold and silver concealed
about the premises, though having no proof thereof, they
never made any very extensive search. Spiritualists and
people with "divining rods," have, however, dug up a
large portion of the field near where his house stood,
though without success.

After Mr. Bakeman's death, his oldest son, Francis
Evans Bakeman, succeeded to the estate, and became a
very successful ship-builder. During the occupation of
Castine by the British, in 1814, his shipping was all seized,
and nothing left him but his homestead. Many of Mr.
Bakeman's descendants still reside in Castine and vicinity.

BANKS, AARON.

The subject of this sketch was born in York, Maine,
June 1, 1738. He married Mary Perkins, of York, who
was a sister of John and Daniel Perkins, of Bagaduce.
His death occurred on the ninth of August, 1823, at
Penobscot.

At the age of twenty-one years, Mr. Banks enlisted in
the provincial army, for the defense of the colonies against
the French and Indians. He was first stationed at Fort
Pownal, and assisted in building that fort, early in the
summer of 1759. In July of that year, he was transferred to General Amherst's command, and was with that
command at the capture of Ticonderoga. He was also
with General Amherst, at the capture of Montreal, September 7, 1760. A treaty of peace was made at Paris,
between England and France, February 10, 1763. In
consequence of this, Mr. Banks was honorably discharged,
early in the winter of 1764. He, and twelve others, were
obliged to walk through the wilderness from Montreal to
York, in the depth of winter, with no covering for their
couch at night but the "starry decked heavens," and
depending for their food upon the game shot upon the
way.

In the spring of 1765, Mr. Banks brought his wife and
infant daughter to Bagaduce. He is said to have bought
the farm first settled by Reuben Gray, on the Neck—

being that now principally owned by Charles J. Abbott, Esq.—and to have built his house near the deep gully, not far from Mr. Webb's house.

At the time of the skirmish at the half-moon battery, during the siege of 1779, Mr. Banks' house was burned by the Americans. He and his family were detained, for upwards of three weeks, as prisoners on board the British sloop *North*. After peace was declared, he moved to that part of Bagaduce which is now Penobscot, where he remained until his death. No descendants bearing his name exist at this day. His daughter Elizabeth, however, who was married to Colonel Jeremiah Wardwell, became the mother of a family of seven sons and four daughters. She died in Penobscot, November 26, 1853, aged 89 years 5 months and 21 days.

CUNNINGHAM. DYCE. PHILLIPS.

Messrs. Cunningham and family, Dyce and family, and Nathan Phillips, are referred to in the Orderly Book of Sergeant Lawrence, as being residents of this place, and as noted for their *Tory* proclivities. Mr. John Jacob Dyce had a house situated somewhere near the old French fort, and owned the whole lower portion of the peninsula, which is named from him, "Dice's Head." His wife's name was Ockabena. Nothing further is known to the author concerning any of these persons, but it is not unlikely that they were driven away by the *Notification* of 1784.

HAINEY, ARCHIBALD.

Frequent allusion is made in the accounts of the siege of the town, to a family of the name of Hainey, but nothing is known about them except that *Mrs.* Hainey is spoken of as being a *Tory*. No reference to any such family is to be found in the town records of Penobscot or Castine. There was a man of that name, however, and probably a descendant of this family, living on Cape Rozier, some years ago ; and William and Edward Haney, of Penobscot, and Charles Haney of Belfast, are also descendants.

HATCH, MARK.

Mr. Mark Hatch, was born August 14, 1746, in the town of Scituate, Plymouth County, Massachusetts. His wife's name was Abigail. She was born in Marshfield, Massa-

chusetts, May 20, 1746, and died in this town on November
30, 1831.   Mr. Hatch was one of the four original settlers
here prior to the Revolutionary war.   He owned the northeastern portion of the peninsula.   He removed his family
sometime after the British took possesssion of the place, at
the time of the Revolution, but returned here about 1785.
He is said to have been the builder of the windmill which
formerly stood near the west entrance of the cemetery.
He had four sons.   Mark Hatch, Jr., was born at this place,
November 6, 1771, it being then a part of Lincoln County;
Jonathan, was born August 28, 1774 ; John, was born
October 19th, 1777 ; and James, October 21, 1779.   He
had also three daughters ; Abigail, born March 9, 1783,
died December 27, 1796 ; Eggathy Phillips, born April 19,
1785 ; and Lucy, born March 20, 1787.   Mr. Hatch, the
father, died in this town, November 30, 1831.

HUTCHINGS, CHARLES.

Mr. Charles Hutchings was born in York, Maine, October 10, 1742.   His mother dying during his infancy, he
was brought up by his elder sister, until he was seventeen
years old, when he enlisted in the army raised for the
reduction of Louisburg, Cape Breton.   He was with Lord
Loudon, at Halifax.   After the failure of this expedition,
he sailed for Boston, and was wrecked on the *Londoner*,
off Cape Ann.   He was afterward at Albany, New York,
where he was noted for his diminutive size, and great
strength.   He was honorably discharged at the close of
the war, and returned to York, where he soon after married
Miss Mary Perkins.   He moved to Penobscot, in 1768, and
took up the farm now owned and occupied by his son, Eben
Hutchings, who is now in his eighty-sixth year.

During the siege of Bagaduce, in 1779, he, with Daniel,
Isaac and Jacob Perkins, lay in ambush on Hainey's Point,
and fired into the English guard-boat as it passed.   They
were informed against by a Tory, and Mr. Hutchings
was obliged to take his family, consisting of his wife and
eight children, and flee for his life.   He took a canoe,
crossed the Penobscot river to Fort Pownal, and walked
through the wilderness to Damariscotta, where he resided
until the peace of 1783.   In this journey through the
woods, two of the children were so small that he and his
wife were obliged to carry them all the way in their arms.

They lodged on the bare ground. Their only cooking utensil was a camp kettle, holding about two gallons. Their only means of obtaining food, was afforded by his gun.

The daughter Mary, is said to have been the first white female child, born of English parents, within the present limits of the town of Penobscot.

Mr. Hutchings died in Penobscot, in June, 1835, aged 92 years and 8 months.

HUTCHINGS, WILLIAM.

Mr. William Hutchings was born at York, Maine, October 6, 1764. He died at Penobscot, May 2, 1866, aged one hundred and one years six months and twenty-six days. His father, Charles Hutchings, moved to Plan-

tation Number Three,—now the town of Penobscot—
when he was four years old. He was an eye-witness of
nearly all the transactions connected with the siege of
Majabagaduce, in 1779 ; and when the British were building Fort George, he assisted in carrying the first log that
was used in the southeast bastion. After the destruction
of the American fleet, his father refusing to take an oath
of allegiance to the British Sovereign, his family were
obliged to flee to a place of safety. He went to Newcastle,
Maine, where he remained until the close of the war, when
he returned to Penobscot, and settled down upon the
same farm that his father had formerly occupied. While
at Newcastle, he voluntarily enlisted, though only fifteen
years of age, into the service of the United States. His
declaration, made for the purpose of obtaining a pension
as a soldier of the Revolution, is on file in the Pension
Office at Washington. According to this statement, he
enlisted in a Massachusetts regiment, commanded by
Colonel Samuel McCobb, and was in Captain Benjamin
Lemont's Company. He was mustered in at Newcastle,
in 1780 or '81, for six months service. He joined his
regiment at a place known then as Cox's Head, upon the
Kennebec river. He was stationed there during the
entire period of his service, and was discharged at that
place. He received a pension of twenty-one dollars and
sixty-six cents per annum ; which was afterwards, in
1865, increased to three hundred dollars—there being at
that time but four Revolutionary soldiers surviving. His
chief occupation in life was farming and lumbering,
though he engaged somewhat in the coasting business.
He was a member of the Methodist church, for many
years. In the latter part of his life, he was a " total
abstinence " man. He had one son, Eliakim, who served
in the war of 1812. He had also a grandson, and several
great grandsons, who served in Maine regiments, in the
late civil war.

At the commencement of our civil conflict, Mr. Hutchings took a decided stand in favor of maintaining, at all
hazard, the supremacy of the union. It was his earnest
wish that he might be spared to see the complete restoration of the country, and that wish was granted.

In 1865, when over one hundred years old, he accepted
an invitation from the municipal authorities of Bangor, to
join in the celebration of the Fourth of July, in that city.

A revenue cutter was detailed for his conveyance, and as he passed up the Penobscot river, the guns of Fort Knox fired a salute of welcome. The ovation, which was bestowed on the occasion, exceeded that ever before given to any person in the State. Multitudes rushed to catch a glimpse of the old man, and the sincere and grateful plaudits which constantly greeted him, as, surrounded by a guard of honor, he was escorted through the streets, constituted the marked feature of the day. His strength and power of endurance, under the excitement, were remarkable. At the close of the oration, which was delivered by Senator Hamlin, he responded at some length to a toast. ' My friends told me,' he said, ' that the effort to be here might cause my death ; but I thought I could never die any better than by celebrating the glorious Fourth.' "

His funeral occurred Monday, May 7, 1866. Reverend Mr. Plummer preached the funeral sermon, from the text which had been selected by Mr. Hutchings himself :— Mathew xxii. 40 ; " On these two commandments hang all the law and the prophets." An address was afterwards made by Reverend Mr. Ives, of Castine.

" One of the last requests of Mr. Hutchings was, that the American flag should cover his remains, and be unfurled at his burial. This was done ; and in the stillness of a bright Spring afternoon, in the midst of an assembled multitude, upon the farm which for nearly a century had been his home, all that was mortal of the old hero was removed from earthly sight, while the stars and stripes he had so long honored, floated above his grave."*

McCULLOM, FINLEY.

In regard to Mr. Finley McCullom, nothing is known, except that he is referred to in Calef's Journal, as one of the few individuals who were allowed access to the Fort at all times, without a pass; and that he is mentioned in Peters' field-book of the survey of Penobscot, as having settled on lot Number Eighty-Seven, prior to the year 1787. Duncan McCullom—or Malcomb, as Peters spells it— settled on lot Number Eighty-Eight. These lots were at the head of Northern Bay.

*He was the last New England pensioner, and the last but one upon the rolls.

PERKINS, DANIEL.

Mr. Daniel Perkins was a native of York, Maine, where he was born in 1754. He married Abigail Penney, who was of Welsh parentage, and very shortly after, came to Penobscot, to engage in farming, having previously spent one or two winters here, in lumbering. In the war of the Revolution, his sympathies for the Americans were so well known that, as he declined to take the oath of allegiance to the English Crown, he was for a time imprisoned, and then banished to the " Enemy's Country." His cattle and crops were confiscated, and his house was taken down and removed to the " Neck," for barracks. At the close of the war, returning with his family from York—where they had spent that period—he again, himself, took down his house, moved it across the waters of the Bagaduce, and rebuilt it upon his farm, where he spent the remainder of his life. He died in 1831, at the age of seventy-seven years.

PERKINS, JOHN.

Captain John Perkins was born in York, Maine, May 21, 1745; and was married May 21, 1765, to Miss Phebe Perkins, of the same town. He died April 2, 1817, aged seventy-two years. His wife was born November 23, 1745, at York, and died March 22, 1811, aged sixty-six years. Shortly after their marriage, they moved to this town, where they remained until their death. They had ten children, viz:

Lydia,—born November 22, 1766; married to James Russell, March 26, 1782; died Sept. 10, 1815.
Lucy,—born February 10, 1770; died May 4, 1782.
Phebe,—born August 12, 1771; married Moses Gay, March 3, 1795; died February 11, 1843.
Betsey,—born March 8, 1773; married Thomas Stevens, July 20, 1798; died December 27, 1849.
Sally,—born August 10, 1775; married Elisha Dyer, November 17, 1796; died August 1, 1852.
Ruth,—born November 6, 1777; married Samuel A Whitney, July 28, 1801; died September 15th, 1849.
Temperance,—born June 2, 1779; married Daniel Johnston, Jan. 6, 1805; date of death unknown.
Robert,—born November 5, 1781; married Miriam C. Plummer, November 30, 1808; died March 26, 1854.
Lucy,—born February 16, 1785; married Henry Whiting, March 27, 1808; date of death unknown.

Polly,—born November 15, 1787 ; married Frederic Spof-
ford, April 9, 1811 ; date of death unknown.

Captain Perkins was a very prominent man in the town,
during its early municipal period, and was one of the
wealthiest of the old citizens. The frequent allusions
made to him in the foregoing pages, show the estimation
in which he was held, in all things pertaining to public or
business matters ; and the testimony of his numerous
descendants is an evidence that he was held in equal
esteem in his domestic life.

PERKINS, JOSEPH.

Mr. Joseph Perkins was born October 19, 1746, in York,
Maine. He married Phebe Ware. She was born in York,
December 16, 1748, and died in this town, August 20,
1815. They had ten children.*

Mr. Perkins was one of the wealthy men of the town at
that period, and was more engaged in commerce and navigation than any other individual. He owned at one time
eight thousand feet of wharf property. He was a very
prominent man, and his name appears in the early town
records more frequently, perhaps, than that of any other
citizen. He was chairman of the first board of Selectmen, chosen by the town of Penobscot. He died in this
town, August 28, 1818, aged seventy-one years ten months
and one day.

WESCOTT, WILLIAM.

The genealogy of the Wescott family is quite complete,
although but little is known of the life of the subject of
this sketch. His father, also named William, was a resident of York, Maine, where the son was born, March 10,
1734. He came here several years before the Revolutionary War, and was one of those who returned here just
prior to the incorporation of Penobscot. He was married, December 29th, 1756, to Elizabeth Perkins. His wife
was born January 6, 1737, but *where*, the record does not
state. They had twelve children, viz:—

John,—born June 4. 1757 ; was lost at sea in 1781.
Deborah,—born April 28, 1758; died in April, 1783.
Elizabeth,—born February 6, 1760; died in 1761.
William,—born October 8, 1764; died on April 7, 1785.

*The list of their names is given in Part III.

Experience,—born April 28, 1766; date of death unknown.
Theodosia,—born June 12, 1767; died June 21, 1805.
Amos,—born January 12, 1769; date of death unknown.
Nancy,—born May 15, 1771; date of death unknown.
Thomas,—born March 18, 1773; died August 18, 1795.
David,—born June 15, 1775; date of death unknown.
Anne,—born October 17, 1777; date of death unknown.
Joseph,—born May 20, 1779; died July 30, 1830.

The last named married, December 10, 1801, Miss Lucy
Stover. She was born August 23, 1779; and died April
5, 1862. They had eleven children, viz —
Joseph,—born October 31, 1802.
William S.,—born September 2, 1804; died June 18, 1866.
George, } born June 13, 1809; died December 3, 1827.
Lucy,   } "   "   "   "   date of death unknown.
Isaiah,—born December 27, 1813; date of death unknown.
Eliza,—date of birth and death both unknown.
Josiah,—born March 11, 1816.
Theodosia,—born August 27, 1817.
Sarah M., born March 27, 1819.
Two infants, (unnamed) date of birth and death unknown.

Joseph Wescott—the second—married Sarah Dyer,
August 2, 1829. She was born February 17, 1808; and
died June 28, 1870. They had seven children. Elisha D.
died October 21, 1855; and Helen M. died November 3,
1865. The others are still living, as is also their father, at
an advanced age, but much respected. The date of Mr.
William Wescott's death is not known. The name of this
family was formerly written Wescutt.

WASSON, SAMUEL.

Samuel Wasson was born in Worcester, Massachusetts,
June 12, 1760. He died in Brooksville, October 16, 1838.

Mr. Wasson enlisted in the American army, on the
breaking out of the Revolution. He was at the siege of
Boston, in 1776; and was under the immediate command
of Washington, when he entered the city upon its evacuation by General Howe. He was in the service during the
remainder of the war, when he received an honorable discharge. About the year 1783, he came to Bagaduce, and
devoted himself to agricultural pursuits. He took, as was
natural, a great interest in military affairs, and his marked
ability as a drill officer, caused his election as Captain

of the Militia. Mr. Wasson married Elizabeth Parker, daughter of Judge Oliver Parker, by whom he had three sons and three daughters. Two of the former are still living. David Wasson, Esq.,—now in his eighty-first year— has been a prominent merchant of Brooksville, and has done as much, at least, as any other person, to promote the material advancement of that town. Honorable Samuel Wasson, of Surry, Maine, is well known in political, but more especially in agricultural circles—having been for some years a member of the State Board of Agriculture.

<h2 style="text-align:center">CLERGYMEN.</h2>

LITTLE, GEORGE BARKER.

Mr. Little was born in Castine, December 21, 1821. He was the youngest of the ten children of Otis and Dorothy P. Little. September 18, 1850, he married Sarah Edwards, daughter of the late Reverend Elias Cornelius. His death occurred at West Newton, Mass., July 20, 1860.

Mr. Little's early instruction was received in the schools of his native town. He afterwards attended the Academy at Leicester, Massachusetts. He was graduated at Bowdoin College, in 1843. He entered the Theological Institution at Andover, Massachusetts, in 1846, and left it in 1849. On October 11, 1849, he was ordained pastor of the First Congregational Church in Bangor, Maine. He remained over this church nearly eight years, but was at last obliged to resign, on account of poor health. He was settled at West Newton, November 12, 1857, and remained there until his death.

" His mind was characterized by keen perception, penetration, and discrimination. His attainments in scholarship were remarkable. As a preacher, he was thoughtful, perspicuous, definite, and bold. People knew what he meant, and knew that he was in earnest. All who knew him, recognized warm and generous impulses, remarkably combined with clearness of thought, definiteness, promptness, decision, and steadfastness of purpose. His domestic virtues made him lovely and happy at home. Wit, intelligence, vivacity, and sympathy made him genial in social intercourse. His Christian faith and love will be manifest to all who read his memorial."

MASON, WILLIAM.

Reverend William Mason was the eldest son of Thomas and Mary Mason, and was born at Princeton, Massachusetts, November 19, 1764. His early life was very similar to that of other young men of that day, who were not born to affluence. He was brought up to hard work on a farm, and had to struggle hard for an education. He entered Harvard College in 1788, and was graduated in 1792. Where, and with whom, he studied for the ministry, is not known; but he was licensed to preach by the Cambridge Association. He removed to Castine in 1798, to assume the duties of pastor of the First Parish. On October 3, 1799, he was married to Miss Abigail Watson, of Leicester, Massachusetts. While a resident of this town, he was annually elected Treasurer of the town, for a period of twenty-six years, and was, for nearly the same length of time, a prominent member of the School Committee. He was much interested in everything relating to education, and was the originator of the Castine Social Library Association.

He resigned his charge over the First Parish, and removed with his family to Bangor, sometime in the year 1834. His departure from town was regretted by all—some, even of his most zealous theological opponents being warm personal friends and admirers. His death occurred at Bangor, March 24, 1847. His excellent wife died at the same place, March 24, 1865. They had six sons and four daughters,—two of whom, John and William, became eminent in the Medical profession. Doctor John Mason practised in Bangor, where he died in 1870. Doctor William Mason is still alive, and in full practice of his profession in Charlestown, Massachusetts. We quote the following from a friend and descendant of Mr. Mason, whose name we are under obligations to withhold.

" Eminently genial and social in his feelings, he was ever generous and hospitable to strangers and friends—as far as his limited means would permit. His love for his people was evinced by his frequent parochial calls to all classes—the poor and distressed, as well as those who had an abundance—and by his readiness at all times to aid by word and deed, in everything that had for its object the promotion of their welfare. He took a lively interest in the mental improvement of the young, and devoted much of his time to the various educational interests of the town. He was strongly attached to the friends of his younger days, and particularly to those who were associated with him during his college life—for whom he retained an ardent affection during his life. In all the relations of life, his aim was to do good ; and it was his endeavor to perform, to the extent of his ability, the various duties devolving upon him, faithfully and conscientiously.

In his theological views, he harmonized with those who were denominated Arians—afterwards called Unitarians. He believed in one supreme God, and not in a Trinity ; in the pre-existence and divinity, but not in the deity, of Christ—believing that he held a subordinate rank to the supreme God; in what he considered the Scriptural, but not in the Calvinistic, doctrine of the Atonement ; and in future retribution—though he believed that *destiny* was in accordance with *character.*"

POWERS, JONATHAN.

The first settled minister in Penobscot, was Reverend Jonathan Powers. He was born in March, 1762. His father was a minister in Deer Isle ; but whether the son was born there, is not known. He was a graduate of Dartmouth College, and was a class-mate of " Father Sawyer " (who lived to be over one hundred years old). He is said to have been a very devoted Christian, even during his college life. He settled in Penobscot, in the year 1795, and remained there until his death. His salary was paid by the town; and his daughter remembers that Major Leach once came to pay him, bringing the money in a *stocking*. Mr. Powers. took the occasion to reprove him for some irregularities in his life. Mr. Leach replied : " I do not think you ought to talk so to me, when I come to bring you *money.*"

Mr. Powers married a Miss Thurston,— sister of a lawyer of that name, in Boston. Mrs. Powers, in a letter to her brother, on one occasion, mentioned the fact that they were almost out of corn meal, but said, in a spirit of Christian hopefulness, that she had no doubt more would come, when that was gone. Mr. Powers had a vacation of two months every year, in which he was employed by the Massachusetts Missionary Society. This contributed considerably to his support. He went to Boston in 1807, to attend the meetings of this society. He spent the last night away from home at the house of Esquire Thurston, in Sedgwick, where he stopped upon his return. He must have suffered from exposure on his way back from Boston, as he was taken ill with Pneumonia immediately after his return, and died, in consequence, November 8, 1807. Doctor Moulton, of Bucksport, was his attending physician. He asked him, just before he died, if he was comfortable in his mind." Mr. Power's reply was : " I have great peace. I will praise him in life and death, and through eternity." Reverend Mr. Fisher, of Bluehill, preached his funeral sermon, from the text : " I have fought the good fight." His remains were interred in the burying-place at North Castine. It is situated in the enclosure back of Mr. George H. Emerson's house. His grave-stone is still legible.

LAWYERS.

ABBOTT, WILLIAM.

William Abbott, Esq., was born at Wilton, Hillsboro' County, New Hampshire, November 15, 1773. The father, Mr. William Abbott, was a native of Andover, Massachusetts. He was a descendant of George Abbott, who emigrated from Yorkshire, England, in 1644, and who was one of the first settlers of Andover. The subject of this sketch, passed his early years on a farm. He was prepared for College in 1790, in a town school kept by Jonathan Fisher, afterwards a minister at Bluehill. In 1793, he entered Harvard College. He was graduated in 1797, at which time he delivered a poem on " Music." After graduation, he studied law with William Gordon, of Amherst, New Hampshire, and was admitted to the bar in 1800. He came to Castine in 1801. In 1802, he married Rebecca Atherton. In 1803, he was appointed Register of Probate, which office he held eighteen years. In 1816, he was chosen one of the Electors for President. In this year he was also elected a member of the Brunswick Convention ; and in 1819, of the Convention at Portland. At the latter Convention, he was appointed upon a committee to determine the name of the new State. He was the first Representative from this town to the Legislature of Maine, and also represented the town in the years 1823, 1826, and 1827. In 1829, he removed to

HON. WILLIAM ABBOTT.

(From a Photograph)

Bangor, where he was for a long time a member of the Board of Selectmen. The charter of the city of Bangor, was drafted by him. He was chairman of the Superintending School Committee, of that place, for twelve years. He was elected Mayor of the city in 1848, and 1850. His death occurred in August of the latter year. He had five sons and two daughters. Of the sons, Charles Jeffrey is still a resident of this town, in which, like his father, he has practiced law with ability and success for many years; has taken a warm interest in educational matters, and in everything pertaining to the interests of the town; and has filled, acceptably, many offices of honor and importance, both in State and town. He was graduated at Bowdoin College, in 1825, in the class with S. P. Benson, Jonathan Cilley, Nathaniel Hawthorne, and Henry W. Longfellow.

In regard to the legal abilities of the father, we cannot do better than to quote the following, from the pen of Honorable William Willis:

"His intellect was clear, strong, and discriminating, rather than brilliant, imaginative, and original. It was well balanced and logical; its pre-eminent characteristic was practical common sense. He possessed a great influence with juries, whose reason and sense of moral right he addressed, rather than their feelings or their prejudices. He was regarded by his legal brethren and compeers as a sound lawyer, thoroughly versed in his profession, learned, astute, and able, and was greatly respected by them." In politics, he was, early in life, a Federalist, but he became afterwards a member of the Whig party. In his religious views, he was a firm and decided Unitarian, of the Channing school. While a resident in this town, he joined Reverend Mr. Mason's church, and after his removal to Bangor, he united with the Unitarian church in that city. His funeral sermon was preached by Reverend Doctor Hedge, who thus sums up his character:—"It is no small praise to say of any man, what in strict truth can be said of him, that he was blameless, and led from the first commencement of his active existence until its close, a blameless life. To be possessed of some one distinguished virtue is less infrequent than to be without reproach. He was one to whom no scandal or breath of suspicion could ever attach, whose pure fame no obloquy ever dared to assail, whom to know was to respect, whom to name was to praise." The estimation in which he was held in Bangor,

28

is shown by the important offices he filled while there, and
by his name being given to one of the principal public
squares of that city. The frequent allusion to his name
in this book is evidence of the esteem in which he was
held by the citizens of Castine. [See Courts and Lawyers
of Maine.]

NELSON, JOB.

Mr. Nelson was born in the town of Middleborough,
Massachusetts, in 1766. He was a graduate of Brown
University, in the class of 1790. He studied law in the
office of Honorable Seth Paddleford, at Taunton, Massachusetts; and came to this town in the year 1793. He
married Miss Margaret Farwell. He was the Representative of this town in the General Court of Massachusetts,
for the year 1801. He was appointed upon the Committee
of Public Safety, and also upon several of the committees
formed to draft resolutions, at the time of the troubles connected with the passage of the Embargo laws, and the
declaration of war with Great Britain, in 1810-'12. In
1804, he was appointed Judge of Probate, and continued
to hold this office for thirty-two years. In 1836, he
removed to Boston, but remained only two years before he
became dissatisfied, and returned to this town. Shortly
after his return, he met with a great loss in the destruction of his house by fire. This was the occasion of his
removal to Orland, where he owned a farm. He died in that
town, July 2, 1850, aged eighty-four years, and his remains
were brought here for interment. Although not a man
of more than average ability, he possessed an excellent
reputation for promptness and fidelity in his business, and
was held in great esteem here. [From Courts and Lawyers of Maine.]

PARKER, ISAAC.

Mr. Parker was born in Boston, June 17, 1768. He
was graduated at Harvard College, in 1786, with high
honor, although but eighteen years of age. He studied
law in the office of Judge Tudor, of Boston. He was
admitted to the bar in 1789, and came here very shortly
after. He was the first regular practitioner of law in this
section of the State. From 1791 to 1795, inclusive, he

represented the town of Penobscot in the General Court of Massachusetts; and was the first Representative from Castine, in 1796. From 1796 to 1798, he was a Representative to Congress from this district. In the year 1799, he was appointed United States Marshal, for the District of Maine,—and about this time he removed to Portland. He was appointed an Associate Judge of the Supreme Court of Massachusetts, in 1806; and was raised to the dignity of Chief Justice in the same Court, in 1814. He was the author of all the first twenty-seven law reports of Massachusetts, except the first volume of all. In 1800, he delivered, at Portland, a eulogy on the death of Washington. He was for eleven years one of the Trustees of Bowdoin College; and was, for twenty years, an Overseer of Harvard College. In 1810, he was appointed Royall Professor of Law in the latter College. He received from Harvard the degree of LL. D., in 1814. Judge Whitman once said of him :—" Parker was one of the pleasantest men I ever knew,—kind, courteous, and amiable. At times he was very eloquent; and always from his candid, honest manner, had great weight with the jury." Honorable William Willis says, in the work from which this sketch is derived :—" No man was ever more free from affectation or pretension, than Judge Parker; modest, unassuming, unaffectedly great, he despised all the accessories and expedients to which weak and mean men resort to acquire notoriety." Judge Parker married Rebecca Hall. She was a daughter of Joseph Hall, of Medford, Massachusetts, who was a descendant from John Hall, who settled in Concord in 1658. They had three sóns,–Edward, Charles A., and John; and three daughters,—Ann, who was married to Henry Wainwright, of Boston; Margaret, who died unmarried; and Emily, who was married to a Mr. Davis, of Boston. Judge Parker was not only learned in the law, but was also a polished writer, and a graceful speaker. His popularity as a man was unbounded, and his reputation as a lawyer and an advocate, attracted many students to his office. [From Courts and Lawyers of Maine.]

PARKER, OLIVER.

Oliver Parker was of English descent, and was born in Worcester, Massachusetts, about the year 1738. He was appointed a Justice of the Peace for Worcester County, by King George, shortly after he had attained his majority. During the war of the Revolution, he was an active loyalist. He became very offensive to his neighbors, in consequence of his adherence to the Crown of England, and was, on this account, obliged to leave his native country, when peace was declared. He went to St. John, New Brunswick, where he resided some ten years. While there, he was engaged in mercantile business, and accumulated considerable property, which he is said to have lost through the dishonesty of his partner in business. Mr. Parker moved to Castine in 1794, and bought the farm now owned by Mr. Alexander G. Perkins. About the year 1800, he was appointed by Governor Strong, Judge of the Court of Common Pleas. This office he held nearly fifteen years. Judge Parker was much interested in religious matters, and was instrumental in having the meeting-house built at North Castine—then Penobscot. He was a member of Reverend Mr. Mason's church, and, for a short time, was one of the deacons. From 1787 to 1790, and again in 1792, he was chosen one of the Board of Selectmen of Penobscot. It is related of him, that, being inveigled by others into some iniquitous transaction, he was brought as a prisoner before the bar of the very Court over which he had once presided. The finding of the Court in his case we do not know; but it is claimed that whatever this may have been, he was free from intentional wrong-doing. Judge Parker was twice married, and brought up a family of three sons and four daughters. Two of the latter married John and Samuel Wasson, of Brooksville. Judge Parker died in Brooksville, in the year 1818, aged about eighty years.

STORY, ISAAC.

Isaac Story, Esq., was the second son of Reverend Isaac Story, of Marblehead, Massachusetts. He was born in that town, in 1774. He was graduated at Harvard College, in 1792, and came here in 1797, and commenced the practice of law. He was, however, much fonder of literature than of law, and gave the greater portion of his time while here to editing the *Castine Journal*. His career was short, though brilliant. After a residence here of some two or three years only, he removed to Massachusetts, and died at his

father's house, in Marblehead, in July, 1803. He wrote
" Essays from the Desk of Beri Hesdin;" a volume of letters entitled " The Traveller ;" and a poem entitled " The
Parnassian Shop, by Peter Quince." A writer in the
Salem Register thus speaks of him :—" A gentleman well
known by numerous productions in polite literature. In
his manners, bland, social, and affectionate ; in his disposition, sportive and convivial ; in his morals, pure, generous,
and unaffected. Wit and humor were provinces in which
he sought peculiar favor, though he not unfrequently
mingled in his poetic effusions the gravity of sententious-
ness with the lighter graces." His kinsman, Judge Story,
of Massachusetts, wrote an elegy upon his death. [Courts
and Lawyers of Maine.]

WETMORE, WILLIAM.

William Wetmore was born in Connecticut, in 1749.
He was graduated at Harvard College, in 1770. He first
practiced law in Salem, Massachusetts, and afterwards
came to Castine—probably about 1777 or '78· He was a
Judge of Probate, for Hancock County, for a number of
years. In 1804, he removed to Boston, and was for many
years a Judge of the Court of Common Pleas, in that city.
Judge Wetmore was married, and had one daughter, who
was married to Judge Story. Whether there were any
other children, is unknown to the writer. Judge Wetmore was one of the *six* lawyers in Maine who were ever
raised to the degree of a *Barrister*. He died at Boston, in
the year 1830, at the age of eighty-one years.

WILLIAMS, HEZEKIAH.
See Citizens Prominent in Nation, &c.

PHYSICIANS.*

CRAWFORD, WILLIAM.

Doctor William Crawford was born in Worcester, Massachusetts, in August, 1730. He was graduated at the
College of New Jersey—then located either in Newark or

*This account of the Physicians of Castine is from the pen of Doctor Joseph
L. Stevens, to whom the entire credit is due for all except what relates to
Doctor Crawford, some of the facts in regard to Doctor Calef, and a portion
of what refers to himself.

Elizabethtown—on the tenth of October, 1755.   He married Miss Mary Brewer, of Westtown, in October, 1763. She was a sister of Colonel Brewer, the former proprietor of the town of Brewer, from whom the place took its name. He had two sons, James and William, who settled in this town.   Doctor Crawford, although never a resident of this town, is mentioned in this chapter from the fact that he was the nearest physician to the earliest settlers of Plantation Number 3, and often came here on professional visits. Doctor Crawford was a Surgeon and Chaplain in the army of General Wolfe, and was attached to his staff at the time of the death of the latter, at Quebec.   He came to this region several years before the war of the Revolution, and located at what is now Fort Point.   It is a family tradition that he was the one to marry the first couple that were ever wedded, according to Protestant forms, in the Penobscot region.   He died at the age of forty-six years, at Fort Pownal, in the town of Prospect (*now* Fort Point, in the town of Stockton).   His diploma, written on parchment nearly one hundred and twenty years ago, highly embellished and with illuminated letters, is in the possession of his grandson, Mr. James B. Crawford, of this town, to whom we are mainly indebted for this sketch.

Doctor Crawford was not only a physician, but for three or four years he officiated as Chaplain, and preached in the chapel at Fort Pownal, which was erected by Colonel Goldthwaite, who was, afterwards, for a short time, a resident of this place.   In regard to his preaching, the following anecdote is related:—One of his parishoners, named James Martin, was observed to be usually absent from divine service on Sunday.   Doctor Crawford called on him to learn the reason of his absence.   Martin informed him that there was no necessity for his attending.   " Why ?" said the Doctor.   " Because," replied Martin, "I have heard your sermon so often that I know it all by heart." " Let me hear you prove it," said the Doctor.   He accordingly repeated the discourse nearly in the very language of the Doctor.   " I declare," said the Doctor, "I must alter my method of preaching, in the future."

Doctor Crawford is represented as a very kind and worthy man, though of an ardent and impetuous temperament.   He was of Scotch descent.

From its peculiar, isolated situation—relatively to other towns in the vicinity—its small population, and its remarkable exemption from acute diseases, for the treatment of which medical men achieve their best reputation, and receive their highest rewards, Castine cannot be entitled a "Paradise for Doctors." It is known that not one has accumulated a fortune, and it is believed that not one has acquired even a competence here by professional means.

CALEF, JOHN.*

The first physician known to have resided, as well as practiced, in town, was Doctor John Calef—often written Calf. He was a man of good education, who came here as a refugee from Massachusetts, on account of his obnoxious political opinions. As there were, at that time, many sympathizers with him, likewise refugees, it is supposed he practiced with them, as well as with the citizens of the town. It is known that he did with one family, at least, the descendants of which are still residents here. He lived, so says tradition, in the house so long owned by Doctor Mann, and probably built it. It is now the oldest house in town, and, when erected, faced the street, which run differently then from Perkins street as now laid out. [Query? See chapter IX.] The Doctor was a son of Robert and Margaret Calef, and was born in Ipswich, in 1725. He married a daughter of Reverend Jedediah Jewett, of Rowley, Massachusetts. Whether he had any offspring, is unknown. Prior to his coming to this part of the country, he was for several years in the General Court of Massachusetts. During the British occupation of this place, in 1779, he was a volunteer Surgeon, and an acting Chaplain to their forces. After peace was declared, he settled in St. Andrews, New Brunswick, where he died in 1812, aged eighty-seven years. He made one visit here after his removal, and called upon the family to which allusion has been made, and left a slight memorial of his interest in it.

MANN, OLIVER.

The earliest settled physician of whom we have any accurate knowledge, was Doctor Oliver Mann, who was

*The name seems to be an old Scandinavian patronymic.—See Sinding's History of Scandinavia, pp. 162, 163.

likewise from Massachusetts. He must have come here very soon after the close of the war. He had seen service as Assistant Surgeon in a hospital ; and, as there was no other practitioner nearer than Doctor Skinner, of Brewer, must have had an extensive and remunerative practice in this and the adjacent towns and islands. He was a man of firm constitution, strong powers of endurance, and temperate habits ; but of warm temper and passions, and, when excited, was in the habit of using intemperate language. By his early friends his opinions were considered infallible, from which there should be no appeal. Late in life, he became a Methodist, with a radical change in language and demeanor. As he had been a medical officer in the war, he became entitled to a pension; to procure which he made a journey to Bangor. The day before, he contracted a severe catarrh by going through wet grass to visit a patient out of town. The additional exposure of his journey, brought on a violent attack of Acute Laryngitis. The writer attended him until his death. He died July 4, 1832, aged seventy-six years. In addition to his professional labors, he was engaged somewhat in navigation, and was also a prominent political man in the town. He was a Representative to the General Court for several years, and filled many other offices of honor and responsibility. He was a large owner of real estate here, and on Cape Rozier.

KITTREDGE, THOMAS, AND OTHERS.

During the closing years of the last century, several physicians—whose names, even, have not come down to us—came here, but staid only a short time. In the early years of the present century, Doctor Kittredge, afterwards of Mount Desert, is said to have staid a short time in what is now called North Castine.

ADAMS, MOSES.

About this same time Doctor Moses Adams came here. He remained a short time, and then removed to Ellsworth. While there he was charged with the murder of his wife, was brought here for trial, and was acquitted for lack of evidence. Public opinion, however, was so adverse that, although he married again, confidence in him was not restored, it is believed, sufficiently for him to regain practice.

THURSTON.

About the year 1809, Doctor Thurston came here from Massachusetts. He was a man liberally educated, of good abilities, and practiced in the best families in town. He staid only two or three years, however, before he removed to Portsmouth, New Hampshire, where it is supposed he lived until his death. The date of his death, and his age, are both unknown.

PECK, CALVIN.

Doctor Calvin Peck, from Western Massachusetts, succeeded Doctor Thurston. While he was attending the lectures of Harvard Medical School, (he was a fellow boarder with the writer) a letter was received by the Professors from prominent citizens in this town—among the names of whom the writer remembers seeing that of William Abbott, Esq.,—requesting them to recommend some young man desirous to settle. Doctor Peck, then about to graduate, was advised to go. The writer assisted him in putting his effects in a sleigh, and saw him start for Castine; little thinking he should ever follow him to the same place to reside. Doctor Peck staid here a year or two, but a better opening offering in Ellsworth, he went there, where he died in 1849, aged fifty-seven years.

D'AYEZ, MADAME.

Some years prior to Doctor Peck's residence here—probably about 1810—a female practitioner, Madame D'Ayez, by name, arrived in town.* She was an extraordinary woman: fully impressed with a sense of "Woman's rights," which she exercised to the fullest extent consistent with law and usage as then existing. She was said to be a daughter of a medical man, and had been a nurse in a hospital, from which source she had gathered quite a harvest of medical lore. She practiced not only in this, but in neighboring towns, and by her shrewdness and address, caused much trouble and vexation to her male competitors. A specimen of her shrewdness is shown by a wonderful plaster she often made. This plaster—made of some simple material—was spread on the nicest scarlet cloth, and

*Commonly pronounced, in this vicinity, "M'am Daggey."

29

when applied to certain portions of the body was *sure* to " draw out " and eradicate all crossness and ill-nature from babies and young children. The price was one dollar a plaster; and, considering its inestimable value, *if true*, could not be considered unreasonable. Unluckily for distressed mothers, for whose special benefit this remarkable article was made, the secret died with her. The following case shows her mode of treatment:—An ancestor of one of our present citizens, got poisoned, it is presumed neither very severely or dangerously so. She was applied to for aid. To treat the case, she took some common salt, dried, pounded and manipulated it for a long time, colored it with some innocent ingredient, and then, with much ceremony, gave it to the patient, who, of course, soon recovered. A lady well acquainted with her devices, expostulating with her upon the deception, asked her why she could not inform the family, and let them procure so simple a remedy. " Oh! " says she, in her broken English, " M'am L—, it taint do to let de folks know *everything*."

GAGE, MOSES.

Soon after Doctor Peck's departure was known, Doctor Moses Gage settled here. He was a native of Rowley, Massachusetts, and a recent graduate from Harvard. He practiced in Duxbury a few months. He came here in 1815. He was a gentleman of superior talents; prompt, energetic, and decided in practice, especially in surgery; and, had he lived, in good health and under favorable circumstances, would have become a distinguished surgeon. An unusually strong predisposition to Consumption compelled him to make a voyage to Havana, with the hope of regaining good health. He soon became much better, and had a large and lucrative practice with the Americans resident there. In 1821, he visited this place and staid a few weeks with his friends, but his disease increasing, he was obliged to return to Havana. He died there in 1822, aged thirty-one years.

STEVENS, JOSEPH L. [Portrait on opposite page.]

Just before the first departure of Doctor Gage for Havana—as mentioned in the preceding sketch—he wrote to the compiler of these sketches (Doctor Joseph L.

Stevens, a native of Gloucester, Massachusetts,) advising
him to take his place, and offering to recommend him to
his friends. They had been fellow students at North
Andover, with Dr. Thomas Kittridge, and were intimate
friends. He accordingly came on, arriving here in January,
1819, the day after Doctor Gage sailed. An interview
with the citizens, mutually satisfactory, induced him to
settle his business in the town where he had been residing,
and to return here, March 2, 1819, where he has since
lived. He has practiced here now for a period of fifty-five
years, varied occasionally, and intermitted by several
severe attacks of illness. Notwithstanding the latter, he
is still in tolerable health, and his physical powers are
pretty well preserved, considering his age, and his mental,
as good as ever, in his own conceit at least.*

[It only remains to be added to the above, that Doctor
Stevens is a graduate of both the Classical and Medical
departments of Harvard College ;† is a man of culture and
refinement, and has had, in his day, a wide-spread reputation as a physician, and more especially as a surgeon.
Although eighty-four years of age, he still keeps up his
interest in professional matters, and practices occasionally.
As he is still living, it would be improper, in this place, to
speak of his character and disposition; but it cannot be out
of place for us to bear testimony to the general esteem in
which he is now, and has ever been, held by the community
in which he has so long lived.]

POOR, EBEN.

In 1822, Doctor Eben Poor came here as Clerk of the
Courts, for the County of Hancock. He had been practicing in Belfast, then a part of the above County. He was
born in Andover, Massachusetts, October 28, 1765. He
studied his profession with Doctor Thomas Kittredge, of
Andover. After practicing for some years in Massachusetts, he removed to Andover, Maine, in 1804, where he
continued in practice until December, 1814, when he
removed to Belfast. While a resident of Andover, he
was appointed principal Assessor of the Sixth Collection

*This is his own language.

†While a student he attended the lectures of Dr. John Warren, the first
Professor of Anatomy and Surgery, in the Harvard Medical School, and one
of its Founders, and likewise heard the first lecture delivered by his son,
Doctor John C. Warren, when appointed Adjunct Professor.

District, in the then District of Maine. He likewise represented the County of Oxford, in the Legislature of Massachusetts. He continued to reside and practice in Castine
till 1817, when he removed to Penobscot, and married
there a widowed lady, who died in 1828. His first wife,
Elizabeth Stevens Poor, died in Castine, November 7,
1824. In 1829, he removed back to Andover, Maine,
where, honored and respected, he practiced until his death,
which occurred January 18, 1837.

Doctor Poor was a judicious and safe practitioner,
though his treatment was what is technically called
" heroic." This kind of treatment was, however, as the
writer well knows, strictly confined to his own person.
He treated his patients with more discrimination than he
did himself. Although always an invalid, and his treatment of himself bordering upon the extreme, yet he lived
to an advanced age, far beyond the period usually allotted
to mankind.

BRIDGHAM, ROLAND H.

In 1834, Doctor Roland H. Bridgham—a native of
Minot—came here as Collector of the Customs for this
port, appointed by President Jackson. Doctor Bridgham
first settled in Sullivan, Maine, where he practiced many
years. For two years prior to his appointment as Collector, he had represented that town in the Legislature, in
which he was active and influential in procuring the passage of the beneficial Act, authorizing towns to cause a
general vaccination to be made. At the expiration of
Pierce's administration, he retired from office ; but a year
or two afterwards, he represented this Senatorial district,
in the Legislature. During his term of office, he practiced
occasionally; and after its expiration, did so very generally
and acceptably to his many friends. He had always had
great influence in the political party to which he belonged,
which continued as long as his activity lasted. About
two years before death, he had a slight attack of general
Paralysis, which, with other signs, indicated the general
wreck of brain sure, sooner or later, to follow. He con-
tinned in business some time after—gradually failing—till
two months before death, when he became delirious, then
unconscious, and died January 25, 1871, aged seventy
years and eight months. He was buried with Masonic
honors.

MILITARY OFFICERS.

JOHANNOT, GABRIEL.

Gabriel Johannot was, probably, of Huguenot descent. He was born in Boston, in the year 1748. He came here soon after the close of the Revolutionary war. The exact time is not known; but as early as 1784, he was living upon this peninsula, having settled upon Lot Number Six, of the original survey. He is said to have had command of one of the militia regiments, but of which one we have been unable to ascertain. He was a prominent man in town affairs, and was the second Representative of the town of Penobscot to the General Court of Massachusetts. He was a prominent Free-mason—having been one of the charter members of Hancock Lodge at its formation, and its first Senior Warden. He removed to the town of Hampden, Maine, where he died, in 1820.

LEE, JOSEPH.

Mr. Joseph Lee was born in Royalston, Massachusetts, in August, 1774. He came, at an early age, to live with his uncle, Mr. John Lee, the first Collector of Customs at Castine. In 1800, he was married to Priscilla Sparhawk, of Templeton, Massachusetts. In 1807, he removed to Bucksport, where he remained until the winter of 1826, when he moved to Milo. How long he resided in the latter place we do not know; but he returned again to Bucksport, where he died, in April, 1861, aged eighty-seven years four months. There were several daughters, but only one son, in his family. The eldest daughter was married to C. A. Swazey, of Bucksport; the second, to Eben Greenleaf, of Williamsburgh, Maine; and the youngest to William Brown, of Brownville, Maine. His son, Joseph A. Lee, was married, about the year 1836, to Miss Mary L. Sawyer, of Calais, Maine.

During his residence in Castine, Mr. Lee assisted his uncle in the duties of the Custom-House. He had considerable predilection for the military service, and we find him mentioned in 1800, as a Lieutenant of the Castine Artillery Company; and ten years later—after he had moved to Bucksport—he is mentioned as resigning his office as Colonel of the Regiment. In regard to his subsequent career, we have received no information.

LITTLE, OTIS.

See Citizens Prominent in Nation, State, &c.

AUTHORS AND PUBLISHERS.

WATERS, DANIEL S.

Neither the old town of Penobscot, nor either of the present towns derived from it, has produced any author of special repute, except such as have been already mentioned amongst its professional men. There have been three editors and publishers, but of this number we have been able to obtain no account of either one, except the subject of this sketch.

Mr. Daniel Waters was the son of Mr. William Waters, of Boston, and learned his trade—as a printer—of Messrs. Adams and Rhodes, of that city. He came here about 1797 or '98; and in 1799, commenced the publication of a paper, under the name of the *Castine Journal, and Eastern Advertiser*. He remained here but a short time, having, about the year 1802, removed his establishment to Hampden—where, however, he remained but one year. He went from Hampden to Richmond, Virginia, where he died, a few months after, at an early age. He was a member of the Masonic fraternity.

CITIZENS PROMINENT IN NATION, STATE, OR TOWN.

LITTLE, OTIS.

Mr. Otis Little was born in Marshfield, Massachusetts, March 27, 1769. He came to Castine—then a part of Penobscot—in 1794. On January 21, 1800, he married Miss Dorothy Perkins, a daughter of Captain Joseph Perkins. A few years after Mr. Little selected this peninsula as his permanent home, he turned his attention to mercantile pursuits, in which he continued for more than forty years. During this period he was also interested, to a considerable degree, in commerce and navigation. He possessed the confidence of his fellow citizens, who repeatedly elected him to offices of responsibility and trust. For four years he represented this town in the General Court of Massachusetts. He was afterwards chosen Representative to the Legislature of Maine, for three successive terms. He was one of the Governor's Council in 1830;

and, during a period of some fourteen years, was one of the Selectmen of Castine. He had some experience in the military service, being chosen first a Sergeant, then Lieutenant, and afterwards a Captain of the Castine Artillery Company. The commissioned officers of the artillery companies of. Bangor, Belfast and Castine, then composing a brigade, elected him Major, by which title he was thereafter always called.

Major Little ever took a lively interest in town improvements, and was always ready to contribute time and money for such purposes. He planted nearly all the shade trees on Green Street, and a large proportion of the noble elms and maples on Court Street. He died February 15, 1846, aged seventy-seven years eighteen days. His wife survived him over ten years, her death occurring November 3, 1856, at the age of seventy-seven years four months and eighteen days.

WILLIAMS, HEZEKIAH.

Hezekiah Williams was born in the year 1798, in Woodstock, Vermont. He was graduated at Dartmouth College, in 1820. He chose law as a profession, and in 1825, settled in this town. In May, of the year following, he was married to Miss Eliza Patterson, of Belfast. Although a respected member of Hancock Bar, he was more extensively known in political than in professional circles. He held at different times, various offices of honor and trust in town and State, and in 1845–1847 he represented this District in Congress. He belonged to the Democratic party. Mr Williams was a prominent and zealous member of the Masonic Order. He was at one time the Master of Hancock Lodge, and in 1841, was elected Grand Master of the Grand Lodge of Maine. He had four sons and four daughters. All four of his sons were in the service of the United States during the war of the Rebellion. Three of them were Army Officers, one of them, Hezekiah, being at one time a Medical Director of the Army of the West. The second son, Edward Patterson Williams, was born in this town, in February, 1833. He was educated at the High School and was afterwards appointed a Cadet at the Naval School in Annapolis, Maryland. After his graduation at the Naval School, he entered the Navy as a Midshipman, but soon rose to the rank of a Lieutenant. He was one of the party who made the night attack on Fort Sumpter, in 1861, and was taken prisoner at that time and received very harsh treatment. After peace was declared, he was promoted to the command of the *Oneida*, which ship was run down by the English steamer *Bombay*, while coming out of the harbor of Yokahoma, Japan, in 1870, and sank with nearly all on board. His conduct at that time was truly heroic, even though unwise. He would not leave his post on the bridge of the vessel, and when urged to do so, replied " I go down with my ship. " A petty officer again urged him to go. He grasped the iron rail and said, "No, this is my place and here I remain." His age at the time was thirty-seven years. But one son and one daughter of this family now remain. Mr. Williams died at Castine, October 23, 1856, aged fifty-eight years and .thirteen months. His wife died in Dixon, Illinois, August 19, 1866, aged sixty-four years. Her remains are interred at Castine.

WILLSON, DAVID.

Micahel Willson, father of the subject of this sketch, emigrated from 'England, and settled in Ipswich, Massachusetts. He was a weaver by trade. For several years he was a member of the Colonial Legislature of Massachusetts. He subsequently settled in Wells, Maine.

His son David, was born in Wells, in April, 1753. He came to this place previous to the breaking out of the war of the Revolution, and, while here, assisted the American forces in erecting the batteries at Hainey's and Wescott's. He remained here until the Americans were defeated. He then enlisted in the army, and was present at Yorktown, when Cornwallis surrendered. After peace was declared, he returned with his family to Castine, and settled on his farm, about two miles from the village. For seventeen years in succession, he was chosen one of the Selectmen—the greater part of the time First Selectman and Assessor—and then felt obliged to decline any longer service in that capacity. He served as a deacon of the First Congregational Society for the term of thirty-three years. He died in Castine, April 29, 1833, aged eighty years and two days. He was married to Miss Marian Littlefield, who was born in York, Maine, March 22, 1756, and who died March 23, 1830, aged seventy-four years. They had three sons: Nathaniel, who died in Castine, in April, 1864, aged eighty-three years ; Benjamin, who was lost at sea, from the brig *Castine*, August 30, 1815, at the age of twenty-eight years ; and Josiah, who died in Penobscot, in 1870, aged about eighty-four years. Nathaniel was married to Christiana Gardner, who was born in Hingham, Massachusetts, and who was a descendant, in a direct line, of one of the Pilgrims who came over in the *Mayflower*. She died in this town, in December, 1861, aged eighty-four years.

MARINERS.

PERKINS, EBENEZER.

Captain Ebenezer Perkins, the fourth son of Joseph and Phœbe Ware Perkins, was born in York, Maine, June 8, 1771; and died in Castine, July 26, 1827, aged fifty-six years. He married Mehitable Littlefield, who was born in Wells, Maine, March 14, 1784. She died at Camden, Maine, November 12, 1857, aged seventy-three years.

" Early in life he chose the vocation of a sailor, and his life was somewhat of an eventful one. In the employment of his father, he was, when quite young, appointed to the command of a vessel. During the existence of the Berlin and Milan Decrees, his vessel was captured, and he was confined for some time in a French prison.

Soon after the declaration of War between Great Britain and the United States, he, being then in command of the ship *Liverpool Trader*, belonging to his father, lying at Poughkeepsie, New York, received orders to bring his vessel to Hampden, that being supposed to be a place of safety. Soon after his arrival, however, some of the British fleet sailed up the Penobscot, and burned the *Liverpool Trader*, together with one of the United States. vessels lying there.

The next interesting event of his life occurred during the year 1820, he then being in command of a vessel named the *Camden*. At that time the coast of Cuba was infested with pirates, and on the passage of that vessel from St. Iago de Cuba to Boston, he was captured by them, near the Isle of Pines. The cargo of the vessel, consisting of coffee, sugar, pimento, and other produce of the island, together with himself and crew, was taken on board piratical vessels, and the *Camden* burned.

While on board a piratical vessel, the captain, mate and crew, seventeen in all, were somewhat at variance as to what disposition should be made of the crew of the *Camden;* whether they should be shot, or landed on a small desolate island near by, called Bahia Honda. It was finally determined to submit the matter to a ballot. The whole crew were called together, the ballots distributed, and it was found, upon counting, that there were nine in favor of shooting them, and eight in favor of landing them on Bahia Honda. The captain of the pirate was among the nine, and the mate among the eight. Captain Perkins belonged to the order of Free-Masons, and so did also the mate of the pirate. A quarrel arose between the captain of the latter and his mate, on this account, which resulted in a duel, in which the captain fell; and in consequence of this, the crew of the *Camden* were landed on the island. This island was found to be quite barren, producing only a few mangrove bushes; and not a spring of fresh water could be found upon it. The unfortunate men subsisted for eight days on the few shell-fish found on its shores, depending on the dew found upon the mangrove leaves in the morning and evening, to quench their thirst. At the end of the eighth day, a small Spanish coasting vessel anchored within a mile of the shore of the island, to which they made signals; but whether these were seen or not, no attention was paid to them. Among the crew of the *Camden*, was an apprentice boy of Captain Perkins', a Dane, named William. He was a very expert swimmer, and volunteered to swim to the vessel (in spite of sharks, and other voracious fish) and endeavor to prevail on her captain to bring her nearer the island, and take them on board. A favorite spaniel of Captain Perkins', which the pirates permitted him to take with him, was very much attached to William, and plunged with him into the sea, and swam by his side until they both reached the vessel in safety. William prevailed on the captain to take them all on board, and they soon set sail for Havana, where they arrived in a few days. A short time after Captain Perkins' arrival in Havana, he saw his vessel's cargo landed. He appealed to the United States

Consul for advice—which he gave in a few words, viz:—
' If you value your LIFE, say nothing about the cargo.'
Such was the state of things in Cuba in those days; and
recent events show that there has been but little improvement since.

The next vessel Captain Perkins commanded was the
brig *Draco*. While loading her in Boston, and when
nearly ready for sea, the United States sloop-of-war *Hornet*, having captured the piratical vessel which destroyed
the *Camden*, brought the crew to Charleston, South Caro-
lina, for trial. Among them was the mate through whose
instrumentality Captain Perkins and the crew of the *Camden* were saved from being shot. Captain Perkins was
summoned to Charleston, to appear as a witness against
them. He could not bear the thought of testifying against
one who was instrumental in saving the life of himself and
crew, and, through the influence of Daniel Webster with
the authorities at Washington, he was permitted to proceed on his voyage. The mate and crew were hung.
Captain Perkins left the sea about two years before his
death."

WHITNEY, SAMUEL AUSTIN.

Samuel Austin, the ninth child of Samuel and Abigail
Whitney, was born in Concord, Massachusetts, September
27, 1770. The most active portion of his life was spent
upon the ocean. He was noted for his intrepidity, contempt
of danger, and perseverance. His indifference to danger
amounted often to rashness. One Fourth of July, happening to pass where a man, torch in hand, was standing by a
loaded cannon, he asked him why he delayed firing it.
The man replied that it was loaded to the muzzle, and no
one dared to fire it. He took the match, touched the fuze,
and the gun burst. He was carried home senseless, his
flesh filled with atoms of powder, and his nose broken.
His exploits in the re-capture of the ship *Hiram*, have already
been narrated. Captain Whitney was married July 28,
1801, to Miss Ruth Perkins, of this town. In 1802, he
moved to Lincolnville, Maine, where he died October 15,
1846, aged seventy-six years. His wife died at Waldoboro',
Maine, September 15, 1849. They had five children, the
descendants of whom, many of them, reside here.

MERCHANTS.

Adams, Samuel.   [Portrait on opposite page.]

Mr. Adams was born in Pembroke, New Hampshire, March 5, 1790. His father, Doctor Thomas Adams, was from Lincoln, Massachusetts, and his mother was from Watertown, in the same State. His father studied medicine with Doctor Spring, of Watertown, and after his marriage moved to Pembroke, where he had an extensive practice until a year previous to his death, which occurred in 1809. At this time Mr. Adams came to Castine as a clerk in the store of Judkins & Adams, the latter named partner being his brother. After the evacuation of the town by the English, in 1815, he went into trade with Thomas E. Hale, Esq.; afterwards, with his brother Thomas. In 1821, he married a daughter of Doctor Moulton, of Bucksport, and went into business alone. In 1835, he took Mr. William Foster, as a partner; and in 1855, he sold his stock to his sons, Samuel, and Alfred P. Upon the death of his son Samuel (in 1861), Deacon Adams purchased back the stock of goods, and resumed business again. He continued in business until 1872, when he sold out to Messrs. Hooper & Shepherd, and retired from all active pursuits. He was principal owner of the ships *Robert Morris, Adams, Samuel Adams, Castine, Saint James, J. P. Whitney,* and of many smaller vessels. He was engaged largely in the Grand Bank and other fisheries, and in the importation of Liverpool and Cadiz salt. He has held many important positions in town, and for thirty-six years has been a deacon in the Second Congregational Society of Castine. He still lives at the advanced age of eighty-four years—a hale old gentleman, with all his faculties unimpaired—cheered by the presence of his worthy wife, and the companionship of his children and a host of friends.

Adams, Thomas.

Mr. Thomas Adams was born at Pembroke, New Hampshire, July 3, 1783. He died at Roxbury, Massachusetts, December 31, 1847. He was married May 23, 1815, to Miss Jane Russell, of St. Andrews, New Brunswick. His active business life was passed at Castine. In 1837, he removed to Boston, and thence, on account of failing health, to Roxbury.   He carried on a prosperous mercantile business here for many years, was a Representative to the General Court of Massachusetts; and for several years was one of the Selectmen of the town.

" He was extensively known and beloved as a man and a Christian, and those who partook of his kindness and shared his hospitality, could not easily forget his winning manners and cordial welcome.   He was associated with two other gentlemen in establishing the Trinitarian church in Castine, and its welfare was near his heart.   Prospered as he was in his mercantile career, and blessed with worldly goods, he did not forget to offer upon the altar of God, a large portion of his gifts.   The poor clergyman, the feeble church, the struggling missionary, can bear testimony to his generous heart.   The Sabbath school in his church was the result of his personal labors, and his heart was warm and his prayers were fervent for his pupils,—he loved them much.   In the prayer meeting, in the Bible class, by the bed-side of the sick and dying, his voice was ever heard; and many were the hearts whose anguish has been soothed, and over whose fleeting spirits came a gleam of consolation and hope, as he guided them to the Saviour.

Two years of extreme illness, and, towards the last, of great suffering, had impaired the powers of his mind, but his last intelligible words were: ' There is *rest* for me in heaven.' "

BRYANT, JOSEPH.

Joseph Bryant, son of Joseph and Sarah (Little) Bryant, was born in Marshfield, Massachusetts, December 3, 1789. His parents both died before he was eight years of age, and he was brought up in the family of his uncle, Mr. Waterman, of Marshfield.   In the year 1800, he came to Castine, and entered the store of his uncle, Otis Little, with whom he remained until he became of age, when he went into business for himself.   During a few years, previous to 1830, Mr. Charles K. Tilden was connected with him.

In 1835 he removed to Bangor, and remained in business there until his death, March 31, 1863.

He was twice married,—first, on September 23, 1816, to Sarah Little, a native of Bremen, Maine, who died May 6,

1822; and second, on November 15, 1824, to Abigail Curtis, a native of Sharon, Massachusetts, who still survives him. While a resident of Castine, he was a member of the House of Representatives of this State, and served several years on the Board of Selectmen.   After his removal to Bangor, he was twice elected Mayor as a Whig and Temperance candidate.   He was in early life a Federalist in politics, afterwards a Whig, and subsequently a Republican.   He was a member of the Unitarian Society of Castine, but after he became a resident of Bangor, he took an active part in establishing the Episcopal Society there—his preference having long been for that mode of worship—and was one of its Wardens from its organization to his death, a period of twenty-seven years.   The following tribute to his character is from the Bangor " Whig and Courier," of a date shortly after his death:

" Mr. Bryant was an honorable merchant, a generous, liberal citizen, an honest man, a consistent Christian.   The poor and needy always found him a ready helper, the young, a judicious and careful adviser, the city a thoughtful counselor, the church a generous giver, while his whole life bore ample evidence of his integrity, his wisdom, and his fidelity.   During his life, and amid the vicissitudes of mercantile life, no one can point a finger to an act that would cast a shadow on his good name, and no words can more appropriately do justice to his memory, than these simple ones—'Semper Fidelis.' "

TILDEN, CHARLES KIRK.

Charles Kirk Tilden was the oldest son of Charles Tilden, who was born in Boston, Massachusetts, in 1768. He was born in Digby, Nova Scotia, February 19, 1793; and died in Castine, January 21, 1860, aged sixty-seven years.   He married Mary, daughter of Judge Nathan Reed, of Belfast, Maine.   They had three children: George F., Mary G., and Charles W.   This family can trace an uninterrupted descent from Sir Richard Tylden, Seneschal to Hugh de Lacy, the Constable of Chester, in the reign of Henry II, who accompanied Richard I, (Coeur de Leon,) in his crusades to the Holy Land. Nathaniel Tilden, a member of the Tenterden branch of the family, emigrated to America in 1623, in the ship *Ann*, and landed at Plymouth.   The subject of this sketch was his descendant by six removes.

Charles Kirk Tilden came to Castine at the age of nine years. He commenced his mercantile life in the employment of Mr. Doty Little. He continued with him a number of years, and became associated with him in business. He subsequently became largely interested with the late Joseph Bryant, in the West India trade. He continued in mercantile pursuits until his death. His worthy and beloved wife survived him for a little more than fourteen years, her death occurring June 23, 1874. The children are all living, and residents of Castine.

WALKER, JOHN.

Mr. John Walker was born in Staffordshire, England, April 22, 1754. He married, about the year 1810, Emma Roundy, a daughter of John Roundy, one of the early settlers of Bluehill. They had six sons and three daughters. He died June 20, 1831, aged seventy-four years two months and eight days.

Mr. Walker enlisted in the British army at the early age of thirteen years. He served under General Burgoyne, in his expedition from Canada into New York, in 1777; and was amongst the number of prisoners of war surrendered by that officer to General Gates at Saratoga, October 17, 1777. He was released on parole, and immediately renounced his allegiance to Great Britain, took the oath of fidelity to the United States, and enlisted in the American army. It is said that he deserted from the American army, was apprehended, and condemned to be shot. That his friends laid the case before Lady Washington, who went to see him in his confinement, and that on her intercession, he was pardoned and restored to his former good standing. This statement is from somewhat doubtful authority, and is probably apocryphal. The fact of his honorable discharge is known with certainty; and he was always regarded by his contemporaries as one who had done the cause of liberty much service.

After the close of the war, Mr. Walker bought a farm on Cunningham's Ridge, in the town of Sedgwick. He remained there a few years, and then moved to Snow's Cove, and engaged in lumbering. Not liking this place, however, he sold it, about the year 1810, and purchased, of Mr. John Lee, the mills situated at the head of the southern branch of the Bagaduce river, in the town of Brooksville. Mr. Walker's descendants are quite numerous. Among them may be mentioned the Honorable Joseph G. Walker, a Commissioner for Hancock County, Captain Amos Walker, and Deacon Joseph Walker—the latter being now in his seventy-seventh year. The subject of this sketch served for many years as a Captain in the Militia, and was always a leading man in the community where he lived. Soon after coming to Brooksville, he was elected a deacon of the First Congregational Church, and continued in this office until his death. Mrs. Thankful Black, of Sedgwick, composed an elegy upon the occasion of his funeral, which was afterwards published.

> " With constant care he lived a holy life,
> And kept the faith, in midst of war and strife.
> For many years the ways of God he tried,
> A saint he lived, and like a saint he died."

WHITNEY, SAMUEL.

Samuel Whitney, the father of Samuel Austin Whitney, was the youngest son of Benjamin Whitney by his second wife, Abigail Bridge. He was born in Marlborough, Massachusetts, September 5, 1734. When about two years old his parents moved to Boston. When three years old, his father died. He was married to Abigail Cutler, October 20, 1757. He went into business in Boston, at first; but moved to Castine when about fifty-nine years of age. He bought timber lands at Orland, and shipped lumber to various foreign and domestic ports. He put up and carried on a rope-walk, built an excellent wharf near where Commercial wharf now is; and built and purchased several ships and other vessels. One of these, the *Hiram*, is famous for its many captures by, and re-captures from the French. Soon after coming to reside here, Mr. Whitney erected a stately mansion—now torn down—in which he continued to reside during the remainder of his days. He died on Sunday, May 29, 1808, aged seventy-four years.

In his religious views, Mr. Whitney was brought up a strict Calvinist, but in the later years of his life he adopted the views of the Universalists. Upon his death bed he turned to one near him and said: "Should they ask how a Universalist could die, tell them that I died in the full belief of God's universal love for all mankind." His wife died in this town, July 2, 1813, aged seventy-nine years. They had twelve sons, and five daughters.

WITHERLE, WILLIAM.

William Witherle, son of Joshua and Rebecca (Howe) Witherle, was born in Boston, where his parents resided, December 15, 1784. His grandfather, Theophilus Witherell, lived on Cape Cod, probably in what is now the town of Truro. In 1798, in the fourteenth year of his age, he came to Castine and went into the store of his uncle, David Howe, where he continued until he attained his majority, shortly after which—on April 28, 1806—he commenced business with Mr. Benjamin Hook, under the name of Hook & Witherle. This connection lasted two years, after which he was without a partner until November 6, 1810, when the firm of Witherle & Jarvis—consisting of himself and Mr. John H. Jarvis—was formed. This partnership was dissolved February 12, 1844; and on March the first, of the same year, he associated with Mr. Benjamin D. Gay, under the name of William Witherle & Co. This firm—of which his son, Mr. William H. Witherle, afterwards became a member—was dissolved February 28, 1855, closing his connection with trade.

His ownership in navigation commenced quite early in life, and continued till his death, which occurred, after a brief sickness, April 13, 1860.

He married, December 25, 1815, Sally Bryant, a native of Marshfield, Massachusetts, and daughter of Joseph and Sarah (Little) Bryant of that town, who survived him less than three months.

Mr. Witherle was a person of regular and temperate habits, and until the last few years of his life—during which he was somewhat of an invalid—in the enjoyment of general good health.

Never in the slightest degree a politician, he had a strong interest in the Free-Soil movement, and a desire for the success of the Republican party.

His father was a member of Reverend John Murray's religious society in Boston; and he, himself, of the Unitarian and Universalist societies, during their existence here;

and though but little inclined to theological controversy, he always entertained to the close of his life, a deep regard for the religious views known as liberal, and a firm belief in them.

At the time of his death, and for some years previously, no *man* was living on the peninsula of Castine, who was there when he came to it.   There were several older persons, but no one who had been so long a resident.

His sons, William H. and George H. Witherle, still reside and do business in this town.

CHAPTER XI.

MUNICIPAL HISTORY OF BROOKSVILLE.

The town of Brooksville was incorporated by act of the General Court of Massachusetts, on June 13, 1817. It was named after Honorable John Brooks, the Governor of the Commonwealth of Massachusetts, at that time. The general history of Brooksville, prior to its incorporation, is included in that of Penobscot and Castine—of which it formerly composed a part—with the exception of the small portion derived from Sedgwick. In the half century that has elapsed since its incorporation, so little of public interest has transpired in this section of the State, especially in Hancock County, that the municipal history of so comparatively young a town cannot reasonably be expected to equal that of older or more thickly settled communities. This town has, like Penobscot, been obliged to bestow its principal attention for many years upon the matter of its roads. Its records contain, as will be seen from the following summary, but few matters of general interest; and for the facts relating to its ecclesiastical and military history the reader is referred to Chapters V and VII.

ABSTRACT OF RECORDS.

1817. The first town meeting in Brooksville, was held sometime in the fall of 1817, at the house of Mr. John Bray. At this meeting Mr. John Wasson was chosen Moderator; and Rogers Lawrence, Joseph G. Parker, and Elisha Smith, were elected as the first Board of Selectmen. The town also, at this time, chose Solomon Billings, Israel Redman, Timothy Condon, John Hawes, William Parker, Cunningham Lymburner, and John Blodgett, as a committee to district the town for schools.

1818. The annual meeting of the town, in 1818, was held at the house of Mr. Benjamin Rea. The town this year made its first appropriation for schools, and elected its first School Committee. The amount appropriated was two hundred dollars. The School Committee consisted of David Walker, John Douglass, William Blodgett, John Lord, Ephraim Blake, Phineas Norton, and John M. Foster.

1819. In 1819, the town voted, by a very decided majority against a separation of the District of Maine, from the Commonwealth of Massachusetts.

1821. The town at its annual meeting in 1821, voted its usual appropriation of two hundred dollars for schools; and at a subsequent meeting voted an additional amount of one hundred and ninety dollars.

1822. The appropriation for the support of schools, was four hundred dollars, in 1822.

1823. In the year 1823, the town instructed the Selectmen to arrange with the municipal officers of Castine, the proportion which Brooksville should pay annually, for the support of a ferry, at what was formerly called Lymburner's Ferry—between North Castine, and West Brooksville. The town this year, instructed the Selectmen to negotiate for suitable burying grounds, in different portions of its territory. For the next twenty years nothing of special interest occurs in the records of the town.

1833—1843. In 1833, the amount of school money appropriated by the town was increased to four hundred and forty dollars; and in 1843, it was raised to four hundred and eighty dollars.

1846. At its annual meeting in 1846, the town voted to build a town-house, and to have it located in Sylvester Condon's pasture, near the southwest corner; John Hawes, Andrew Gray, and Simeon Allen, were chosen as a building committee. At another, and later, meeting the town decided to have the building placed in the same pasture, but "on the north side of the bars leading from the highway." An attempt had been made for many years to induce the town to provide a settled place for its annual meetings, but the article in the warrant in relation to the matter, had heretofore invariably been passed over.

1853—1856. The appropriation for schools in 1853, was six hundred dollars; and in 1856, the amount was increased to eight hundred and fifty.

1862—1865. In 1862, the appropriation for the support of schools was eight hundred and sixty dollars; and this is about the amount generally raised by the town, for this purpose, in subsequent years. From this time until the close of the war of the Rebellion, nothing occurs in the town records of any particular interest, except what relates to the appropriation of money for bounties, for the support of the families of volunteers, and for other purposes connected, directly or indirectly, with the war then being carried on. As these amounts are all included in another place, they are in consequence omitted here. [See pages 168, 169.]

For several years after the incorporation of the town, the inhabitants of Brooksville, were without a Post Office, and were obliged to cross the water to Castine, or go to Penobscot, or Sedgwick, for their mail. The letters were usually obtained from these towns, and distributed to the inhabitants by one or more carriers. As the population increased, however, the difficulty of transmitting the mail to different portions of the town increased also, and accordingly a Post Office was established there about the year 1830, and John R. Redman was appointed postmaster at that time. At the present time offices are established in each section of the town. [See Brooksville Directory.]

CHAPTER XII.

PRESENT AND FUTURE OF THE THREE TOWNS.

Brooksville, according to the census of 1870, contains a population of one thousand two hundred and seventy-six souls. Its valuation is, Polls, three hundred and twenty-two ; Estates, two hundred and thirty-eight thousand nine hundred and eighty-seven dollars. Its principal business consists in navigation; although the granite quarries in South Brooksville afford employment the greater portion of the time, to a large number of persons. The navigation of the town consists mostly of small.coasting vessels, some of them rather old. These vessels, though of comparatively small intrinsic value, carry freights as cheaply as those of much greater cost, and consequently afford a very much greater percentage of profit. The inhabitants of the Cape are mostly engaged in fishing. Numbers of them go to the Banks of Newfoundland, in vessels owned principally in, and sailing from, towns on Cape Ann. The remainder are chiefly engaged in shore fishing, and the obtaining of shell-fish. Brooksville was the latest of the three towns, whose history has been narrated, to be incorporated into a separate municipality. It was, indeed, a sort of off-shoot from the towns of Castine and Penohscot, and in its earlier years, offered less inducements to settlers than either of these towns. The aspect of things, however, has changed very much, of late years. There is now growing up in West Brooksville a thrifty little village, which threatens, ere many years, to completely cast into the shade its more favored rivals. The causes which have led to the rather rapid growth of this town within recent years, are said by an aged merchant—of this vicinity, but not a resident of the town—a gentleman of sound judgment, and of large information in regard to the business affairs of these communities, to be as follows : *First*—the early and steadfast encouragement to the cause of temperance reform. This cause gave the first impetus not only to the social happiness of the citizens, but to the financial prosperity of the community. *Secondly* — the advance made by the town in educational matters. *Thirdly*—the inducements held out to the young men of the town, to marry and settle at home, instead of seeking their fortune abroad, as is too often the case in New England towns. Possibly the reason first given is the cause of the other two. If so, what more glowing encomium could be paid to the cause of temperance, than the mere recital of the fact! The growth of Brooksville being due to the causes mentioned, it requires no prophetic power to predict a continued prosperity, so long as these same causes shall remain in operation. This town having no great agricultural capabilities, must, however, continue in the future to extract its wealth, as it has in the past, from its granite hills, draw it from the bosom of the deep, or increase it by maritime enterprise.

The town of Penobscot, though like most of the neighboring towns, it has lost in population during the last decade, has increased in wealth. Its present population is about one thousand four hundred and eighteen souls. Its valuation in 1870 was, Polls, three hundred and twenty-nine; Estates, two hundred and twenty-seven thousand three hundred and fifty-six dollars. This town is engaged somewhat in navigation, and in small manufactures, but is, on the whole, to be considered as an agricultural town. Its increased prosperity of late years, notwithstanding its marked falling off in population, is, doubtless, due to the temperance, frugality and industry of its citizens. It is simply the slow and natural growth in wealth that every town *ought* to show, where no extrinsic causes have interfered to produce a decline. Its financial growth is due partly, of course, to the new vessels that have been built, and to the manufactures that have sprung up; but is due mainly to the increased value of its farms. The situation and soil of Penobscot is such, however, that it can never compare, agriculturally, with the more favorable soils of many other places in the State. Its future prosperity will depend principally upon the encouragement extended to Manufactures. It possesses sufficient water power to enable it to carry on manufactories of a small kind to an almost unlimited extent; and its facilities for navigation would even, it is thought, render the employment of steam power profitable. The manufacture of

brick has been carried on there for a long period, but the
business has never been conducted to the fullest extent of
which it is capable. With good farms, tolerable facilities
for navigation, excellent chances for manufactures of all
kinds, and an industrious and hard-working population,
there is no reason to doubt the continued prosperity of
the town.

The past and present condition of Castine has been so
fully treated in the chapter upon the commercial history
of the town, that but little remains to be added. Within
the last decade, this town has declined, both in population
and in its valuation. Its population in 1870, was one
thousand three hundred and four. Its valuation, at that
time, was, Polls, two hundred and fifty-eight; Estates,
four hundred and sixty-one thousand three hundred and
forty-three dollars. In 1860, the valuation of the Estates
was seven hundred and sixty-four thousand five hundred
and seventy-one dollars. This apparently excessive depre-
ciation of property is due, in great part, to the fact that
the valuations for some years had been altogether too high,
and had consequently been reduced. Notwithstanding
this fact, however, there has undoubtedly been a decline
in the wealth of the town, within the last ten or fifteen
years—as well as for a much longer period. While it
might be an error to state that the business of the town
was still on the decline, it cannot be said to be on the
increase. The location here of the State Normal School,
and the starting of a factory for the canning of lobsters
and shell-fish have, in a measure, counteracted the failure of
certain other branches of business; and the financial condition of the town is probably what it was at the last census.
What outlook does the future offer? The town cannot
again, within the present century, at least, reasonably
expect to see the day when it will be possible for any one
to utter the boast that he " could go from the upper to the
lower wharf upon the decks of vessels;" but nevertheless,
shipping must continue to be, to a certain extent, one of
the sources of its prosperity. To what extent this will be
the case, will depend upon the degree in which navigation
is revived throughout New England. Its limited territory
forbids any hopes of its ever becoming an important agricultural town. Its farms can never supply even the home
demand. Its want of water power, and its limited supply
of fresh water needed for steam power, will prevent its

ever becoming, to any great extent, a manufacturing town; unless, indeed, the advances made in scientific knowledge should some day enable the immense power of the *ocean tides* to be made available. The only reasonable prospect for the *immediate* future lies in encouraging, as much as possible, the current of summer travel, which has already begun to flow in this direction. The natural advantages of the town as a place of summer resort, are already too well and widely known, to need any special advertisement. All that is needed, on the part of our people, is a spirit of fairness, in all their transactions, to offset the extortionate demands of our more celebrated watering-places.

Penobscot, Castine, and Brooksville possess a common origin, and the same history. They are bound together by the ties of neighborhood and of consanguinity. Their business interests do not conflict with one another; and whatever tends to increase the general well-being and prosperity of one, will inevitably benefit the others also. As they were one in origin, it is to be hoped that they may continue to accord, in all their aims and efforts.

PART III.

DOCUMENTARY.

"The grounds I work upon."

Shak.—All's well that ends well. iii—4.

DOCUMENTS RELATING TO THE ANTE-REVOLUTIONARY PERIOD.

CONSISTING OF TRANSLATIONS OF THE "DOCUMENTS COLLECTED IN FRANCE," NOW IN THE ARCHIVES OF THE COMMONWEALTH OF MASSACHUSETTS, AND SUNDRY OTHER SIMILAR DOCUMENTS FROM BOTH ENGLISH AND FRENCH SOURCES, ARRANGED IN CHRONOLOGICAL ORDER.

1.

Deposition of Edward Naylor.

" The Testomony of Edward Naylor aged $= 32 =$ yeares or ther Aboutes Sartifieth that haveing the charge and command of Negew Belonging to Penobscott for the acct $=$ of Coll^e Tempells $=$ Now $=$ Sr Thomas Tempells That In Aprill $= 1662 =$ Leiueftennant Gardner $=$ commander^r of Penobscott for ye sayed Coll^e Tempells Accompt Writt $=$ to me that Coll^e Tempell had Left y^e fortes & that Capt. Thomas Bredion had Taken Poshion [*sic*] of them & had Dismissed him & the Rest of the men from y^e sayed Tempells Imply : & sarves & Plased a Mr Gladman Governor of the fortt^e & other offeseres & soldiers : the sayed Gardner $=$ having Received a Commission from y^e sayed Bredon [*sic*] : & : Commanded mee In his Magestys mane [*sic*] to Declare to the men that they wear the all Discharged **f**rom Coll^e Tempelles sarves & to be opon the Accompt of Capt. Thomas Bredion fiom that Time : & allso $=$ they sayed gardner sayed that Capt. Bredion : had a Commishon from his magesty : opon the obedences of which hey sorendred the ffortt & Trad$^e =$ & $=$ y^e Goodes $=$ deposed in Generall Court 25 of octobre 1666. p Edw. Rawsŏn Secret. [Mass. Records, Vol. 67. p. 115.]

2.

Extract from a letter of Sir Thomas Temple's to the Lords of the Council, November 24, 1668.

" May it please your Lordships, 'Tis my duty to acquaint you that I received his Majesty's Letter dated the 31st of

December, 1667, for the delivering up of the Country of
Acadia, the 20th of *October*, 1668, by Monsieur *Morillon* du
Bourg, deputed by the most Christian King, under the
Great Seal of *France*, to receive the same; * * * *
I thought fit also to let your Lordships know, that those
Ports and Places named in my first Order, were a part of
one of the Colonies of *New England*, viz: *Pentagöet*,
belonging to *New Plymouth*, which has given the Magistrates here [Query. In Boston?] great Cause of Fear,
and Apprehensions of so potent a Neighbour, which may
be of dangerous Consequence to his Majesty's Service and
Subjects, the Caribbee Islands having most of their Provisions from these Parts, and that Mons. du Bourg, informs
me that the most Christian King intended to plant a Colony
at *Pentagöet*, and make a Passage by Land to *Quebec*, his
greatest Town in *Canada*, being but three Day's Journey
distant."
[Memorials of the Eng. and French Commissaries concerning the Limits of Nova Scotia or Acadia, pp. 588, 589.]

3.

Instructions for Monsieur le Chevalier de Grandfontaine.

LA ROCHELLE, March 5, 1670.
The said Sieur de Grandfontaine will understand that
the said province of Acadia, which is included within the
whole extent of coast, which is found from, and includes
Kennebec and Pentagöet, extending towards the north, to
Canso, and Cape Breton, and all that land which is in this
same extent of this coast, stretching to the west as far as
the Great River St. Lawrence, having been put under the
authority and government of his Majesty, in the year 1630,
by means of the possession which had then been taken by
Monsieur the Commander de Razillai—charged with the
orders of his Majesty to that end; that this possession had
some interruptions upon the part of the English, which interruptions were followed by several treaties, by which the
restitution of it has always been promised and conceded to
his Majesty. Among others by the first article of the
treaty made at Paris, in the month of March, in the year
1632, between Isaac Houac, Ambassador of his said Britannic
Majesty, and Messrs. de Bouillon and Bouthillier, Commissioners upon the part of the King, by which article, it
is precisely stated that the said Sieur de Houac promises,

in the name of his said Britannic Majesty, to cause to be surrendered to his said Majesty, all the places occupied in New France, Acadia, and Canada, and to give, for that purpose, the necessary copies of the treaty to those who command, on the part of his said Britannic Majesty, at Port Royal. And again by article tenth, of the treaty of Breda, in the year 1667—upon the last invasion of said country, by the English, in the year 1654—it is again expressly declared that the King of Great Britain, shall likewise make restitution to the Most Christian King, or to such person as shall be proposed for it, by his order, well and duly attested by the Great Seal of France, of the country in North America, called Acadia, which the Most Christian King possessed heretofore, and to that end the said King of Great Britain, immediately after the exchange of the ratifications of peace, will deliver, or will cause to be delivered, to the said Most Christian King, or to some one who shall be commissioned by him, all the memoranda and orders necessary for the said restitution.

The Sieur de Grandfontaine should know that it is in execution of this article, that the King of Great Britain, has caused to be delivered, the orders of which Sieur de Grandfontaine is bearer to him, as well as [bearer] of the commission of his Majesty, well and duly attested by the Great Seal of France.

And as the eleventh article of the same treaty of Breda, decides what should be done with respect to the inhabitants of the said country of Acadia, who shall desire to leave, the purport of it will be inserted here, in order that the said Sieur de Grandfontaine, may observe it, and that he may have for it all proper regard.

Article eleventh of the Treaty of Breda:

" But if any of the inhabitants of the said country called Acadia, prefer or desire to be under the rule of the King of Great Britain, it shall be permitted them to depart from it within the space of one year, reckoning from the day of the restitution of the country, and to sell, to pass in account, or otherwise dispose of, as shall appear advantageous to them, their lands, slaves and all other movable or immovable property, and such persons as shall contract with them for that purpose shall be obliged to draw up their contracts under the authority of the Most Christian King—but if they prefer to depart and carry with them their household goods, slaves, cattle, silver, and all other movable things, he will suffer them to be carried off without any hindrance or molestation whatever.

(Signed)   ARLINGTON."

As regards the restitution which is demanded in execution of the said articles, and of the orders whereof the said Sieur de Grandfontaine is bearer, he should know that it is the lands, country, ports, rivers, and places, or forts, which are from and include the said place of Kennebec, and Pentagöet, as far as Canso, and Cape Breton included, and all the extent of territory, as far as the river St. Lawrence,—without any reservation or exception. And that he ought particularly to stick to Pentagöet, the restitution of which has always been demanded by his Most Christian Majesty, as well as the forts upon the river St. John, and Port Royal, even as it appears from the letters of his Most Christian Majesty, of January 30, and October 7, 1658, written by Monsieur de Bordeaux, at that time his Ambassador in England, concerning the last invasion made by the English upon said forts, in the year 1654.

The said Sieur de Grandfontaine, having obtained this restitution, and having been put in possession of the said territory, will be able in his discretion and prudence to decide where he will make his principal establishment—which it appears to us ought to be at Pentagöet, as being the place nearest the territory under the English rule, and where he will be better able to support and protect the lands under the rule of his Majesty, which are, as has been said before, extending towards the north, from the middle of Pentagöet, as far as Cape Breton.

And when the Sieur de Grandfontaine shall be settled, he ought to pay great attention in regard to putting himself promptly in a state of defense, and protecting himself against all the accidents which might happen in the course of time and of affairs, by fortifying himself and providing himself with everything necessary for that purpose—for which, besides that already furnished him, his Majesty will provide for what more will be necessary for him in the memoranda of them which he will take care to send.

In resuming possession of the aforesaid things, the said Sieur de Grandfontaine will take care to have instructive memoranda made of the condition of those places which shall be given up to him, including the fortifications, build-

ings, the number and quality of inhabitants, and the means
and conveniences for their subsistence and trade.

He will use all the authority which is given him by his
Majesty, and all the forces which are, and shall be entrusted to him, to strengthen the traffic that his Majesty
may in future be able to make on the said coast of Acadia
—either for permanent or transient fishing, dressing of furs,
erecting of dwellings, tillage of lands, or such other things
as they desire to attempt there—and that without exclusion of any one, allowing full and entire liberty to all the
subjects of his said Majesty, to go and come, and to carry
on such traffic as they shall wish; but interdicting and
taking away this same freedom of trade and residence from
all strangers, unless they are provided with an express
order of the King; having regard all the time, that in this
exclusion from residence he ought not to include the English who are settled in the country, and places which shall
be restored and delivered to the King; but should require of
them an oath of fidelity and submission to his Majesty, such
as good and faithful subjects ought to make and keep.

And as, for the maintenance of the said country of Acadia, it appears that there is nothing more important to do
than to open communication with the inhabitants of the
French Colonies, which are upon the river St. Lawrence,
the Sieur de Grandfontaine should give particular attention to find the means; and he should go to work without
losing a moment of time—and it appears that this communication can better be found by way of the river St. John
with that of the Savages, or that of Pentagöet with that of
the Saut, otherwise called Chaudiere, than by any other
places. For the examination and discussion of the best
means for this communication, by any other places, as well
as of all other things, he will have as much acquaintance
and correspondence as he can, with Monsieur de Cour-
celles, Governor, and Lieutenant General for the King in
Canada, and the country of New France, and Monsieur
Talon, Intendant of the said conntry,—to follow in everything their instructions and advice.

And supposing—what is not to be believed—that the
said Sieur de Grandfontaine finds insurmountable obsta-
cles to the restitution of the country before mentioned, and
to taking possession of it, he must know that it would not
be expedient for the service of his Majesty, that he should
return to France, with the people who shall be placed un-

der his command; but that he ought to endeavor to take a
position in some place, upon the said coast of Acadia,
either at La Heve, or such other place as he shall judge
fit, in order to give account of his anxieties, and of the
difficulties that he will have met in the execution of his
orders, whereupon his Majesty will let him know what he
shall do.

(Signed) COLBERT DE TERROU.

["Documents Collected in France" Vol. II, page 211, et
seq.]

4.

*Act of Surrender of Fort Pentagöet, in Acadia, by Captain
Richard Walker, to the Chevalier de Grand-Fontaine,
August 5, 1670, with a detailed account of the condition
of the said Fort, and of all the things that were and did
remain in the said Fort, at the time of its surrender to the
said Chevalier de Grand-Fontaine.*

The fifth Day of *August*, 1670, being in the Fort of
Pentagöet, in the Countries of *Acadia*, whereof we took
Possession for his most Christian Majesty the Seventeenth
Day of last Month, Captain *Richard Walker*, heretofore
Deputy Governor of the said Fort, and of the said Countries of *Acadia*, representing the Person of Sir *Thomas Temple*, Knight and Baronet, accompanied with *Isaac Garden*,
Gentleman, did jointly require of us, that we should give
a particular Account of the Condition of the said Fort,
and of all Things which were and did remain in the
said Fort, when the Possession thereof was given unto
us by the abovesaid Captain *Richard Walker*, that they
might have an Instrument in Writing indented, to deliver
to the said Sir *Thomas Temple* for their Discharges, whereunto we do accord; and for that End and Purpose, we, in
the Presence of the above named, and of the Sieur *Jean
Maillard*, the King's Scrivener in the Ship of his Majesty,
called the *St. Sebastian*, commanded by Monsieur *la
Clocheterie*, as also of another Secretary, writing under Us,
the said Proceedings in Manner and Form following.

First, at the entring in of the said Fort upon the left
Hand, we found a Court of Guard* of about fifteen
Paces long, and ten broad, having upon the right Hand a
House of the like Length and Breadth, built with hewen

*An old form of expression for Guard-house. See Shakspeare—I King
Henry VI. Act II. Sc. 1, 4th line.

Stone, and covered with Shingles, and above them there is a Chapel of about six Paces long, and four Paces broad, covered with Shingles, and built with Terras,* upon which there is a small Turret, wherein there is a little Bell, weighing about eighteen Pounds.

More, upon the left Hand as we entered into the Court, there is a Magazine, having two Stories, built with Stone, and covered with Shingles, being in Length about thirty-six Paces Long, and ten in Breadth, which Magazine is very old, and wanted much Reparation, and which there is [a] little Cellar, wherein there is a Well.

And upon the other Side of the said Court, being on the right Hand, as we enter into the said Court, there is a House of the same Length and Breadth as the Magazine is, being half covered with Shingles, and the rest uncovered, and wanted much Reparation ; these we have exactly viewed, and taken notice of.

Upon the Rampart of the said Fort, and in Presence of our Canonier, whom we caused to be there present, to take a View of the several Pieces of Cannon, are as followeth.

First, six Iron Guns carrying a Ball of six Pounds, whereof two are furnished with new Carriages, and the other four with old Carriages and new Wheels; Two of them weighing eighteen hundred and fifty Pounds, each of them ; Three weighing each of them fifteen hundred Pounds; the other weighing two Thousand two hundred and Thirty Pounds.

More, two Iron Guns, carrying a Ball of four Pounds, having old Carriages and new Wheels, one weighing one Thousand three hundred and ten Pounds, the other weighing one Thousand two Hundred and thirty-two.

More, two small Iron Culverines, carrying a Ball of three Pounds, having their Carriages old and their Wheels new, weighing each of them nine Hundred twenty-five Pounds.

Afterwards we went out of the said fort and came to a little Plat-form near adjoining to the Sea, upon which we surveyed two Iron Guns, carrying a Ball of eight Pounds, furnished with new Carriages and new Wheels, the one weighing three Thousand two Hundred Pounds, and the other three Thousand one Hundred Pounds.

Which are twelve Iron Guns, weighing twenty one Thousand one Hundred twenty and two.

*The French is " bâtie sur une terrasse."

More, we do find in the said Fort, six Murtherers without Chambers, weighing twelve hundred Pounds.

More, two hundred Iron Bullets, from three to eight Pounds.

Lastly, about thirty or forty Paces from the said Fort, there is a small Out-house, being about twenty Paces in Length and eight in Breadth, built with Planks, and half covered with Shingles, which do not serve for any Use but to house Cattle.

More, about fifty Paces from the said Out-house, there is a square Garden, inclosed with Rails, in which Garden there are fifty or sixty Trees bearing Fruit.

All which Things above Writ, we have exactly viewed and taken notice of in the Presence of the Persons underwritten; and I do acknowledge that they are in the Quality and Condition as is above declared; whereof we have given this particular Account, that the Value thereof may be made good to the said Sir *Thomas Temple*, or to his Heirs or his Assignees, or to whom it shall belong; whereunto we, with the above named, have put our Hands, and caused our Secretary to witness the same, the Day and Year above writ. Signed *le Chevalier de Grand-Fontaine, Jean Maillard, Richard Walker. Isaac Garner, Marshal* Secretary.

I do hereby certify that this Paper is a true Copy compared with the Original in the Books of this Office. Plantation Office, Whitehall, July the 12th, 1750.

Signed THOMAS HILL.

[From " The Memorials of the English and French Commissaries concerning the Limits of Nova Scotia or Acadia. London : M DCC LV." pp. 606–610.—In the Library of the Boston Athenæum.]

5.

Condition of the Fort and post of Pentagöet as it was in the year 1670, *the sixth of August, when the English surrendered it.*

First, a fort with four bastions, well flanked, which bastions, taking them as far as the verge of the terrace inside, are sixteen feet.

The terraces on the inside are eight feet within [en] the curtains.

On entering in at the said fort there is upon the left hand a guard-house that is from twelve to thirteen paces in length and six in breadth.

Upon the same side is a low Magazine with another of equal size and length, being thirty-six paces in length and about twelve in breadth, covered with shingles, under which Magazines there is a small cellar nearly half as large as the Magazines, in which there is a well.

Upon the right hand on entering into said fort there is a house of the same size as the aforesaid guard-house, in which there are three rooms.

Above the passage which is between the guard-house and the house which is upon the right, there is a chapel, eight paces in length, and six in breadth, built of timber, and with mud walls, [Bouzillage,] upon which is a small steeple, in which is a metallic bell weighing eighteen pounds, the whole covered with shingles.

Upon the right hand is a house, of the like length and breadth as the magazine, of the same character except that it is not all covered, and that it has no cellar. All of which houses are built of stone from Mayenne, [in the places] where a little repair is necessary.

Sixty paces from the place there is a shed—half covered with plank—twenty-five paces long and twelve wide, which serves to house the cattle.

About one hundred and forty paces from the place, there is a garden, which has been found in quite good condition, in which there are seventy or eighty feet of fruit trees.

In regard to the Artillery upon the rampart of the said fort, the following cannon were found, first:

Six iron guns carrying 6-lb. balls, two having new carriages, and the other four old, and the wheels new, which six pieces weigh, according to their marks,

One	1800	pounds,
One	1230	"
Three others	1500	"
One	1350	"

Besides two pieces carrying 2-lb balls, having old carriages and new wheels, weighing

One	1310	pounds,
The other	1232	"

Besides, two iron Culverins, 3-lbers., with their carriages old and wheels new, weighing each 925 pounds.

Besides, upon a platform overlooking the sea and outside of the fort, two iron guns carrying an eight pound ball, having new carriages,

One weighing	3200	pounds,
The other	3100	"

In the fort is found 200 bullets from three to eight pounds in size. Lastly, upon the ramparts there are six iron guns without stock, and dismounted, that they judge to weigh 1200 pounds. [" French Documents," page 227 et seq.]

6.

Memorial of Monsieur Talon to the King.

QUEBEC, November 10, 1670.

*   *   *   *   *   *   *   *

I have entertained two Frenchmen and two Savages sent by the Chevalier de Grandfontaine, Governor of Acadia, with letters which show that the English have given back to him, in good faith, the portion for the restitution of which the King of Great Britain had engaged himself by the treaty of Breda. That he has been very well received and that there is reason to believe that he will easily bring about commercial relations with Boston if his Majesty judges it useful to his service.

That he has found at Pentagöet the Fort, of which I send the plan under the apprehension that that which he had caused to go by the St. Sebastian might be lost. That there is some timber suitable for the Navy, safe harbors and abundant fisheries throughout all the extent of Acadia.

That the privilege of fishing is only granted by the English upon paying a duty of twenty-five crowns per boat. That this duty is collected by Colonel Temple or by his creditors for the discharge of his debts. It is of consequence to know whether the King desires that they should continue to give, in his name, the same permission to the English, and upon what terms.

That the ground in the vicinity of Pentagöet is not the most suitable for cultivation, but is much like that of Port Royal and the river St. John.

That almost all the soldiers desire to settle.

That there was a place in the vicinity much better adapted to receive a more regular fortification and of better security than the post that he was occupying, which is commanded [by the high land?] and that his opinion was that he should work there and in this direction his inclination appears to me to incline him.

That the English had seized a vessel which had been apparently taken away from Jamaica by a Frenchman from

St. Malo, named La Fontaine, and by him conducted to Boston, loaded with Merchandise estimated at more than 100,000 crowns and carrying some forty pieces of cannon, a part iron and a part brass.

That this La Fontaine has escaped and that they mistrust that this vessel belongs to the King.

To this letter I have replied in advance, and, under the good pleasure of his Majesty, I have made it known to the Chevalier de Grandfontaine that my opinion was that he should not give any cause for jealousy to the English, by new fortifications and new works, nor cause for belief that the King wishes to become the master of all the fisheries which are for his convenience, by excluding them and refusing permission [to fish] until the authority of his Majesty was acknowledged and his troops well confirmed in the post of Pentagöet—for the repair and fortification of which it imports him to give his first and chief attention and his aid in establishing the soldiers and their families.

And [to give] his attention to bringing about a connexion and correspondence with Boston in order to get from there what he wants, and for other reasons which I cannot lay down, since this correspondence may be useful in this beginning of the settlement and may be broken when it pleases his Majesty.

And as to the matter of the vessels—I have sent letters to Colonel Temple, and to the Governor and Council of Boston, by which I make entreaty with all for that which they preserve, and the crew of the vessel, its rigging and appurtenances, and the merchandise which they have taken charge of, beseeching them to send me by the lieutenant of Monsieur de Grandfontaine, who must be carrier of the letters, the duplicates of the *proces verbal*, *inventories* and other legal instruments which have been drawn up in regard to the detention of this vessel, so that if it is proved that it belongs to his Majesty, I might make, in his name, the claim in a Court of Justice.

(" He has well answered."—*Colbert.*)

[" French Documents," Vol. 2d, Page 231 et seq.

7.

Memoir of Monsieur Talon to the King.

QUEBEC, 2d November, 1671.

*   *   *   *   *   *   *   *   *   *

The Sieur de Marson, lieutenant of the Chevalier de

Grandfontaine, with whom he has fallen out, has come here from Pentagöet, with the consent of his captain. Both have given me their respective causes of complaint, which I shall examine, nevertheless I do not believe that it was for the King's service to dismiss the said lieutenant within his gate, before having either tried or settled his quarrel; because their animosity appears too great, in order that the two parties should not proceed to any extreme in sight of the English, and as I know that the service of the King requires that I should make a voyage to Acadia before I return to France, I have kept near me the said lieutenant, who will accompany me on my journey, that I shall make, if my health returns, either this winter, upon snow-shoes, or next spring, in canoes.

* * * * * * * * * *

I shall observe the condition of the two principal posts of Pentagöet and Port Royal, and if they need any repair, I will cause work to be done [on them.]

[" French Documents," Vol. 1, page 247.]

8.

Extract from a letter of Governor Leverett, to Mr. John Collins, dated August 24, 1674.

" Our neighbors, the Dutch, have been very neighborly since they had certaine intelligence of the peace. One of their captains have bin upon the French forts, taken Penobscot, with loss of men on both sides; what they have done further east, we understand not."

[From the Hutchinson Papers, p. 464.]

9.

Memorial from Count Frontenac to the Minister.

QUEBEC, November 14, 1674.

Although I am in despair at having to write to you news little agreeable, I cannot refrain from giving you notice of the disaster which has happened to Monsieur Chambly, of his wound, of his confinement in prison, and of the capture of Pentagöet, together with that of Genesee, in the St. John's river, and of Monsieur Marson, who commanded there.

What I have learned, from a letter that Monsieur Chambly has written me, is, that he was attacked by a crew of buccaneers, who had just come from St. Domingo, and who had crossed over from Boston, with one hundred and ten men, who, after landing, kept up their attack for an hour.

He received a musket-shot through the body, that compelled him to leave the field, and which also injured his ensign; and the rest of his garrison which, with the inhabitants, was composed of only thirty disaffected and badly armed men, surrendered at discretion. The pirates have pillaged the fort, carrying away all the guns; and while they ought to have brought Monsieur Chambly to Boston with Monsieur Marson, he has been taken to the St. John's river, by a detachment who hold him as a ransom, and wish to make him pay a thousand beavers.

As I received this news only the last of September, through the savages whom Monsieur Chambly sent me with his ensign, praying me to give an order for his ransom, and as there remains not more than a month of navigation, I shall, in the inability of sending to Acadia for help—even although I may have the necessary things for that—content myself with sending some soldiers in canoes, in order to get news of the state in which they have left the fort; and if no invasion is made against Port Royal, to give orders to bring back the girl of Marson's, and those who are retained in the St. John's river, and to send to a correspondent that Monsieur Formont has provided for me at Boston, bills of exchange for the ransom of Monsieur Chambly, which I am obliged to discharge by my merchant at Rochelle, not thinking it for the glory of the King—for which I shall always sacrifice what little property I may have—to leave for the consideration of our neighbors a Governor in the hands of pirates, who would have brought him with them where one may be killed; besides, that this poor gentleman is assuredly, on account of his merit and his long service, worthy of a better destiny.

I have also written a letter to the Governor of Boston, of which I send you a copy, by which I express my astonishment to him, that while there has been no rupture between His Majesty and the King of England, he gives shelter to these pirates and these vagrants and men without employment, after they have insulted us so; and, as for me, I shall believe in failing [to carry out] the orders

I have had, to keep up a good correspondence with them if I had opportunity for anything of the kind.

I am persuaded that these people from Boston have employed these men there to do us this injury, they having given them even an English pilot to conduct them, they impatiently enduring our neighborhood, and the fear which this gives them for their fisheries and their trade.

I do not know if those that I have sent you will be able to return before the departure of the vessels; or whether I may be able to send other, more particular, news. But my Lord, by what I have written you now, and by what Monsieur Chambly will write you the first opportunity he finds, you will be able to discover the orders that you should give for the safety of Acadia, and what you wish I should do, since you know I am unable to do any good as 82. 25. 12. 17. 69. 14. 17. 92. 5. to be able there, failing 105. 33. 17. 29. 14. 57. 67. 104. 24. 18. 32. 12. of all things 18. 86. 14. 106. 14. 20. 68. 37. 24. 39. 17. 7. 79. 28. 17.* and that you expressly forbid me making any extraordinary expense, which I shall observe with the utmost care.

It is very much to the purpose, I think, that I finish this letter, which ought to weary you, it has already been so long; and that I add only those protestations that I will make to you, even to the last breath of my life.

My Lord,
Your very humble, very
obedient, and very
obliged servant,
FRONTENAC.
[" French Documents," Vol. 2, p. 287, et seq.]

10.

Letter of Monsieur de Colbert to Monsieur de Frontenac.

St. Germain-en Laye, 15th March, 1675.
* * * * * * *

His Majesty has been surprised to learn that the forts of Pentagöet, and of Genesee, have been seized and pillaged by the crew of a privateer; he cannot persuade himself that there has not been a little negligence upon the part of Sieur de Chambly. He wishes nevertheless, that you may do all that you possibly can to bring it [the captured

*Perhaps the reader will decipher this; we confess our inability to do so.

vessel] back from Boston, together with the soldiers and other persons taken with it, and to repair this mishap, in regard to the vessel which has been built in Canada. You have done well to compel the Sieur Baguire, agent of the company, to advance some money for the finishing of this construction. His re-imbursement will be provided for, and I will give the necessary orders to Monsieur de Demain, Intendant of the Navy, at Rochefort, to carry by the first vessels which shall go to Canada, all the rigging, appurtenances, arms, and ammunition necessary for the armament of this vessel, and to conduct it into one of the ports of the kingdom, his Majesty not wishing to confer such a favor upon this country as you propose.

[" French Documents—" vol. 2, page 291.]

11.

Order of Mr. Palmer, Judge of New York, to Thomas Sharpe, Captain of a vessel.

NEW YORK, July 23, 1686.

He will go to Pentagöet, and will send his letter to Sieur de St. Castin.

He will go to the places where are the wines which he had seized, in the name of his Britannic Majesty, and will put aboard his vessel, all which he can take.

If he finds upon his return some ships or vessels negotiating to, or having put some merchandise ashore in the country, belonging to the English, he will seize them and will bring them to Pemaquid.

[" French Documents," vol. 3, page 187.]

12.

Synopsis of a letter from Mr. Palmer, to the Sieur de St. Castin.

NEW YORK, July 31, 1686.

As he learns that vessels are transporting contraband goods, he has sent one on a cruise upon the coasts subject to the jurisdiction of New York.

He commands him in the name of His Britannic Majesty not to hinder the carrying off of the wine which has been found at Pentagöet. He warns him not to threaten the subjects of the English King, among others those who dwell on the island of Martinique; and that he will not be allowed on English 'territory if he intends to aid the Savages.

Having orders from His Britannic Majesty to give lands to those who shall wish any, and to confirm to others that which tiity have marked for said Sieur de St. Castin, [having orders] that, as he pretends to own a portion, he should summon him on the part of the said King, in order to learn what lands he wished to possess, which would be granted him in the name of His said Britannic Majesty, on his becoming his subject.

[" French Documents," Vol. 3, p. 188.]

13.

Report of Monsieur de Denonville to the Minister.

QUEBEC, 10 November, 1686.

*　　*　　*　　*　　*　　*　　*　　*

There is at Pentagöet the Sieur de St. Castin, who is a gentlemanly officer in the Carignans. He is very daring and enterprising and cherishes the interests of the King, having his life all the time at stake from the English with the Savages of the country of which he has become the ruler.

They assure me that he has recently come into the inheritance in France of £5000 a year, that he is a man of sound understanding, hating the English who fear him.

If Monsieur Perrot dislikes him on account of his government, St. Castin, by the report they have given me of him, should be a true man to give chase to the pirates and to encourage the fisheries of Monsieur de Chenvy, I have requested him to come to see me in order to become better acquainted with him and to engage him to go to France, if he should appear to me fit for anything.

He is quite solicitous of honor, [and] having some property, this will be a great help in sustaining a post like that of Port Royal, especially if he is not selfish.

It is true that he has been addicted in the past to libertinism; but they assure me that he has very much reformed and has very good sentiments.

My Lord our Bishop has returned from Acadia where he has made his visit to all the dwellings with great fatigue. He will send you an account of the great amount of disorder which there is in the forest from the wretched libertines who have been for a long time like the Savages, doing nothing towards cultivating the land.

I have written strongly about it to Monsieur Perrot. When we shall be at leisure it will be well for Monsieur de

Champigny and myself to make a tour there. I learn this on all sides, both that there is scarcely any left of the Savages and that they are for the most part destroyed by excessive drinking of brandy.

Monsieur l'Evesque sends three priests there with the Sieur Petit whom I understand talks to much advantage.

They assure me that the English have destroyed all the fish upon their coast and that they continue to fish upon ours; they will soon drive them away; for they do not come ashore like us to work the fish—throwing into the sea all the heads and garbage which become putrid and infect the bottom.

What has hindered the progress of the Colony in Acadia is the trade in the beaver, which has turned the brains of the inhabitants of Acadia as well as others, and which hinders the success of the permanent fisheries for which there ought to be small houses and ordinances in the places where the soil is good.

It is a shame that the people who have dwelt in this place for fifty years—father and son—have not received a bushel of corn, and have not even gardens. It is a shame that I have been upbraided by some people in this country, whom I have threatened to dispossess if they did not clear the ground.

It is proper that you should know that piracies are daily committed in our bay and upon our coasts, which proceed from New England alone.

Monsieur de Champigny will inform you how Dombour, a captain of a vessel which has brought him here, has given chase to a corsair which had taken a fishing vessel from Bayonne, which was released by the firmness of Dombour who was not in too good condition to give combat. I perceive that all our captains are very much disgusted at the news which they have had that there was at Boston a frigate of 25 guns destined to cruise in the bay and straits of the Hudson. Monsieur Perrot writes me thus, and that the people of Boston boast strongly.

[" French Documents," Vol. 3, p. 233 et seq.]

14.

Summary of a letter from Monsieur Perrot to Colonel Dongan.

PORT ROYAL, 29th August, 1686.

I complain that people have come to Pentagöet by order

of the Sieur Palmer to confiscate the goods which have
been discharged from an English vessel.

Although the pretenses of the said Sieur Dongan are
that his government has posession of the French coast even
to the river St. Croix, he does not believe that he desires
to decide the dispute by violence before the decision of
the Kings of France and England.

The said Palmer ought not to commit the act which he
has on the lands of the King, the fort of Pentagöet belonging to His Majesty by the treaty of Breda.   He expects
justice of Sieur Dongan that he may not be obliged to do
it himself.   ["French Documents," Vol. 3, p. 191.]

15.

Note by the Minister—1686.

The early part of the last year Monsieur Perrot was
compelled to borrow money of the Sieur de St. Castin in
order to buy two ketches, but when they had arrived he
found none of the inhabitants who would undertake to go
on board and on that account was obliged to make use of
English fishermen under the flag of France.   The enterprise has not prospered [on account of] the knavish talk
of these fishermen, who steal the greater part of the fish
which they send to Boston; so that the Sieur Perrot, in
order not to fail, was compelled to return the two ketches
to the seller and to relinquish what fish remained.
["French Documents," Vol. 3, p. 231.]

16.

*Memorial concerning some wines seized at Pentagöet, pre-
sented to the King of England by the Ministers of France
about* 1687.

The undersigned Ambassador and Envoy Extraordinary
of France, Commissaries appointed for the execution of the
Treaty of neutrality in regard to America, represent to
your Majesty that the person called Philip Syuret, master
of a vessel called the Jane, having departed from Malgue
for New France, entrusted with Merchandise for the account
of the Messrs. Nelson, Watkins and partners, and having
delivered them, agreeably to his bill of lading, to the Sieur
Vincent de Castène, merchant established at Pentagöet,
situated in the province of Acadia; the Judge of Pemaquid,
who is under the authority of your Majesty, caused to

be fitted out a vessel which he sent to Pentagöet, from whence he carried off the said merchandise as being contraband, and pretending that Pentagöet belonged to your Majesty, seized the vessel of the said Syuret, and refuses, even now, to restore it. But as by the articles X and XI of the Treaty of Breda, it is expressly declared that Acadia belongs to the King, our master; and as in execution of this Treaty, the late King of England, by his dispatch of the 6-16* of August, 1669, has sent his orders to Chevalier Temple, then Governor at Boston, to surrender Acadia into the hands of the Chevalier de Grand-Fontaine, and especially the forts and dwellings of Pentagöet, which are a part of it; and besides the said Chevalier Temple, after the reception of this order, being ill, conferred authority upon Captain Richard Walker, by a writing of the 7-17 July, 1670, to give back in his absence the said province of Acadia, and especially the forts and dwellings of Pentagöet, into the hands of the said Chevalier de Grand-Fontaine, authorized by the King our master to receive it; besides that the said Captain Walker obliged the Chevalier de Grand-Fontaine to give him a writing dated the 5th of August 1670, by which he acknowledges that Captain Walker is acquitted of the trust that he had received from the Chevalier Thomas Temple, and that he has surrendered to him, the Chevalier de Grand-Fontaine, the province of Acadia, and especially the forts and habitations of Pentagöet.

The said undersigned Ambassador and Envoy have confidence in the justice of your Majesty, that after having taken cognizance of all these things, she will disavow the proceeding of the Judge of Pemaquid, will prohibit his committing similar infractions of the law in future, and will order that all the merchandise of the said Syuret shall be restored to him, or the just value thereof, that his vessel shall be restored to him immediately, and that he shall be imdemnified for all the expenses that this interruption in his commerce has caused him.

(Signed)   BARILLON & BONREPAUS.

[From "The Memorials of the English and French Commissaries concerning the Limits of Nova Scotia or Acadia." pp. 615, 616.]

*The first number denotes *old style*, and the last *new style*.

17

Letter of the Baron de St. Castin, to Monsieur the Marquis of Denonville.

PENTAGÖET, 2d July, 1687.

I make use of the means of these two Savages, whom I have charged to make all possible diligence, to inform you that two days after having returned from Port Royal, the English came with fifty men, to take possession of this place, and went everywhere along the coast as far as the river St. Croix, which is about 40 leagues from here towards the east, where they say their boundary is. They have given me to understand that it was adjusted thus between the two kingdoms; as I had no orders from M. Perrot, I have told them that I have no answer for them; that I am only a private individual, and an inhabitant only of this place. They have forbid me any longer to receive the orders of the French, as well as the two inhabitants, who are about two leagues from here. They have been in all the places where there are Savages, in order to say as much to them, and have made them many presents. It is necessary that I should acknowledge to you that I have been surprised, and that if there had been no ruler in this country, I should have tried to prolong this business until I had received some orders from you; but I have been very badly received by Monsieur our Governor, who has made a slight pretext the past year of opposing the English, who came to seize some wine, about a quarter of a league from my house; and I believe, from the disposition I know he has, that he would ask nothing better, to make me pass wholly for a seditious person, and a man who would encroach upon his authority by undertaking something without order. If I was not on bad terms with him, from a feeling that every upright man ought to have, when he is ill-treated by his ruler as I have been, I should have informed you of his conduct; but I prefer to suffer a little longer, and that the matter should come to you through the letters of M. Petit, priest at Port Royal, who will not fail to acquaint you with all, without passion, which I might not be able to do; I will only tell you that he has detained me from the 21st of April to June 9th, under pretense of some weakness that I have for some women; and he has even told me that he had orders from you to do it. But that is not what vexes him; and as I do not think there is another man under heaven whom self-interest would lead to more base actions than to vend, himself, in his own house, before strangers, brandy by the pint and half-pint, not trusting a single one of his domestics to do it for him, I understand well his trouble; he wishes to be the only dealer in Acadia, as please God, he may, for all me; for as long as he shall be in this country, I shall aim not to displease him in this respect. He has never been willing to give me permission to go to Isle Perceè* [l'Isle percèe] because he fears that I will go perhaps even to Quebec,—nor will he permit me to send to Boston, after some millstones, for a mill, which the commonalty of Port Royal has desired me to construct for them, although he had promised it before the mill was commenced, and now it is finished, and the mill-stones are paid for. He has changed his mind, and makes no difficulty about sending M. Villebon, who only returned from there fifteen days ago, and who must go there again towards the first of September, to go after a bark that he has had built there. If I were not afraid of wearying you, I would inform you of many other particulars concerning the affairs of this country, which are in a strange disorder, especially at Port Royal, where M. Petit certainly suffers much.

I will close, Monsieur, by assuring you that I am, with all possible respect,

Your very humble and very obedient servant,

ST. CASTIN.

I forgot to tell you that going away from Port Royal, M. Perrot drew me one side, and whispered in my ear that if the English should come here, I should say nothing, and that it was not necessary to say anything. This I immediately after told to M. Petit, not understanding what it meant. I departed from the above place, and two days after that I had arrived here the English came, who said, in presence of the French, who are here, that M. Perrot had twice sent M. Villebon as deputy to the Governor at Boston; besides whom there was no one else to whom he had communicated anything else in the world. This that I say is very true; not that I am certain of anything; for

*Where this "Isle Perceè" is, we do not know. Williamson [Hist. of Me., Vol. 1. p. 596,] mentions a French settlement by that name, apparently between Chedabuctoo and St. John. In a sketch from the "NoVus Atlas" —1642—[in Documentary History of Maine, between pp. 314 and 315,] there is an island at the mouth of the St. John river, called "Isle Esperce."

I ought not to advance anything that I cannot sustain, even to the last word, and which also cannot be confirmed in the course of time. I know too well that this matter may go a great way for me to desire to advance anything which is not very true.

["French Documents," Vol. 3, p. 259, et seq.]

18.

Letter of the Marquis de Denonville to the Minister.

AT VILLE MARIE, 25th August, 1687.

* * * * * * *

I receive letters from Acadia which inform me that the English are not sparing of making an attempt upon the lands of the King upon that coast. I send you the letter which the Sieur de St. Castin has written me about it, who appears to wish me to understand that M. Perrot is in concert with the Governor at Boston. If this lasts, my Lord, he has no more means of resistance. I would much prefer to make war against them than against the Iroquois, and if they are taken the Iroquois would be put in order and forced to follow our will. * * * * *

["French Documents," Vol. 3, p. 266.]

19.

Summary of a Letter of the Sieur de Badie, Baron de St. Castin, to M. de Menneval.

PENTAGÖET, 15th September, 1687.

The fort at Pentagöet, where he is, is very advantageous for the coast of Acadia. He requires 30 soldiers in order to be able to maintain himself there against the continual insults of the English, who, up to the present time, have all that they could do to gain possession of it, and to conciliate the savages. He says that for a little assistance which is given him he will make a settlement of 400 savages, so much the more easily as they are the natural enemies of the English, and as they have entire confidence in him.

["French Documents," Vol. 3, p. 266.]

20.

Summary of a Memoir upon Acadia by M. de Menneval.

PORT ROYAL, 1st December, 1687.

* * * * * * *

The Sieur de St. Castin has communicated the intelligence to the said Sieur de Menneval that the English have enticed the Iroquois upon the coast of Pentagöet in order to corrupt the savages called Canibas who are in this quarter and by that to cause a kind of indirect war with the Colony.

The lands under the rule of His Majesty upon the English side are bounded by the river St. George, which is eleven leagues or thereabouts from that of Pentagöet.

* * * * * * *

The Sieur de St. Castin is absolute master of the savages, the Canibas, and of all their business, being in the forest with them since 1665, and having with him two daughters of the chief of these savages by whom he has many children.

This man has promised to quit the life that he has led up to the present time, and to proceed to establish himself at Port Royal; but having learned that the Sieur Perrot had intention of causing his arrest with the view of seizing his trade, he has not come. The Sieur de Menneval is ordered by his instruction to declare to the said Sieur de St. Castin that His Majesty will pardon him the past, if he will conduct himself differently, and make his settlement real.

This gentleman who has acquired a great deal would contribute to the construction of the fort that the Sieur de Menneval proposes to make at Pentagöet. It is important, nevertheless, to consider, in regard to this fort, whether it would not be more proper to construct it upon the river St. George.

The said Sieur de Menneval has had news that the English were coming to Port Royal, to demand payment of what is owed to them by the inhabitants, and he asks what his conduct should be, on this occasion.

The said inhabitants are reduced to great want, all that which they have made up to the present time having been sufficient only to pay what they owed to the said English who had sold to them at a very high price all that they needed, in order to recover themselves after the invasion of the said English.

["French Documents," Vol. 3, p. 281 et seq.]

21.

Instructions from the King to Sieur de Menneval.

*   *   *   *   *   *   *

Although what His Majesty has just explained to him of his intentions, for finding an outlet for the wood trade that has been the sole employment of five or six of the old and chief settlements, and to oblige those who are there to undertake enterprises for cultivating the soil and for carrying on the fisheries, ought to be applied to the matter of the Sieur de St. Castin's doing the principal business upon the river Pentagöet, without fixed dwellings, nevertheless His Majesty is well pleased with causing him to look to that which particularly regards him, viz: that he carry on with the savages the trade that he carries on solely with the English ; and that, as His Majesty is informed that he has derived great advantage from what he has done up to the present time, it is necessary that he commence without delay a settlement conformed to the intentions of His Majesty, cultivating the soil, undertaking the fisheries, and causing to pass through French hands the furs which he shall trade for with the savages who shall come to traffic with him at his house, and he shall know that for conforming himself to the will of His Majesty and to what one ought to expect from a conduct more becoming a Gentleman, he will take notice of it and will give him some tokens of his satisfaction.

[" French Documents," Vol. 3, p. 286.]

22.

Report of M. de Menneval, Governor of Acadia.

PORT ROYAL, 10th September, 1688.

*   *   *   *.   *   *   *

France has formerly had a fort at the river of Pentagöet where the Chevalier de Grandfontaine has commanded, and from which it is now nearly 20 years [since] the English drove him away. The Sieur de St. Castin, who was his Lieutenant escaped from their hands and since that time has his customary residence there, refusing always to recognize the English although he has been many times summoned with threats to do it, preserving thus the possession to France. *   *   *   *   *

The only man who could give any explanation in regard to this business is the Sieur de St. Castin. [In regard to the limits of the English occupation.]

* * * * * * *

I have induced the Sieur de St. Castin to live a more regular life. He has quitted his traffic with the English, his debauchery with the savages, he is married, and has promised me to labor to make a settlement in this country; and to that end he ought to demand a concession from M. de Denonville to whom he has gone, by his order, on account of the War with the Iroquois. He has rendered me an account of the affairs of the Savages in his country. There are two different races between the river of Pentagöet and the Kennebec; the Canibas, in small number, are in the region of Pentagöet, and the Abenakis, much more numerous, towards Kennebec. They are quite devoted to the French and hate the English. But whereas nothing is done for them, and as, on the contrary, the English make them presents and provide them lavishly with those things which they need, this will cause in the end that they will gain them over and will, in the course of time, be benefitted by them against the French. They appear quite inclined to prayer and to receive instruction in religion; but some expense is necessary for that.

I have driven off the English from the traffic that they were carrying on there and have sent back three or four small vessels, which were carrying goods there. This has a little displeased the inhabitants who were obtaining relief; but they will easily be comforted if the company continues to carry the same relief to them as it has done before.

["French Documents," Vol. 3, p. 317.]

23.

Memoir of the Colony at Acadia.

(Date not given.)

The parties concerned in the said company, pray very humbly for the favor of giving orders to the officers of the Admiralty of Rochelle, to cause to be returned to them a fly-boat of about twenty-two tons, which the English pirates who plundered the colony of Chedabouctou, gave to the crew of their ship, that they may return to France.

The said fly-boat belonging to the Sieur de St. Castin, having been taken by the pirates, in returning from Quebec, on the way to Port Royal. The said pirates gave a long-boat belonging to the said company, to the ship's crew of the fly-boat to bring them to Port Royal. Meanwhile a man named Gitton, of Rochelle, pretending to act for the said Sieur de St. Castin, has arrested the said fly-boat. It was proved by the *proces verbal* of the trial of said crew, that the said long-boat of the company, had been given to the ship's crew of the fly-boat; moreover, the Sieur de St. Castin had made amends, and that the said company suffer a loss of about one hundred and fifty livres, by the depredations of said pirates, who have carried away about sixty of their engaged men.

["French Documents," vol. 3, p 325.]

24.

Letter from the Marquis de Denonville to the Minister.

QUEBEC, October 30, 1688.

*   *   *   The first of this month two messengers from Monsieur Andros, Governor of New England, arrived, who were the bearers of letters to me, of which I send you a copy, together with my reply.

It is very much to the purpose, My Lord, that you see them, for by them, you perceive that the spirit and the sentiments of Dongan, have passed into the heart of Monsieur Andros, who may have less passion and be less moved, but who will be at least opposed to us as much and may be more dangerous, with his flexibility and mildness, than the other with his passion and violence.

What he has caused to be done at Pentagöet, pillaging the house of St. Castin, because he was not willing to acknowledge that he was a dependent of his; what he has just done to the Iroquois, pretending that they are under his government; the hinderances in the way of coming to find me, [all these things] are proofs that neither he nor the other English Governors, any more than all the people, will ever forbear from doing to this colony, whatever evil they can do.

There is certainly room for believing that the inhabitants of Boston, have a great part in the pillage, which has been done in Campseaux, and at Chedabouctou, whatever disavowal of it the Governor and the inhabitants may make.

["French Documents," vol. 3, p. 335.]

25.

Remarks concerning Acadia, by Monsieur Pasquine.

VERSAILLES, December 14, 1688.

If, my Lord, you are willing to give some time after my return from Acadia, in addition to that which I have employed, without cessation and without intermission, in order to have the honor of sending to you the map, plans and estimates which concern this colony, before my departure for Cayenne, I will use it, to give a full account of the observations which I have made there, not only of the boundaries, but also of that which concerns the firm establishment of that new colony ; and I hope to have the honor of an audience about certain things, which I cannot now write. But for the present, I will take the liberty of representing the importance of preventing the peace of the Iroquois with our Kennebec savages, which is only being brought about by the solicitation of the English. Last spring the Iroquois sent a Commission to the Kennebecs of the Hamourahiganiaques, allies and friends of the Kennebecs, accompanied by some Sonconaquin people, savages, from New York. They took for a present a necklace of porcelain, and from the doubt they had of not being favorably heard, these deputies did not go as far as Pentagöet. They descended to the river Amirganganeque —6 or 7 leagues further west than that of Kennebec.

A short time after, those near the river Amirganganeque wished to carry this present to the eastern coast, namely, towards St. George and Pentagöet. But the chiefs of the Kennebecs disapproving strongly the advances they had made, [and] not approving what they had done, caused them to be told that they were not willing. Among others, the Sagamore Madockawando, their General in war, who accompanied me, appeared very unwilling. He is a good Frenchman,—a brave, upright man, and of acute and subtle understanding, whom Monsieur Andros, Governor-general of New England, treats with great caution, searching for him when they went to Pentagöet, to pillage the abode of the Sieur de St. Castin, and takes the trouble himself of going to see him, carrying him a present, as he says, of

14 blue blankets,
12 shirts,
3 rolls [of cloth,]
2 barrels of wine—which he received
—although he does not esteem or love him, the Kennebecs being naturally the sworn enemies of the English.

The Iroquois will come in September, to conclude this peace ; it is very important for the quiet of our settlement in Canada, but still more particularly for that of Acadia, that this peace should not be made, or should be broken, if it should be made—this is not difficult to manage.

My time being exceedingly limited, I will have the · honor to tell my lord in a few words, and in general, that the principal establishment upon the coast of Acadia should not be made at Port Royal, [it being] too much out of the way, and of too difficult access, on account of the variable-ness of the winds which it is necessary to have to get there, and [it being] out of the way of all commerce. The finest and best place on the coast is the Port Rasoir.

Upon my return from Cayenne, if my lord directs me, I will present to him an account of everything concerning this colony, and with so much the more ease as I hope he will do me the kindness to give me a private room in the building which he will pass over to me in Cayenne, where I shall be able to work.

[" French Documents."]

26.

Census of Pentagöet—1689.
Priest, 1.
Married Men, 1.
Boys under 15 years of age, 1.
Married Women, 1.
[" French Documents," Vol. 3, p. 379.]

27.

Report of M. de Monseignat to the Minister.
QUEBEC, 10th September, 1691.
MY LORD.   *   *   *   *

M. le Comte has recently received some letters from the

Sieur de St. Castin. He dispatches a canoe to him in order to send him two letters that the Governor at Boston, and the Sieur de Nelson had written him. They were quite sincere and aimed to engage him to return the prisoners which were in the hands of the Abenakis and other Savages. They would make him remember the obligations that their colony had for some time been under to him and they implored him to continue the same good will in spite of the inevitable war in which the French and English would engage. He answered them somewhat in the same style, and that if they wished to recover theirs [i. e. the prisoners of the Abenakis,] it would in the first place be necessary that they should surrender the Chevalier d'Eau who, against the law of nations, being sent by him, had been taken by the Iroquois, those who had accompanied him burned, and was still retained at Manath; that it was no more according to law to break the terms of surrender agreed upon [with] the Sieur de Menneval, Governor of Port Royal, and his garrison, who were still for the most part prisoners; that when they had given satisfaction for these infractions of the laws of honorable warfare, they would think of a general exchange of the prisoners, who might be in the hands of each nation or of the Savage allies.

For news, the Sieur de St. Castin tells him that New England was in an extremely low condition; that they had lost many islands; that there was a great disunion at Manath between the English and Dutch, since the death of their Governor, and that they were having a kind of civil war; that all these conferences in regard to an exchange of prisoners was only to induce our savages to peace, and that he would oppose it with all his strength.

[" French Documents," Vol. 4, page 113. et seq.]

28.

Summary of a memoir upon the affairs of Canada, Acadia, and Newfoundland.

PARIS, 17th February, 1692.

From the war with the Iroquois, Flemish and Bostonians, Phipps has gone to seek assistance in old England. There is some news from the Sieur de St. Castin about the French soldiers who are in prison at Boston. The Abenakis struck several blows last Autumn. ["French Documents," Vol. 4, p. 130.]

29.

Memoir upon the Abduction of the Sieur de St. Castin— 1692.

The men called James Peter Pau and St. Aubin, inhabitants of the Country of Acadia, having been forcibly carried off by the English, with their families, and carried to Boston, the Governor of New England selected them, with two French deserters from the army, to go to carry off by force the Sieur de St. Castin, detaining their wives and children.

These two inhabitants have disclosed the purpose for which they were sent and have given up the two deserters. Upon this condition of things the Sieur de Villebon, commanding at Acadia, and the Sieurs Desgoutins and Bonnaventure, thought it necessary on account of this service to give 554 livres to these two inhabitants, destitute of everything, and to give them the means of recovering their wives and children from the hands of the English, in consideration of their fidelity.

["French Documents," Vol. 4, p. 168.]

30.

Report of M. de Champigny.

QUEBEC, November 4, 1693.

   *   *   *   *   *   *

*   * This intelligence confirming that which had come through the French, who had attempted the abduction or the murder of the Sieur St. Castin, at Acadia, obliged Messrs. de Frontenac, and de Champigny, to hasten the fortifications of Quebec, and of Montreal, in order not to be surprised, and to warn the savages of Acadia to hold themselves in readiness to come to the relief of Quebec—upon the first news they should have of the departure of the fleet.   *   *   *   *

["French Documents," Vol. 4, p. 245.]

31.

Account of what has transpired in Canada—1696.

* * * * * * *

There was a project for making an exchange of prisoners, of which the Sieur de St. Castin would take the sole charge in the name of Monsieur, the Count Frontenac. They could not choose a more zealous agent, or a more intelligent one.

["French Documents," Vol. 4, p. 409.]

32.

Synopsis of a letter from M. de Villebon, to the Minister.

He informs us by his letter of the fourth of October, 1698, that the English having, during the early part of that same year, carried on the traffic in all the French abodes, they had taken the beaver at from 3. to 3.10 livres per pound—English weight—that is to say, fourteen ounces to the pound, which had compelled him, in order not to offend the inhabitants, to pay them fifty-five sous per pound, for winter beaver.

That the English will always run the risk of making trade and commerce in Acadia, and especially at Pentagöet, where the French who are there make a rendezvous ; the man named Caldin [or Alden?]* having been at Pentagöet about the 15th of August last, where he had traded much in furs, and had given goods to a son-in-law of the Sieur de St. Castin, and to three Frenchmen who were at Pentagöet.

In order to destroy this traffic, M. de Villebon proposes to compel them to establish themselves at Pessemoncadi, where the land and the fishing is good, and where the English will not trust the Savages.

That he has implored M. de Chambault, missionary priest at Pentagöet, to drive off the English from the neighborhood of Pentagöet, when they shall come there, but that he believes he has followed his own self-interest, and that it has just been told him that he will die, unless he shall be able to assure it.

That John Mathew said Le Page, being at Boston when peace was announced last winter, had joined with an

*It is difficult to tell from the manuscript whether the word is Caldin or Alden.

Englishman, in order to carry on trade in Acadia, where they arrived at Port Royal without letting him know. The Sieur le Borgne and the Sieur de Pleine, his brother-in-law had begun to assume the powers of Lord and of Governor, having made the master of the English vessel pay 50 livres for permission to sell and to land his goods ; this they have continued to do to two others who have come here. That the Sieur John Mathew being joined with Joseph Guyon, they have left with the English, to go to Pessemoncadi, where they have traded with the Savages along the coast, as far as Majaja.

That they have given the Savages English brandy, which has caused a terrible riot.

That having written to Sieur de Thury to engage the Savages to make a party early against the English, Ville-bon having no news of peace, he has sent his letter to him by a Savage, who, having been met by Matthew and Guyon, they took the letter from him, and showing the seal to the Savages, persuaded them that the English were trading by his order.

He complains that the priests continue their trade, and that the one at Pentagöet had done so more openly than those who had preceded him.

That for the settlement they desired to make upon the eastern coast, it is necessary to fortify Pentagöet as an important post, and if they made two forts upon this coast, it was important that one should be at Pentagöet.

That the English in Boston very much desired to have the coal trade, and that they had written to him urgently, but that this will go for little, because Boston would consume no more of it than four vessels would carry, with what vessels from England bring them as ballast.

[" French Documents," Vol. 4, p. 563.]

33.

Synopsis of a letter from M. de Bonnaventure to the Minister.

(His vessel, l'Envieux, arrived at Rochelle, October 9th, 1698.)

He said that the inhabitants of Pentagöet did not wish to deliver their furs, on account of the facility they had for trading with the English, as they have since done, there having arrived there a vessel which neither the Sieur de St. Castin, nor the inhabitants have been willing to conduct to the river St. George, nor to show them the fine forests, saying that they did not know them, not·even in Pentagöet, where there are some very fine oak groves, looking upon themselves as the proprietors of Pentagöet, trading only, and not cultivating a single garden.

That an English ketch had been with the man called Petit, to Mouscoudabouct, to take there an Englishman who belonged there; the savages having told him that the English had traded at the Cape St. Zambre.

["French Documents," Vol. 4, p. 565.]

34.

Summary of a letter of the Sieur de Villieu, to the Minister.

20th OCTOBER, 1700.

He has sent to the Governor of New England, to inquire after the new converted French, who had fled from Chibouctou, where they had been settled by the company of the Pesche Sedentaire, [permanent fisheries] and who had taken away the goods of this Company.

Mousieur the Count Bellamont, happening to be away upon the arrival of his messenger, the Governor at Boston, had said to him for his complete answer, that he ought to know that thieves would find protection in a foreign kingdom.

He has permitted one called Basset, a Frenchman, married at Boston, to go there in search of his wife, in accordance with the instruction that His Majesty has given him. He has charged him to inform the people of that place who are the fishermen of Molue, [near by] the coast of Acadia, that His Majesty is willing to permit it to them if they take a passport of the Governor of Acadia, *viséed* by the Sieur de Goutins, secretary of the King, on the payment of a certain fee, in proportion to the size of the vessels, upon condition of receiving some French upon their ship,—but he doubts whether they will accept this last condition, and he believes that it will be more suitable to take, in the beginning, some English seamen upon the French vessels,

in order to render our people capable of carrying on this
fishing.

He complains of the trade that the Sieur de St. Castin,
a gentleman settled at Pentagöet, which is the land nearest to the English, has had with the English from Boston,
and the small hamlets upon the coast, to whom he had carried furs, and had carried back in payment English goods,
which hindered the sale of the French.   The said Sieur de
St. Castin, and the Missionary at Pentagöet, have absolute
control over the savages of this country, who have refused
this year the presents of His Majesty, that the late Sieur de
Villebon had charged him to carry to them, not having
found them sufficiently great.

The said Sieur de Villebon had charged him to draw a
map of the river St. George, before going to Pentagöet.
He has drawn it as accurately as he could, and has sent a
copy.   He besought him to concede to him the office of the
said Sieur de Villebon.   He represents that he serves His
Majesty since 1674, and that he has served in Flanders, in
Germany, and in Catalonia, and that having been taken by
the English, during the last war, he had acquired much
familiarity with them.

Note by the Minister.

The missionary of Pentagöet has written that it is not
out of contempt that the savages have refused the presents,
but it was because the said Sieur de Villieu, wished at the
same time to sell them brandy, which they did not wish
to purchase, foreseeing the excess into which they fall when
they are intoxicated.

During the war, the King relied upon the annual sum of
four thousand livres, to be spent in purchasing ammunition—reduced after the peace to four hundred and fifty
livres, to make presents to the chiefs alone.

If the war was renewed it would be necessary to sustain
this colony against the English—upon whom they have
waged a sanguinary war, which has obliged them to be continually upon the defensive.

(Written to St. Castin.)

["French Documents," Vol. 5, p. 23.]

35.

Abridgment of a Letter of Monsieur de Brouillau to the Minister.

PORT ROYAL, 30 October, 1701.

Having arrived at Port Royal he caused the inhabitants to assemble in order to propose to them that they should make efforts to protect themselves from the insults of the English. He found them at first opposed to this opinion— believing that it was a bondage which he wished to impose upon them, having told him very freely that they would not assist if it were for an alliance—saying arrogantly that they would prefer being with the English ; but he found means of bringing them back, and as soon as they consented to what he desired, he went, without waste of time, to the river St. John, the fort of which appeared very odious to him ; and with the aid of the equipage of the fleet of the Gironde, which Sieur de Maurville gave him he razed the fortifications to the dust. He put on board this fleet all that could serve for the construction of a new fort at Port Royal, where he carried it all.

All the Religious Superiors who are missionaries to Acadia obtained a salary which the King gives them, so that these poor missionaries finding themselves without it, they were not obliged to abandon them. He begs that he may order those things which Sieur Monte delivered to them, to be sent to them by the King's vessels.

The missionary of the Malassites prays them to make it convenient for him to make his abode at Passamaquoddy, which is much more accessible to Port Royal than the place where he actually resides. This missionary hopes to persuade these savages to cultivate the soil at this place, and to devote themselves to fishing, whereby they would be less miserable.

The Sieur Gaulin, who has charge of the mission of Pentagöct, appears very pious, and strongly desirous of keeping the savages in the interests of France. The Sieur Guay, late missionary at Pentagöet, returned to Rochefort, pursuant to the orders which he had received. He appears to be a good priest, and an upright man.

It is certain that Father Bigot, who has charge of the

mission at Kennebec, has not the same opinions, not having forbidden the savages to converse with the English, who have gone so far as to receive presents and promises of making peace with them, which would have been done, but that the English had wished to exact from them that they should have no more communication with the French, which had prevented the savages from deciding; but no one knows whether they had done it since.

The Sieur de St. Castin, whom they accuse of carrying on trade with the English, returns to France, to render an account of his conduct. It is certain that he has kept in the interests of France the savages of the frontier where he dwells; and as these savages have confidence in him, he is very capable of keeping them there. The Sieur de St. Castin would request a grant upon the river de la Point au Hestre; he believes that it is proper to concede it to him, having a design to establish a fishery in Molue, and to remove the savages there.

It appears to him of consequence to continue to give presents to the savages of the frontier, to hinder them from taking vengeance upon the party of English who have established within their reach store-houses, where they would be able to carry the goods that were necessary to them, and this expense is afterwards levelled upon all the English colony.

He has not believed it necessary, this year to make any attempt upon the English, who have made a fishery upon the coast of Acadia, not being in a condition to sustain what ought to be done, but as it appears to him that the English would not abstain from this fishery, according to the answer which the delegate from Boston had made to a letter which he had written to my Lord Bellamont, he is disposed to take some of their boats next summer.

The officer, whom he had dispatched to Boston to carry this letter, told him that they had made new fortifications at the entrance of that Port, that he saw there three vessels of war, and that he believed from the report that they expected two others, with the Governor-General for New England, and for New York.

Monsieur l'Evesque says the Jesuits have left.

["French Documents," Vol. 5, p. 103, et seq.]

36.

Substance of a letter from the Sieur de St. Castin.

LA ROCHELLE, 21 November, 1701.

He has gone to France, to justify his conduct as regards the complaints that have been made that he traded with the English.

He grants that residing upon the frontier of the colony, where no Frenchman has carried thus far any goods, and not having been permitted to buy at Quebec or in New-foundland, he has been obliged to take them from the English for his most urgent wants, and that he has no other traffic with them than this.

["French Documents," Vol. 5, p. 109.]

37.

Memoranda of things necessary to have at Pescadoué, for the month of October—by the Sieur de St. Castin.

[Not dated.]

6,000 lbs. of powder.
8,000 musket-balls.
30,000 selected gunflints.
3,000 firewads (firebours.)
1,000 aleves à point carrée.
1,000 clasp-knives.
1,000 " aulnes melis" for sails, tents, and sacks.
1,000 axes.
  30 lbs. of thread.
  15 " " measured thread.
  10 lines.
125 barrels of bacon of 200 lbs.
5,000 "quentos" of sea-biscuit.
4,000 lbs. of lead, for fowlers.
1,000 lbs. of Brazillian tobacco.
3,000 "quentos" of meal.
  700 bushels of peas.
  10 barrels of brandy.
  100 bushels of salt.

["French Documents," Vol. 5, p. 147.]

37

38.

Substance of a Letter from M. de Subercase.

PORT ROYAL, October 25, 1706.

*   *   *   *   *   ´ *

It is very important always to have a man of character amongst the savages, to watch over their conduct in order to give him information of it.   The son of the Sieur de St. Castin, is very suitable for that, because his mother is of their nation, and besides he is a very wise and very capable young gentleman.   He proposes to grant him a commission of Second Lieutenant, in the Navy, with the salary, and he is certain that no one in the colony will better earn his money than he.   *   *   *   *

["French Documents," Vol. 5, p. 307.]

39.

Summary of a Letter from M. de Subercase to the Minister.

AT PORT ROYAL, IN ACADIA, July 26, 1707.

*   *   *   *   *   *   *

The Sieur de St. Castin when he had put [himself, or some one] at the head of the inhabitants there had perfectly well performed his duty.

The savage Canibas, and those of Pentagöet, tired of waiting for the assistance of the French, from Acadia, have taken the road to New York, where they have made a treaty.   This has sent them back with the Iroquois, so that it is to be feared that it engages them all to wage war against the French.   He sees no other way of warding off this blow, than to furnish these first savages with goods, at the same rate, almost, at which the English give them to them, and he designs to carry to Pentagöet, and to Kennebec, some provisions and 4 or 500 of goods, in order to give them to them at a fixed price.

["French Documents," Vol. 5, p. 343.]

40.

Transcript from the Register of the Parish of St. Jean Baptiste, at Port Royal.

" 31, Oct. 1707.   Gaulin, Missionary priest of the Seminary of Quebec, being at Port Royal, married Anselm de

St. Castin, baron de St. Castin, son of Sieur Jean Vincent, baron de St. Castin, and of Dame Mathilde, of the parish of the 'Sainte famille,' at Pentagöet, and damoiselle Charlotte l'Amours, daughter of St. Louis d'Amours, ensign of a company at Port Royal, etc.

"4, Dec. 1707. Married le Sieur Alexander le Borgne, de Belleisle, (etc.) to the damoiselle Anastasie de St. Castin, fille du Sieur Vincent, ecuyer, baron de St. Castin et de dame Mathilde.

"4, Dec. 1707. Philip de Ponbomcou is married to Therese de St. Castin, daughter of the Baron and of Dame Marie Pidianiskge."

[From "Centennial Celebration at Bangor" p. 24, Note.]

41.

Letter of L'Auverjat to Father de La Chasse.

PANOUAMSKE*, July 8, 1728.

Very dear Brother:

The insolence of the Messrs. de St. Castin has come to be so excessive that they no longer set bounds to it, in their conduct to me, or before God.

The elder, who does not care to marry, and not satisfied with spreading corruption through the whole village, in addition to that, now makes a business of selling brandy, openly, in company with his nephew, the son of Monsieur de Belle Isle. They have been the means of one man being drowned, already, on account of it, and are like to be the destruction of many others. The younger of the Messrs. de St. Castin never comes into the village, without getting drunk in public, and putting the whole village in an uproar.

Both of them, prompted by the supplies they receive, pretend to be on my side, and in the interests of the King; but behind my back, they do not cease to work against me, and to oppose every enterprise I undertake in the service of God and the King.

Excessively puffed up with the commission and with the salary they have obtained from the King, through M. de Vaudreuil, the earth is not good enough for them to stand upon. They believe that they have a right, through this commission, to rule, absolutely, and to seize and dis-

*Supposed to be Oldtown.

pose of everything at their will; and if any one thinks of opposing them, they threaten him with nothing less than death or massacre.

They are going to Canada; and they will not fail to boast of their services, and to seem very much attached to the interests of the colony. But here is what I believe before God.

That, before the savages had begun the war against the English, they did everything in the world they could, to prevent their undertaking it—and this in spite of all the exhortations I made to the savages, on the part of M. de Vaudreuil, and notwithstanding all that M. de Vaudreuil himself had said to them.

That, after I had, in spite of them, engaged the savages to determine upon a war against the English, they broke up the first expedition I had formed, and prevented it from starting.

That, after I had organized another war-party, and had sent it off, they stopped it on the way, and would have absolutely prevented the war from breaking out, if I had not gone down to the sea-shore and persuaded my people to proceed with it.

That, not having been able to prevent the attacks upon the English, they pretended to be neutral (except that they made money out of the booty taken from the English, and that for two whole years) on the pretext that they were Frenchmen and not natives.

That, when they could no longer abstain from deciding for one side or the other—M. de Vaudreuil having given them to understand, particularly, that their qualities as Frenchmen did not take from them their rights and, consequently, their duties, as savages—the younger, actually and in earnest, did go on an expedition, and signalized himself; but the elder contented himself with showing himself once only, and, although he received a hundred affronts from the English, by whom he was taken twice, by treachery, and robbed, yet far from dreaming of taking revenge on them, he has sought their protection and asked favors of them.

That, towards the end of the war, when I went to Canada, by your orders—the English having sent a hostage here, during my absence, to propose peace—the Messrs. de St. Castin were the first to suggest that a favorable answer should be made to the English, and disbanded an expedition that had just set out, by my orders, to make reprisals on the English, who had treacherously sent an expedition against us, the previous winter, while at another point they assured us against peace.*

That, since that time, these same gentlemen have not ceased to urge the savages to make peace with the English, and to accept their propositions, without caring what the French might think about it.

All this I am positively certain about, and am ready to make oath to, and this, added to all the other irregularities that these gentlemen are guilty of, such as selling at false weight and at false measure, cheating people so out of one-quarter to one-third of all they buy, is sufficient reason that their pay should be stopped, and that what they have not drawn of their salary should be confiscated. [From Historical Magazine, Vol. 2d, 3d Ser. No. 3, p. 126 et seq.]

*Mr. Prentiss thinks this to have been the Heath Expedition.

II.

DOCUMENTS RELATING TO THE REVOLU-
TIONARY PERIOD.

1.

*Calef's Journal of the Siege.**

The Siege of Penobscot by the Rebels;
containing a
Journal of the proceedings of his Majesty's Forces detached from the 74th and 82d Regiments, consisting of
about 700 Rank and File, under the Command of Brigadier-
General Francis McLean,
and of
Three of his Majesty's Sloops of War, of 16 guns each,
under the Command of Captain Henry Mowatt, Senior
Officer—
when besieged by
Three Thousand Three hundred (Rebel) Land Forces,
under the Command of Brigadier General Solomon Lovell,
and
Seventeen Rebel Ships and Vessels of War under the Command of G. Saltonstall, Commodore.
To which is annexed
A Proclamation issued June 15, 1779, by General McLean
and Captain Barclay, to the Inhabitants;
Also
Brigadier General Lovell's Proclamation to the Inhabitants; and his Letter to Commodore Saltonstall found on
board the Rebel Ship Hunter;
Together with
the Names, Force, and Commanders of the Rebel Ships
destroyed in Penobscot Bay and River, August 14 and
15th, 1779,
With
A Chart of the Peninsula of Majabigwaduce, and of Penobscot River,

*From a Volume belonging to Harvard College Library. The spelling and
punctuation are the same as in the original edition.

well bastion of which was not yet begun, nor the seamen's* quite finished; but, on the appearance of the Enemy, the works were put in a more defensible state; some cannon were mounted, and the little army was in garrison early the next morning. Guard-boats, during the night, watched the motions of the Enemy, who were discovered to have come to an anchor about three or four leagues off, in the narrows of Penobscot.

July 25. At 10 A. M., a brig appeared at some distance from the harbour's mouth, and after reconnoitring the situation of the men of war, stood back into the fleet. At noon, the Enemy's fleet, consisting of thirty-seven sail of ships, brigs, and transports, arrived in the bay of the harbour. The transports proceeded about half a mile up Penobscot river and came to anchor, while the armed ships and brigs, stood off and on, and a boat from each ship repaired on board their flag-ship, which had thrown out a signal for that purpose. At 3 P. M., nine ships, forming into three divisions, stood towards the King's ships, and, as they advanced in the line, hove to and engaged. A very brisk cannonade continued four glasses, when the Enemy bore up, and came to an anchor in the bay without. The King's ships suffered only in their rigging. The fire of the Enemy was random and irregular; and their manœuvres, as to backing and filling, bespoke confusion, particularly in the first division, which scarcely got from the line of fire when the second began to engage. The second and third divisions appeared to have but one object in view, that of cutting the springs of the men of war, to swing them from the bearings of their broadsides, and thereby to afford an entrance into the harbour. During the cannonade with the shipping, the Enemy made an attempt to land their troops on Bagwaduce, but were repulsed with some loss. On the retreat of the Enemy's troops and ships, the garrison manned their works, and gave three cheers to the men of war, which were returned; and soon after, the general and field officers went down to the beach, and also gave three cheers, which were returned from the ships. Guard-boats, and ship's companies, during the night, lay at their quarters.

July 26. At 10 A. M., the Enemy's ships got under

*So called from being the work of the Seamen only.

weigh, and, forming their divisions as yesterday, stood in
and engaged the King's ships four glasses and a half.
The damages sustained this day, also, were chiefly in the
rigging at the extreme ends of the ships ; and the fire of the
Enemy appears again to be directed to the moorings ;
which attempt not proving successful, they bore up and
anchored without. The Enemy again attempted to land
their troops, but were driven back with some little loss.
At 6 P. M., the Enemy having stationed two brigs of fourteen guns and one sloop of twelve, on the east side of
Nautilus island, landed 200 men and dislodging a party of
twenty marines, took possession of four 4-pounders (two
not mounted,) and a small quantity of ammunition. At 9
P. M., it being found that the Enemy were very busy at
work, and that they had landed some heavy artillery, which
they were getting up to the heights of the island, and
against which the men of war could not act in their present
station, it was judged expedient to move them further up
the river. This was accordingly done, and the line formed
as before; the transports moved up at the same time, and
anchored with the men of war. Guard-boats, and the
ship's companies, as usual, lying at their quarters.

July 27. Pretty quiet all this day. A few shots from
some ships of the Enemy were aimed at the small battery
on Majabigwaduce point; which were returned with a
degree of success, one ship having been driven from her
station. Observed the Enemy very busy in erecting their
battery on Nautilus Island. The garrison being much in
want of cannon, some guns from the transports, and from
the off-side of the men of war, were landed, and, being
dragged by the seamen up to the fort, were disposed of for
its use. At 3 P. M., a boat, passing from the Enemy's ships
to Nautilus island, was sunk by a random shot from the
fort. At 11 P. M., the guard boats from the King's ships
fell in and exchanged a few shot with the Enemy's.

July 28. At 3 A. M., under cover of their ship's fire,
the Enemy made good their landing on Majabigwaduce,
and, from their great superiority of numbers, obliged the
King's troops to retreat to the garrison. The Enemy's
right pressed hard, and in force, upon the left of the King's
troops, and attempted to cut off a party of men at the
small battery; but the judgement and experience of a
brave officer (Lieut. Caffrae, of the 82d,) counteracted
their designs; and a retreat was effected with all the order

and regularity necessary on such occasions. An attempt was made to demolish the guns; but the Enemy pushed their force to this ground so rapidly as not to suffer it. The position of this battery afforded their ships a nearer station, on which they immediately seized. At 6 A. M., the Enemy opened their battery of 18 and 12-pounders from Nautilus island, and kept up the whole day a brisk and well-directed fire against the men of war. The King's ships cannonaded the battery for two glasses, and killed some men at it; but their light metal (6-pounders) was found to be of little service, in comparison to the damage they sustained from such heavy metal brought against them. At 10 A. M., the *Warren*, of 32 guns, the Commodore's ship, which as yet had not been in action, got under weigh, and, with three more ships, showed an appearance of entering the harbour, but hauled by the wind at a long shot distance. A brisk fire was kept up for half an hour, when the Enemy bore up, and came to anchor again without. The *Warren* suffered considerably; her mainmast shot through in two places, the gammoning of her bowsprit cut to pieces, and her fore-stay shot away. Their confusion appeared to be great, and very nearly occasioned her getting on shore; so that they were obliged to let go an anchor, and drop into the inlet between Majabigwaduce head and the point, where the ship lay this and the next day, repairing her damages. The battery on the island still keeping up a heavy fire, and the ships' crews being exposed without the least benefit to the service, Captain Mowat thought proper to move further up the harbour, which was done in the night, and the line formed again; he being firmly resolved to dispute the harbour to the last extremity, as on that entirely depended the safety of the garrison, whose communication with the men of war was of the utmost importance. The dispositions on shore and on the water co-operating, and perfectly supporting each other, foiled the Enemy in their purposes; their troops were yet confined to a spot they could not move from; and, while the harbour was secure, their intention of making approaches, and investing the fort on all sides, could by no means be put in execution. The present station of the men of war being such as rendered it impossible for the Enemy's ships to act but at particular periods, the marines [whose service, in their particular line of duty, was not immediately required on board] were ordered on shore to garrison duty, holding themselves in readiness to embark at a moment's notice, which with ease they could have effected in ten or fifteen minutes. Guard-boats as usual during the night.

July 29. At 6 A. M., the Enemy's ships weighed, and, altering their positions, came to an anchor again. The state of the fortress requiring more cannon, some remaining off-side guns were landed from the men of war, and dragged by the seamen up to the fortress, for its use and that of the batteries; and though the task, to be performed up a steep hill, over rocks and innumerable stumps of fallen trees, was laborious, yet their cheerfulness and zeal for the service, surmounted every difficulty. P. M.—The Enemy opened their batteries on the heights of Majabigwaduce, and kept up a warm and incessant fire against the fortress. The commanding ground of the Enemy's works, and the short distance from the fortress, gave them some advantages with their grape, as well as round shot, which considerably damaged the store-house in the garrison.

Six pieces of cannon at the half-moon battery, near Bank's house, and which belonged to the fortress, being now found necessary for its particular defence, were moved up to it, and replaced with some ship's guns, under the direction of the gunner of the *Albany*, with a party of seamen. Captain Mowat having obtained intelligence, that the Enemy, in despair of reducing the King's ships by means of their own, or of getting possession of the harbour, had come to the resolution of joining their whole force in troops, marines, and seamen, to storm the fortress the next morning at daybreak, he judged it expedient to reinforce the garrison with what seamen could be conveniently spared; and, for this purpose, at the close of the evening, 140 men, under the command of Lieut. Brooke, were sent into garrison: part of these were immediately detached to reinforce the troops on the outline piquets, others manned the facing of their own bastion, while the remainder were busily employed in raising cavaliers in the fort. In all these operations, a brotherly affection appeared to unite the forces, both by sea and land, and to direct their views all to one point, much to their credit, and to the honour and benefit of the service. During the night the Enemy threw a number of shells into the fortress. At 10 P. M., a few shot between the Enemy's guard-boats and those from the King's ships.

July 30. The Enemy's ships preserve their disposition

of yesterday. A brisk cannonade the whole day, between the fortress and the Enemy's batteries on the height; and a number of shells thrown on both sides. The store-houses being apprehended to be in danger, some seamen were ordered to move the provisions out of the fortress into the ditch in its rear; as likewise a quantity at another store-house. Guard-boats as usual.

July 31. At 2 A. M., the seamen and marines of the Enemy's fleet, landed to the westward of the half-moon battery, and, under cover of the night, attacked the piquet, and by heavy platoon firing, obliged them to retreat; but an alert reinforcement of fifty men who, were detached from the garrison, under the command of Lieut. Graham of the 82d regiment, to the support of the piquet, drove the Enemy back with some loss—in killed, wounded and taken, amounting in the whole, according to the best information, to about 100; the loss on the part of the King's forces, amounting to thirteen killed, wounded and missing, fell chiefly on the seamen and marines, who composed the piquet this night. Lieut. Graham unfortunately received a dangerous wound in this action.

August 1. A slack fire on all sides. At 4 P. M., the Enemy's fleet getting under weigh, and the wind and tide serving them to enter the harbour, the embodied seamen were immediately called on board their respective ships; but it afterwards appeared that the Enemy only weighed to form a closer line. Guard-boats as usual.

August 2. At 10 A. M., three of the Enemy's ships weighed, and came to anchor nearer the harbour's mouth. Some cannonading between the fortress and the Enemy's batteries on the height. The outer magazine of the fortress being too much exposed, as lying in front and between the two fires, the marines were charged with the duty of bringing it to the magazine in the fortress, which was performed without any loss. P. M. A flag of truce from the Enemy, to treat for the exchange of a lieutenant of their fleet, taken (wounded) at the half-moon battery, on the 31st ult.; but he had died of his wounds this morning. This day the Enemy posted some marksmen behind trees, within musket shot of the fortress, and killed and wounded some sentinels.

August 3. A slack fire the whole day. Perceived the Enemy busy in erecting a battery to the northward, on the main, above the King's ships. By a deserter from the Enemy's fleet, we learn, the force landed below the half-moon battery was 1000 seamen and marines, joined on their landing by 200 troops; that their intentions were, to storm the fortress in the rear, while the army from the heights made their attack in front; that it was not intended to storm the half-moon battery, but that they had mistaken their road, in endeavoring to get in the rear of the fortress, when they received the first fire of the piquet; which led them to suppose that their design had been discovered, and that they were ambushed. The army also, believing this to be the case, retreated to their ground. At 2 P. M., some seamen were sent to the fortress to assist in working the cannon, and another party for the defence of the Seamen's bastion, where a number of swivels from the men of war were planted, loaded with grape shot, as a precaution against any attempt of the Enemy to storm the works. By request of the General, a number of pikes were also brought from the King's ships to the fortress, and put in the hands of the seamen, to prevent the enemy from *boarding* their bastion. Guard-boats out as usual.

August 4. The Enemy's ships retain their former situation. A smart cannonading between the fortress and the batteries on the heights, and a great number of shells thrown on both sides. Some ship's buckets for the use of the garrison brought on shore, in case the fascines at the well bastion, or store-houses, might be fired by the Enemy's shells. At 9 A. M., the Enemy opened their new battery near Wescoat's house, on the main, to the northward of the shipping. A brisk fire was kept up the whole day, and the men of war suffered much in their rigging and hulls; being too far from the battery for the light metal of the ships to produce any effect, their companies were ordered below. P. M. Some skirmishing between the piquets, and trifling losses on both sides; on the Enemy's, some Indians were killed. During the day, several accidents happened by cannon shot in the fort: among others, the boatswain of the *Nautilus* was wounded by grape, and a seaman belonging to the *North* killed by an 18-pounder, at the guns they were stationed at in the fortress.

August 5. Cannonading the greatest part of the day between the fortress and the Enemy's batteries on the height, and from the north battery against the men of war, damaging their hulls and rigging. A. M. The remaining off-side guns from His Majesty's sloop *North* brought on shore, and mounted in the cavalier in the fortress. P. M. The garrison, being much in want of wads and match, was supplied from the men of war, as also with some six-pound shot, together with a quantity of twelve-pound shot, in which it is deficient. The north battery on the main having the commmand of the opposite shore on the peninsula of Majabagwaduce, where the Enemy, under its protection, might make lodgments in their approaches towards the heights opposite the men of war and within shot of the fortress, and might thereby destroy communication between them and the garrison; Captain Mowat judged it necessary to erect a work in order to preserve this communication; a square redoubt was therefore marked out, to be manned with fifty seamen, and to mount eight ship's guns *en barbette*. Guard-boats as usual during the night.

August 6. Slack fire between the fortress and batterles on the heights; and a few shot from the north battery against the men of war, cutting their rigging, and dismounting a six-pounder on board the *North*. At four A. M., seventy seamen from the different ships, under the direction of Lieut. Brooke, of the *North*, sent on shore to raise the Seamen's redoubt on the height. P. M. A quantity of musquet cartridges (of which the garrison was in want) brought on shore from the men of war. Guard-boats as usual. At 11, a few shot exchanged between the Guard-boats.

August 7. The Enemy's ships preserve their positions. At 9 A. M., three of their brigs got under weigh, and stood down the bay, supposed to be on the lookout. Some skirmishing between the piquets, with loss to the Enemy. Lieut. McNeil, of the 82d, and one private, wounded. Slack fire between the batteries and the fortress, and the north battery perfectly silent. At 4 P. M., discovered a boat crossing the southeast bay to Hainey's plantation, where the Enemy kept a piquet. Lieut. Congalton, of the *Nautilus*, chaces with the boats from the men of war, and took her; but her crew, with those of a whale boat, and a gondola for transporting cannon, got safe on shore, and joined the piquet. Capt. Farnham, of the *Nautilus*, with Lieut. Brooke and fifty seamen. joined by a party of soldiers from the garrison, landed and scoured the woods;

the Enemy fled immediately, and so effectually concealed
themselves as not to be discovered; some had left their
arms, ammunition and blankets, which were taken and
brought on board. Guard-boats as usual during the night.
By a deserter from the Enemy we learn that General
Lovell had sent out small parties from his army round the
country, and brought in a great number of loyal inhabitants, who were sent on board their fleet, and thrust down
the holds, heavily laden with irons, both on the hands and
feet; their milch cows, and other stock, killed for the
Enemy's use; all their moveables destroyed or plundered,
and their wives and children left destitute of every support
of life.

August 8. A constant cannonade the whole day between the fortress and the Enemy's battery on the heights;
and from the north battery against the men of war, but
returned only with a musquet. At 10 A. M., the Enemy
brought a field-piece to play from the main on the seamen
working at the redoubt; but the facing towards the
Enemy being the first raised, for the purpose of covering
the party, it was impossible to dislodge them; and a
covering party daily attending from the garrison, prevented a nearer approach on any other ground. This
evening the redoubt was finished, and, to the credit of the
seamen, met with the approbation of the General and
Engineers. Guard-boats as usual during the night.

August 9. Cannonading as usual. At 9 A. M., a new
battery on the left of the Enemy's lines, was opened
against the fortress, and its chief fire, as well as the shells,
directed against the northwest bastion, raised with fascines only. P. M.—Discovered the Enemy had moved
their piquet from Hainey's plantation and given up their
design of carrying on a work for two 18-pounders against
the men of war. Guard-boats as usual during the night.

August 10. The Enemy's ships in their former position. A slack fire on all sides; and nothing material.

August 11. A smart cannonading from all the batteries,
and some shot from the north battery well directed at the
men of war.

August 12. Slack fire on all sides, and no material operations the whole day: but at 9 P. M., a large body of seamen and marines, from the Enemy's fleet, landed below
Banks' house to the westward, and setting a fire to some

barns, houses, and a quantity of lumber, boards, &c., on the beach, retreated to their ships again.

August 13. Some skirmishing at daybreak, between the piquets, but no material loss on either side. At 1 P. M., came in some deserters from the Enemy's ships, who say, the boat chaced on shore at Hainey's plantation had in her the Commodore and some officers of their fleet, who, having escaped, returned to their ships, after lying two days and a night in the woods; that one of the officers (Capt. Ross of the Monmouth) had broke his leg in the woods; and that they were much disconcerted at the loss of the gondola, which was intended to carry over some 18-pounders to the battery on the plantation. Captain Mowat also (by his usual diligence) obtained information, that a degree of mutiny prevailed in the Enemy's fleet against their Commodore, who, notwithstanding the resolves of several councils of war, and the urgent solicitations of the General to make another attempt on the King's ships had hitherto declined it through fear of losing some ships; but that, in consequence of another council held this morning on board the *Warren*, it was determined to force the harbour next tide, and take or destroy the men of war; that five ships were destined for this service, one of which was the *Warren;* but that the *Putnam*, of twenty guns, was to lead; and that each ship was doubly manned with picked men. This information was confirmed at noon by five of their fleet getting under weigh, and coming to an anchor in a line, the *Putnam* being the headmost ship. The marines were now called on board their respective ships, the barricades strengthened, guns double-shotted, and every disposition made for the most vigorous defence. The *St. Helena* transport had been brought into the line, and fitted out with what guns could be procured, and the crews of the transports (now scuttled and laid on shore, to prevent them from falling into the Enemy's hands) turned on board to fight her, and the General had also advanced five pieces of cannon, under cover of an épaulement, to salute them as they came in. But at 5 P. M., the appearance of some strange sails in the offing, disconcerted the Enemy's plan; and the five ships, getting under weigh again, stood off and on the whole night. Guard-boats watching the motions of the Enemy's fleet; and the ships' companies standing at their quarters until daylight. This night had been fixed

39

upon to storm the north battery, with sixty seamen, under the command of Lieut. Brooke, supported by Lieut. Caffrae, of the 82d, with fifty soldiers ; but the Enemy's operations, and the appearance of the strange fleet, prevented the execution of it.

August 14. At daybreak this morning it was discovered that the Enemy had during the night, moved off their cannon, and quitting the heights of Majabigwaduce, silently embarked in small vessels. At 4 A. M., after firing a shot or two, they also evacuated Nautilus island; and leaving their cannon spiked and dismounted, got on board a brig lying to receive them, and made sail with the transports up the Penobscot river. The whole fleet got under weigh, and upon one of the brigs heaving in sight, off the harbour's mouth, with various signals abroad, they bore up with all sail after the transports. There remaining now no doubt but the strange fleet was the relief expected, the off-side guns of the *Albany*, *North*, and *Nautilus*, were got down from the fortress, and being taken on board, the three ships slipped their stern moorings, hove up their bower anchors, and working out of the harbour, joined in about the centre of the King's fleet, in pursuit of the flying Enemy, who were now crowding with every sail they could set. The *Hunter*, and *Hampden*, two of the Enemy's ships, of twenty guns each, attempted to escape through the passage of Long Island, but were cut off and taken; the former ran in shore, all standing, and was instantly deserted by her crew, who got safe on shore; and the *Raisonable*, Sir George Collier, being the sternmost ship in the fleet, took possession, and got her off, and came to anchor near her. The rest of His Majesty's ships continued in chace of the Enemy, until it grew so dark, as to render the narrow navigation exceedingly dangerous; and then were obliged to anchor for the night, while the Enemy, having good pilots, ran some miles further up the river. The *Defiance* brig, of fourteen guns, ran into an inlet, where she could not be pursued, and was set on fire by her crew. During the night the Enemy set fire to several ships and brigs, which blew up with vast explosions. In short, the harmony and good understanding that subsisted amongst the forces by sea, and by land, enabled them to effect almost prodigies, for so ardently did they vie with each other in the general service, that it may be truly said, not a single Officer, Sailor, or Soldier, was once seen to shrink from his duty, difficult and hazardous as it was. The flying scout of fifty men, commanded by Lieut. Caffrae, of the 82d, in particular, distinguished themselves to admiration, marching frequently almost round the peninsula, both by day and by night, and with drum and fife playing the tune called *Yankee*, which greatly dispirited the Enemy, and prevented their small parties from galling our men at their works. In one instance, they even drove back to their encampment, 300 of the Enemy, who had been sent to storm an out-work. The manœuvres of the Three Sloops of War, under the direction of Captain Mowat, were, moreover, such as enabled the King's forces to hold out a close siege of twenty-one days, against a fleet and army, of more than six times their number, and strength; insomuch that, on the first appearance of the reinforcement from New York, in the offing, the Enemy debarked their troops, and sailed with their whole fleet up Penobscot river, where they burnt their shipping, and from thence marched to their respective homes: and the loyal inhabitants, who were taken in the time of the siege, and were cruelly treated on board their ships, had their irons taken off, and were set at liberty.*

Thus did this little Garrison, with Three Sloops of War, by the unwearied exertions of Soldiers, and Seamen, whose bravery cannot be too much extolled, under the judicious conduct of Officers, whose zeal is hardly to be paralleled, succeed in an enterprise of great importance, against difficulties apparently insurmountable, under circumstances exceedingly critical, and in a manner strongly expressive of their faithful and spirited attachment to the interests of their King and Country.

*"To give them a cool airing, as the Enemy called it, once a day the irons were knocked off their feet, and they were put into a boat alongside the ship, where they remained about an hour, and had the filth of the ship poured upon their heads."

2.

A List of the Enemy's Ships, &c., taken and destroyed in Penobscot River.[1,2]

[By Calef.]

Names.	Commanders.	Guns.	No. of Men.	Metal.	
Ships.					
Warren,	Saltonstall,	32	250	18 & 12	Burnt.
Sally,	Holmes,	22	200	9 & 6	do
Putnam,	Waters,	20	130	9	do
Hector,	Cairns,	20	130	9	do
Revenge,	Hallett,	20	120	6	do
Monmouth,	Ross,	20	100	6	do
Hampden,	Salter,	20	130	9 & 6	Taken.
Hunter,	Brown,	20	130	6	do
Vengeance,	Thomas,	18	140	9 & 6	Burnt.
B ack Prince,	West,	18	100	6	do
Sky Rocket,	Burke,	16	120	6	do
Brigs.					
Hazard,	Williams,	18	100	6	do
Active,		16	100	6	do
Tyrannicide,	Cathcart,	14	90	6	do
Defiance,		14	90	6	do
Diligence,	Brown,	14	90	4	do
Pallas.	Johnstone,	14	80	4	do
Sloop.					
Providence,	Hacker,	12	50	6	do

1. Killed, wounded and taken—on the Enemy's side, ...474
   Killed, wounded and missing of His Majesty's Sea and Land forces, ..70
2. With 9 Sail of Transport vessels, ...taken.
   With 10 Sail of Transport and Ordnance Vessels, ...burnt.
                 Total, ...37

3.

PROCLAMATION

By Brigadier-General Francis McLean, and Andrew Barclay, Esq., commanding Detachments of His Majesty's Land and Naval Forces in the River Penobscot.

Whereas it is well known that there are in the several Colonies in North America, now in open rebellion, many persons who still retain a sense of their duty, and who are only deterred from an open profession of it by the fear of becoming objects of cruel treatment, which they had seen exercised on others, by persons who, having plunged their country into the horrors and distresses it now labors under, industriously seize every opportunity of gratifying their avaricious and wicked dispositions, by the wanton oppression of individuals :

And whereas it hath been represented, that the greater part of the inhabitants on the river Penobscot, and the several islands therein, are well affected to His Majesty's person, and the ancient constitution under which they formerly flourished, and from the restoration of which they can alone expect relief from the distressed situation they are now in :

Their Excellencies, the Commanders in Chief of His Majesty's naval and land forces in North America, taking the good dispositions of the inhabitants above mentioned (as represented to them) into their consideration, and desirous of encouraging and protecting the persons professing them, and securing them from any molestation on that account, have ordered here the forces under our respective commands for that purpose. We, therefore, in obedience to their directions, hereby invite, and earnestly request, the inhabitants on river Penobscot, and the islands therein in general, to be the first to return to that state of good order and government to which the whole must, in the end, submit, and openly to profess that loyalty and allegiance from which they have been led to swerve by arguments and apprehensions, of the falsehood of which they must long ago have been sensible, as well as of the views of those who promoted them.

We call on all those, also, in whom these principles have never been shaken, to embrace the present opportunity of manifesting them without dread or apprehension, as we hereby assure them of every protection in the power of the forces under our respective commands to bestow. And, to quiet the apprehensions of any persons who might be deterred from embracing this opportunity by the dread of being punished for any former acts of rebellion which they may have been led to commit, we, hereby, declare that we will extend our protection, and give every encouragement, to all persons of whatever denomination, without any retrospect to their former behavior, who shall, within eight days from the date hereof, take the oaths of allegiance and fidelity to His Majesty, before such persons as we shall appoint, either at the headquarters of His Majesty's troops at Majabigwaduce Neck, or at Fort Pownal; which oaths of allegiance and fidelity we require all persons whatever to come and take within the required time, and not, by neglecting to give such testimony of their loyalty, give room to look on them as desirous of continuing in an obstinate and unavailing rebellion, and subject themselves to the treatment such conduct deserves.

To all persons, who, by returning to their allegiance, shall merit it, we not only promise protection and encouragement, with the relief that shall be in our power to alleviate their present distresses; but we also declare that we will employ the forces under our command to punish all persons whatever who shall attempt in any manner to molest them, either in person or property, on account of their conduct or loyalty towards us; and if forced by their behavior to punish any men, or set of men, on the above mentioned account, we declare that we will do it in such an exemplary manner as we hope will deter others from obliging us to have recourse to such severe means in future.

And whereas, the inhabitants to whom this proclamation is addressed, as well as those in general settled in that part of the country called the Province of Maine, have settled themselves on lands, and cultivated them, without any grant or title by which their possessions can be secured to them or their posterity, we, therefore, declare that we have full power to promise, and we do hereby promise, that no person whatever, who shall take the oaths of allegiance as above required, and give such other testimony of their attachment to the constitution, as we, or other officers commanding His Majesty's forces, may require, shall be disturbed in their possessions; but that whenever civil government takes place, they shall receive gratuitous grants from His Majesty (who alone has the power of giving them) of all lands they may have actually cultivated and improved.

And whereas, the leaders of the present rebellion, in pursuit of the views which first instigated them to foment it, and probably to blind the people with regard to the cause of the severe distress under which they now labour, have industriously propagated a notion, that the officers of His Majesty's sea and land forces willingly add to their sufferings; we, therefore, to remove such prejudices, and, as far as in us lies, to alleviate the misery of the inhabitants of the villages and islands along the coast of New England, hereby declare that such of them as behave themselves in a peaceable and orderly manner, shall have full liberty to fish in their ordinary coast-fishing craft, without any molestation on our part; on the contrary, they shall be protected in it by all vessels and parties under our command.

Given on board His Majesty's Ship Blande, in Majabig-waduce river, the 15th of June, 1779.

[Signed] { FRANCIS McLEAN
{ ANDREW BARKLAY.

4.

PROCLAMATION.

By Solomon Lovell, Esq., Brigadier-General and Commander in Chief of the Forces of the State of Massachusetts Bay, and employed on an Expedition against the Army of the King of Great Britain, at Penobscot.

Whereas it hath been represented to Government, that an armament of some sea and land forces belonging to the King of Great Britain, under the encouragement of divers of the inhabitants of these parts, inimically disposed to the United States of America, have made a descent on Penobscot, and the parts adjacent; and, after propagating various false reports of a general insurrection of the Eastern and Northern Indians in their favour, a Proclamation has been issued on the 15th of June last, signed Francis McLean and Andrew Barclay, said to be in behalf and by authority of said King, promising grants of lands which he never owned, and of which he has now forfeited the jurisdiction by an avowed breach of that compact between him and his subjects, whereon said jurisdiction was founded, and terrifying by threatnings which his power in this land is unable to execute, unless his servants have recourse to their wonted methods of midnight slaughter and savage devastation, all designed to induce the free inhabitants of this part of the State to submit to their power, and to take an oath of allegiance to their King, whereby they must greatly profane the name of God, and solemnly intangle themselves in an obligation to give up their cattle, provisions, and labour, to the will of every officer pretending the authority of said King, and finally to take up arms against their brethren whenever called upon; and it appears some persons have been induced out of fear, and by the

force of compulsion, to take said oath, who may so far be
imposed on as to think themselves bound to act in
conformity thereto:

I have thought proper to issue this Proclamation, hereby declaring that the allegiance due to the *ancient constitution*, obliges to resist to the last extremity the present system of tyranny in the British Government, which has now
overset it; that by this mode of government the people
have been reduced to a state of nature, and it is utterly
unlawful to require any obedience to their forfeited authority; and all acts recognizing such authority, are sinful in
their nature; no oaths promising it can be lawful; since,
if any act be sin itself no oath can make it a duty: the very
taking of such an oath is a crime, of which every act adher-
ing to it is a repetition with dreadful aggravations.

In all cases where oaths are imposed, and persons compelled to submit to them, by threats of immediate destruction, which they cannot otherwise avoid, it is manifest that,
however obligatory they may be to the conscience of the
compeller, whose interest and meaning is thereby so solemnly witnessed, *it can have no force on the compelled*,
whose interest was known by the compulsion itself, to be
the very reverse of the words in which it is expressed.

At the same time I do assure the inhabitants of Penobscot, and the country adjacent, that if they are found to be
so lost to all the virtues of good citizens, as to comply with
advice of said pretended Proclamation, by becoming the
first to desert the cause of freedom, of virtue, and of God,
which the whole force of Britain, and all its auxiliaries,
now find themselves unable to overthrow, they must expect
also to be the first to experience the just resentment of this
injured and betrayed Country, in the condign punishment
which their treason deserves. From this punishment their
invaders will be very unlike to protect them, as it is now
known they are not able to protect themselves in any part
of America; and as the protection, on which those pro-
claiming Gentlemen say they have only *power* to *promise*,
can be afforded by nothing but the forces which they command, and of these forces by the blessing of God, I doubt
not in a very short time, to be put in possession; so there
is no more reason to expect it from the Indian nations
around, as good part of them are now in my encampment,
and several hundreds more on their way speedily to join
me; and I have the best evidences from all the rest, that

they steadfastly refused to accept of any presents, sign the papers, or do any of the barbarous acts assigned them by our Enemies; and, on the contrary, hold themselves in readiness, 'on the shortest notice, to turn out for the defence of any place which these men may attack.

Therefore, as the authority committed to me necessitates my executing my best endeavours to rid this much-abused country, not only of its foreign, but also from its domestic enemies, I do therefore declare, that when, by the blessing of Heaven on the American arms, we shall have brought the forces that have invaded us to the state they deserve, it shall be my care that the laws of this State be duly executed upon such inhabitants thereof as have traitorously abetted or encouraged them in their lawless attempts.

And that proper discrimination may be made between them and the faithful and liege subjects of the United States, I further declare, that all persons within the Eastern Country, that have taken the oath prescribed by the Enemy and shall not within forty-eight hours after receiving notice of this Proclamation, repair to my camp at Majabigwaduce, with such arms and accoutrements as they now possess, shall be considered as traitors, who have voluntarily combined with the Common Enemy in the common ruin; but all such as shall appear at head-quarters within said term and give proper testimony of their determination to continue cordially in allegiance to the United States of America, shall be recognized as good and faithful members of the community, and treated accordingly, anything obnoxious in their taking the oath, notwithstanding.

Given at Head Quarters on the Heights of Majabigwaduce, this 29th Day of July, Anno Domini 1779, and in the Fourth Year of the Independence of America.

(Signed) S. LOVELL, *Brig. General.*

By Command of the General.

(Signed) JOHN MARSTON, *Secretary.*

. 5.

*Copy of General Lovell's Letter to Commodore Saltonstall;
taken with other Papers on board the Transport.*

HEAD QUARTERS, MAJABIGWADUCE HEIGHTS,)
August 11, 1779.)

SIR:

In this alarming posture of affairs, I am once more
obliged to request the most speedy service in your department; and that a moment be no longer delayed to put in
execution what I have been given to understand was the
determination of your last council.

The destruction of the Enemy's ships must be effected
at any rate, although it might cost us half our own; but I
cannot possibly conceive that danger, or that the attempt
will miscarry. I mean not to determine on your mode of
attack; but it appears to me so very practicable, that any
further delay must be infamous; and I have it this moment
by a deserter from one of their ships, that the moment you
enter the harbour they will destroy them; which will effectually answer our purpose.

The idea of more batteries against them was sufficiently
reprobated; and, would the situation of ground admit of
such proceeding, it would *now* take up *dangerous time;* and
we have already experienced their obstinacy in that respect.
You cannot but be sensible of my ardent desire to co-operate
with you; and of this the guard at Westcot's is a sufficient
proof, and which, I think, a hazardous distance from my
encampment. My situation is confined; and while the
Enemy's ships are safe, the operations of the army cannot
possibly be extended an inch beyond the present limits;
the alternative now remains, to destroy the ships, or raise
the siege. The information of the British ships at the
Hook (probably sailed before this) is not to be despised;
not a moment is to be lost; we must determine instantly,
or it may be productive of disgrace, loss of ships and men;
as to the troops, their retreat is secure, although I would
die to save the necessity of it.

I feel for the honor of America, in an expedition which
a nobler exertion had long before this crowned with success; and I have now only to repeat the absolute necessity

of undertaking the destruction of the ships, or quitting the place; and with these opinions I shall, impatiently, wait your answer.

I am, Sir, Yours, &c.

[Signed.] S. LOVELL, Brig. General.

To Commodore Saltonstall.

6.

POSTSCRIPT.

[To Doctor Calef's Journal.]

Inasmuch as the Country of Penobscot has, till lately, been but little known or considered by Britons, the Editor [John Calef] has thought proper to give the Public the following short Account of it; having of late years travelled eight times through the same, and made himself acquainted with the most respectable persons in each Town, and with the minutest circumstances which respect that District.

Penobscot, sometimes called the territory of Sagadahock, lies in the eastern part of the Province of Massachusetts Bay, having the Province of Nova Scotia (viz: Passamaquodie) for its Eastern, the Province of Main (viz: Kennebec River its Western; Canada its Northern, and the Ocean its Southern boundary; and is nearly as large as the kingdom of Ireland. The French were formerly in possession of part of this Country, viz: from Penobscot River, eastward; they had a Fort on the Peninsula of Majabigwaduce, commanded by Monsieur Castine, and a great number of French inhabitants settled upon Penobscot, and on other rivers, and along the sea-coast to Nova Scotia. On the reduction of Louisburg, in the year 1745, Monsieur Castine demolished the Fort; and all the inhabitants of this District broke up, and removed to Canada.

At the end of the last war, viz: in 1763, the General Assembly of Massachusetts Bay granted thirteen Townships, each of six miles square, lying on the East side of Penobscot River, to thirteen Companies of Proprietors, who proceeded to lay out the said Townships, and returned plans thereof to the General Assembly, which were approved and accepted. In consequence of this measure, about sixty families settled on each Township, and made great improvements of the land. These settlers employed the then Agent for the said Province at the Court of Great Britain, to solicit the Royal approbation of those grants; and in the year 1773, as also in the last year (1780,) they sent an Agent, expressly on their own account, for the same purpose, and further, to pray that His Majesty would be graciously pleased to sever that District from the Province of Massachusetts Bay, and erect it into a Government under the authority of the Crown; which solicitation has hitherto, however, been without effect.

The inhabitants of this Country are in general loyal, except those of the Township of Machias, who have at that place a small Fort, under the direction of Congress, and about 135 Indian warriors of the Machias tribe, in their interest; all the other tribes of Northern Indians are in the King's peace.

The soil of this Country is good, and well adapted to the culture of every sort of English grain, as well as hemp, flax, &c., but it is more especially proper for grazing (in which it excels every other part of America) and for breeding cattle, sheep, swine, and horses. Its woods abound with moose, and other kinds of deer, beaver, and several kinds of game good for food.

A few miles from the sea-coast are large tracts of land, covered with pine trees, suitable for masts of the largest size.* Timber for ship-building, staves, boards, and all other sorts of lumber. On the rivers and streams there were more than 200 saw-mills, when the rebellion broke out, and many more might be erected. The rivers abound with salmon and various other kinds of fish; several of which rivers are navigable 50 or 60 miles for ships of 300 tons, and much further for small craft. There are, on the sea-coast from Falmouth to Passamaquoddy, which is about 70 leagues, more than twenty harbours; many of them are very large, with deep water, and good bottom, and are not incommoded with ice in the winter season,— viz: Falmouth, Sheepscut, Townsend, George's Islands, Penobscot, Algemogin, Bass, Cranberry Islands, Frenchman's Bay, Gouldsborough, Machias, Narraguagus, and East Passamaquodie. In each of these harbours, ships of

*For this article Britain has been obliged to the Northern powers, Russia in particular.

the largest size may ride in safety, in the most violent winds.

In the harbour of Majabigwaduce, is a large sandy beach; the tide flows from fifteen to eighteen feet, and a˙ dock-yard may be erected there, at a small expence, for the collection of masts, lumber, &c., and to heave down the largest men of war. Near the entrance of the harbour, is good fishing ground, where cod, shell, and several other kinds of fish are taken in plenty.

In October, 1772, there were in this District, forty-two towns, and 2,638 families,* who have since greatly increased, at least in the proportion of one-fourth, which is 659 families, making, in the whole, 3,297 families:—Reckoning, then, five souls to each family (which is a moderate computation) there are now 16,485 souls.

To this New Country, the Loyalists resort with their families, (last summer, particularly, a great number of families were preparing to remove thither) from the New England Provinces, and find an asylum from the tyranny of Congress, and their taxgatherers, as well as daily employment, in fishing, lumbering, clearing and preparing land for their subsistence; and there they continue in full hope, and pleasing expectation, that they may soon re-enjoy the liberties and privileges which would be best secured to them by laws, and under a form of government, modelled after the British Constitution; and that they may be covered in their possessions, agreeably to the Petition to the Throne in 1773; which was renewed last year.

Should this District be severed from the Province of Massachusetts Bay, and erected into a Province under the authority of the Crown and the inhabitants *quieted* in their *possessions*, it would be settled with amazing rapidity; the Royal Navy, West India Islands, and other parts of His Majesty's Dominions, well and plentifully served for centuries to come, from this District, with every article above mentioned, without being obliged to other Powers for the same; and the profits of the whole would, fall into the lap of Great Britain, in return for her Manufactures. Roads would, moreover, be opened for communication with other of His Majesty's Provinces, which might be travelled, in a short time, by the following routes:—

* " As appears by a list taken by a respectable person."

Distance from Quebeck to Passadonkeag, Indian
   Oldtown, on Penobscot river.   65 Miles.
Souadabscook,   35   "
Fort Halifax, on Kennebec river,   19   "
Pownalborough,   33
Falmouth,   54
Portsmouth,   53
Boston,   65

                                   324

Distance from Annapolis, Nova Scotia, to St.
   John's, 16 leagues,   48 Miles.
Penobscot River,   55   "
Fort Halifax,   19   "
Boston,   205

                                 327   "

N. B. from Boston to Halifax, is a good Cart Road.

7.

SERGEANT LAWRENCE'S JOURNAL.

Remarks on the Siege of Majabiguaduce from July 24th to August 14th, 1779.

Sat. July 24th. Saw a large fleet of Ships, Brigs, Sloops and Schooners, amounting to 37 sail or upwards.

Sun. 25. This morning the Fleet, belonging to the Rebels, anchored in this harbour, and in the afternoon came and attacked our little fleet very warmly, and was returned as smartly both by our Ships and Batteries. They were endeavoring to land their forces this afternoon, but were repulsed, and obliged to return to their shipping with a considerable loss.

Mon. 26. They were very busy in landing their men at Matthew's Point, opposite the neck, and we were as busy in preparing platforms, &c., to annoy the Rebels, if any attack on the fort should be made. A constant firing of Cannon commenced between both sides again, with the shipping and our batteries from about two o'clock until 3— when the Rebels returned back till about six, when they once more ventured the second attack, and so continued till dark—though not much damage supposed to be done on either side. This evening they landed some men on Banks' island, with a design to sink our ships and play on our fort.

Tues. 27. We were pretty quiet all day, except a few cannon fired at our Batteries, which was accordingly returned by us with as good sulphur as Britons could give, and we hope they did proper execution. This night they were very busy about making a Battery on Banks' island. They also attempted to land on our neck, but our picquet repulsed those poor and misled conquerors, as they thought themselves, by dividing their plunder and selling their shares one among another, at as high a price as the billings-gate leaders does the furniture.

They drew close in shore, in order to cover their landing, which they effected by a constant firing from their shipping—they landed their troops in all, at that time, about 600. Although our picquet behaved with the usual spirit of Britons they were forced to retreat to the fort, with the loss of several killed and wounded, but not one-half part was our loss to what the rebels were. One principal officer of the Rebels was killed by a soldier of the 82d Regt., as he was endeavoring to penetrate his way through a constant fire of small arms, and climbing a steep hill. The remainder part of the day some cannon was fired from us to divert the Yankees, besides some small arms.

Thurs. 29. This morning they opened a battery at Nautilus island consisting of two 18-pounders and one 12-pounder—their rebellious spirit they begun to show by firing on our Ships, Fort and Batteries—we did not spare powder and ball to the Rebels in part of payment for their compliment of this morning. Our ships were obliged to remove their stations, and go further up the harbour, as they met with some small damage by their heavy metal. There was two men wounded on board the ships, one of which is since dead. One of their 18-pounder shot they sent into our fort, which killed a bullock on the parade— thus they finished this day's malice.

Frid. 30. This morning they opened a battery in the Avenero, distance from us about 488 yards, consisting of one 18-Pr. and two 12-Prs. from which they kept a continual firing on purpose to make a breach through our works, but their attempts proved in vain, for they could not obtain their vile intentions, as we was well lined with brave Britons. This afternoon they killed two of the additional gunners, belonging to the 74th Regt., with their cannon. They also began to throw small shells at us. We also began to throw a few small pills at them in partnership with our broad *Arr. Gentlemen*, which without doubt they paid their journey well.

Sat. 31. The usual sport of cannonading at each other commenced. This night the Rebels, under cover of the dark of night and a thick fog, they surrounded our battery at Banks' house, and, like skulking savages lay concealed till this morning, when about two o'clock in the morning they were discovered, and a very smart attack with small arms commenced on both sides, considering our strength, which did not exceed forty officers and privates—the Rebels were upwards of 300—they drove our party from the works awhile, but daylight coming on, our brave soldiers advanced on them again, and drove them from our lost Battery. We had in the first retreat and advancing six men killed and five wounded, one of which was Lieut. Graham, of the 82d Regt.—they this once more begun their cruelty by setting on their most outrageous villains with the Indians, scalping and stripping our men after they were dead—but the brave spirit of our soldiers would not let them deal so with them after they drove those scoundrels, but showed them mercy; for when they retreated they left fifteen prisoners, some of which was wounded, one of those was a Lieutenant, who died since. They also intended to storm our fort, but was most badly disappointed in a shameful manner.

Mond. Aug. 2. All last night the Rebels were very hurried in making a battery at the back of Waistcoat's house, to damage our shipping—we were constantly cannonading each other all this day. We had two additional gunners belonging to the 74th Regt. killed, one carpenter killed, and the boatswain of the Nautilus wounded by their cannon shot.

Tues. Aug. 3. The Rebels still at work at their battery to play on our ships, and we as busy as possible, throwing shells and cannonading them, which pass away time very merrily. We were always in expectation of their coming to storm us, and we were as ready to receive them on the point of our bayonets. We met with no damage this day, worth mentioning.

Wed. 4. We begin with the old story on both sides. They killed one man on board the *North*, from the battery on Nautilus Island. The Rebels this day opened their battery at Wescutt's, consisting of two 18-Prs., and one 12-Pr.—they sent one ball into the *Nautilus*—this was all the damage done by the villains this day. Lieut. Carfrey, of the 82d Regt., with a party of light infantry, played them Yankee Doodle in open defiance, in front of their battery, but the cowardly boasters dare not attempt to face him.

Thurs. 5. Early this morning the Rebels begun on our ships, from Nautilus Island and Wescott's battery, as also a smart fire with small arms, which lasted half an hour. We had one man killed and one wounded. One Indian and one Yankee were killed in plain view, and without doubt, many more fell in the action. Their batteries kept a continual fire on our ships, Batteries, and on the Fort, which we returned with the spirit of Britons. Their batteries hulled the *Nautilus* three times; they wounded one man on board in both hands. This afternoon our chief Engineer was " diverted " in raising a battery for our seamen, in case they had been obliged to leave their shipping, and secure their retreat, and maintain a constant communication with the Fort.

Fri. 6. This morning one of the 74th Regt. was killed, and in payment for their trouble one of our marines shot a Rebel in open view, in front of the 74th old Camp ground. A constant cannonading on both sides, but no damage received on ours—the seamen at work on their reserve battery, with great expedition.

Sat. 7. This morning commenced with the common game of exchanging shot on both sides, and one Corporal of the 74th stood in the way of a stranger, as he was passing over our fort, taking his way through the Commissary's store, made bold to take the Corporal's head off his shoulders, without asking any other pay for his journey. This afternoon a smart skirmish began with the Rebels and a party of our light infantry, Lieut. McNeil of the 82d, was wounded, and one private. We may well suppose the Yankees did not return without loss, as they were forced to fly to the woods for shelter, like a cowardly crew, and seen to carry several, either killed or wounded with them. A detachment from the Fort joined the seamen, and was sent to a place called Hainey's Point, opposite our shipping, where the Rebels intended to erect a Battery, which of consequence would have done much damage to every vessel in our harbour belonging to His Majesty—in which case, the mistaken pickaroons fired a few small arms at our boats, as they were landing their men, and so fled to the woods, as usual, for safety, and left their boats to be towed along side our ships—they being content to pad the hoof through woods, swamps, and briars, &c. This evening, the Rebels set fire to Master Banks' and Dyce's houses and Barns—both these was true friends to government.

Sund. 8. Only a few cannon shot exchanged, by reason of a heavy rain.

Mon. 9. All day pretty quiet till night, when a cannon ball was sent from the Rebels, and killed one of the 74th. We are always in hopes we paid them for their trouble, as we commonly play as good a stick as they.

Tues. 10. This morning a few cannon shot was fired in exchange, till we discovered one piece of Ordnance in a new work, directly in a line from our works. But we soon rooted them from that work, with the usual alertness of Britons. This afternoon came in a deserter from the Rebels, and informed us of some ships cruising off the harbour, which was no disagreeable news to us, as we expected a reinforcement to assist us to give these two bold commanders of the Yankees a proper disabling, and teach them the quickstep.

Wed. 11. This morning they fired on our picquet, and killed one man and wounded another. This evening Lieut. Carfrey of the 82d, and his light infantry went to reconnoitre round the neck and fell in with a party of the Rebels, consisting of about 300 scarecrows, at Banks' Battery—Our Lieut. ordered to give them a volley of small arms and a tap of the Grenadier's march, accompanied with Yankee Doodle, which so daunted these poor devils that they hove some of their arms away and ran to the woods—they threw a few Balls out of their mortars at us, but did us no damage. We closed the day by sending them plenty of 12-Pr. shot.

Thurs. 12. This morning the Rebels seemed as if they had meant to make an attack on the fort, for at daybreak they opened all their batteries on the fort and shipping. We also employed ourselves to make them a recompense for their extravagances. The General and all our principal officers were of opinion the Yankees had taken courage to storm our fort, which seemed very likely by their landing many of their troops and often forming them in open view of our scouting parties. We were this afternoon busy in raising a bit of a battery for four 6-Prs. to play on their shipping, if in case they should make an attempt to approach ours, which would sooner have perished in the attack than have fallen a prey to these savage plunderers. This evening they set fire to Perkins' house and barn, and also many feet of boards and other lumber, which would, they thought, have been of use to us. This day we closed, but the Rebels did not make their attempt, as we could have wished them to have done.

Frid. 13. This morning we were pretty quiet till about noon, when they opened their batteries and some field pieces on us, as we were hauling our cannon to the new Battery to interpose their shipping, if in case of an attempt on ours. Towards the evening the Rebels advanced towards Joseph Perkins' house, but we soon deprived them of that design by the opening of both round and grape shot among them, both from our batteries and shipping— at the same time we discovered some large ships off the harbour, which glorious sight put our whole soldiers in fresh spirits, as we made no doubt but they were friends and would soon be in pursuit of the Rebels, as it seemed very probable by their signal vessel coming with all speed and making many different signals to their Commodore—at the same time we fired some signal guns from the fort to our supposed friends, which was returned by firing some guns to Leeward and hoisting English colors. We soon observed the rebel fleet to be in great confusion. At dusk they fired one 18-Pr. which was the last they fired—at which time they killed a Corporal of the 82d Regt. Thus ended the exploits of this day, with the Rebels all in surprise not knowing which way their course to steer.

Sat. 14. This morn to our great satisfaction we found what we expected from the night before. But the morning being entirely calm our shipping could not get under weigh till about nine o'clock, when they threw the Rebels in nothing but a rapid confusion. The Genl. detached parteys to their different posts and found them all evacuated. A party was also sent to Matthew's Cove, which party was joined by the Artificers, covered by two 3-Prs. to endeavor to stop them from carrying their cannon away, and if possible to catch some prisoners, but they having too much the start of us, we was disappointed and could only stop one rebel; which was effected by one of the carpenters named

Stanford, as he was attempting to make his escape thro' a corn-field. By this time the Rebel fleet was all in readiness to make their last attempt some way or other, as to fighting we thought it was not their intention, for they left the soldier part, or forgot it, when they came from Yankee town. About noon they got to be all in a line, and soon after he was the best fellow who could run and sail the fastest, for Sir George Collier and his fleet came so fast on them, that some ran on shore, some taken, burnt, or blown up, so that none got liberty to go back to carry the news to Yankee town, except what poor creatures can travel through a most miserable, fatiguing, and almost starved country, and most lost all expectation of driving us from Maj. In the afternoon we fired a royal salute from the fort, and by accident of a gun hanging fire, one of the Artillery had his right arm broke, and his thumb blown off.

Now the Siege is raised, our fears are ended, we will return thanks to God that he has delivered us from outrageous men, and Rebels, such that was commanded by General Lovell.

[The spelling of the foregoing journal has been corrected in a few places, but otherwise, in style and grammar, this is a correct copy of the original. Lawrence was an Orderly Sergeant of the Royal Artillery. He with another soldier of that corps was sent across from Boston to Cambridge, on the evening before the march to Lexington, to instruct the Infantry how to throw hand-grenades —was on the Common when the first gun was fired—afterwards fought and was wounded at Breed's Hill. He was in Castine during the whole of the Siege, and at the conclusion of peace was honorably discharged. He afterwards settled in Bucksport, where he died not very many years ago, at an advanced age.]

8.

Extracts from Sergeant Lawrence's Orderly Book—1779.

[Substantially correct, but not *verbatim.*]

[The first entry occurs July 11th, 1779, and is an order to parade.]

1779. July 20. Small change is so scarce that dollars are cut into five pieces, by command of the General, each part to pass for one shilling. Soldiers are forbidden to take up any potatoes belonging to the inhabitants, nnder pain of severe punishment.

July 28th. Soldiers are forbidden to leave the fort, without permission. Marauding is forbidden, and also smoking within the fort.

August 5. Strict injunctions against soldiers leaving the fort without permission, for the purpose of shooting at the enemy—as had been done.

August 11. None of the inhabitants allowed within the fort, except those employed in His Majesty's service, viz: Mr. Nathan Phillips; Mr. Cunningham, family and driver; Mr. Dyce and family; and Mr. Finley McCullom.

August 18. The General thanks the officers and soldiers for their spirited conduct while the enemy were in the wood. Hereafter nothing is to be taken from any of the inhabitants, without payment.

August 19. Soldiers are forbidden to set fire to the houses of the inhabitants, without the General's orders.

August 21. Lieutenant Wilson is ordered to send a man from the Artillery, with a Gin, for weighing the guns of those ships that were burned.

August 29. Parties of Rebels reported to be lurking in the woods, and officers recommended to be careful about going into them.

August 30. A detachment sent up the river for lumber, with two days' provisions.

September 25. All Rebel firelocks are ordered to be brought in by the inhabitants, and the sum of three dollars each to be paid for them.

November 14. Owing to fraudulent practices, the cut pieces of dollars are to be called in. Doctor Calef is appointed as Overseer and Commissary of the inhabitants. Mr. MacZachlar is to be Barrack Master, and to act as Quarter Master General. General McLean is preparing to leave, and Colonel Campbell has taken the command.

November 16. The inhabitants are not allowed to leave the peninsula, without a written pass from Doctor Calef.

November 22. All the inhabitants drawing provisions from the King's stores are allowed till the twenty-ninth inst. to make their dwellings comfortable and convenient. On that day all (who are fit) are to be employed on the

King's works, at reasonable wages, and those who refuse are to have their names struck from the list of those who draw provisions.

December 5. The inhabitants having neglected to comply with the order of the fifth inst., none are to receive provisions except those who produce a certificate from the chief Engineer or from Doctor Calef. Mr. Archibald, Nathan Phillips and David Cunningham, being considered as always engaged, do not need certificates.

December 24. The inhabitants are forbiden to sell liquor to any one.

1780. Jan. 2. Soldiers are restricted to two-thirds an allowance of Rum and Butter.

January 27. All strangers intending to stay over night are ordered to report to Doctor Calef. No persons are allowed to go on or off the peninsula after sunset without permission from Doctor Calef. All persons not reporting to Doctor Calef are to be fined or corporally punished. This order to be publicly posted and copies of it sent to the neighboring towns. No person known to be disaffected is to be allowed to dwell on the peninsula. All the inhabitants are to be armed and accoutred and ready for action at a moments notice. The inhabitants are also to be mustered and inspected once each week by their Overseer.

[The rest of the Orderly Book is filled with countersigns, paroles, &c., &c.—The last date in the book is Feb. 28, 1780.]

9.

William Hutchings' Narrative of the Siege, and other reminiscences.

[The following account was narrated to Mr. Joseph L. Stevens, Jr., in August, 1855, by Mr. William Hutchings of Penobscot.]

The British landed in front of Joseph L. Perkins' house, June 17, 1779, which stood on what is now the south eastern corner of Main and Water streets. They seemed as frightened as a flock of sheep, and kept looking around them as if they expected to be fired on by an enemy hid behind the trees. This day they did not stop, but returned to their vessels. The next day they came on shore, and encamped on the open land east of where the fort now stands. They immediately began to fortify the place. In a short time the American expedition came, and orders were sent out for the inhabitants to come in and work. I helped to haul the first log into the south bastion. It was on the Sunday before the Americans arrived, and was the only Sunday on which I had to work in my life. The peninsula was then covered with a heavy growth of trees. When the fort was built it was mostly spruce, and the trees were rather small, but farther to the westward there was a good deal of maple, beech, birch, etc.

General Lovell built his works mostly of logs and brush. He had to cut away a great many trees to make a passage for his cannon balls to the fort. General McLean expected to be taken, and when his troops were driven back into the fort, the morning the American troops landed—July 28, 1779—he stood with the pennant halliards in his own hands all ready to strike the colors himself. He said he had been in nineteen battles without getting beaten, but he expected he should be beaten in the twentieth one. The walls of the fort were so low at that time that I heard a soldier say he could jump over with a musket in each hand. McLean considered that every day the Americans delayed the attack was as good to him as another thousand men. My father was among the patriots who joined the Americans. He was stationed part of the time at Hainey's point, and always thought he killed an English soldier there. A party of English came to drive the Americans away, and most of them speedily retreated; but my father and a few others stopped to give them a parting shot, when the boat should come in good range. One of the guard afterward said to him at Mrs. Hainey's house that when my father fired he saw a soldier in one of the boats fall, and heard him cry out. Mrs. Hainey was along and she subsequently reported this at head quarters, and we supposed it the reason of our family being driven away. I worked on the battery at Wescott's, in all, eight days.

*   *   *   *   *   *   *

We kept up a hot fire on the ships, and drove the men ashore and below. There were three frigates—the *Albany*, *North*, and *Nautilus*. We could hear our shot go—*thud*—into them. We cut away an anchor hanging at the bows of one of them. I marked where it fell, as I thought sometime or other I might want to get it up. When the siege was raised the guns were carried across to Matthews' point to be put on board the transports. In the hurry of getting them on board a brass four-pounder was lost overboard. One night the Americans undertook to surprise the English but they fell in with the British guard at Banks's battery, and had a sharp fight. Quite a number were killed on both sides. I afterwards saw, up by the narrows, some bloody uniforms, tied up in a blanket, that had been stripped from the English soldiers killed that night. Major Sawyer was killed, or drowned, in a boat that was sunk by a cannon ball fired from the fort, while it was passing from the fleet to to Nautilus Island. A cannon shot from the battery on Nautilus Island came in the fort gate and passing between General McLean and one of his officers, killed an ox belonging to my father—which he had raised himself. Hatch's barn was used as a hospital. I was there after the siege was raised, and the floor was then covered with beds so thick that there was scarcely room to pass between them. The poor fellows groaned a good deal when the doctors dressed their wounds. I believe most of those who died there were buried on the lower side of the road. Being so young I was allowed to go off and on the peninsula, but the soldiers sometimes used to call me "a damned little rebel." It was reported that there was to be a combined attack on the fort and frigates, at a set time, by the Americans. I went with a number of others to the high land in Brooksville, opposite Negro Island, but it did not take place. At that, or another time, I recollect seeing some of the American fleet drop in behind Nautilus Island and fire across the bar at the English ships. Their last shot ploughed up the dry sod near Hatch's house, and set considerable of it on fire. A drummer was killed, the night of the skirmish, at the battery near Banks' house, and, for a good many years after, people used to say that they could hear *his ghost drumming there at midnight.* I saw both Lovell and Wadsworth. I did not like the appearance of Lovell very well, but Wadsworth was a beautiful man. There was no canal dug across the neck at that time.

A good many years ago, I used to know a man named Conolly, who told me that he once found near the *second* Narrows, on or near the shore, a kind of chest pretty much covered over with moss or grass, as if it had been exposed to the weather many years. On opening it he found French goods, such as handkerchiefs, etc. As long ago as I can remember there was what was called the " Old French Fort," down by the shore below Banks's house. There were a great many spruce poles around it and posts in the shore, when I was a boy. There used to be a considerable growth of oak there. I do not remember ever hearing that there were in old times any Mills about here belonging to Frenchmen—what used to be called the " Winslow" farm, at the head of Northern Bay, was a great while ago called " Frenchman's" farm, and the pond at the head of a stream that runs through it, was called " Frenchman's" pond, when I was a boy, and there was an old cellar there they used to call the old Frenchman's cellar. It may be all gone now. If not, you will find it between Perkins' store and the shore.

Hutchings' Narrative to Joseph Williamson, Esq., in February, 1860.

* * * * * *

In Wescott's battery there were three guns, one 12-lb., one 6-lb., and one 3-lb. brass field piece, which was lost overboard off Stover Perkins' point, when the Americans were trying to carry it off. It lays there now, I suppose—a little way from the shore. The transport must have come as nigh as she could. It probably slipped out of the slings.

I saw as many as 50 or 60 cannon the English got from the fleet up the river. They all lay at high water mark on the shore, loaded, and were fired off, to see if they were cracked, or anything the matter with them.

Doctor Calf [Calef] built the old Mann house about a year before the British came. He was a Tory refugee.

We shot an anchor from Wescott's battery off the *Santillana* [St. Helena] near Hatch's Point. Three or four ships lay along there. I saw it at low tide, and suppose I might have got it, if I had had spunk enough.

The old wreck on the shore down below Hatch's was the *Providence.** The *St. Helena* was a letter-of-marque,

---

*This is corroborated by a letter from J. Snelling, Esq., of Halifax, to the wife of Col. Goldthwaite, at Bagaduce. This letter was dated Dec. 17, 1779, and communicates the information that the *St. Helena* had recently been cast away, with great loss of life, at some place, the name of which we cannot decipher from the manuscript, but which certainly was not Penobscot or Bagaduce. The word looks like " Salu—ing."

of fourteen guns. She was not in the regular service. The *Providence* was an old transport, that troops came over in. She fell over there, I believe, and stove her side in.

The *Albany* carried sixteen guns, the *Nautilus* twenty-two, and the *North* twenty-eight. She was an old French ship, and was not good for much of anything. Her guns were light-mounted.

Nautilus Island was named after the *Nautilus*, and I suppose I saw the caper that was the occasion of it. The *Hazard* and other vessels, ran in behind the island, and fired across the bar, and raked the ships that lay across the mouth of the harbor. They cut or slipped their cables, and dropped up further. Nautilus Island used to be called Banks' Island; was called Nautilus Island after that.

The guard at Hainey's Point all ran off but five, who fired and killed one man—the first who was killed. My father is said to have done it on the second shot, and the Tories (the commanding officer didn't say it) said he would be hung. Mrs. Hainey told of it, and my mother was so frightened we had to move away. Ah! hard and trying times those were!

· The *Santillana* was a very nice ship. The old *Providence* was an old vessel. She fell over and stove her broadside in. She was one of the British fleet. They hauled the transports ashore, when the Americans came. Otter Rock was named for the ship *Otter*, which went on the rock close by, at the eastward of it, going out, I think.

I went aboard the *Nautilus*. I was a boy. One of my countrymen took me down below, and fed me pretty well, then told me he was a pressed man. He had tried to run away, and got flogged for it. I saw two men flogged on the *Albany*. They can say what they please, when tied up, and one man told the officer he should run away again every chance. An English soldier joined us on the Kennebec, and then ran into the country. He was brought back and court martialed, and sentenced to 200 lashes. The blood ran down and filled his shoes. When he had received 100, they had to take him down. About that ship *Providence*, you needn't be afeared to assert it as truth, because I know all about it. * * * The frigate *Blande* was one of the convoy that came with McLean. She did not come in, but lay outside of the harbor. I used to go on board, to sell milk, &c. She was a beautiful ship—was not here at the time of the siege, had gone away. The *Albany* was commanded by an American. Mowatt was a Portland man.

I remember when Pomroy was cut out by Little. He chased Pomroy about, but couldn't bring him to an engagement. Little said he would have him, if he followed him to h—ll. Pomroy had taken a coasting vessel which Little retook. Little got a whale-boat at Fox Islands, which he left with some men, below Nautilus Island, to make his escape in, if necessary. Pomroy had a 14-gun Brig; Little had a 12-gun Sloop. He came in on the top of the tide, just at the close of the day—before dark. When the sentry hailed him, he replied that he was a prize from Fox Island. " Who commands her? " " Peter Littlejohn." He ran alongside of the brig, and told them to heave him a warp, as he had lost both anchors in Fox Island thoroughfare. He had his men all ready, and jumped aboard with them, and took her. The sloop kept right on, and stood out of the harbor, but the brig had to make a couple of tacks. The people collected to look on, and Captain Little afterwards said he might have swept the streets as he went by. He was fired on from the fort, and men ran down to the old French fort and fired. Commissary Mc-Laughlin told a man (I heard him) that he delivered out 1700 rounds. It was said that Little picked up bullets by the bucketful from his deck, where they fell, after striking among the sails and rigging. A shot from the sloop, or brig, when going out of the harbor, struck a crowbar, and drove it through a hogshead of rum that stood in the King's store, about ten rods below the Fort gate. William Redhead told me that shot cost him one hogshead of rum. He was a sort of deputy Commissary, and came over with the British. He married old Banks' daughter. Pomroy was a Tory. He and most of his crew were ashore. Next day the British officers laughed at him. They thought very much of Little.

*   *   *   *

When the British came I was at Fox Islands, with my uncle—where we went fishing in an open boat. We had news of their coming, and when the fleet came in sight, uncle said, " there comes the devils." We started for home, and when the fleet followed us up we knew it was them. We reached Castine when they were firing guns for pilots. Nine of the vessels came in. They anchored off Dice's Head, I should think by eleven o'clock. Their boats came ashore down at the beach, below Johnson's corner. I was there when they landed. As many as twenty officers came ashore. They looked all around as if they were considerably frightened. They didn't do much that day. I went home that night. Can't say if troops came next day or day after. When I went down they were camped in tents on the ridge to northeast of where the fort is.

When Little came, I had come back from the Kennebec, (a year before father) and worked about here with the neighbors. I was then at old Mr. Samuel Wescott's. I had gone up to go to bed, and was leaning on a chest by the window. I heard a great firing of guns, and couldn't think what it all meant. Wescott was on the peninsula, and when he came home he told us all about it. I went down next day and saw Pomroy, who looked as if he had been stealing sheep, and had lost all the friends he had in the world. General McLean was an excellent officer. He was very angry because the Tories drove off so many of the Americans by saying that the English were going to hang them. The old General didn't go about much, but the other officers used to. They went to Orland, to see Old Vyles' daughters.   *   *   *   *   *

As soon as the boats went off, the guard ran off. We thought they would come in above and cut us off. My father came near shooting one of our men who had run off. He was in the bushes, and started up. Father saw him and brought his gun to fire on him. He had a fur cap on, and father saw a mark on the back of it.

10.

Letter from David Perham, giving Colonel Brewer's account of the Expedition against Penobscot, in 1779.

[From Bangor *Whig and Courier,* of August 13, 1846.]

" Early in the month of June 1779, General Francis McLean, who commanded the King's troops in Nova Scotia, entered Penobscot Bay, with 650 men in transports, escorted by three sloops, and took possession of the Peninsula (now called Castine) formed by the waters of Penobscot Bay, and the Majabagaduce River, which struck the inhabitants with terror—especially the women and children. At this time provisions were very scarce, and the inhabitants almost destitute of arms and ammunition. A meeting was called of the principal officers, to determine on defence, or submission; at which it was concluded to send a committee to treat with the General; and myself [Colonel Brewer] and Captain Smith of Marsh Bay, were chosen. We proceeded on our mission, and obtained assurance that, if the inhabitants would mind their business, and be peaceable, they should not be disturbed in person or property; but afterwards they were called upon to take the Oath of Allegiance, or of *Neutrality*. Nothing further occurs to my mind worthy of relating, till a few days before the American Fleet arrived in the Bay, when Captain Smith and myself were again called upon by the people to wait upon General McLean to transact certain business, which we accomplished to our satisfaction, and obtained our pass to return home. I then had a full view of their works. About four o'clock P. M., I observed a very rapid movement of the troops, and told Captain Smith it was time for us to be off. We proceeded immediately to our boat, and had just gotten from the shore, when the Grand Rounds went for no one to leave the Peninsula. We continued our course, with a small breeze, up the Penobscot River, when casting our eyes down the Bay we discovered a large fleet of shipping standing up, and knew pretty well what it must be, for myself and others had kept a birch canoe passing every few days from my house to Camden, for information. We stood up the river about six miles, where we staid all night; but got little sleep for joy at what we had seen, and what we expected would take place. Next morning, July 26th, we went down in our boat about three miles, to make further discovery of the fleet; but the fog being so thick we could not see it. We then stood up the river to old Fort Point, there landed and went back about half a mile, when the fog cleared away, and we had a full view of the fleet, which had just got under weigh, standing up with a small breeze, in line of battle,—as they passed they discharged their guns at the British shipping, then lying in the river. This drew our attention for sometime, but casting my eyes westward, I discovered, under the bank, a number of whale boats full of armed men, and I

told Captain Smith it was no place for us. We started for
our boat, which we had regained, and were getting up
our sails, when the boats came up with us and ordered us
to stand; and who should it be but my brother (Colonel
Josiah Brewer) who was sent with a detachment of soldiers as an advance guard to be stationed at Buckstown, to
stop communication. He ordered us to get under weigh
as soon as possible, came on board with one or two of his
men, and we arrived at Buckstown, about five o'clock P. M.
Having stationed his guard and taken some refreshments,
he manned a boat and, taking Captain Smith and myself
with him, set out to go on board of the fleet, which, on account of darkness and fog, we did not reach until after
sunrise in the morning. We went on board of General
Lovell's vessel, and being introduced by my brother, were
very politely received by the General, who, on being informed that Captain Smith and myself had left the Peninsula about four o'clock, on the 25th, sent immediately for
Commodore Saltonstall to come on board. When he arrived, my brother told them whatever information we
should give, might be relied upon. We were then invited
into the cabin. I told them at four o'clock—as above
stated—I reviewed all their works, and was in their Fort.
That the Northerly side next to the Cove was about four
feet high, the Easterly and Westerly ends were something
like a stonewall, laid up sloping; from the back side to the
front there was but one sag, and the ground not broken.
On the backside the ditch was about three feet deep,—the
ends were sloping according to the height of the wall—not
a platform laid, nor a gun carriage up to the Fort. I also
told him a part of the troops were stationed near the upper
end, on the heath; but there was no appearance of Artillery. That there was one six gun battery at Dice's Point,
(as it is called) and that was all they would have to con-
tend with on the land. I told him, likewise, there was a
small battery begun on Cape Rozier. There was Captain
Moat's [Mowatt's] ship mounting twenty guns, and one
other mounting ten, which I thought lay nearly opposite
the Fort. General Lovell seemed much pleased with the information. I then told the Commodore that being all the
force he would have to meet, I thought that as the wind
breezed up he might go in with his shipping, silence the
two vessels and the six-gun battery, and land the troops
under cover of his own guns, and in half an hour make

everything his own.   In reply to which he hove up his long chin, and said, " You seem to be d—n knowing about the matter! I am not going to risk my shipping in that d—d hole !"

Captain Smith and myself returned home, having received orders from my brother, then my colonel, to return immediately with half of my company—I being then a captain.   This order I obeyed ; but my family not then being in a situation to leave, my men were put under the command of another captain, and I returned home for one week, when I again repaired to my post.   Next morning we discovered a party of the British going down from the head of the Point, and supposing it to be their intention to come on the rear of us, I marched out my company to attack them ; but we soon perceived their object to be fishing, which a few shot defeated, and they hurried back again.   Nothing important appearing to be going on, I again returned home ; and the next information I had was from my brother, who came up in a boat, double-manned, said he did not think anything would be done, and was unwilling to leave his wife and effects.   He staid about two hours, when he took his wife and best furniture, and returned down the river.   His wife was landed at Camden, and his furniture was put on board the General's ship, which I afterwards saw on Captain Moat's ship.

The next information was received from Doctor Downing, Chief Surgeon of the army, with whom I had formerly been acquainted.   He arrived at my house on the morning of the fourteenth of August, with the sick and wounded Americans, and said the siege was raised, and the fleet and army of the Americans, between 3000 and 4000, were on their way up the river, followed by Sir George Collier, with the British fleet.   The Doctor stopped, dressed the wounded, got some refreshments, and enquired where would be the best place of safety for the men under his care.   I directed him to Major Treat's, about two miles above navigation, where he landed and left them, under the care of Doctor Herberd, leaving with him his medicine chest.   Before night, such of the shipping as were not taken or destroyed below, appeared, which were blown up and burnt the next morning, and the troops took their flight into the woods.

The next day I was again requested by the inhabitants to wait on General McLean to know our fate, which I did

in company with Captain Ginn. We accordingly proceeded
on that duty.   At the Narrows, where the ship *Blande* lay
at anchor, we were hailed and went on board.   The Captain being informed what our business was, gave us a pass,
and we proceeded to the Peninsula.   When I called on the
General he received me very politely, and said, 'Mr. Brewer,
you have come to see me again, what is the news up the
river? and where are the rebels? have they dispersed?'   I
told him they had.   He replied: 'I believe the commanders
were a pack of cowards or they would have taken me.   I
was in no situation to defend myself, I only meant to give
them one or two guns, so as not to be called a coward,
and then have struck my colors, which I stood for some
time to do, as I did not wish to throw away the lives of my
men for nothing.'   He then said: 'What is your request?'
I told him that the inhabitants were in distress, waiting to
know his determination.   If it be favorable, they will stay
at home; if not, they will quit their houses and take to the
wood, which some have already done.   To which he made
answer: 'Go home and tell them if they will stay in their
houses and live peaceably and mind their business, they
shall not be hurt; but if not, all the houses that are left
shall be burnt.'   My next request was to know what
should be done with the sick and wounded men who had
been left.   He asked:—'What is your wish?'   I replied
that they might be conveyed to their friends, as soon as
convenient.   To which he said: 'Go up and get a vessel,
if you can; if not, I will provide one.'   I told him I had
one in view that I could get.   'Then get it,' he said; 'fit
her out in good order, and take all the sick and wounded
on board; come down with them, and return me a list of
their names, and I will give you a pass, or a cartel, to
deliver them where it will be most convenient for the
men.'   I told him there would be some stores wanted, that
could not be procured up the river.   He replied: 'Get
what you can, and make out a memorandum of what you
want more, and I will supply you here.'   I then returned
home, and on the way chartered a schooner, shipped a
master and hands, and the next day she came up the
river, and went to Bangor, there to be fitted up with platforms and bunks convenient for the purpose.   In a few
days Captain Moat came up the river, and anchored his
ship off my cove.   At night when I came down I was
hailed, gave my name and told them I lived abreast his

ship—which was communicated to Captain Moat. He returned,—that he wished me to call on him in the morning; which I did, and informed him what my orders were, from the General, in relation to the sick and wounded. He wished me to accomplish the business as soon as I could. He frequently called me on board when I was passing, and enquired after the sick and wounded, and often invited me into his cabin to take a glass of wine or brandy. This friendship subsisted till the schooner was completed, when he went up to see the same previous to her sailing. When in readiness I informed him the schooner would be down in the evening, and in the following morning he gave me a pass to General McLean.

On my way, at Marsh Bay, I heard of Captain George Ross and his cabin boy, and sent the boat on shore with Doctor Herberd, to bring off Captain Ross. He had commanded one of the 20-gun ships, and was wounded the day he landed. He and the boy were brought on board, and I entered his name, George Ross, on my list, likewise the brig's name, and proceeded down to the General's quarters, and presented him with my list, which he appeared to be very much pleased with. I made out a memorandum of what was wanted, which, by his order, was furnished and put on board. He then gave a pass for the schooner, as a cartel, to proceed to Boston, or other places where it would be most convenient for the men; and I then returned home late at night, much fatigued with the tour. Before I got home, Ichabod Colson, then of Marsh Bay, went up and informed Captain Moat that I had sent my boat on shore, and taken off Captain Ross and his cabin boy. Early in the morning after my return, Moat sent his boat on shore, with a message for me to go on board his ship. I sent in reply that I was much fatigued, having been out most of the night, but that I would call on board in the afternoon. When I had gotten ready to go, I saw him land on the opposite point of land below my house; and I took my canoe and passed over to him. He saw me coming and walked towards me; we met at a little distance from the shore, and were together about a quarter of an hour, and our meeting was not very cordial. The first compliment I received was: 'you damned rebel, I understand that you stopped at Marsh Bay, and took on board Captain Ross, one of the finest officers there was in the Navy. I meant to have kept him and had two of my captains for him, he was such a fine fellow. Did you return him as a Captain?' 'No! I returned him as George Ross.' Making use of the same opprobrious language, he added, 'Did you not know that I had not given you orders to take any man on board?' I answered, 'yes.' Then said he, with his sword flourishing over my head, 'how dare you do it?' 'Because,' said I, 'I received my orders another way.' 'Which way?' said he. I answered: 'from General McLean, your Master.' It may well be supposed, from my answer, that I was somewhat agitated. He stepped back, and drawing his sword out of its scabbard, said: 'You d—d rebel! I have a good mind to run you through.' I opened my breast and told him: 'there is your mark, do it if you dare! I am in your power.' He turned on his heel and stepped back a little, then turned and advanced, flourishing his sword with more passion than could be well expressed, said, 'before sunrise to-morrow morning, your buildings shall be laid in ashes.' I told him it was in his power to do it, but I asked him what he thought I should be doing in the meantime. Upon which he turned on his heel again and marched off to his boat, and I to mine. I came home and told Mrs. Brewer, what had passed, so that she might not be surprised if he proceeded to put his threat in execution—though I did not believe he would. I always kept a good musket well loaded, and intended to do what lay in my power to defend myself. However, we did not have so good a night's rest as usual; but nothing further occurred, worthy of remark, till the next day about four o'clock P. M.,—at which time I saw Captain Moat come on shore at my landing. I told Mrs. Brewer of it, and it put her in a panic. He walked along very moderately, till he got nearly up with my door, when I stepped out and met him. He very politely asked me how I and my family did; I invited him to walk in, which he readily did; and Mrs. Brewer was introduced to him, which took off most of her panic. He took a seat and opened most of the conversation by stating how much he regretted the situation of the inhabitants, and felt for their distress; and went into a very social conversation for two or three hours, and took coffee with us. He inquired into the situation of my family—how many children we had, and whether it would not be very difficult for me to support them without assistance. I told him I should try.

He then said: 'If you think you cannot, I will supply you with such things as you want for your family, to the amount of £1000 sterling, at the first cost at Halifax. If you make out a memorandum, I will send by the first vessel for them.' I thanked him for his good will, and we separated.

At all other times than the one above stated, both before and after, he appeared very friendly. Soon after his first arrival he called all hands on deck and, in my presence, told them if they took one thing out of my garden, or field, they should be punished; and they strictly adhered to his orders during their whole stay. I supplied him with milk, garden vegetation, and pigeons, for his cabin—which he generously paid me for in money. Before he left this place he agreed with me for $200, to take down my brother's house, which was nearly as much as the building was worth. In the situation of things, I considered the house of very little value to my brother, especially as the enemy claimed the right of doing as they saw fit—and so indeed they did with all others—and that it is as well to save something as to have the whole lost. He was to send up a vessel to carry the materials of which the house was composed, to the Fort. But soon after he left, some person, in the night, took out all the windows and concealed them. Upon which I had to report what had taken place to General McLean—for that being the orders in all cases where there was a contract. I accordingly went down to the Fort and called upon the General, and was very civilly received. He said: 'Well, Mr. Brewer, you have called on me again. What is the news? and what is your request?' 'It is to report to you that I agreed with Captain Moat to take down a house for him, which he was to send a vessel for. But on a certain night, some persons unknown to me, took out all the windows, and have carried them off.' To which he replied: 'Well, *man*, you must get them again.' I told him I could not, for I knew not where they were nor whom to suspect. He answered: 'Then *man*, you must stay here till you produce them.' I told him that would be impossible for me to do without having liberty to search for them. To which he replied, 'well, *man*, I guess you know as well where they are as anybody! I will give you a week, or fortnight, to go home and get them, and if you don't bring them here within that time, I will put you under confinement.' I thanked him for his lenity, bid him good bye, and went directly home; but instead of making search for those windows, I hid my own, together with my other things, and packed up my beds and clothing—that I pretended to take with me—and made the best of my way out of his control.

Major George Ulmer, then having a command at Camden, was up the river, at my house, with a large boat and a party of soldiers, getting what remained from the destruction of the vessels, &c. He offered his services to take my family with him to Camden, which then consisted of nine beside myself, which he, with my small effects, safely landed at Camden. I collected about half of my stock of cattle, — one yoke of oxen, three cows, and my horse,—joined stock with Mr. John Crosby and others, making about thirty head in the whole, and laid our course through the woods, as direct as possible, for Camden, where we arrived in three or four days. Thence I took my family to the westward of Boston — where we remained till peace was restored, when I again returned with my family to my former residence in Penobscot."

I am, sir, with respect,

Your obedient servant,
[Signed]   DAVID PERHAM.

To William D. Williamson, Esq.

[The foregoing account was contained in a letter from Colonel Brewer to David Perham, and was found among the papers of the latter at his decease.]

11.

Account of a Skirmish at Biguyduce, July 28, 1779, *By Lieutenant (afterwards Sir John) Moore.* [From British Plutarch page 243.]

"On the 28th, after a sharp cannonade from the shipping on the wood, to the great surprise of General McLean and the garrison, the Americans effected a landing. I happened to be on piquet that morning, under the command of a Captain of the 74th Regiment, who, after giving them one fire, instead of encouraging his men—who naturally had been a little startled by the cannonade—to do their duty, ordered them to retreat, leaving me and about twenty men to shift for ourselves.

After standing for some time I was obliged to retreat to the Fort, having five or six of my men killed and several wounded. I was lucky to escape untouched."

12.

MacZachlar's Order.

FORT GEORGE'S, PENOBSCOT, Octr. 1780.

For His Majesty's Service:

You are hereby Ordered and Directed to Bring down to this Place all the Cord Wood that you can find upon the Shores of Northern Bay, Majebagwaduce River, belonging to Sparks Perkins, Charles Hutchings, Jack* Perkins, Daniel Perkins, and such oth^r Inhabitants as have left their Possessions and Gone to Enemy's Country by Commandant's Orders.

For Jeremiah Wardwell and }
Thomas Cutter, Inhabitants. } [Signed]

Northern Bay, Majabagwaduce River.

P. W. MacZACHLER, ASST. DPT.
Q^r. M^r. General.

[The *original* order is in the possession of Mr. Hosea Wardwell, of Penobscot.]

*Probably a mistake for Jacob, as Jack is the synonym for John, and Mr. John Perkins is not known to have had any lot at the Head of the Bay, while Jacob Perkins resided there at that time.

III.

DOCUMENTS RELATING TO THE MUNICIPAL PERIOD.

1.

RESOLVE.

Confirming a grant of land to David Marsh and others conditionally.

November 17, 1786.

The committee on the subject of unappropriated lands in the county of *Lincoln*, when they made their report on the 17th of March, 1785, on the petition of Enoch Bartlett and others, praying for the confirmation of six townships lying between *Penobscot* river, and the *Union* river, which were conditionally granted to David Marsh and others, on the second day of March, 1762, omitted to report respecting the township No. 3, commonly called Majabigwaduce, for reasons therein set forth; but having since examined into the state of the said township, so far as circumstances would permit, now take leave to report,

That in their opinion, it will be expedient to confirm to the said Marsh and others, the said township No. 3, on the conditions contained in the following articles:

1st.   That the proprietors heretofore known, as proprietors of the said township, or as holding under David Marsh and others, do grant, allot, and mete out one hundred acres of land unto each settler on the said township, his heirs or assigns who before the first day of January 1784, settled thereon, and made separate improvement, the same to be laid out in one lot, in such manner as best to include his improvements.   And where any original settler has sold, or otherwise disposed of his improvements to any other person, the purchaser or his heirs and assigns shall hold the same lands, which such original settler would have held, by virtue of this article, if there had been no such sale or disposition.

2nd. That in like manner there be allotted and meted out unto each proprietor, his heirs or assigns, who, before the first day of January, 1784 settled thereon, and made a separate improvement, two hundred acres of land, one hundred acres of which to be in consideration of his being a settler; the same to be laid out in such manner as best to include his improvements.

3d. That in the said township there be allotted, reserved and appropriated four lots of land of three hundred acres each, in situation and quality equal in general to the lots in the division, for the following purposes, *viz.* One lot for the first settled minister, his heirs and assigns; one for the use of the ministry; one to and for the future appropriation of government; and one for the use of a school forever.

4th. That each settler mentioned in article 1st, his heirs or assigns, who has not already done it, shall within five years, build a house, not less than eighteen feet square, and seven feet stud; and clear and cultivate five acres of land fit for mowing or tillage; and pay within six months into the treasury of the propriety of the said townships, *thirty shillings*, to be appropriated to defray the expense of surveying and dividing the said township, and laying out, clearing, and repairing of roads within the same.

5th. That where a settler has made improvement, by clearing or inclosing with a good fence, more than one hundred acres, he shall have the liberty to purchase the lands so improved at a reasonable price, estimating the same as if in a state of nature; or to receive of the proprietor or proprietors of such land, a reasonable allowance for extra improvements at the settler's election; and in case of any disagreement about the said price; or allowance, or any other matter relating to a settlement, that the same be decided by disinterested men, one of whom shall be chosen by the proprietor or proprietors, one by the settler, and in case they cannot agree, the third by the two chosen as aforesaid.

6th. That after the allotments to the settlers, resident proprietors, and for public uses, are made as aforementioned, the residue and remainder of the said lands shall be divided to, and among the proprietors heretofore known as the proprietors of the said township, or as holding under David Marsh and others to whom the said township was conditionally granted, their heirs or assigns in proportion to the respective shares or rights, held in the original division of the said town.

7th. That the division and allotments in the said township be made conformably to the foregoing articles, within the space of twelve months from this time, and a return thereof be made on or before the expiration of the said term of time to the committee on the subject of unappropriated lands in the county of *Lincoln*, specifying and describing therein the lots, number of each, names of the persons to whom allotted, and those for public uses, under their particular heads. And if it shall appear by the said return, that a quantity of land exceeding six thousand acres, has been allotted, meted and assigned by the said proprietors, to that class of settlers included in article 1st and by virtue of the same in manner aforesaid, then there shall be granted and conveyed to the said proprietors, their heirs and assigns, in some parts of the township No. 7, in the first division of townships east of Penobscot river, adjoining southerly on the township No. 6 of the same division in part and partly on township No. 1, of the second division of townships, and lying on both sides of *Union* river, so many acres as shall be equal to the quantity of land above six thousand acres which shall be allotted and assigned to the settlers as aforesaid.

8th. If no return be made to the said committee, as required in the preceding article, the said committee shall appoint, and they are hereby accordingly empowered to appoint three disinterested persons as commissioners, to report to the said township, to make the division and return required, and allot and divide the same conformably to the articles 1, 2 and 3, and make return thereof to the said committee, and conformably to the seventh article ; and the said commissioners shall, six weeks at least, before they proceed on the said business, give public notice in Adams and Nourse's Independent Chronicle, the Portland newspaper, and by a written notification, posted up in some convenient place in the said township, of their appointment and of the time when they shall proceed on the said business, that all persons interested therein may be apprised thereof ; and the lots the said commissioner shall lay out to the resident proprietors and settlers as provided for in article first and second shall be confirmed unto them, and the remaining lots shall be subject to the order and disposal of the General Court, and the expense arising from said appointment of commissioners, shall be defrayed by the resident proprietors and settlers of said township, provided they have prevented or obstructed the division as provided for in articles 2nd, 3d, and 6th; otherwise, so much of the remainder of the lands (after allotments and divisions made to the resident proprietors, settlers, and for public uses as aforesaid) shall be sold by the said committee, as shall be sufficient to defray the said expence.

9th. That notwithstanding the conditions and regulations contained in the foregoing articles, if the proprietors and settlers of the said township, shall agree among themselves, and settle all matters in dispute, relating to the quantities of land respectively to be held and retained by them, and such other matters and things as immediately respect the settlement of said lands, and make a report of the same to the said committee, within six months from this time, with the names of the settlers and proprietors resident and non-resident, the quantity allotted to each, and the right reserved for public uses, conformably to article 3d, in such case the said committee shall have full authority to confirm the said township; but in case no report shall be made as aforesaid to the said committee, nor return as in the 7th article is required, the said committee shall appoint commissioners, as provided for in the 8th article (twelve months having been expired, as mentioned in the said 7th article) who shall proceed on their business as pointed out in the said 8th article.

10th. It shall be understood, notwithstanding anything contained in the foregoing articles, that the final confirmation of the said township, shall not be made until there be in the said town, sixty dwelling-houses not less than eighteen feet square, and seven feet stud; sixty protestant families, and also five acres of land cleared on each share, fit for mowing and tillage; also a meeting-house for the public worship of God; and until the proprietors and settlers of said township, shall have settled a learned and protestant minister, and provided for his comfortable support, for which purposes five years shall be allowed.

SAMUEL PHILLIPS, jun. ⎫
NATHANIEL WELLS,   ⎬ Committee.
JOHN BROOKS,   ⎭

44

BOSTON, Nov. 4, 1786.

Read and accepted, and thereupon Resolved, That, the
township No. 3, commonly called Majorbigwaduce, conditionally granted to David Marsh and others, on the second
of March, 1762, be, and it is hereby confirmed to the said
Marsh and others, on the conditions and with the reserva-
tions which in the foregoing report are specified.

2.

Act of Incorporation of the Town of Penobscot.

COMMONWEALTH OF MASSACHUSETTS.

In the year one thousand seven hundred and eighty-
seven.

An Act for Incorporating a certain plantation in the
County of Lincoln, called Majorbigwaduce, or Number
Three, into a town by the name of Penobscot.

Whereas, the Inhabitants of the said plantation, labor
under many difficulties and inconveniences for want of
being Incorporated into a town, therefore,

Be it enacted by the Senate and House of Representatives in General Court assembled, and by the Authority of
the same, that all the Lands lying within the following
limits, with the Inhabitants thereon, viz: Beginning at
Buck's Harbor, so called, on the dividing line between
Number Three, and Number Four; and from thence running Northeasterly on the westerly line of Number Four,
Number Five, and Six to the Southerly Corner of Number
Two; thence westerly on the Southerly line of Number
Two to Penobscot River; thence Southerly down the same
river and Penobscot Bay, to the Southwesternmost part of
Cape Rozier; thence Easterly, including Spectacle Island,
to Buck's Harbor, aforesaid, the place of beginning,
be and are hereby Incorporated into a town by the name of
Penobscot, and the said Town is hereby invested with all
the powers, privileges, and immunities that the towns of
this Commonwealth are entitled to according to Law.

And be it further enacted, that Joseph Hibberd, Esq.,
be, and he hereby is, empowered to issue his warrant to some
principal inhabitant of said town, to warn the Inhabitants
thereof to assemble at such time and place in said town, as
by said warrant shall be appointed, to elect such Town

Officers as are empowered by Law to be chosen annually in the month of March or April, and the said Inhabitants being so assembled, shall be, and hereby are empowered to choose such Officers accordingly.

Provided, nevertheless, that nothing in this Act shall in any manner affect the right of Soil in the lands aforesaid, or discharge the taxes already assessed, or ordered to be assessed, in the said plantation, but the said town shall be considered as held to pay all such taxes which remained due, unpaid, from the said plantation.

In the House of Representatives, February 22, A. D. 1787.

This bill having had three successive readings passed to be Enacted.

[Signed.] ARTEMAS WARD, Speaker of House.

In Senate, February 23, A. D. 1787: This bill having had two several readings passed to be Enacted.

[Signed.] SAMUEL PHILLIPS, Jr.,
President of Senate.

By the Governor, Approved.
[Signed.] JAMES BOWDOIN.

A true copy,
[Signed.] JOHN AVERY, Jr., Secretary.

3.

Act of Incorporation of the Town of Castine.

COMMONWEALTH OF MASSACHUSETTS.

In the year of our Lord one thousand seven hundred and ninety-six.

An Act to divide the Town of Penobscot into two distinct towns, and to incorporate the southerly part thereof into a Town by the name of Castine.

Be it enacted by the Senate and House of Representatives in General Court assembled, and by authority of the same, that the Town of Penobscot in the County of Hancock, be, and hereby is, divided into two separate and distinct towns, and that the southerly part thereof, bounded as follows, viz: beginning at the northwest corner of Andrew Steele's lot of land on Penobscot Bay, or river, so called, thence running on said Steele's northerly line till it strikes the center line, so called, dividing the lots on each side of the neck of land; thence down said center line a southwesterly course till it comes to the dividing line between Oliver Parker, Esq., and Peter Mograge; thence by said dividing line a southerly course to Moore's Cove, so called; from thence over the waters of Majabiguaduce river, so called, including the whole of the Peninsula, to the northerly line of land belonging to John Condon, in the Cove opposite the Peninsula; thence running south seventy-eight and three-quarters of a degree east, to the line dividing Penobscot from Sedgwick; thence southwesterly adjoining the Town of Sedgwick, to Buck's Harbor, so called; thence following the course of the Bay round Cape Rozier to the northwestern extremity of the Peninsula of Penobscot; thence round the Bay called Penobscot Bay, or river, to the northwesterly corner of Andrew Steele's lot aforesaid; together with all Islands included within said lines; and the Inhabitants within the same be, and they hereby are, Incorporated into a Town by the name of Castine, with all the powers, privileges, and authority of other towns in this Commonwealth.

And whereas, the Courts of Common Pleas, and Court of General Sessions of the Peace for the County of Hancock, have been heretofore holden in that part of the Town of Penobscot now hereby incorporated:

Be it further enacted by the Authority aforesaid, that the said Courts shall continue to be holden in said Town of Castine; and that the said Town of Castine shall be, and hereby is constituted the Shire Town of said County of Hancock; and all writs, precepts, and judicial proceedings whatever, which are, or may be, returnable to either of the Courts aforesaid, shall be accepted, adjudged and considered by the said Courts in the said Town of Castine, any law to the contrary notwithstanding.

And be it further enacted by the Authority aforesaid, that until a new general valuation is taken, the State taxes which may be called for from the aforesaid towns, shall be levied in the following proportion, viz: three-fifths of the whole sum on the Town of Castine, and two-fifths thereof on the Town of Penobscot; and each of the aforesaid towns shall be holden to pay such proportion accordingly.

And be it further enacted by the Authority aforesaid, that Oliver Parker, Esq., be, and hereby is, authorized and directed to issue his warrant to some principal inhabitant of the said Town of Castine, requiring him to notify the Inhabitants of said town, qualified as the law directs, to assemble at the time and place by him appointed, to elect such Town Officers as they are by law empowered to elect in the months of March or April annually:—

Provided, however, that nothing in this Act contained, shall be construed as a relinquishment of any Property, which either of the towns aforesaid may claim, as belonging to Township Number Three, before its incorporation.

In the House of Representatives, February the eighth, one thousand seven hundred and ninety-six. This bill having had three several readings passed to be enacted.

[Signed] EDWIN H. ROBBINS, Speaker.

In Senate, February the eighth, one thousand seven hundred and ninety-six. This bill having had two several readings passed to be enacted.

[Signed] THOMAS DAWES, President *pro. tem.*

By the Governor, Approved February the thirteenth, one thousand seven hundred and ninety-six.

[Signed] SAMUEL ADAMS.

A true copy—Attest

[Signed] JOHN AVERY, Jr., Secretary.

Attest

[Signed] THOMAS PHILLIPS, Town Clerk.

[From the Town Records.]

4.

A List of the Families belonging to the Town of Castine, November, 1796.

No.	Names.	Born in Town of	County of	Time of Birth.	Time of Death.
1.	Joseph Perkins,	Old York,	York,	October 18, 1746,	August 20, 1818.
2.	Phebe Perkins, his wife,	"	"	December 1768,	(?) In 1815.
3.	Mary Perkins, their daughter,	"	"	December 27, 1770,	December 3, 1833.
4.	William Perkins, their son,	"	"	[Date unk own.]	[Date unk own.]
5.	Joseph Perkins, Jr., their son,	"	"	July 28, 1774,	"
6.	James Perkins, their son,	Majabigwaduce,	Lincoln,	March 26, 1776,	September 12. 1815.
7.	Dolly Perkins, their daughter,	Old York,	York,	June 15, 1779,	November 3, 1856.
8.	Ebenezer Perkins, their son,	Majabigwaduce,	Lincoln,	June 3, 1781,	July 26, 1827.
9.	Rufus Perkins, their son,	Penobscot,	"	June 4, 1785,	(?) In 1818.
10.	Phebe Perkins, their daughter,	"	"	April 12, 87,	[Date unkn.]
11.	Abigail Perkins, their daughter,	"	Hancock,	November 8, 1788,	" "
12.	Peggy Perkins, their daughter,	"	York,	April 19, 90,	January 30, 1838.
13.	David Wh.,	Old York,	"	March 23, 1753,	April 23, 1833.
14.	Miriam, his wife,	Wells,	Lincoln,	March 7, 1757,	March [date unkn.]
15.	Nathaniel Willson, their son,	Wells,	"	May 29, 1782,	[Date
16.	Benjamin Willson, their son,	Majabigwaduce,	"	February 5. 1785,	" "
17.	Josiah Willson, their son,	Penobscot,	Hancock,	March 18, 1787,	" "
18.	Susannah Willson, their daughter,	"	"	September 3. 1789,	" "
19.	Mary Willson, their daughter,	"		January 21, 1792,	May 22, 1799.
20.	David Willson, their son,	[Unknown.]	[Unknown.]	March 6, 1794,	[Date unknown.]
21.	John Lee,	"	"	[Date unknown.]	"
22.	Sally Lee, his wife,	Majabigwaduce,	Lincoln,		October 18, 1786.
23.	Lucy Lee, their daughter,	"	"	September 3, 1785,	[Date unl own.]
24.	John Lee, Jr., their son,	"	"	March, 6, 1787,	April 6, 1789.
25.	Joseph Lee, their son,	Penobscot,	Hancock,	November 18, 1788,	November 29. 1842.
26.	Chloe — natural daughter of Patience,	Boston,	Suffolk,	April 10, 1795,	November 3, 1828.
27.	David Howe,	Boston,	"	March 25, 1759,	September 14, 1807.
28.	Margaret Howe, his wife,	Boston,	"	October 29, 1761,	[Date unknown.]
29.	Mary Franks (an apprentice to Mr. Howe),	Pembroke,	Plymouth,	February, 1785,	" "
30.	William,	Old York,	York,	August 8, 1749,	
31.	Lucy, his wife,			August 13, 1757,	

No.	Names.	Born in Town of	County of	Time of Birth.	Time of Death.
32.	Mary Turner, their daughter,	Penobscot,	Hancock,	May 21, 1792,	[Date unknown].
33.	William Turner, Jr., their son,	"	"	July 3, 1794,	"
34.	Deborah Orr,	Lynn,	Essex,	July 25, 1761,	"
35.	Deborah Orr, dr son.	Boston,	Suffolk,	January 9, 1778,	"
36.	Winthrop Gray Orr. dr son.	Boston,		April 8, 1783.	
37.	Rachel Dobbie (apprentice to Mrs. Orr,)	Penobscot,	Hancock,	August, 1793,	
38.	Jno Orcutt,		No record in the book—other than this.		
39.	Abigail Orcutt, his wife,			"	
40.	Malachi Orcutt, their son,			"	
41.	Pamela Orcutt, their daughter.			"	
42.	Jacob Orcutt, Jr., their son.			"	
43.	Hannah Orcutt, their daughter,			"	
44.	Thomas Orcutt, their son,			"	
45.	James Orcutt, their son,			"	
46.	Galen Orcutt, their son,			"	[Date unknown].
47.	Abigail Orcutt, their daughter,	Georgetown,	Lincoln,	June 23, 1766,	"
48.	Andrew Melziar Blake,	"	"	June 26, 1762,	"
49.	Susannah Blake, his wife,	Majabigwaduce,	"	October 23, 1785,	"
50.	Prudence Blake, their daughter,	"	"	October 5, 1787,	"
51.	Susannah Blake,	Penobscot,	Hancock,	October 29, 1789,	"
52.	Andrew Blake, their son,	"	"	October 14, 1791,	"
53.	Ruth Blake, their daughter,			November 13, 1793,	"
54.	Richard Blake, their son,			February 16, 1767,	"
55.	Israel Reedman,	Scarborough,		July 2, 1766,	"
56.	Abigail Reedman, his wife,	Salem,	Essex,	August 9, 1788,	"
57.	Mehitabel Reedman, their daughter,	Sedgwick,	Lincoln,	September 29, 1789,	"
58.	Abigail Reedman, " "	Penobscot,	Hancock,	December 23, 91,	October 4, 1792.
59.	Sarah Reedman, " "	"	"	July 13, 1793,	September 16,
60.	Polly Reedman, " "	"	"	February 6, 1795,	August 16, 1795.
61.	Robert Reedman, their son,	Union River,		October 12, 1789,	[Date
62.	Mathew Montgomery.	Rencleven,	Perth in Scotland.	June 10, 60,	January 6, 1849.
63.	James Scott, in the Parish of	Westerly,	State of Rhode Isla	March 14, 1751,	March 24, 1849.
64.	Huldah Scott, his wife,	Penobscot,	Lincoln,	April 16, 1783,	[Date unknown.]
65.	Elinor Scott, their daughter,	St. Andrews,	Charlotte (N. B.),	April 1, 1785,	"
66.	Mary Scott, their daughter,	Scituate,	Plymouth,	August 14, 1746,	August 5, 1833.
67.	Mark Hatch,				

No.	Names.	Born in Town of	County of	Time of Birth.	Time of Death.
68.	Abigail Hatch, his wife,	Marshfield,	Plymouth,	May 7, 1776,	November 30, 1831.
69.	Mark Hatch, Jr., their son,	Majabigwaduce,	Lincoln,	Mar 6, 1771,	[Date unknown.]
70.	Nathan Hatch, " "	"	"	August 28, 1774,	"
71.	John Hatch " "	"	"	October 19, 1777,	"
72.	James Hatch, " "	"	"	October 21, 1779,	"
73.	Abigail Hatch, their daughter,	"	"	March 9, 1783,	December 27, 1796.
74.	Eggathy Phillips Hatch, their daughter,	"	"	April 19, 1785,	[Date unknown.]
75.	Lucy Hatch,	Penobscot,	"	April 25, 1793,	"
76.	Bill, (a negro boy in the family)				"
77.	John Collins,	Mount Desert,	Hancock,	July 24, 1770,	"
78.	Polly Collins, his wife,	Westerly,	Province of Maine,	July 1, 1771,	"
79.	David Collins, their son,	Penobscot,	State of R. Island,	October 24, 1792,	"
80.	Asa Collins, " "	Castine,	Hancock,	October 10, 94,	"
81.	James Collins, " "	Majabigwaduce,	"	January 9, 97,	"
82.	William Collins,	Beverly,	Lincoln,	October 1, 1781,	"
83.	Benjamin Rea,	"	Essex,	September 6, 1751,	"
84.	Lydia Rea, his wife,		"	November 29, 1754.	"
85.	... Rea, Jr., their son,			August 8, 1775.	"
86.	Hannah Rea, ... their daughter,	Lunenburgh,	Worcester,	November , 118,	"
87.	J...a Rea, their son,	Fitchburg,	"	July 30, 180,	"
88.	Lucy Rea, their daughter,	Newbury,	Essex.	May 15, 1782.	"
89.	Nancy Rea, " "	"	"	January 27, 1784,	"
90.	Sally Rea, " "			February 2, 1786	"
91.	Hiley Rea, " "	Deer Isle,	Lincoln,	January 6, 90,	"
92.	Polly Rea, " "	Penobscot,	Hancock,	October 4, 192,	"
93.	Gritha Rea, " "	"	"	March 19, 1794.	"
94.	...er Rea, their son,	"	"	July 26, 1795,	"
95.	Emma Rea, their daughter	"	"	May 19, 1797,	April, 1841.
96.	...er Perkins	Castine,	[not given.]	February 13, 1751,	[not given.]
97.	Lydia Perkins, his wife,	[not given]	"	13, 1752,	"
98.	Lydia Perkins, their daughter,	"	"	December 11, 1775,	"
99.	J...n Perkins, their son,	"	"	April 1, 1777,	"
100.	James Perkins, Jr.,	"	"	May 4, 181,	"
101.	Stover Perkins, Jr., their son,	"	"	June 29, 1784,	"
102.	...na Perkins, their daughter,	"	"	July 30, 1786,	"

No.	Names.	Born in Town of	County of	Time of Birth.	Time of Death.
103.	Mark Per cihs, their son,	[Not given.]	[Not given.]	Fber 27, 788,	[Date unknown]
104.	irh Perkins, their son;	"	"	Mar 25, 1791,	"
105.	Jonathan P rkin se "	"	"	uuary 17, 1796,	"
106.	Benjamin nay,	Gloucester,	Essex,	March 3, 769,	"
107.	byil Courtney, his wife,	Harpswell,	Cumberland,	August 20, 1770,	"
108.	Sally uuly, their daughter,	Penobscot,	Hancock,	Mar 23, 1794,	"
109.	Peggy may, their daughter,	Vinalhaven,	"	July 8, 1796,	"
110.	Samuel Courtney, their son,	Castine,		ober 23, 1797,	"
111.	Ephraim Blake,	East Nottingham,	State of N. H.	August 19, 1752,	"
112.	Mary Blake, his wife,	Fort Pownal, (Penobscot River),	P.of Me.	Not given.]	"
113.	Elisha Bd, their son,	Majabigwaduce,	Lincoln,	April 10, 1776,	"
114.	Edward Be, their son,	"	"	April 2, 1778,	"
115.	Mary Blake, their their,			ust 4, 1780,	"
116.	Ephraim d, Jr., their son,	[Not given.]	[Not given.]	[N t given.]	"
117.	Hannah Blake, their uh,	"	"		"
118.	Israel Bd, their son,	"	"	"	"
119.	Sarah Blake, their daughter,	"	"	"	"
120.	Betsey Blake, "	"	"	"	"
121.	John (Ban,	Scarborough,			"
122.	Margaret (Bn, his wife,	Bristol,		"	"
123.	Sally (Bn, their daughter,	[Not given.]	[Not given.]	"	"
124.	John Redman, Jr., their son,	"	"	"	"
125.	Benjamin (Ban, their son,	"	"	"	"
126.	Jenny (Ban, their daughter,	"	"	"	"
127.	Margaret (Ban, their daughter,	"	"	"	"
128.	John (Ban (d), their son,	"	"	"	"
129.	Peggy and, their daughter,	"	"	"	"
130.	Jonathan Foster,	Ipswich,	Essex,	June 21, 1749,	"
131.	Bd der, his wife,	"	"	May 27, 1749,	"
132.	i Sah For, their i der,	"	"	September 15, 1773,	"
133.	Eel ter, their daughter,	"	"	Mch 13, 1705,	"
B4.	dn (ter, their son,	Fox Islands,	Lincoln,	De 19, 1777,	"
135.	Jaes (Gr, their son,	"	"	September 11, 1780,	"
136.	Hannah (ter, their daughter,	"	"	July 25, 1782,	"
137.	Eli bah Foster, their daughter,	"	"	Mch 19, 1784,	"
138.	Barbara Foster, their daughter,	Lincoln,	Lincoln,	ober 3, 1785,	[Date unknown.]
139.	Joshua B. Foster, t their son,	"	"	July 12, 1787,	Still living.

45

No.	Names.	Born in Town of	County of	Time of Birth.	Time of Death.
140.	Hepzibah Foster, their daughter,	Fox Islands,	Lincoln,	August 3, 1789,	[Date unknown.]
141.	Abigail Foster, their daughter,			December 16, 1790,	"
142.	Barnabas Higgins,		Hancock,	November 12, 1745,	"
143.	Abigail Higgins, his wife,	Wellfleet,	Barnstable,	April 12, 1743,	"
144.	?oah Higgins, ?ir daughter,	"	"	October 8, 1771,	December, 1794,
145.	Barnabas Higgins, Jr., } twin children,	"	"	November 22, 1774,	[Date unknown.]
146.	Abigail Higgins,	"	"	"	"
147.	M?a Atwood Higgins, their daughter,	Majabigwaduce,	Lincoln,	January 23, 1786,	"
148.	?an Holbrook,	Georgetown,	Province of Maine,	February 1, 1768,	"
149.	Easter Holbrook, his wife,	Hollis,	Hampshire,	?er 8, 1766,	"
150.	Harriet Holbrook, their daughter,	Penobscot,	Lincoln,	January 13, 1794,	"
151.	Ruth Holbrook, th?ir daughter,	Castine,	Hancock,	May 9, 1796,	"
152.	Holbr ?o Martine,	Marblehead,	Essex,	January 28, 1773,	"
153.	Lydia ?a?is wife,	Concord,	Mas?,	?er 1, 1771,	"
154.	Silas Hosmer Martine, his wife,	Penobscot,	Hancock,	July 18, 95,	"
155.	Lucy Lee ?r?, ?ir daughter,	Castine,	"	May 23, 1797,	"
156.	Joseph Young,	Hampton Falls,	New Hampshire,	February 12, 1727,	"
157.	M?rtha Y?ung, ?his wife,	Stratham,	"	August 13, 1733,	"
158.	Sally Young, their daughter,	"	"	June 13, ?9,	"
159.	??a Young, ?ir ?r,	Majabigwaduce,	Province of Maine,	May 28, 1771,	"
160.	John Bakeman, Jr.,	Stratham,	New Hampshire,	March 26, 1764,	"
161.	Sally Bakeman, his wife,	Penobscot,	Hancock,	June 13, 1769,	"
162.	J?neBakeman (3d), his son,	"	"	July 26, 1790,	"
163.	Sally Bakeman, ?ir daughter,	"	"	July 4, 1792,	"
164.	Nancy Young Bakeman, their daughter,	"	"	August 18, 1794,	"
165.	Luther Bakeman, ?ir son,	Castine,	[Not given],	February 8, 97,	: "
166.	William ??th,	Summersworth,	Province of Maine.	?st 19, 1765,	"
167.	a?ha Wi ?rth, his wife,	Majabigwaduce,	Hancock,	?er 29, 1771,	"
168.	William Wintworth, their ?o	Frankfort,	"	March 27, 1791,	"
169.	Thomas Wintworth, ?ir son,	"	"	July 22, 1793,	"
170.	J?ha Wintworth, their s?,	"	"	August 30, 1795,	"
171.	Charles Winship Hall, son of Warr ?eHall,	Castine,		[Not given.]	

[Copied from the Town Records—Remarks in brackets excepted.]
On page 74, the population of the town is given as 178. This is an error arising from our supposing that the foregoing was—what it purports to b —accorrect list. We are s?id, v ?ar, that the above list is only of those living in the village of Castine. At all ev?ts it is an incomplete one of the ?hole t?wn.

5.

An Act to incorporate the town of Brooksville.

SEC. 1. BE *it enacted by the Senate and House of Representatives in General Court assembled, and by the authority of the same,* That those parts of the towns of Castine, Penobscot, and Sedgwick, included in the following boundaries, viz: Beginning at the water on the line between Castine and Penobscot, there bounded by the waters of the harbour of Castine, and by Castine river, to land of John Walker, on the southerly side of said river; thence on the line of said lot, including the same to the water; thence from the outlet of Walker's Pond, so called, southwesterly, to the southerly line of Isaac Billings' land; thence, on said southerly line, to the sea; thence running by the sea-shore round Cape Rozier, and by the shores of Castine harbour, to the first mentioned bounds; together with the inhabitants thereon, be, and are hereby incorporated into a town, by the name of Brooksville; and the said town is hereby vested with all the privileges and immunities which other towns do, or may enjoy by the Constitution and laws of this Commonwealth: *Provided,* that the inhabitants within the boundaries aforesaid, shall be holden to pay to the several towns, to which they have heretofore belonged, their several proportions of all taxes voted by said towns, together with all state and county taxes, apportioned on said towns, before the passing of this act.

SEC. 2. *Be it further enacted,* That in all state taxes, which shall hereafter be granted by the General Court of this Commonwealth, until a new valuation shall be settled, one-eighth part of the taxes which would have been set to the town of Sedgwick, one-fifth part which would have been set to the town of Penobscot, and one-fifth part which would have been set to Castine, according to the last valnation, shall be taken from said towns and set to the said town of Brooksville.

SEC. 3. *Be it further enacted,* That William Abbott, Esquire, be, and he is hereby authorized to issue a warrant, directed to some suitable inhabitant of said town of Brooksville, requiring him to notify the inhabitants thereof, to meet at such time and place as shall be appointed in said warrant, for the election of all such officers as towns are entitled to choose in the month of March, or April annually. —Approved by the Governor, June 13, 1817.—
[Laws of Massachusetts—1817.]

6.

An Act to set off a part of the town of Penobscot, and annex the same to the town of Castine.

SEC. 1. BE *it enacted by the Senate and House of Representatives, in General Court assembled, and by the authority of the same,* That that part of the town of Penobscot, in the county of Hancock, hereafter described, and the inhabitants thereon, be annexed to the town of Castine, in said county, viz: That part of said Penobscot lying between Penobscot and Castine rivers, and southerly and westerly of t e following lines, viz: Beginning at the first narrows in Castine river, on the northerly line of Lot Number sixty, laid out to Pelatiah Freeman, deceased, and surveyed by John Peters, and John Peters, Jun.; thence on the northerly line of said Lot Number sixty, north-westerly to the centre line; thence northerly on the centre line, to the southerly line of Lot Number twenty-two; thence westerly to the easterly end of Lot Number twenty-three; thence northerly on the head or easterly end of Lot Number twenty-three, and continuing the same course to the stream, which empties into Morse's Cove, so called; thence down said stream to said Cove.

SEC. 2. *Be it further enacted,* That the inhabitants of the said part of the town of Penobscot, by this act annexed to the said town of Castine, shall be holden to pay such taxes as have been assessed, or ordered to be assessed on them by the said town of Penobscot, previous to passing of this act.

SEC. 3. *Be it further enacted,* That in all state taxes, which shall hereafter be granted, by the General Court of this Commonwealth, until a new valuation shall be settled, one quarter part of the taxes which would have been set to the town of Penobscot, according to the last valuation, shall be taken therefrom and set to the town of Castine.

SEC. 4. *Be it further enacted,* That no person who is now supported wholly or in part, by any town in this Commonwealth, shall, by the passing of this act, thereby gain a settlement in said town of Castine.

—Approved by the Governor, June 16, 1817.—
[Laws of Massachusetts, 1817—p. 420.]

7.

General Sherbrook's Account of the Capture of Castine.

[From an English Paper.]

DOWNING STREET, October 9, 1814.

Major Addison has arrived with the following despatch from Lieutenant General Sherbrook, dated:

Castine, at the entrance to the Penobscot, Sept. 18.

MY LORD:

I have now the honor to inform your Lordship that, after closing my despatch, on the 26th ult.—in which I mentioned my intention of proceeding to the Penobscot—Rear Admiral Griffith and myself lost no time in sailing from Halifax, with such a naval force as he deemed necessary, and the troops as per margin,* to accomplish the object we had in view.

Very early in the morning of the 30th, we fell in with the *Rifleman*, Sloop of war, when Captain Pearse informed us that the United States frigate *Adams*, had got into the Penobscot, but from the apprehension of being attacked by your cruisers, if she remained at the entrance of the river, she ran up as high as Hampden, where she had landed her guns, and mounted them on shore for her protection.

On leaving Halifax, it was my original intention to have taken possession of Machias, on our way hither; but on receiving this intelligence, the Admiral and myself were of opinion that no time should be lost in proceeding to our destination, and we arrived here very early on the morning of the first instant.

The Fort of Castine, which is situated upon a peninsula, of the eastern side of the Penobscot, near the entrance of that river, was summoned a little after sunrise; but the American officer refused to surrender it, and immediately opened a fire from four 24-pounders upon a small schooner that had been sent with Lieutenant Colonel Nicholls (commanding the Royal Engineers) to reconnoitre the work.

Arrangements were immediately made for disembarking the troops; and before a landing could be effected, the enemy blew up his magazine, and escaped up the Majetaquadous river, carrying off in the boats with them two field-pieces.

As we had no means of ascertaining what force the

*See note on p. 356.

Americans had on this peninsula, I landed a detachment of Royal Artillery, with two companies of the 60th and 98th regiments, under Colonel Douglass, in the rear of it, with orders to secure the isthmus, and to take possession of the heights which commanded the town; but I soon learned that there was no regulars at Castine, except the party which had blown up the magazine and escaped, and that the militia which were assembled there had dispersed immediately on our landing.

Rear Admiral Griffith and myself next turned our attention to obtaining possession of the *Adams*, or, if that could not be done, to destroying her. The arrangements for this service having been made, the Rear Admiral entrusted the execution of it to Captain Barrie, Royal Navy, and as the co-operation of the land force was necessary, I directed Lieutenant Colonel John, with a detachment of artillery, the flank companies of the 29th, 62d, and 98th regiments, and one rifle company of the 60th, to accompany and co-operate with Captain Barrie on this occasion; but as Hampden is twenty-seven miles above Castine, it appeared to be a necessary measure of precaution first to occupy a port on the western bank, which might afford support, if necessary, to the force going up the river, and at the same time prevent the armed population, which is very numerous to the southward and westward, from annoying the British in their operations on the *Adams*.

Upon inquiry, I found that Belfast, which is upon the high road leading from Hampden to Boston, and which perfectly commands the bridge, was likely to answer both these purposes, and I consequently directed Major General Gosselin to occupy that place with the 29th regiment, and to maintain it till further orders.

As soon as this was accomplished, and the tide served, Rear Admiral Griffith directed Captain Barrie to proceed to his destination, and the remainder of the troops were landed that evening at Castine.

Understanding that a strong party of militia from the neighboring township, had assembled at about four miles from Castine, on the road leading to Bluehill, I sent out a strong patrol on the morning of the second, before day-break. On arriving at the place, I was informed that the militia of the county had assembled thereon, the alarm guns being fired at the Fort at Castine, upon our first appearance, but that the main body had since dispersed and returned to their respective homes. Some stragglers were, however, left, who fired upon our advanced guard, and then took to the woods; a few of whom were made prisoners. No intelligence having reached us from Captain Barrie on Saturday night, I marched with about 700 men and two light field-pieces on Buckstown, at three o'clock on Sunday morning, the fourth inst., for the purpose of learning what progress he had made, and of affording him assistance, if required. This place is about eighteen miles higher up the Penobscot than Castine, and on the eastern bank of the river. Rear Admiral Griffith accompanied me on this occasion, and as we had reason to believe that the light guns which had been taken from Castine were secreted in the neighborhood of Buckstown, we threatened to destroy the town, unless they were delivered up, and the two brass 3-pounders on travelling carriages were, in consequence, brought to us in the course of the day, and are now in our possession.

At Buckstown we received very satisfactory accounts of the success which had attended the force employed up the river. We learned that Captain Barrie proceeded from Hampden to Bangor; and the Admiral sent an officer in a boat from Buckstown to communicate with him, when finding there was no necessity for the troops remaining longer at Buckstown, they marched back to Castine the next day.

Having ascertained that the object of the expedition up the Penobscot had been attained, it was no longer necessary for me to occupy Belfast, I therefore, on the evening of the sixth, directed Major General Gosselin to embark the troops and join me here.

Machias being the only place now remaining where the enemy had a post between the Penobscot and Passamaquoddy Bay, I ordered Lieutenant Colonel Pilkington to proceed with a detachment of Royal Artillery and the 27th regiment to occupy it; and as naval assistance was required, Rear Admiral Griffith directed Captain Parker, of the *Tenedos*, to co-operate with Lieutenant Colonel Pilkington on this occasion.

On the morning of the ninth Captain Barrie, with Lieutenant Colonel John, and the troops which had been employed with him up the Penobscot, returned to Castine. It seems the enemy blew up the *Adams*, on his strong position at Hampden being attacked; but all his artillery, two stands of colors, and a standard, with several merchant vessels, fell into our hands. This, I am happy to say, was accomplished with very little loss on our part; and your Lordship will perceive, by the return sent herewith, that the only officer wounded in this affair is Captain Gell, of the 29th Grenadiers.

[Signed.]   J. C. SHERBROOK.

*First Company Royal Artillery, two rifle companies of the 7th batt. 60th Regt. 29th, 62d and 98th regiments.

8.

Deeds of Peninsula School Lot.

1. *Joseph Perkins to Treasurer of Castine.*

KNOW ALL MEN BY THESE PRESENTS,
That I, Joseph Perkins, of Castine, County of Hancock, Commonwealth of Massachusetts, Merchant, in consideration of ninety dollars to me in hand paid by William Mason, of Castine, aforesaid, Clerk and Treasurer of the Town of Castine, aforesaid, in behalf of the Inhabitants of the school district in said town, commonly known and called by the name of the Peninsula School District, the receipt whereof, I do hereby acknowledge, do give, grant, sell, and convey to the said William Mason, a certain tract, or lot of land lying in said Castine, bounded and described as follows, to wit: Beginning on Center street, fifty-one feet northwest from the west corner of land belonging to the heirs of Samuel Whitney, deceased; thence running northeasterly, at right angles from said street, one hundred feet; thence northwesterly on a line parallel with said street, thirty feet; thence southwesterly on a line parallel with the line just above described, one hundred feet to said street; and thence southeasterly on said street thirty feet to the first mentioned bounds. To Have and to Hold the aforegranted premises to him the said William Mason, his successors in the said office or assigns, in trust to and for the sole use and benefit of the Inhabitants of the said School District, for the purpose of erecting thereon a building for the accommodation of said District for a school house forever. And I do covenant with the said William Mason,

his successors and assigns, that I am lawfully seized of the aforegranted premises; that they are free of all incumbrances; that I have a good right to sell and convey the same, in manner aforesaid; and that I, my heirs, executors, and administrators will warrant and defend the same to the said William Mason, his successors in said office or assigns, against the lawful claims and demands of all persons. In witness whereof, I, the said Joseph Perkins, together with Phœbe, wife of the said Joseph, she hereby relinquishing her right of dower, have hereunto set our hands and seals this twenty-eighth day of September, in the year of our Lord one thousand eight hundred and eleven.

Signed, Sealed and delivered in presence of us,

David Willson. } [Signed] JOSEPH PERKINS. [Seal.]
William Abbott. } [Signed] PHŒBE PERKINS. [Seal.]

HANCOCK ss. Castine, November 4, 1811. Personally appeared the above named Joseph Perkins, and acknowledged the foregoing instrument to be his free act and deed.

Before me, [Signed] WILLIAM ABBOTT, J. P.

2. John Perkins to Treasurer of Castine.

KNOW ALL MEN BY THESE PRESENTS, that I, John Perkins, of Castine, in the County of Hancock, Merchant, in consideration of ninety dollars to me paid by William Mason, of Castine aforesaid, Clerk and Treasurer of the Town of Castine, aforesaid, in behalf of the Inhabitants of the school district in said town, commonly known and called by the name of the Peninsula School District, the receipt whereof I do hereby acknowledge, do give, grant, sell and convey to the said William Mason a certain tract or lot of land lying in said Castine, bounded and described as follows, to wit: beginning on Center street, twenty-one feet northwest from the west corner of land belonging to the heirs of Samuel Whitney, deceased; thence running northeasterly at right angles from said street one hundred feet; thence northwesterly on a line parallel with said street thirty feet; thence southwesterly on a line parallel with the line first above described one

46

hundred feet to said street; and then southeasterly on said street to the bounds first mentioned.

To Have and to Hold the aforegranted premises to him the said William Mason, his successors in the said office or assigns, in trust to and for the sole use and benefit of the Inhabitants of the said School District, for the purpose of erecting thereon a building for the accommodation of said District for a school house forever. And I do covenant with the said William Mason, his successors and assigns, that I am lawfully seized of the premises; that they are free of all incumbrances; that I have good right to sell and convey the same in manner aforesaid; and that I, my heirs, executors and administrators, will warrant and defend the same to the said William Mason, his successors in said office or assigns, against the lawful claims and demands of all persons. In witness whereof, I the said John Perkins, have hereunto set my hand and seal this twenty-eighth day of September, in the year of our Lord eighteen hundred and eleven.

[Signed]   JOHN PERKINS,   [L. S.]
                      his X mark.

Signed, Sealed and delivered in presence of us.
The words " in trust " interlined
before signing, [Signed] B. HALL.

HANCOCK ss. Castine, November 4, 1811. Then the aforenamed John Perkins acknowledged the aforegoing instrument to be his free act and deed.

Before me, [Signed]   B. HALL, Justice of Peace.

9.

Deed of Meeting-House Lot, &c.

John Perkins to Inhabitants of Castine.

KNOW ALL MEN BY THESE PRESENTS,
That I, John Perkins, of Castine, in the County of Hancock, and Commonwealth of Massachusetts, Gentleman, in consideration of ten dollars, paid by the Inhabitants of Castine, in said County, the receipt whereof I do hereby acknowledge, do hereby give, grant, sell and convey unto the said Inhabitants a certain piece or lot of land lying and being in said Town of Castine,' and bounded as fol-

lows, viz:—Beginning at the northerly corner bounds of a piece of land lately conveyed by Captain Joseph Perkins to the Inhabitants of the County of Hancock; thence running northeast by land improved by James Perkins, Henry Whitney and myself, to land belonging to William Freeman, Esq., to a post, being the west corner bound of said Freeman's land; thence southeast by said Freeman's land to Court street; thence southwest on said Court street to said land conveyed as aforesaid to said Inhabitants of said County; thence northwest on the same land to the bound first mentioned. Said land is hereby conveyed to said Inhabitants of said Castine, for the public buildings of said town, and other public uses—on which the Meeting House and School House now stand—whenever the premises shall cease to be improved by said Inhabitants for said purposes, the same shall then revert to the said John Perkins and his heirs: reserving however a free passage to said Whitney from his dwelling house to said Court street. To have and to Hold the aforegranted premises to the said Inhabitants of said Castine for said purposes, to their use and behoof forever. And I do covenant with the said Inhabitants of said Castine and their successors, that I am lawfully seized in Fee of the afore-granted premises; that they are free of all incumbrances; that I have good right to sell and convey the same to the said Inhabitants of the said Castine; and that I will warrant and defend the same premises to the said Inhabitants of said Castine and their successors forever, against the lawful claims and demands of all persons.

In witness whereof, I, the said John Perkins, have hereunto set my hand and seal this seventh day of June, in the year of our Lord one thousand eight hundred and fifteen.

Signed, sealed and delivered
    in presence of us,

Mason Shaw. ⎱ [Signed.]
Doty Little. ⎰

[Signed.]   JOHN PERKINS,   [L. S.]
        his X mark.

HANCOCK ss. CASTINE, June 7, 1815. Then the above named John Perkins, personally appeared and acknowledged the above instrument to be his free Act and Deed.

Before me,
[Signed.]   MASON SHAW, Justice of Peace.

10.

Deeds of Common Lot.

1. *Winslow Lewis to Inhabitants of Castine.*

KNOW ALL MEN BY THESE PRESENTS,

That I, Winslow Lewis, of Boston, in the Commonwealth of Massachusetts, Physician, in consideration of seventy-five dollars, to me paid by the Inhabitants of the Town of Castine, in the County of Hancock, in the State of Maine, the receipt whereof is hereby acknowledged, do by these presents grant, remise, release, and forever QUIT CLAIM, unto the said Inhabitants, and their successors, and assigns, all my right, title, interest and estate in and to a certain piece or parcel of land situated in said Castine, and known as the Common Lot, upon which the County Buildings of the said County of Hancock were placed, and bounded as follows, namely: northwesterly by land of the heirs of the late Peggy Brooks, and by land of William Witherell, and Charles J. Abbott; southeasterly by Court street; northeasterly by Castine Common; and southwesterly by land of Otis Little; being the same lot assigned to Rufus Perkins, by Commissioners of Division, as will appear by their Report in Hancock County Probate Office. To have and to hold the above described Premises, to them the said Inhabitants, their successors and assigns, to their use and behoof forever.

And I do covenant for my heirs, executors, and administrators, to and with them, their successors and assigns, that I will and my heirs shall warrant and defend the said Premises unto them, their successors and assigns, against the lawful claims of all persons claiming by, through, or under me but not otherwise.

And for the consideration aforesaid, and for divers other good and valuable considerations, I, Emeline Lewis, wife of the said Winslow Lewis, do hereby release, and Quit Claim unto the said Inhabitants, their successors and assigns, all my right, claim, or possibility of dower, in or out of the afore-described premises.

In witness whereof, we, the said Winslow Lewis and Emeline Lewis, have hereunto set our hands and seals this twenty-ninth day of April, in the year of our Lord eighteen hundred and forty.

Signed, sealed and delivered
    in presence of us,
The words " by Commissioners of Division " previously interlined.

John A. Andrew. }
A. H. Fiske.   } [Signed]

[Signed]   WINSLOW LEWIS. [L. S.]
[Signed]   EMELINE LEWIS. [L. S.]
[Signed] RACHEL CARLETON, { Witness to signature of Emeline Lewis.

COMMONWEALTH OF MASSACHUSETTS.

SUFFOLK ss. 29th April, A. D. 1840.   Then personally appeared the above-named Winslow Lewis, and acknowledged the foregoing instrument to be his free act and deed. Before me [Signed]   A. H. FISKE, Justice of Peace. [Recorded in Book No. 72, Page 506.]

2.   *Otis Little to Inhabitants of Castine.*

KNOW ALL MEN BY THESE PRESENTS,

That I, Otis Little, of Castine, in the County of Hancock, and State of Maine, Esq., and Dorothy Little, my wife, in her right, in consideration of fifty dollars, paid by Silas H. Martin, Rowland H. Bridgham, and Jonathan Perkins, Selectmen of Castine, and in behalf of the Inhabitants of said town, the receipt whereof we do hereby acknowledge, do hereby remise, release, bargain, sell and convey, and forever QUIT CLAIM unto the said Inhabitants of Castine, their heirs and assigns forever, all our right, title, and interest in and to a certain piece of land situated in Castine, and bounded as follows, viz: Beginning at the corner post of Otis Little's garden fence; thence northwesterly by the Town House, eighteen inches from the same, seventy-six feet eight inches to a stake and stones at the corner of the Town House, eighteen inches from the same; thence northeasterly nineteen feet eight inches to a stake and stones; thence southeasterly seventy-six feet four inches to the street; thence southwesterly twenty-one feet four inches to the bounds first mentioned;

it being part of the ground on which the Town House now stands. To Have and to Hold the same, together with all the privileges and appurtenances thereunto belonging to the said Inhabitants of Castine, their heirs and assigns forever, against the lawful claims and demands of all persons claiming by, through, or under me. IN WITNESS WHEREOF, we, the said Otis Little and Dorothy Little, have hereunto set our hands and seals this twenty-sixth day of August, in the year of our Lord one thousand eight hundred and forty-one.

Signed, Sealed and delivered
    in presence of
[Signed] Thomas Cobb.
      [Signed] OTIS LITTLE.   [L. S.]
      [Signed] DOROTHY LITTLE. [L. S.]

HANCOCK ss. August 26, 1841. Personally appeared the above named Otis Little and Dorothy Little, and acknowledge the above instrument to be their free act and deed.

Before me,   [Signed] THOMAS COBB,
                     Justice of Peace.
    [Recorded in Book No. 72, Page 506.]

*A list of the Residents of Majabigwaduce, who were Soldiers in the French and Indian War, in 1759.**

Aaron Banks,	Andrew Herrick,
Hate-evil Colson,	Charles Hutchings,
Josiah Colson,	Nathaniel Veazie.

*A List of the Residents of Plantation No. 3, who were Soldiers in the War of the Revolution.**

Theodore Bowden,	Stephen Kevan,
Edmund Bridges,	Alexander McCarslin,
Hate-evil Colson,	Noah Norton,
Henry Dorr,	Nathaniel Patten,
David Dunbar,	Moses Veazie,
William Hutchings,	Daniel Webber,

William Webber.

*This list is derived from traditional and not from documentary sources, and may not contain all the names that belong in it.

Soldiers of the War of 1812,—*Residents of Castine,* (*Including Brooksville.*)*

Benjamin Bolton,
Nehemiah Bowden,
Oliver Bridges,†
James Collins,†
Joshua Foster,
Cornelius McGee,
John Gray,
Henry Keeler,
Eben Richardson. †

Soldiers of the War of 1812.—*Residents of Penobscot.*

Nicholas Bartlett,‡
Nehemiah Bowden,
Ralph Bowden,
Cyrus Buker,
Henry Dorr,
Stephen Ellis,
Aaron Gray,
John Gray.
Eliakim W. Hutchings,
David Leach,
Joseph Leach,
William Leach,
Alexander McCarslin,
Adam McCarslin,§
Andrew McCarslin,§
James McCarslin,§
Reuben McCarslin,§
Mark S. Patten,
Mighill Patten,‖
Abijah Pray,
John Springfield,
Joel Wardwell,¶
Lewis Wardwell,
Samuel Weaver,
David Wescott.**

11.

List of the members of the Hancock Guards who went to the Aroostook, in 1839.††

Captain Charles H. Wing,
J. Selden Burbank,
Charles A. Cate,‡‡
Mr. —Crehore, Orderly Sg't.
Charles Fitz,
Oakman Gardner,
Thomas E. Hale,
John Heath, Drummer,
Ithiel Lawrence,‡‡
J. Haskell Noyes,
Robert Perkins, Jr.,
John Prim,
Robert Straw,
Wm. B. Walker,
Benj. J. Wilson,
John B. Wilson.

*This list is derived from traditional and not from documentary sources, and may not contain all the names that belong in it.
†Still living.
‡He lost a leg at Plattsburg.
§Sons of Alexander McCarslin.
‖The only one living, in Penobscot, in Sept., 1874.
¶He died at Plattsburg.
**He died in Canada.
††Only the sixteen first mentioned were actually members of the Hancock Guards, though the others were constructively so.
‡‡Started with the company, but provided substitutes on the way.

The following persons also went at this time, either as substitutes, or in some other company:

Samuel Bowden, John Rea,
Elijah Orcutt, John Snowman,
Fayette Buker, David Montgomery, Teamsters.

12.

Roster of Castine Light Infantry,—1858—1860.

COMMANDING OFFICERS.

S. K. Devereux, Captain, A. F. Adams, 3d Lieut.,
C. W. Tilden, 1st Lieut., J. B. Wilson, 4th Lieut.,
S. W. Webster, 2d Lieut.,

John M. Dennett, Standard Bearer.

NON-COMMISSIONED OFFICERS.

Sergeants.

D. D. Wardwell, Jas. C. Collins,
H. B. Robbins, P. J. Hooke.

Corporals.

Charles E. Jarvis, H. L. Macomber,
Isaac Doyle, William T. Hooper.

S. C. Murch, *Musician.*

Privates.

Otis Hatch, John S. Perkins,
J. H. Noyes, Geo. E. Noyes,
S. P. Hatch, Charles Blaisdell,
Z. H. Webber, Samuel B. Stevens,
R. H. Bridgham, A. M. Noyes,
J. S. Norton, E. H. Buker,
R. A. Bridgham, Wm. S. Wescott,
Jeremiah Wescott, Joel Perkins,
John H. Crawford, Mark P. Hatch, Jr.,
E. F. Davies, Otis T. Hooper,
Samuel Bowden, John Lewis,
Elisha D. Perkins, John Taylor,
Sewall Perkins, John McLaughlin,
M. P. Perkins, James Christian,

William Jarvis,
Andrew Collins,
A. B. Osgood,
E. S. Perkins,
Geo. W. Jarvis,
John Clark,
James B. Crawford,
Geo. I. Brown,
E. F. Collins,
I. G. Shepherd,
F. A. Hooke,
James S. Moore,
Richard Tibbetts,

Edward A. Lawrence,
Orville D. Webber,
Wm. M. Lawrence,
Ellis Peterson,
Charles Veazie,
Wilson Hutchins,
Thomas Reynolds,
John Donahue,
Daniel Bridges,
Amos Clark,
B. W. Darling,
John F. Surry,
Augustus Wescott,

Albert King.

HONORARY MEMBERS.

John R. Redman,
James Brophy,
John W. Dresser,

Geo. S. Vose,
S. K. Whiting,
B. B. Foster,

F. H. Jarvis.

47

DOCUMENTARY.

13.

List of Soldiers and Sailors in the War of the Rebellion.

[Compiled from the Reports of the Adjutant General of Maine.]

CASTINE ARMY LIST.

No.	Name.	Rank.	Reg't.	Co.	Date of Enlistment.	Date of Discharge or Death—and Remarks.
1.	Ams, Alvin G.	Priv.	2d Me.	B,	May 28, 1861,	Re-enlisted in 6 D, 31st Regt.—prom. Serg't, wounded May
2.	Ames, Rufus C.	"	"	B,	" "	Mustered out Jue 4, 1863. [21, died June 23, '64.
3.	Bickford, Elisha F.	Corp.	16 Me.	K,	August 14, 1862,	Killed at ..., July 1, 1863.
4.	Blodgett, John J.	Priv.	"	K,	" "	Transferred to V. R. Corps.
5.	..., Edward L.	"	1st H. Art'y.	G,	——1864,	Died in 1865, for disability.
6.	Bowden, Frank M.	"	16th Me.	K,	——1862,	Died from wounds, July 20, 1863.—Interred at Gettysburg.
7.	Bowden, G. W.	"	1B,	F,	Dec. 10, 1861,	Re-enlisted in Co. G, 8th Regt., in 1864. Died out in 1866.
8.	..., Lorenzo D.	"	16th,	K,	——1862,	Transferred to V. R. Cos.
9.	Bowden, Sewall P.	"	2d,	B,	May 28, 1861,	Killed at Bull un, July 21, 161.
10.	..., Wilson	"	14th,	A,	Dec. 3, 1861,	Re-enl ...—p om. to Sergt. in '65—transferred to 14th M.
11.	Bridges, Mary C.	Corp.	8th,	H,	Sept. 7, 1861,	Re-enlisted in 1864—Mustered ot in 166. [Battery.
12.	Bridges, Giles	Priv.	2d,	B,	May 28, 1861,	Prom. to Sergt.—Mustered out in '63,—afterwards Q. Master
13.	Bridges, Daniel	"	8th,	H,	Sept. 7, 1861,	Re-enlisted in 1864.—Died Oct. 11, 1864. [of a colored Regt.
14.	Bridges, G. W.	"	26th,	E,	Oct. 11, 1862,	Mustered out Aug. 17, 1863.—Re-enlisted in Co. A, Coast
15.	Brewster, Lewis	"	2d,	B,	May 28, 1861,	Discharged di ...ity in 1862. [...als and prom. Sergt.
16.	Brown, G. I	Serg't.	2d,	B,	" "	Prom. to 1st Lieut.—discharged for prom. in U. S. Vols.
17.	Butler, Henry B.	Priv.	16th,	K,	——1862,	Prom. to Sergt., died of ...ls March 2, 1865.
18.	Butler, Josiah G.	"	26th,	E,	October 11, 1862,	Re-enlisted in Co. D, 31st Regt. in 1864;—pr m. to ...
19.	Clark, Delmont	"	14th,	B'y B	March 26, 1864,	Discharged for disability Dec. 31, 1864. [Mustered out, ...
20.	Clark, John	"	26th,	E,	...er 11, 63,	Mustered out Aug. 17, 1863, Wd at Irish Bend. Apr.
21.	Collins, G. E.	Serg't.	2d,	B,	May 28, 1861,	Mu-tered out June 4, 1863. [14, 63.
22.	Collins, James C.	Mus'n.	"	B,	" "	Prom. to 2d Lieut.—Mustered ot June 4, 1863.
23.	Collins, Joseph H.	Priv.	31st,	D,	March 11, 1864,	Mustered out July 15, 1865.
24.	..., John W.	"	14th,	A,	——1864,	Mustered out.
25.	Crawford, Danl. A.	"	Coast Guards,	B'y A	February 16, 165,	Mustered out August 28, 1865
26.	Crossgrove, Robert	"	D. C. t.	G,	January 28, 164,	Transferred to 6. I. 1st M. Cav., discharged May, '65.
27.	Crossgrove, Wm. C.		——			Enlisted in 4th N'w York Artillery.
28.	1 ..., John	Priv.	31st,	D,	...er 10, 864,	Prom. Mustered ot July 15, 1865.

No.	Names.	Rank.	Reg't.	Co.	Date of Enlistment.	Date of Discharge or Death—and Remarks.
29.	Davies, Edward F.	Sergt.	16th,	K,	August, 14, 1862,	Prom. to 1st Lt.—to Capt. o'd. C. Taken prisoner Aug. 18, '64, escaped—mustered ut June 5, 1865.
30.	Devereux, Frank	Priv.	"	K,	" "	Prom. Corporal.—Killed at ', Aug in '63.—Interred th ae in Grave No. 1.
31.	Devereux, Seth K.	Capt.	d,	B,	May 28, 1861,	Resign ed on account of nt as Collector of Cs- [toms h e.
32.	Dimond, John					to m in 42d New York Reg't.
33.	Eaton, Charles	Priv.	D. C. Cav.	G,	February 8, 1864,	Transferr ed to C L, 1st M. Cav.—Prom. Corp. in B. Mustered nt Aug. 1, 165.
34.	Emerson, Henry E.	"	14th,	A,	December 14, 1861,	Re-enlisted—Wounded Q. 9 64. Prom. Corp. Trans. to 14th Me. Batt. in '65. that Aug. 28, '65.
35.	Foster, Charles W.	"	D. C. Cav.	F,	——1864,	Mt out.
36.	Gardner, Wm. N.	"	d,	B,	May 28, 1861,	1 Sol ued of disability, October 2, 1861.
37.	Grindle, Joseph	"	"	B,	October 25, 1861,	Mt to 20th Me., Co. A. Discharged Dec. 24, 1865.
38.	Grindle, Reuben	"	Coast Guards,	A,	——1864,	Md d.
39.	Hackett, Edward	"	2d Cav.	K,	December 24, 1863,	Died September 28, 1864. Interred at Barancas, Fla. Grave No. 6.
40.	Hackett, Joseph	"	2d Inf.	B,	May 28, 1861,	Re-enlisted in C. K, 2d Cav., in 1863. Mustered out in 1865.
41.	Haley, Charles	"	"	E,	Or 17, 1861,	Transferred to Co. B, 20th Me. Discharged for disability, in 63. [tom Kenduskeeg.]
42.	Hamlin, James H.	"	16th,	K,	September 7, 163,	Transferred to Navy.
43.	Hatch, Mark E.	"	"	K,	Ast 14, 1862,	" "
44.	Hawes, N. A.	"	D. C. Cav.	G,	——1864,	Cd to Castine. Trans. to Co. L, 1st Me. Cav. Dis- charg ed June, 85.
45.	Heath, Lorenzo J.	"	2d,	B,	1860, 1864,	Transferred to Co. E, Me. Cav. Discharged June 1, 1865.
46.	Hooper, Charles H.	Corp.	16th,	K,	May 28, 1861,	Discharged of disabi lity, Gt 23, 1861.
47.	Hooper, Samuel	Priv.	26th,	E,	Mt 4, 1862,	Discharged for kibi lity in 163.
48.	Ives, Alfred E.	"	16th,	K,	Or 11, 1862,	Prom. to Corporal. Mustered out August 17, 1863.
49.	Jarvis, Andrew J.	Mus'n.	2d,	B,	Sat 14, 1862,	Ml for isibility, December 1862.
50.	Lawrence, Edward A.	Priv.	14th,	B,	May 28, 1861,	Cd in '65, in 1st Army Corps—Hancock Vet. Vols.
51.	Lewis, John	"	26th,	B,	" "	Md on Nov. 14, 1861.
52.	Little, Edward F.	"	1st H. Arty,	A,	December 14, 1861,	Discharged in Me., Sept. 12, 1863. Died subsequently.
53.	McCausland, Decattur	"	2d,	E,	Or 1, 1862,	Md out August 17, 1863.
54.	McLaughlin, John	"		G,	——1 64,	Mtd out Septem br 1, 1865.
55.	Moores, Alonzo D.	"		B,	May 3, 6,	Re-enlisted in Co. K, 2d Cav., Dec. 24, 1863. Transferred to Nly July 15,' 6.

No.	Name.	Rank.	Regt.	Co.	Date of Enlistment.	Date of Discharge or Death—and Remarks.
56.	Moore, Hezekiah C.	Priv.	1st H. Arty.	M,	Mary 1, 1864,	Discharged for disability in 1865.
57.	Moore, Samuel W.	Mus'n,	"	M,		Mld ut Mr 11, 4. [1864. Disch. July '65.
58.	Morey, Geo. W.	Priv.	D. C. Cav.	G,	My 22, 1864,	Mld to 1st M. Gr., G. L. T ken isoner in Ar-
59.	Morris, Chas. S.	"	d,	B,	May 28, 61,	Mld out J ne 4, 1863, A fr at Libby, a-
60.	Morgridge, Andrew J.	"	h,	B,	August 4, 1862,	Mld out de 5, 4. [sonville ad Tuscal ea.
61.	Morgridge, Samuel T.	"	D. C. Gv.	K,	January 19, 364,	Transferred to G. I, at M. Gv. (in Regt. Band). M-
						tered ut in '65.
62.	Murch, Augustus S.	"	31st,	D,	March 1, 4,	Prom. 4. Mld ut July 15, 4.
63.	Murch, Simeon C.	Corp.	2d,	B,	May ", 1861,	Mally vld at Hanover C. H., My 27, 1862.
64.	Noyes, George E.		"	B,	" "	Prom. 4. Mld ut J ne 9, 63.
65.	Noyes, Nelson P.	Priv.	"	B,	May 28, 1861,	Dch. for disability July 61. Re-enlisted in 7th Me, Co.
						A, in 6. Rns. to 1st H. Arty. Prom. Sergt. Mus-
66.	Ordway, Frederick	"	1st H. Arty.	M,	1863,	Died de 3, 66. [d ut d. 1, 1866.
67.	Ott. William H.	"	8th,	G,	January 4, 1864,	Mustered ut January 3, 66.
68.	Perkins, Chas. M.	Sergt.	2d,	B,	May 28, 1861,	Dged for disabili June 3, 491.
69.	Perkins, Elisha S.	Priv.	"	B,	" "	" " Or 14, "
70.	Perkins, Francis L.	"	"	B,	" "	" " Jly 14, "
71.	Perkins, John S.		31st,	D,	March 11, 1864,	" " 12, 1865.
72.	Perkins, Frank R.	Corp.	"	D,		Ki Md at Gd Harbor, de 3, 1864. Buried on he field.
73.	Rea, he R.	Priv.	"	D,		Died d'wounds, August 9, 64. Ild at Arlington.
74.	Sawyer, David, Jr.	"	d,	B,	May 3, 61,	Died at Hall's Hill, Feb. 24, 62.
75.	Shepherd, Isaac G.	"	Gh,	E,	October 11, 1862,	Must. ut Aug. 63. Re-enlis ed in D. C. Cav. in '64.
76.	8th, John					Trans. to 1st M. Gv. Disch. de 5. 63.
77.	Staples, Thomas D.	"	Gh,	E,	St. 16 8,	Tm. to Gp. Trans. to Gh M. Mld ut Jly
78.	Straw, Geo. W.	"	2d,	B,	N8, 8,	Mld ut June 4, 6. [16, 6.
79.	Straw, William C.	"	"	B,	" "	Tm. to 1st Serg't.
80.	Stevens, Charles L.	Sergt.	14th,	A,	do. 3, 6.	Prom. to 1st Lieut., G. H. Ts. to G. A. Died from
81.	Stockbridge, Joseph S.	Priv.	Gh,	E,	Mor 11, 62,	ds, July 24, 6. Ild at Ge.
						Mld in 64, in D. C. Gv. Trans. to Me. Gv. G.
						B. Did An. 20,' 6. Ild at An, Va., gruve
						No. 5161.
82.	Surry, Joseph L.	"	2d,	B,	Mh 22, 1863,	Mld in G. A, Gh Me. Mld ut in 6.
83.	Sylvester, Charles E.	"	1st H. Arty.	D,	1863,	Td to Navy.
84.	Sylvester, Joseph H.	Sergt.	2d,	B,	May 28, 1861,	Mld out Ine h, 63.

No.	Name.	Rank.	Regt.	Co.	Date of Enlistment.	Date of Discharge or Death—and Remarks.
85.	Taylor, John	Priv.	2d,	C,	May 28, 1861,	Mustered out June 9, 1863.
86.	Tibbetts, Richard	Corp.	"	C,	" "	" " 4th "
87.	Tilden, Chas. W.*	1st Lt.	"	C,	" "	Prom. Capt. Ap.Lt. Col., 6th Me., July 9, '62. Prom. Col. " " July 1, 1863. Escaped from lly in pris. Aug. 18, '64.—Escaped. Brev. Feb. 10, '64. Brig. G., U.S. Vol. 1ly 16, 1865. ed Brig.
88.	Turner, Reuben H.	Priv.	1st H. Art'y,	M,	1ly 5, 1864,	Transferred to V. R. Corps in 18.
89.	Varnum, 1ph G.	"	1st Cav.,	D,	February 8, 1864,	From D. C. Cav. Mt out 1st, 1865.
90.	Varnum, 1n B.	Sergt.	6th,	V,	1st 14, 1862,	rd to V. R. Corps Dec. 30, 1863.
91.	Veazie, Arthur	Mus'n.	D. C. Cav.,	G,	1ly 22, 1864,	No further official report.
92.	Veazie, 1ds W.	Priv.	2d,	B,	1ly 28, 18.	Tl er par June 29, 164.
93.	Veazie, 1les A.	"	6th,	K,	August 14, 8,	Mtd out 1de 4, 1863.
94.	Veazie, Jol n R.	"	2d,	B,	May 28, 63,	Ng at 1le d Fredericksburg.
95.	Veazie, Moses	"	"	B,	" "	Mtd out June 4, 1863.
96.	1m, 1les H.	"	3st,	D,	Mh 11, 1864,	D1 1br 12, 1862.
97.	1er, Forester	"	4th,	G,	December 28, 1861,	Mtd out July 15, 1865.
98.	1er, Orville D.	"	2d,	B,	1or 25, 63,	1d to G. A. Discharged for disability June 27, '62.
99.	Wardwell, David D.	2d Lt.	"	B,	May 28, 61,	Discharged for 1ility, in 1863.
100.	Webster, Albert	Priv.	14th,	A,	1ber 28, 81,	Discharged for 1st 6, 1861.
101.	Webster, Littleton	"	"	E,	1ober 1, 62,	1lty March 63.
102.	1, George L.	"	"	E,	" "	Dtl r6m wounds. May 27, 63.
103.	Wescott, Augustus R.	Sergt.	2l,	B,	1ly 28, 63,	Promoted Sergt. Mtd out 1st 17, 1863.
104.	Wescott, George	Priv.	28th,	I,	1or 6, 1862,	Re-enlisted in 3st M. in 164. Prom. to 1st Lieut. Must.
10.	Wescott, Henry B.	"	6th,	K,	August 14, 62,	Mustered out 1st 31, 1863. [out July 15, 1865.
106.	1lam, Charles H.	"	31st,	D,	March 11, 1864,	Prom. to 1oral. 1ed 1t June 5, 1865. Ded of 1ease, May 6, 1865.

NAVY LIST.

1. Bowden, Nehemi 1h
2. Bryant, Robert
3. 1llin', John
4. Gardner, Wm. N.
5. Greene, David
6. Foster, Charles

7. Haskett, Edward
8. Hamlin, James H.
9. Hatch, Mark E.
10. Heath, Zebediah
11. Howard, 1u
12. Hooper, 1h
13. 1an, 1n

14. Perkins, Jeremiah
15. Perkins, Lafayette
16. 1dn, Robert
17. Sylvester, Chas. E.
18. Webster, Thomas H.
19. Woodbury, Jacob

1st 1gt. of S. Guards.

1s of G. E.

S. K. Devereux, Capt., } Com.
Bently Grindle, 1st Lieut., } Aug. 3,
Wm. H. 1, 2d " } 1863.

1fn 1ke 16th, his Military his- 1n wh 1e pr 1s 1g in this volume. 1 may be found 1r 1s 1, an 1br 1t of 1t to 1kw 1t his unwritten record rewards him 1 as an 1br, it is 1l of the 1r wo participated in 1o 1ch 1e 1ll d 1r was 1e of the

*The Adjutant General's Report (Maine) 1, p. 472, says of this
tory was thoroughly identified with that of 1s
Should it 'fail to do adequate credit to his superior 1ds, but 1o 1m 1e 1ll d
a high place, not only in the esteem of his co 1lly prison, in February, 1864
the memorable escape through a tunnel, from

BROOKSVILLE ARMY LIST.

No.	Name	Rank.	Regt.	Co.	Date of Enlistment.	Date of Discharge or Death—and Remarks.
1.	Allen, ?on E.	Priv.	1st H. Art'y,	G,	August 21, 1862,	Wed the ?, and died in July, 1864.
2.	?in, John	Corp.	2d,	H,	October 11, 186?,	Mustered out ?st 17, 1863.
3.	Billings, Adoniram J.		13th,	F,	May 28, ?er 6?,	Died in 1862.
4.	Billings, David F.	Priv.	2d,	B,		Dropped from Rolls, in 1862.
5.	Blake, John S.	"	1st Cav.,	K,	February 16, 1864,	Prom. to Corporal. ?d out August 1, 1865.
6.	Blake, Wils ?	"	?R,	H,	?er 11, 1862,	Mustered out August 17, 1863.
7.	?t, Geo. W.	"	"	H,		" " "
8.	?in, ?d		16th,	K,	?ary 3, ?8,	
9.	?s, Erastus					Discharged June 21, 1865.
10.	Condon, Sylvester C.	"	26th,	H,	October 11, 1862,	Enlisted in 19th Mass. Regt.
11.	Dodge, Harlan P.					Mustered out ?st 17, 1863.
12.	Emerton, Andrew L.	Priv.	4th,	H,	?ber 9, 1861,	Enlisted in an Illinois Regt. Trans. to 19th Me. ?t—sick—at Muster out of Regt. [in 1865.
13.	Farnham, Geo. L.	Mus'n.	26th,	H,	?er 11, 1862,	Mustered out ?t 17, 1863.
14.	Farnham, Otis L.	Priv.	26th,	H,	"	Left sick at Buffalo, August 6, 1863, on return of regiment.
15.	?y, Edmund B.	"	Mtd. Art y,	2d B'y	?ary 15, 1864,	Mustered out June 16, 1865.
16.	?y, Francis	"	1st Cav.	L,	?uary 26, 1864,	Discharged by General ?r No. 77, in 1865.
17.	?y, Otis	"	2d Cav.,	K,	December 24, 1863,	Transferred to Navy.
18.	?s ?as	"	"	K,	"	" "
19.	?t, Pearl S.					Enlisted in 15th Mass. Regt.
20.	?n, James	Priv.	26th,	H,	May 28, 1861,	Mustered out August 17, 1863.
21.	Grindle, Bentley	"	2d,	B,	" 25, 1861,	" "
22.	Grindle, Emery M.	"	26th,	H,	?er 11, 1862,	?d out August 17, 1863.
23.	Grindle, Frank L.	"	2d,	B,	" 7, 1861,	" " 9, " Re-enlisted in 20th Me. Trans. [to Navy.
24.	Grindle, Joseph	"	20th,	A,	Agust 21, ?8,	Discharged Dec. 24, 1864.
25.	?t, Kenney S.	Corp.	1st H. Art'y,	G,	October 11, ?2,	Transferred to Navy.
26.	Grindle, Mark H.	Priv.	26th,	H,	—1864,	?d out August, 17, 1863.
27.	Holland, Samuel A.	"	Coast Guards,	A,		?d out.
28.	Howard, Albert	"	1st ?,	I,	January 19, 1864,	Died ?r, 1864.
29.	Howard, Hollis	"	"	A,	February 19, 1864,	Died in one of the Rebel prisons.
30.	?s, George V.	"	2d,	B,	September 6, 1862,	?s. to Co. C. 20th Me. Disch. July 18, 1865.
31.	Perkins, Eben F.	"	"	B,	May 28, 1861,	Killed July 21, 186?.
32.	Perkins, John D.	"	"	B,		M? ?ed out June 9, 1863.
33.	Roberts, Cyrus	"	26th,	H,	?er 11, 1862,	" August 17, 1863.

No.	Name.	Rank.	Regt.	Co.	Date of Enlistment.	Date of Discharge or Death—and Remarks.
34.	Smith, William M.	Priv.	2d,	B,	May 28, 1861,	Mustered out June 4, 1863.
35.	Snow, Charles E.	"	26th,	H,	October 11, 1862,	" August 17, 1863.
36.	Tapley, Benj. W.	"	2d,	B,	July 31, 1862,	Transferred to 20th Me. Transferred to Navy.
37.	Tibbetts, James B.	"	26th,	H,	October 11, 1862,	Died May 24, 1863.
38.	Walker, John	"	11th,	H,	—1864,	Discharged in 1865.
39.	Webber, David B.	"	2d,	B,	May 28, 1861,	Killed at battle of Grovetown, August 30, 1862.
40.	Wescott, Chas. E.	"	26th,	H,	October 11, 1862,	Re-enlisted in 2d Cavalry. Mered out December 6, 1865.
41.	Wessell, John M.	"	"	H,	" "	Mustered out August 17, 1863.
42.	Williams, John	"	16th,	B,	Sept. 10, 1862.	Recorded as a deserter in 1863.

NAVY LIST.

1. Allen, James
2. Austin, Henry
3. Beninga, Peter F.
4. Boyd, James
5. Boyd, Thomas
6. Br oks, John
7. Burns, Daniel*
8. Clary, Daniel
9. Chill, James*
10. Collins, Adams*
11. Cross, Wm. E.

12. Davis, John*
13. Devine, Geo. H.
14. Duh, John*
15. Duc, Lewis*
16. Fernald, Wm. H.
17. Fritz, Lewis
18. Gray, Geo.†
19. ..., Thomas†
20. ..., Fnk L.†
21. Grindle, Kenney S.†
22. Hanson, Andrew*

23. Harvey, William
24. Henry, William S.
25. Howison, Robert*
26. ..., Edward
27. Joh nan, Harry*
28. Ludbury, Fred*
29. Mann, Peter*
30. ..., Isaac P.*
31. McGowin, Job
32. Morris, J hn
33. Palmer, Dvid M.*

34. Porter, Willi m*
35. Se tt, George*
36. Solomon, Andrew
37. Smith, Frank
38. Smith, G. W.
39. ..th, William
40. Stanton, ...
41. Tapley, Benj. W.†
42. ..., 1 M*
43. Van Zandt, Wm. V. R.

*These are substitutes for drafted men.
†These have served in the Army also.

PENOBSCOT ARMY LIST.

No.	Name.	Rank.	Regt.	Co.	Date of Enlistment.	Date of Discharge or Death—and Remarks.
1.	...s, Elias W.	Priv.	28th,	L,	October 16, 1862,	...d out August 31, 1863. [charged Sept. 15, 1864.
2.	Bridges, ...tus K.	Sergt.	18th,	G,	August 21, 1862,	...ed to H. Art. Prom. 2d Lt., Co. M. Dis- Regt.
3.	Bridges, Nelson	Corp.	"	G,	"	Prom. Sergt. and 2d Lieut. Died ...or 20, 1864.
4.	Bowden, Elisha R.	Priv.	28th,	L,	...er 16, "	Discharged for disability in December, 1862.
5.	Bowden, Henry S.		14th,	A,	December 3, "	Died December 24, 1861.
6.	Bowden, ...n'l Jr.	Corp.	1st Cav.	D,	...er ..., "	Pr. m. Sergt. Re-enlisted. ...ged ...ne 5, 1865.
7.	Boyd, William C.	Priv.	1st S.S.	C,	November 29, '64,	Pr m. Corporal. Trans. to 20th Me. ...d out July [16, 1865.
8.	Cain, ...lon P.	"	28th,	L,	...er 16 1862,	Discharged for disability in December, 1862.
9.	...er, Francis M.	"	14th.	G,	December 28, 1861,	Transferred to Co. A. Died May 24, 1862.
10.	Carpenter, Wils ...	"	4th,	H,	m...er 9, 1861,	...ged June 25, 1862.
11.	..., Willard C.	A't S'n,	26th	A,	September 23, 1862,	Mustered out August 17, 1863.
12.	...r, Edwin	Priv.	14th,	A,	December 14, 1861,	Prom. to ...al. Died in December, 1862.
13.	..., Benj. H.	"	"	L,	" 3, "	s...ed in 1862.
14.	Cunningham, Ed'n H.	Corp.	28th,	L,	October 16, 1862,	Mustered out August 31, 1863.
15.	Cunningham, ...n T.	Priv.	"	L,	" " "	" " "
16.	..., Benj. H.	Corp.	"	D,	" 19, 1861,	" " in 1864.
17.	Devereux, AugustusR.	"	1st Cav.	K,	...st 14, 1862,	Transferred to V. R. Corps.
18.	Devereux, ...A.	"	16th	B,	May 28, 1861,	Died in prison at Richmond, Va., December 4, 1861.
19.	Devereux, Warren J.	"	2d,	D,	...r 16, 1862,	Transferred to Invalid Corps.
20.	Dunbar, Edward	"	1st Cav.	D,	" 19, 1861,	Prom. to Sergt. ...d June 5, 1864. Discharged June [5, 1865.
21.	Grant, William B.	"	"	L,	...st 21, 1862,	Transferred to Navy.
22.	Gray, Abner K.	"	"	G,	January 23, '65,	Killed May 19, 1864.
23.	Gay, Chas. W.	"	18th,	L,	...st 21, 1862,	Mustered out August 28, 1865.
24.	Gay, Erastus R.	"	14th,	B,	May 28, '63,	Mustered out June 9, 1863,
25.	Grindle, Augustus P.	"	2d,	B,	October 25, "	...ged for ...ty February 24, 1862.
26.	...le, Edwin J.	"	"	B,	November 9, "	Transferred to Invalid ...ps.
27.	...le, Elijah H.	"	4th,	H,	October 11, 1862,	Mustered out August 17, 1863.
28.	Grindle, Charles H.	"	26th,	H,	May 28, 1861,	" June 9,
29.	...le, ...im L.	"	2d,	B,	October 16, 1862,	Died August 11, 1863.
30.	Grindle, John	"	28th,	I,	" "	" June 22d, "
31.	Grindle, ...	"	"	L,	...er 16, 1862,	" in 1862.
32.	Grindle, Pearl L.	Mus'n,	1st Cav.	D,	" 1861,	Mustered out August 31, 1863.
33.	...a, Isaac B.	Priv.	1st H. Arty.	G,	January 12, 1864,	Wounded June 18, 1864. Discharged in 1865.

No.	Name.	Rank.	Regt.	Co.	Date of Enlistment,	Date of Discharge or Death—and Remarks.
34.	Guilford, Wm. H.	Priv.	4th,	H,	November 9, 1861,	Discharged for disability January 5, 1863.
35.	Harriman, Joseph N.	"	1st Cav.,	D,	October 19, "	Prom. to Sergt. Discharged June 5, 1865.
36.	Hatch, Elisha G.	"	18th,	G,	August 21, 1862,	Discharged June, 1865.
37.	Heath, Avery H.	"	6th,	E,	July 15, 1861,	Died August 2d, 1862.
38.	Heath, Josiah	"	28th,	I,	October 11, 1862,	" July 6, 1863.
39.	Herrick, Orlando	"	"	I,	" " "	Mustered out August 31, 1863, "
40.	Hutchings, John C.	"	"	L,	" " "	
41.	Hutchings, Luther D.	"	"	L,	" " "	Died July 6, 1863.
42.	Hutchings, Wm., Jr.	"	6th,	E,	July 15, 1861,	Discharged in 1862.
43.	Hutchings, Wesley T.	"	14th,	A,	January 3, 1862,	Reported as a ...er in 1862. [charged in 1865.
44.	Hutchins, Elm	"	18th,	G,	August 21, "	Trans. from Co. G. Wounded October 19, 1864. Dis-
45.	Hutchins, Geo. W.	"	2d,	B,	May 28, 1861,	Prom. to Corpl. Discharged in 1865.
46.	Hutchins, Ben	"	18th,	G,	August 21, 1862,	Sergeant. Mustered out June 9, 1863.
47.	Hutchins, Wiley H.	"	18th,	G,	" "	Died in 1862.
48.	Hutch, Alt	Corp.	28th,	L,	...er 16, "	Prom. Sergt. Killed June 18, 1864.
49.	...ch, Byron	Priv.	18th,	G,	August 21, 1862,	Died out August 31, 1863.
50.	...ch, Francis N.	"	18th,	G,	" "	Died of wounds June 26, 1864.
51.	...ch, Chas C.	"	"	G,	" 14, "	Discharged for disability February 1863,
52.	Leach, Henry	"	16th,	K,	January 3d, "	Killed at Fredericksburg, Va., ...ber 13, 1862.
53.	Leach, Hiram F.	"	14th,	A,	October 11, "	Trans. from Co. G. Transferred to V. R. Corps.
54.	Leach, ...s M.	"	28th,	I,	" " "	Mustered out August 31, 1863.
55.	Leach, Isac B., Jr.	Corp.	4th,	H,	...ber 9, 1861,	Prom. Sergt. Discharged for disability in 1862.
56.	Leach, ...s	Priv.	11th,	G,	...ust 21, 1862,	Wounded May 19, 1864. Died in 1865.
57.	Leach, ...l	"	11th,	E,	" 10, 1863,	" July 26, " " 1866.
58.	Leach, Parker W.	"	1st Cav	L,	October 19, 1861,	M'd out November 25, 1864. [1865.
59.	Leach, Silas	"	18th,	G,	August 21, 1862,	Taken prisoner June 22, 1862. Discharged the service in
60.	Leach, Uriah B.	"	"	G,	" " "	Wounded " 18, 164. Discharged the service in
61.	McCaslin, John B.	Wag'r,	28th,	I,	...ber 16, "	Mustered out August 31, 1863. [1865.
62.	Norton, ...h F.	1st Lt	14th,	A,	December 30, 1861,	Re-enlisted. Transferred to Navy.
63.	Norway, Edwin	...	28th,	I,	October 11, 1862,	Mustered out Aug't 31, 1863.
64.	Perkins, Chas. A.	Priv.	"	I,	" " "	" " "
65.	Perkins, Jedediah D.	"	"	I,	" " "	Died in 1862.
66.	Perkins, Francis M.	"	2d,	B,	May 28, "	Prom. Sergt. Killed October 27, 1864.
67.	Perkins, Lorenzo D.	Corp.	18th,	G,	August 21, 1862,	

48

No.	Name.	Rank.	Regt.	Co.	Date of Enlistment.	Date of Discharge or Death—and Remarks.
68.	Perkins, Peletiah A.	Priv.	28th,	I,	October 11, 1862,	Died July 23, 1863.
69.	Reed, Charles F.	"	14th,	F,	March 1, 1865,	Mustered out August 28, 1865.
70.	Steele, George W.	"	4th,	H,	November 9, 1861,	Prisoner at ...burg. Escaped. Discharged for disability in 1863.
71.	Steele, Joseph	"	31st,	D,	March 11, 1864,	Discharged for disability July 27, 1865.
72.	Wood, George P.	Sergt.	4th,	H,	November 9, 1861,	Re-enlisted. Trans. to 19th Me. Prom. to Sergt. Prom. to Lieut. Mustered out in 1865.

NAVY LIST.

1. ...k, D...id
2. B...k, William
3. ...n, William
4. Carter, William
5. ...r, Ezra S.
6. ...r, Henry F.
7. Conner, Hugh
8. ...y, ...n
9. Gardner, ...m
10. Grosvenor, Chas. A.
11. Haynes, ...lle P.
12. ...y, ...r K.*
13. Hunter, Charles
14. Jackson, George E.
15. Jenkins, Jacob
16. Kauaka, J seph
17. King, Thomas
18. Lawson, Elias
19. Leach, Samuel T.
20. Littlefield, Joseph B.
21. ...n, William
22. ...vs, ...rles W.
23. Murphy, John
24. ...n, Jn*
25. ...ey, Edwin†
26. Reardon, John
27. ...o, J nes
28. Spaert, ...les
29. ...r, J hn
30. ...s, Joseph
31. ...n, Frank
32. Veazie, ...
33. Vincent, ...rles
34. Wardwell, Hiram F.
35. ...n, Miles R.*
36. Waters, George

*Substitutes for drafted men.
†Have served in the army also.

APPENDIX.

1.

RANUNCULACEÆ (Crow Foot Family). Ane-mone—*Nemorosa* (wood anemone). Hepatica—*triloba.* Ranunculus—*Flammula* (Spearwort), *Acris* (Buttercups), *Abortivus, bulbosus,* (Buttercups), *Pennsylvanicus* (Bristly Crowfoot). Coptis—*trifolia* (Three-leaved Goldthread). Aquilegia—*Canadensis* (wild Columbine.)

NYMPHÆACEÆ (Water-lily Family). Nymphæa-*Odorata* (White Pond Lily). Nuphar—*Advena* (Yellow Pond Lily).

SARRACENIACEÆ (Pitcher Plants). Sarrace-nia—*purpurea* (Side-Saddle Flower).

CRUCIFERÆ (Mustard Family). Capsella— *Burra-Pastoris* (Shepherd's Purse). Cakile—*Americana* (Sea Rocket). Raphanus—*Raphanistrum* (Wild Radish). Sin-apis—*Alba* (White Mustard), *Nigra* (Black Mustard). Sysymbrium—*Officinale* (Hedge Mustard).

VIOLACEÆ (Violet Family). Viola—*blanda* (Sweet White Violet), *Cucullata* (Blue Violet), *Canadensis* (Can-ada Violet), *pubescens* (Yellow Violet).

DROSERACEÆ (Sundew Family). D. *rotundifolia* (Round-leaved Sundew).

HYPERICACEÆ (St. John's Wort Family). Hy-pericum—*Mutilum, Canadense.*

CARYOPHYLLACEÆ (Pink Family). Stellaria (Chickweed)—*longifolia* (Stitchwort), *borealis* (Northern Stitchwort). Cerastium — *arvense* (Field Chickweed). Spergularia — *rubra* (Sandwort), Anychia — *dichotoma* (Forked Chickweed).

PORTULACACEÆ (Purslane Family). Portula-ca—*oleracea* (common Purslane).

MALVACEÆ (Mallow Family). Malva—*sylves-*

tris (High Mallow), *rotundifolia* (Common Mallow), *crispa* (Curled Mallow.)*

TILIACEÆ (LINDEN FAMILY). Tilia — *Americana* (Basswood).

OXALIDACEÆ (WOOD-SORREL FAMILY). Oxalis— *Acetosella* (Common Wood Sorrel), *stricta* (Yellow Wood Sorrel).

GERANIACEÆ (GERANIUM FAMILY). Geranium. *Maculatum* (Wild Cranesbill), *Robertianum* (Herb Robert).

BALSAMINACEÆ (BALSAM FAMILY). Impatiens— *fulva* (Spotted Touch-me-not).

ANACARDIACEÆ (CASHEW FAMILY). Rhus — *typhina* (Staghorn Sumach), *copallina* (Dwarf Sumach).

ACERINEÆ (MAPLE FAMILY). A. *sacharinum* (Sugar or Rock Maple) — Var. *nigrum* (Black Sugar Maple), *dasycarpum* (White Maple), *rubrum* (Red or Swamp Maple), *Pennsylvanicum* (Striped Maple), *Spicatum* (Mountain Maple).

LEGUMINOSÆ (PULSE FAMILY). Trifolium—*repens* (White Clover), *Arvense* (Rabbit-foot or Stone Clover.) *pratense* (Red Clover), *agrarium* (Yellow Clover), Lathyrus —*maritimus* (Beach Pea), *palustris* (Marsh Vetchling), Vicia—*hirsuta* (Common Tare).*

ROSACEÆ (ROSE FAMILY). Prunus — *maritima* (Beach Plum), *pumila* (Dwarf Cherry), *Pennsylvanica* (Wild Red Cherry), *Virginiana* (Choke Cherry). Spiraea —*tomentosa* (Hardhack), *salicifolia* (Meadow Sweet), *Ulmaria** Potentilla—*Argentea* (Five-Finger). Fragaria *vesca* (Wild Strawberry). Rubus—*triflorus* (Dwarf Raspberry), *strigosus* (Wild Red Raspberry), *villosus* (High Blackberry), *Canadensis* (Dewberry), *Hispidus* (Swamp Blackberry. Rosa—*lucida* (Dwarf Wild Rose), *blanda* (Early Wild Rose), *rubiginosa** (True Sweet-Brier). Cratalgus — *coccinea* (Scarlet-fruited Thorn). Pyrus— *arbutifolia* (Choke-berry), *Americana* (Mountain Ash).

SAXIFRAGACEÆ (SAXIFRAGE FAMILY). Ribes— *lacustre* (Swamp Gooseberry), *prostratum* (Fetid Currant).

HAMAMELACEÆ (WITCH-HAZEL FAMILY). Hamamelis. *Virginica* (Witch Hazel).

ONAGRACEÆ (EVENING-PRIMROSE FAMILY). Epi-

*Escaped from the gardens.

lobium—*angustifolium* (Great-Willow Herb), *coloratum.* Œnothera—*biennis* (Common Evening Primrose), *pumila.*

CRASSULACEÆ (ORPINE FAMILY). Sedum— *telephium* (Live-for-ever).* Penthorum—*sedoides.*

UMBELLIFERÆ (PARSLEY FAMILY). Carum—*carui* (Caraway). Ligusticum — *Scoticum* (Scotch Lovage). Sium—*lineare* (Water Parsnip).

ARALIACEÆ (GINSENG FAMILY). Aralia—*racemosa* (Spikenard), *nudicaulis* (Wild Sarsaparilla).

CORNACEÆ (DOGWOOD FAMILY). *C. Canadensis* (Bunch Berry), *florida* (Flowering Dogwood).

CAPRIFOLIACEÆ (HONEYSUCKLE FAMILY)—Linœa—*borealis* (Twin flower). Viburnum—*Opulus* (Cranberry Tree). Sambucus—*Canadensis* (Common Elder), *pubens* (Red-berried Elder).

RUBIACEÆ (MADDER FAMILY)—Galium — *Asprellum* (Rough Bedstraw), *triffidum* (Small Bedstraw). Cephalanthus—*Occidentalis* (Button Bush). Mitchella—*repens* (Partridge Berry). Houstonia—*Cœrulea.*

COMPOSITÆ (COMPOSITE FAMILY). Eupatorium —*perfoliatum* (Thoroughwort—Boneset). Aster (Starworts—Asters)—*Undulatus, Cordifolius, Macrophyllus, dumosus, Tradescanti, longifolius, crecordes, Multiflorus.* Erigeron,—*strigosum* (Fleabane), *annuum.* Solidago (Goldenrod)—*bicolor, altissima, angustifolia.* Ambrosia—*trifida* (Great Ragweed). Bidens —*frondosa* (Beggar-Ticks). Achillea—*Millefolium* (Yarrow—Milfoil). Tanacetum—*vulgare* (Common Tansy).* Artemisia—*Absinthium* (Wormwood). Gnaphalium—*polycephalum* (common Everlasting,) *decurrens* (Everlasting), *uliginosum* (Low Cudweed), *purpureum* (Purple Cudweed). Cirsium—*Lanceolatum* (Common Thistle), *arvense* (Canada Thistle), *pumilum* (Pasture Thistle). Sonchus—*oleraceus* (Sow-Thistle) Nabalus *Frazeri* (Lion's Foot). Taraxicum—*Dens-leonis* (Dandelion). Leontodon—*Autumnale* (Fall Dandelion). Maruta —*Cotula* (Mayweed). Chrysanthemum —*Leucanthemum* (White weed). Erechthites—*Hieracifolia* (Fireweed).

LOBELIACEÆ (LOBELIA FAMILY). Lobelia—*cardinalis* (Cardinal Flower), *inflata* (Indian Tobacco), *Syphilitica* (Great Lobelia).

ERICACEÆ (HEATH FAMILY). Gaylussacia—*resi_*

*Escaped from gardens.

nosa (Black Huckleberry), *frondosa* (Dangleberry—Blue Tangle). Vaccinium—*Pennsylvanicum* (Dwarf Blueberry), *corymbosum* (Swamp Blueberry), *Oxycoccus* (Small Cranberry), *macrocarpon* (Common Cranberry). Kalimia—*latifolia* (Mountain Laurel), *angustifolia* (Lambkill), Pyrola—*monotropa.*

PLANTAGINACEÆ (PLANTAIN FAMILY). Plantago—*Major* (Common Plantain), *maritima* (Sea-side Plantain).

PLUMBAGINACEÆ (LEADWORT FAMILY). Statice—Limonium (Marsh Rosemary).

PRIMULACEÆ (PRIMROSE FAMILY). Lysimachia—*mimulasea* (Loosestrife).

SCROPHULARIACEÆ (FIGWORT FAMILY). Verbascum—*Thapsus* (Mullein).

LABIATÆ (MINT FAMILY). Mentha—*viridis* (Spearmint), *Canadensis* (Wild Mint). Hedeoma—*pulegioides* (Pennyroyal). Nepeta — *cataria* (Catnip,) *Glechoma* (Ground Ivy). Brunella—*vulgaris* (Heal-all), Stachys—*palustris* (Hedge Nettle).

BORRAGINACEÆ (BORAGE FAMILY). Cynoglossum—*Morisoni* (Beggar's Lice).

CONVOLVULACEÆ (CONVOLVULUS FAMILY.) Cuscuta—Gronovii.

SOLANACEÆ (NIGHTSHADE FAMILY). Solanum—*Dulcamara* (Bittersweet).* Datura—*Stramonium* (Jamestown Weed—Thorn Apple).

ASCLEPIADACEÆ (MILKWEED FAMILY). Asclepias—*Cornuti* (Milkweed).

OLEACEÆ (OLIVE FAMILY). Fraxinus—*Americana* (White Ash), *sambucifolia* (Black Ash).

PHYTOLACCACEÆ (POKEWEED FAMILY). Phytolacca—*decandra* (Garget—Pigeon Berry).

CHENOPODIACEÆ (GOOSEFOOT FAMILY). Salicornia—*nubacea* (Glasswort—Samphire). Suæda—*maritima* (Sea Goosefoot). Salsola—*Kali* (Saltwort).

POLYGONACEÆ (BUCKWHEAT FAMILY). Polygonum—*aviculare* (Goose-grass); var. *erectum.* Persicaria—*hydropiperoides* (Mild Water Pepper), *acre* (Smart Weed), *arifolium* (Tear-Thumb), *Convolvulus* (Black Bindweed),

*Escaped from the gardens.

dumetorum (False Buckwheat). Rumex—*orbiculatus, verticillatus* (Swamp Dock), *crispus* (Curled Dock), *acetosella* (Field or Sheep Sorrel).

URTICACEÆ (NETTLE FAMILY). Ulmus—*Americanus* (White Elm). Urtica—*gracilis* (Tall Wild Nettle).

PLATANACEÆ (PLANE TREE FAMILY). Platinus.—*occidentalis* (Sycamore).

CUPULIFERÆ (OAK FAMILY). Quercus—*coccinea.* (Scarlet Oak), *rubra* (Red Oak). Fagus—*ferruginea* (American Beech). Corylus—*Americana* (Wild Hazel-nut Tree). Carpinus—*Americana* (American Hornbeam).

MYRICACEÆ (SWEET-GALE FAMILY). Myrica—*Gale* (Sweet Gale). Comptonia—*asplenifolia* (Sweet Fern).

BETULACEÆ (BIRCH FAMILY. B. *papyracea* (Paper Birch), *lutea* (Black or Sweet Birch), *alba* (White Birch.) Alnus—*incana* (Speckled Alder), *serrulata* (Smooth Alder.)

SALICACEÆ (WILLOW FAMILY). Salix—*cordata* (Heart-leaved Willow), *lucida*, Shining Willow), Populus *tremuloides* (American Aspen), *grandidentata* (Larch), *balsamifera* (Balsam Poplar) — var. *candicans* (Balm of Gilead).

CONIFERÆ (PINE FAMILY). Pinus—*resinosa* (Red Pine), *strobus* (White Pine). Abies—*balsamea* (Balsam Fir), *Canadensis* (Hemlock Spruce), *nigra* (Black Spruce), *alba* (White Spruce). Larix—*Americana* (Black Larch—Hackmatack). Taxus—*Canadensis* (Ground Hemlock). Thuja—*occidentalis* (Arbor Vitæ), var. *ericoides.* Juniperus—*communis* (Juniper).

ARACEÆ (ARUM FAMILY). Arisœma—*triphyllum* (Indian Turnip). Symplocarpus—*fœtidus* (Skunk Cabbage). Acorus—*calamus* (Sweet Flag).

TYPHACEÆ (CAT-TAIL FAMILY). Typha—*latifolia* (Cat-Tail).

ORCHIDACEÆ (ORCHIS FAMILY). Spiranthes—*gracilis* (Ladies' Tresses), *cernua.*

NAIADACEÆ (PONDWEED FAMILY). Zostera—*marina* Eel-grass).

IRIDACEÆ (IRIS FAMILY). Iris—*virginica* (Blue Flag). Sisyrinchium—*Bermudiana* (Blue-eyed Grass).

LILIACEÆ (LILY FAMILY). Trillium—*erectum.* Erythronium—*Americanum* (Yellow Adder's-Tongue).

EQUISETACEÆ (HORSE-TAIL FAMILY). Equisetum—*arvense, sylvaticum, limosum.*

FILICES (FERNS). Polypodium—*Vulgare, Phegopteris.* Pteris—*aquilina* (Common Brake). Osmunda—*cinnamomea* (Cinnamon Fern).

LYCOPODIACEÆ (CLUB-MOSS FAMILY). Lycopodium—*dendroideum* (Ground Pine), *clavatum* (Club-Moss), *complanatum.* Salaginella—*rupestris.*

CYPERACEÆ (SEDGE FAMILY).

GRAMINEÆ* (GRASS FAMILY).

2.

COLLECTORS OF CUSTOMS FOR THE PORT OF CASTINE.

John Lee, from July 31, 1789—1801,
Josiah Hooke, from 1801, to Sept., 1814.
William Newton, (British), Sept., 1814, to April, 1815.
Josiah Hooke, from April, 1815 to 1817.
S. K. Gilman, from 1817 to 1825.
Joshua Carpenter, from 1825 to 1829.
Rowland H. Bridgham, from 1829 to 1841.
B. W. Hinkley,   } from 1841 to 1845.
Charles J. Abbott, }
Rowland H. Bridgham, from 1845 to 1849.
Charles J. Abbott, from 1849 to 1853.
John R. Redman, from 1853 to 1861.
S. K. Devereux, from 1861 to 1870.
William H. Sargent, from 1870 to——.

3.

MEMBERS OF CONGRESS WHO WERE RESIDENTS OF PENOBSCOT OR CASTINE.

Isaac Parker, from 1796 to 1798.
Hezekiah Williams, from 1845 to 1849.

*Represented by many species.

4.

MEMBERS OF GOVERNOR'S COUNCIL.

William B. Webber, Castine, 1825.
Otis Little, Castine, 1830.
John H. Jarvis, Castine, 1836.
William Grindle, Penobscot, 1871—'74.

5.

STATE SENATORS.

Charles Hutchings, Jr., Penobscot, 1830—'31.
Rowland H. Bridgham, Castine, 1832.
John R. Redman, Brooksville, 1837.
Hezekiah Williams, Castine, 1839—1841.
Rowland H. Bridgham, Castine, 1842—1843.
Benjamin Rea, Brooksville, 1849—1850.
John Bridges, Castine, 1851—1853.
William Barker, Brooksville, 1855—'56.
John Bridges, Castine, 1860—'61.
Charles J. Abbott, 1866.

6.

REPRESENTATIVES TO THE LEGISLATURE FROM PENOBSCOT, CASTINE AND BROOKSVILLE.

TO GENERAL COURT OF MASSACHUSETTS.*

George Thatcher, 1788.
Gabriel Johannot, 1789.
Isaac Parker, 1791—1795— 1796.
Oliver Mann, 1798—1807.
Mark Hatch, 1799.
Job Nelson, 1801—1803.
Otis Little, 1806—'09—'12.
David Howe, 1813.
Thomas Adams, 1814.
Thomas E. Hale, 1816—'18.
Samuel Upton, 1819.

TO LEGISLATURE OF MAINE.

[From Records in Office of Secretary of State.]

FROM BROOKSVILLE.

Simeon Allen, 1839.
Robert J. Blodgett, 1874.
James W. Coombs, 1855.
Samuel Condon, Jr., 1864.
John Devereux, 1857.
Kenney Grindle, 1861.
Lowell Grindle, 1867.
John Hawes, 1847.
George V. Mills, 1870.
Joseph P. Parker, 1822—'28.
William Perkins, 1842.
Benjamin Rea, Jr., 1837—'44.
Erastus Redman, 1849.
John R. Redman, 1833.
David Walker, 1830.
Rufus B. Walker, 1851—'52.
David Wasson, 1835.
William Wasson, 1858.

*Compiled from Town Records.

FROM CASTINE.

William Abbott, 1820, '22,   James Hooper, 1837.
  '23, '25, '27·   Ithiel Lawrence, 1863.
Samuel Adams, 1866.   Otis Little, 1829.
John Bridges, 1843, '45·   George Vose, 1833, '35·
John R. Bridges, 1869.   Frederic Webber, 1857, '60·
Joseph Bryant, 1831.   David W. Webster, 1873.
Henry Emerson, 1839, '41·   Benjamin J. Wilson, 1847, '49.
Timothy Fernald, 1854.   Josiah Wilson, 1838.

FROM PENOBSCOT.

John Burnham, 1830.   Pelatiah Leach, 1829,—'48,
Isaac B. Goodwin, 1869.   '50·
Benjamin Gray, 1842.   Uriah B. Leach, 1866.
Jonathan Hatch, Jr., 1846. Dan'l M. Perkins, 1860,—'63.
Charles Hutchings, Jr., 1823, Isaac Perry,—1822.
  '26—1844,—'53.   Leander A. Snowman, 1871.
Ebenezer Hutchings, 1834,— Moses Trussell, 1827.
  1855.   Jeremiah Wardwell, 1836,—
Ebenezer Leach, 1831—'32. '40·

7.

SELECTMEN OF CASTINE.*
[Including the old town of Penobscot.]

1787—1788.

Joseph Perkins,
Jeremiah Wardwell,
Oliver Parker,
Joseph Hibbert,
Joseph Young.

1789.

Joseph Perkins,
Joseph Hibbert,
Oliver Parker,
Pelatiah Leach,
John Wasson.

1790.

Oliver Parker,
Joseph Hibbert,
Daniel Wardwell,
Seth Blodgett,
Oliver Mann.

1791.

John Perkins,
Elijah Littlefield,
David Hawes,
David Wilson,
Pelatiah Leach.

*Compiled from Town Records.

1792.

Oliver Parker,
Oliver Mann,
John Wasson,
John Wilson,
Sparks Perkins.

1793—1794.

Jeremiah Wardwell,
Pelatiah Leach,
John Wasson,
Oliver Mann,
John Wilson.

1795.

Thatcher Avery,
Joseph Binney,
Thomas Wasson.

1796.

Joseph Perkins,
Joseph Young,
David Wilson.

1797.

David Wilson,
David Howe,
Jonathan Foster.

1798.

David Wilson,
David Howe,
Ephraim Blake.

1799—1803.

David Wilson,
David Howe,
Israel Redman.

1804—1806.

David Wilson,
David Howe,
Francis Bakeman.

1807—1809.

David Wilson,
David Howe,
Rogers Lawrence.

1810—1811.

David Wilson,
William Abbott,
Rogers Lawrence.

1812.

David Wilson,
David Howe,
Rogers Lawrence.

1813—1814.

David Wilson,
Thomas Adams,
Rogers Lawrence.

1815.

David Wilson,
Thomas Adams,
Elisha Smith.

1816.

Thomas Adams,
Hezekiah Rowell,
Rogers Lawrence.

1817.

Thomas Adams,
Bradshaw Hall,
Rogers Lawrence.

1818.

Thomas Adams,
Bradshaw Hall,
William Freeman.

1819.

William Abbott,
Otis Little,
John Wilson.

1820.

William Abbott,
Otis Little,
Theodore B. McIntyre.

1821—1824.

Otis Little,
Joseph Bryant,
Theodore B. McIntyre.

1825.

Otis Little,
William Witherle,
Theodore B. McIntyre.

1826—1831.

Otis Little,
Joseph Bryant,
Theodore B. McIntyre.

1832.

Otis Little,
Joseph Byrant,
Henry Emerson.

1833—1835.

Samuel Adams,
Hezekiah Williams,
Henry Emerson.

1836—1838.

Charles J. Abbott,
Charles Rogers,
John A. Avery.

1839.

Charles J. Abbott,
Charles Rogers,
Jonathan Perkins.

1840—1842.

Silas H. Martin,
Rowland H. Bridgham,
Jonathan Perkins.

1843.

Hezekiah· Williams,
Charles Rogers,
William B. Webber.

1844.

Hezekiah Williams,
Charles J. Abbott,
Joseph Wescott.

1845—1847.

Charles J. Abbott,
Stover P. Hatch,
Joseph Wescott.

1848—1849.

Stover P. Hatch,
Charles Rogers,
Joseph Wescott.

1850—1851.

Frederic A. Hooke,
Charles Rogers,
Joseph Wescott.

1852—1854.

Stover P. Hatch,
Charles Rogers,
Joseph Wescott.

1855.

Mark P. Hatch,
Charles Rogers,
Joseph Wescott.

1856—1857.

Charles A. Cate,
Charles Rogers,
Joseph Wescott.

1858.

Frederic A. Hooke,
Stover P. Hatch,
Joseph Wescott.

1859—1860.

Samuel Adams,
Charles Rogers,
Joseph Wescott.

1861.

Stover P. Hatch,
Stephen W. Webster,
Zadoc Witham.

1862.

John R. Redman,
Stephen W. Webster,
Zadoc Witham.

1863—1865.

Frederic A. Hooke,
William H. Witherle,
Jefferson Devereux.

1866.
Frederic A. Hooke,
Otis Hatch,
Jefferson Devereux.
1867—1870.
Josiah B. Woods,
Thomas E. Hale,
Jefferson Devereux.

1871—1873.
Stover P. Hatch,
Philip J. Hooke,
Joseph Wescott.
1874.
Stover P. Hatch,
Philip J. Hooke,
Jefferson Devereux.

8.

TOWN DIRECTORIES. 1874.

CASTINE.

COLLECTOR OF CUSTOMS—Hon. William H. Sargent.
DEPUTY COLLECTOR—L. G. Philbrook, Otis Little.
POSTMASTERS—Charles Rogers; *North*, Samuel Dunbar.
SELECTMEN—Stover P. Hatch, Philip J. Hooke, Jefferson Devereux.
TOWN CLERK—Philip J. Hooke.
TREASURER—Charles H. Hooper.
CONSTABLES—J. M. Dennett, F. Hooper, A. J. Raffnell, S. P. Hatch.
SCHOOL COMMITTEE—J. W. Dresser, S. K. Whiting, D. W. Webster, Jr.
CLERGYMEN—A. E. Ives, *Cong.*; J. H. Moores, *Meth.*; J. W. Winkley, *Unit.*
PHYSICIANS—J. L. Stevens, G. A. Wheeler.
LAWYERS—Chas. J. Abbott.
NOTARY PUBLIC—Chas. J. Abbott.
JUSTICES—Geo. F. Tilden, Chas. J. Abbott, L. G. Philbrook, Daniel J. Crawford, J. W. Dresser, Samuel K. Whiting, William H. Sargent, Samuel Dunbar, *Quorum;* Josiah B. Woods, *Trial;* William H. Sargent, *Dedimus.*
DEPUTY SHERIFF—E. F. Davies.
MERCHANTS—Perkins & Sargent, Witherle & Co., Chas. W. Tilden & Co., R. M. Joyce, J. B. Crawford, Hooper & Shepherd, *dry goods and groceries*; J. W. Dresser, *ship chandlery;* Richard McCluskey, Andrew Brown, *tailors;* Aaron Chamberlain, *toys and confectionery;* H. L. Macomber, *jeweller;* Mrs. L. H. Parker, Miss Isabella Brown, *millinery;* Miss Meheteble Cornwallis, Miss Isadore Cornwallis, Miss Isabella Brown, *dressmakers;* D. J. Crawford,

apothecary; D. J. Crawford, Perkins & Sargent, *books and stationery;* John F. Rea, *wood and lumber;* Geo. S. Vose, *stoves and tin ware; North,* George H. Emerson, Samuel Dunbar, *dry goods and groceries.*

MANUFACTURERS.—John Clark & Son, *boots and shoes;* Edward F. Davies, *furniture;* Geo. F. Tilden & Son, *lobster factory;* Castine Brick Co., F. A Hooke, *Agent;* J. W. Dresser, *rope walk;* James A. Webster, Joel Perkins, S. T. & J. H. Noyes, *master shipwrights;* H. B. Robbins, *pump and block maker;* B. J. Wilson, *boat builder;* John Bridges, A. J. Raffnell, Geo. H. Emerson, *smiths;* Elisha S. Perkins, Frank Perkins, *painters;* Dresser & Surry, *mackerel lines;* E. H. Buker, *mason;* S. W. Webster, William M. Lawrence, Geo. L. Weeks, *master carpenters;* J. M. Dennett, William Morgrage, *sailmakers;* D. W. Webster, Jr., *grist and shingle mill;* Chas. Witham, *boots and shoes.*

SCHOOLS.—Eastern State Normal School. J. W. Dresser, *Member of Board of Trustees;* G. T. Fletcher, *Principal;* Castine Free High School, Edward P. Sampson, *Principal.*

ASSOCIATIONS.—*Masons*—Hancock, No. 4. 1st Thurs. in month. *I. O. G. 'T.*—Rising Virtue, weekly on Sat. eve.

LIVERY STABLES—Hooper Bros. — *North,* Geo. H. Emerson.

HOTELS—Horatio E. Hodsden; *North,* Geo. H. Emerson.

U. S. REVENUE CUTTER—*Dobbin*—Capt. Chas. Abbey, *Commander.*

BELFAST & CASTINE STEAMBOAT—*Pioneer*—Jeremiah Hatch, *Captain.*

BUCKSPORT AND CASTINE STAGE—Office at Hotel.

BELFAST AND CASTINE PACKET—*Spy*—H. D. Hodsdon, *Agent.*

EASTERN EXPRESS AGENT—Chas. W. Tilden.

AGENT FOR STEAMER LEWISTON—Chas. W. Tilden.

BROOKSVILLE.

POSTMASTERS—J. Walker; *South,* L. M. Bates; *West,* Luther Tapley; *North,* Mrs. Emily Blodgett.

SELECTMEN—David Varnum, William Wasson, Joseph Redman.

Town Clerk—C. E. Snow.

Treasurer—Amos Gott.

Constables—Samuel Condon, Richard Condon.

School Supervisor—Lucius M. Perkins.

Clergymen—Vacant; *West*, H. H. Hutchilson, *Cong.;* F. A. Bragdon (Penobscot) *Meth.; South*, T. Shepherdson, *Cong.*

Justices—J. G. Walker, F. P. Billings, D. S. Gray, William Wasson, Jeremiah Jones, *Quorum;* David Wasson, G. V. Mills, *Trial.*

Merchants—S. Babson, L. M. Perkins; *West*, G. H. Emerson,—— Douglas, David Billings; *South*, E. C. Chatto, E. H. Bates, S. D. Gray; *North*, C. Staples, *dry goods and groceries.*

Manufacturers—J. & J. G. Walker, *clothiers and lumber; South*, S. D. Gray, *lumber;* Joseph Wescott & Son, *granite; North*, E. P. Parker, *lumber; West*, J. P. Tapley, *smith.*

Associations—*I. O. G.T.— West*, Bagaduce, Saturday. *C. W. T.*—Saturday.

Hotel—Samuel Babson.

PENOBSCOT.

Postmasters—Sylvia Perkins; *North*, Phebe Osgood; *South*, Edward White.

Selectmen—Charles Leach, Samuel Farnham, Ellery Varnum.

Town Clerk—Ellery Varnum.

Treasurer—Rufus Leach.

Constable and Collector.—Monroe Wardwell.

School Committee—Elizabeth Leach, Peleg G. Staples, S. D. Staples.

Clergymen—F. A. Bragdon, *Meth.;* vacant, *Baptist.*

Justices—W. Grindle, Jr., Peleg G. Staples, James Leach, Charles Leach, William G. Heath, *Quorum;* S. H. Perkins, *Trial.*

Merchants—Josiah Varnum, Horace Perkins, Phebe Osgood, Bowden & Grindle, J. Wesley Leach, *variety;* Mrs. Abbie Condon, *millinery.*

Manufacturers—Isaac B. Goodwin, John D. Gray, *boots and shoes;* James Smith, M. Littlefield, John Wardwell, Benj. Cushman, *coopers* (fish barrels); D. Grindle,

——— White, Grindle & Co., *staves;* W. S. Hutchins & Sons, Smith & Grindle, Penobscot Brick Co., *bricks;* Wardwell Bros., S. Bowden, Stephen Goodwin, *smiths;* John B. Lawrence, R. W. Devereux, *harnesses.*

ASSOCIATIONS—*I. O. G. T.*—Penobscot Bay, Saturday; *North*, Rechab, Saturday.

9.

A Chronological Table of Local Events—Including, also, the Names of the Reigning Monarchs
of England and France, and of the Governors
of the Commonwealth of the State.

1555. Penobscot bay described by Thevét, who refers
to an old French fort in this vicinity.—Reign of Queen
Mary, of England; and Henry II, of France.

1604. Champlain visits this region.— James I, of
England; Henry IV, of France.

1605. Penobscot river and bay explored by James
Rozier.

1611. Father Biàrd visits this region.—Louis XIII, of
France.

1613. Colony of St. Sauvier formed in France. Captain Argall, of Virginia, cast ashore here. First French
fort probably erected here about this time.

1614. Captain John Smith reports finding a settlement
here.

1620. Landing of the Pilgrims at Plymouth.

1626. Trading house established by Isaac Allerton,
under direction of Plymouth Colony of Massachusetts.—
Charles I, of England.

1632. Trading house surprised and rifled by the
French under Rosillon.

1635. Trading house attacked and occupied by Aulney.
Captain Girling and Miles Standish attempt to regain it.
Death of Razillai.

1643. La Tour attacks some of Aulney's men at a
mill. Louis XIV, of France. Confederation of New
England colonies.

1644. La Tour attacks and burns a farm house of
Aulney's. Articles of peace concluded between Aulney
and Endicott, Governor of New England.

1648. Friar Leo lays corner stone of Capuchin chapel.

1651. Death of Aulney. La Tour marries his widow.

50

1654. Pentagöet taken by the English. Oliver Cromwell *Protector*, of England.

1656. Patent of Acadia from Cromwell to La Tour, Temple and Crowne.

1662. Captain Thomas Bredion in command of Fort. Edward Naylor in command of " Negew," of Penobscot. Charles II, of England.

1665. Baron Castin stationed at Quebec. The Dutch surrendered New York the year before.

1667. Treaty of Breda. Pentagöet nominally returned to the French. Arrival of Baron Castin at Pentagöet.

1670. Fort Pentagöet surrendered by Colonel Temple to Grandfontaine.

1671. Sixty passengers, including four girls and one woman, arrive in the *l' Oranger*.

1673. Grandfontaine succeeded by M. Chambly. Population of Pentagöet (white), thirty-one.

1674. Fort Pentagöet taken by a Flemish corsair, under command of Captain Jurriaen Aernoots.

1676. Pentagöet taken by the Dutch.

1686. Seizure of some wines by Thomas Sharp, under orders of Palmer and West. James II, of England. Andros, Governor of New England.

1687. Castin notified by the Government of New England to surrender Pentagöet.

1688. Probable date of Castin's marriage to a daughter of Madockawando. Visit here of Sir Edmund Andros.

1689. Thomas Gyles tortured by the Indians on the heights of Bagaduce. Census of Pentagöet, (whites), four. William III, and Mary, of England.

1690. Sir William Phipps takes possession of the place. King William's War begins.

1692. Attempted abduction of the Baron Castin. The colonies of Plymouth and Massachusetts Bay united. Hanging for *witchcraft* in Massachusetts.

1693. Castin gives in his adhesion to the English. Population of Pentagöet (whites), fourteen.

1694. Sieur Villieu in command. Governor Phipps receives a deed of Pentagöet from Madockawando.

1697. Treaty of Ryswick. Conference between Commissioners and Indians. Death of Madockawando.

1698. One Caldin (or Alden) trades at Pentagöet.

1701. Baron Castin returns to France.—Stoughton, Lt. Governor.

1703. House of Anselm Castin plundered by the English.—Anne, of England. Queen Anne's war began the previous year. Joseph Dudley, Governor.

1704. A daughter of Baron Castin captured by Church. The Castin family remove to Canada.

1707. Anselm Castin takes part in engagement at Port Royal. Accompanies Levingstone to Canada, and saves his life. Marries Charlotte l'Amours. His two sisters marry Frenchmen.

1721. Anselm Castin captured and taken to Boston. —George, of England ; Louis XV, of France.

1722. Anselm goes to Béarne, France.

1725. Joseph Dabadis St. Castin is attacked by the master of an English vessel, and has an English lad taken from him. William Dummer, Lieut. Governor.

1760. Lincoln County established. George III, of England. Sir Francis Bernard, Governor.

1762. Twelve townships granted by the Provincial General Court to David Marsh and others.

1764. William Hutchings born October 6th,—one year before the STAMP ACT.

1776. Chart of Penobscot bay published by order of the English Parliament. Louis XVI, of France. DECLARATION OF INDEPENDENCE.

1779. The English take possession of Majabagaduce, and the Americans make an unsuccessful attempt to recapture it. Fort George and a number of batteries built.

1780. The bay frozen over from here to Camden. General Wadsworth and Major Burton escape from Fort George. John Hancock, Governor of Massachusetts.

1781. General McLean died at Halifax. The English attempt to plant a colony at this place, which they call "New Ireland."

1783. Charles Steward interred in what is now the cemetery of Castine. The first burial there. PEACE with England.

1784. The Tories are ordered by the Federalists to leave this region.

1785. James Bowdoin, Governor of Massachusetts. The General Court confirms the title of Plantation No. 3. Survey of the Plantation made by John Peters.

1787. The town of Penobscot incorporated February 23d. John Hancock, Governor of the Commonwealth.

1788. George Thatcher, first Representative of Penobscot to the General Court of Massachusetts. Constitution of the United States adopted.

1789. Penobscot made a Collection District.

1790. Hancock County established. Penobscot made the shire town.

1791. Reverend Isaac Case removed here from Thomaston. Vermont admitted to the Union.

1793. Some *stocks* erected near the Court House.— Samuel Adams, Lieut. Governor.

1794. Hancock Lodge F. & A. M., chartered. Samuel Adams, Governor.

1795. First tavern in Penobscot kept by Mr. Brewer.

1796. Jonathan Powers settled as first minister in Penobscot. Town of Castine incorporated and made the shire, February 10th. Isaac Parker elected as first Representative. Tennessee admitted to the Union.

1797. Public welcome given to Mr. Parker, on his return from General Court. Increase Sumner, Governor.

1798. Reverend William Mason ordained as first minister in Castine.

1799. Castine Journal published. Moses Gill, Lieut. Governor.

1800. Washington's death commemorated, February 23d. Ship *Hiram* captured by the French and re-captured. First Methodist sermon preached in Castine, by Reverend Joshua Taylor. Caleb Strong, Governor.

1804. Insurrection west of Belfast. Militia ordered to be in readiness for service.

1807. Castine Cemetery purchased. Reverend Jonathan Powers died November 8th. James Sullivan, Governor. EMBARGO.

1809. Fort Point Ferry Co., incorporated. The "Eagle" published. Christopher Gore, Governor. Embargo repealed.

1810. Castine Mechanic Association incorporated.— Elbridge Gerry, Governor.

1811. Ebenezer Ball hung.

1812. Declaration of WAR against England, June 18. Caleb Strong, Governor. Louisiana admitted to the Union.

1813. Memorial of town of Castine against the war.

1814. Castine made a Port of Entry. British occupy the town, dig a *canal* and throw up batteries. Treaty of

Peace, December 24, 1815. British troops evacuate Castine, April 28th. Town illuminated. United States troops take possession.

1816. Castine Bank established. John Brooks, Governor. Indiana admitted to the Union.

1817. Susup tried for the murder of Knight. Doctor Moses Adams tried for the murder of his wife. The town of Brooksville incorporated, June 13th. A part of Penobscot set off to Castine. Mississippi admitted to the Union.

1819. United States abandons Fort George. Alabama admitted to the Union.

1820. Trinitarian Church organized in Castine. Maine admitted to the Union. William King the first Governor of the State.

1824. Arrival of first steamboat at Castine. Albion K. Parris, Governor.

1825. Seth Elliot hung.

1826. First Congregational Society of Brooksville organized. Death of Adams and Jefferson, July 4.

1828. Rope-walk burned, March 6th. " Eastern American " published. Penobscot Steamboat Navigation Co. incorporated. Enoch Lincoln, Governor.

1830. Rope-walk again burned, October 7th. Jonathan G. Hunton, Governor.

1832. Orthodox Church dedicated, May 30th. Samuel E. Smith, Governor.

1833. Castine Poor-farm purchased.

1834. Resignation and departure from town of Reverend William Mason. Robert P. Dunlap, Governor.

1835. Steam Flour Mill erected in Castine.

1836. Town-house built in Penobscot.

1838. Courts removed to Ellsworth. Edward Kent, Governor.

1839. Hancock Guards organized. They go to the Aroostook. John Fairfield, Governor. Boundary troubles between Great Britain and the United States.

1840. Castine purchases the Court-house for a Town-house. Finding of the " Castine Coins." Edward Kent, Governor.

1842. Two houses burned in Castine, March 26th. John Fairfield, Governor.

1845. Bagaduce fire engine purchased. Hugh J. Anderson, Governor.

1846. Town-house built in Brooksville.

1849. Brooksville Manufacturing Co., and South Bay Meadow Dam Co. incorporated. John W. Dana, Governor.

1855. Castine Town Library established. Anson P. Morrill, Governor.

1857. Disastrous fire in Castine, March 1st. Joseph H. Williams, *Acting* Governor.

1858. Castine Light Infantry organized. Lot M. Morrill, Governor.

1861. War of Rebellion. Castine Light Infantry leave town for place of rendezvous, April 27th. Hancock Lodge F. & A. M. re-chartered. Israel Washburn, Jr., Governor.

1863. Finding of the "Copper Plate." Abner Coburn, Governor.

1866. William Hutchings died May 3d. Samuel Cony, Governor.

1867. State Normal School established in Castine. Castine Brick Co. incorporated. Joshua L. Chamberlain, Governor.

1868. Orthodox Church of Castine, re-dedicated.

1873. State Normal School-house dedicated May 22d. Hector Fire-engine purchased. Sidney Perham, Governor.

1874. Edward Griffith (Lord Egmont) died———.

GENERAL INDEX.

Abduction of Castin, attempted, 24, 278.
Abigail, the Schooner, 95.
Abridgement of Letter of Brouillan to Minister, 283—284.
Acadia, 18, 20, 250, 254.
Acadia, Governor of, 17, 19.
Account of Capture of Castine in 1814, 353—356.
Account of Sir John Moore's Skirmish, 336—337.
Account of Town against State, 163—165.
Account of what transpired in Canada in 1696, 279.
Act of Incorporation of Brooksville, 351.
Act of Incorporation of Castine, 343—345.
Act of Incorporation of Penobscot, 342—343.
Act of Surrender of Fort Pentagöet, 1670, 254—256.
Act to set off part of Penobscot to Castine, 352.
Active, the Brig, 38, 46, 304.
Acts of Legislature, &c., 64—66, 73, 76, 81, 140, 239, 342—345, 351, 352.
Adams, the Ship, 232, 353—355.
Adams & Nourse's Independent Chronicle, 340.
Agent for Proprietors, 67, 69.
Agency, 14.
Albany, the Sloop, 40, 291, 292, 296, 302, 323, 326, 327.
Algemogin, 55, 312.
Americans, the, 36—38, 46, 48.
American Attack, 41—44.
  cruisers and privateers, 36.
  dead, burial place of, 42.
  expedition, 37—40, 46.
  fleet, 38, 40, 45.
  landing-place, 41, 42, 192.
  officer, statement of an, 41.
  repulse, 45, 46.
  Ships, list of, 304.
Amirganganeque, the river, 275.
Amount of money donated in 1861, 189.
Amusements, 86—87.
Anecdotes, 25, 27, 48, 49—52, 109—110, 218.
Animals, 58—59.
Anniversaries, 87—88.
Appendix, 375—394.
Appropriations, 68—70, 72, 74, 76, 83, 84, 112, 115, 116, 121, 136, 138, 240, 241.

Area, 56.
Arrival of sick and wounded at Col. Brewer's, 331.
Arrivals of birds, fishes, &c., 60, 63.
Artillery Company, 86, 88, 89, 156, 162.
Associations, 89, 91.
Associated Refugees, the, 65.
Atlantic House, the, 91.
Attack by Captain Girling, 17.
  La Tour, 18, 19.
  the English, 25.
  the Dutch, 30.
  the French, 17.
  Flemish Corsairs, 30.
  Pirates, 260—262.
  on Bangor and Hampden, 355.
  on Belfast, 354.
  on Buckstown, 355.
Authors and Publishers, 92, 93, 129, 226.
Back Cove, the, 51, 158, 191.
Bagaduce Fire Engine, 83, 102.
  House, 92.
  Peninsula of, 55, 75, 111.
  River, course of, 55.
  Names of, 15.
Bakeman's Mountain, 185.
Ball, trial of, &c., 105.
Band, Lawrence's Cornet, 148.
Bangor, a half-shire town, 104.
  Packet the, 159.
Baptisms, Number of, 125.
Baptist Society of Brooksville, 133.
Batteries, 40—43, 158, 189—192, 228.
Battery,—East Point Battery, 190.
  Furieuse, 189.
  Gosselin, 190.
  Griffith, 191.
  Nautilus Island, 192.
  Penobscot, 189—190.
  Sherbrooke, 190.
  Wescott's, 190, 325.
  West Point, 191.
Betsey & Jane, the Schooner, 173.
Bill of sale, a, 171.
Biographical Sketches, 198—238.
Birds, 58.
Black Prince, the Ship, 38, 304.
Blande, the, 45, 307, 327.
Block House, the, 191.
  Point, 41.
Bluehill Mountain, 185.
Board of Health, the, 82.
  War, the State, 38.
Bombay, the Steamer, 228.
Boston Massacre, the, 158.

Boston Regiment, the, 158.
Boundaries, 55, 185.
Bounties, 78, 80, 84, 168, 241.
Breda, treaty of, 20, 251—252.
Brewer's visit to Lovell, 32.
    to McLean, 329, 331-332.
British, the, 20, 30, 31, 36, 37, 40, 41,
    43—48, 52, 77, 150, 155, 157—161,
    170, 173, 174, 177, 183, 188—193, 198,
    199, 219, 328.
Brooksville Manufacturing Company,
    180.
    Sailors in war of Rebellion,
      371.
    Soldiers in war of Rebellion,
      370—371.
    Town of, 13, 55—57, 133—
      136, 158, 162, 168, 169, 180, 181, 185,
      192, 199, 203, 209, 236, 239, 241, 242
      —243.
Buck's Harbor, 73, 135, 185.
Bulwark, the (man-of-war), 157.
Burhante, the Frigate. 157.
By-Laws of Castine, 83.
Calef's Journal of the Siege, 290—303.
Camilla, the, 45.
Camden, capture of the, 229, 231.
Cannon, 192—193, 255—256, 257—259,
    325, 355.
Capture and escape of Wadsworth and
    Burton, 49—52.
Captures by the English, 20, 37, 157—
    159, 353—356.
    of vessels, 44—46, 94—98, 259,
      327.
Capuchins—See Priests
Caribbee Islands, the, 250.
Carignan Salieres, regiment of, 21, 264.
Castin, character of Baron, 22—23.
    concerning sons of Baron, 287
      —289.
    family of, &c., 23, 24—28.
    house of 22.
    garden of 22, 256, 257.
    letters concerning, 264-265, 270
      273, 278, 279, 282, 284, 286,
      287.
    orchard of, 22, 256, 257.
      from, 268—270, 285.
      to, 263—264.
Castine,—Academy, 139—142.
    Bank, 177, 180.
    Brick Company, 180.
    "Coins," 194—195.
    Gazette, the, 92, 93.
    Healthfulness of, 29, 61—62,
      103—104, 219.
    House, the, 92.
    Journal, the, 93.
    Light Infantry, 166—168.
    Mechanic Association, 179.
    Soldiers in War of Rebel-
      lion, 366—369.
    Sailors in War of Rebellion,
      369.
    The Brig, 229, 232.

Castine,—the town of, 13, 55—59, 61,
    65, 70—84, 135—154, 162
    —168, 170—197, 209—212,
    214—229, 232—238, 244,
    245.
    the village of, 85—110, 185—
      197.
Cato, the Sloop, 159.
Cemetery, the, 76, 83, 108, 240.
Census, 32, 276.
Center Street, 142.
Chain Manufactory, 180.
Chapels, 111, 131, 186, 255, 257.
Charts of the Coast. 36, 37.
Chest found at 2d Narrows, 324—325.
Cholera, the, 82, 104.
    Infantum, 103.
Chronological Table, 389—394.
Churches, 64, 68, 69, 75, 89, 112—115, 118,
    120, 129—132.
Church Members, 117, 122, 125, 127.
    Organization, 116, 117, 122,
      126, 130—134.
Citizens Prominent in Nation, State,
    &c., 226—229.
Clergymen, 74, 76, 112, 116—133, 209—
    212.
Climate, 59—63.
Coasting in Street forbidden, 81.
Coast Survey, the U. S., 36.
Cobb House, the, 193.
Coffee House. Woodman's, 88, 91.
Collectors of Customs for Port of Cas-
    tine, 380.
Colony, the French, 16.
    the Plymouth, 16, 17.
Commerce, the Schooner, 99.
Commercial History, 170—183.
Commissioners, 30, 33, 76.
Committee of Public Safety, 78, 79.
Common, the, 80, 83.
Condition of Fort Pentagöet, 1670, 256
    —258.
Confession of Faith and Covenant, 117,
    122.
Congregational Society of Brooksville,
    133—134.
Congregational Society of Castine, 120,
    —126, 126—130.
Congregational Society of Penobscot,
    117—120.
Consumption, Pulmonary, 103.
Contest between Aulney and La Tour,
    18—19.
Copper Plate, the, 195—196.
Correspondence in the Seasons, 63.
Corporations, 179—180.
"Cotton's Head," 196.
Courts and Trials, 104—108.
Court House, 83, 88, 129.
    Martial, 46.
    of Guard, 254.
Courts removed to Ellsworth, 82.
Cove, Maple Juice 48.
    Mathews', 319.
Crescent, the, 93.

Crops, the, 57.
Cross, Island, 40, 292.
Croup, the, 103.
Crows, Bounty for, 78.
Crustaceans, 59.
Customs and Revenue, 177—178.
Deaths by Drowning, 98—99.
Deeds, 33, 115, 142, 145, 355, 356.
Deeds of Common Lot, 360—362.
  Meeting House Lot, 358—359.
  Peninsula School Lot, 356—358.
Defiance, the Sloop, 38, 46, 302, 304.
Delirium Tremens, 103.
Deposition of Edward Naylor, 249.
Descriptive Chapter, 55—63.
Description of Property, 181—182.
Deserters, 159.
Diligence, the Brig, 38, 304.
Diseases, 102—104.
Distances, 55, 314.
District Meetings, 138—146.
Documents relating to Ante-Revolutionary Period, 249—289.
Documents relating to Revolutionary Period, 290—337.
Documents relating to Municipal Period, 338—374.
Domestic Statuary, 196.
Doshen Shore, the, 132.
Draco, the Brig, 231.
Dragon, the (Man-of-war), 157, 161.
Dutch, Occupation by the, 30, 260.
  oven, 190.
Duties, 33, 174—176.
Dyce's Head, 41, 55, 56, 179, 201.
Dysentery, 103.
Eagle, the, 93.
Early Explorations, 14.
  Settlers, 198—209.
  Trade, 170—175.
Earthquakes, 18, 34, 61.
Eastern Advertiser, the, 93,
  American, the, 93.
East Point Battery, 190.
Eclipse of the Sun, 48.
Ecclesiastical Councils, 117—119, 122, 124, 126—129.
  History, 111—134.
Educational History, 135—154.
Elliott, trial of, &c., 107—108.
Ellis House, the, 193.
Embargo, the, 77—80.
Engine men, list of, 102.
English, the—See British.
  Fleet, the, 45, 157, 158.
Epilepsy, 103,
Epilogue to Comedy of Poor Gentleman, 86—87.
Epitaphs, 108—109.
Etchemins, land of the, 13.
Excommunications, 118, 119.
Expedition, American, 37—39.
  English, 159, 328.
  of Colonel Church, 34.

Extract from letter of Gov. Leverett, 260.
Extract from a letter of Sir Thomas Temple, 1668, 249—250.
Families in Castine in 1786, 346—350.
Fantine, the Brig, 160.
Farmhouse, Aulney's, 19.
Farms, 35, 57, 325.
Fauna, 58, 59.
Ferry, Castine and Brooksville, 75, 184, 240.
  Lymburner's, 75.
Fires, 19, 99—102.
Fire Companies, 99—102.
  Engines, 99—102,
Fishes, 59.
Fisheries, the 24, 30, 170, 183, 242, 258, 259, 265, 266, 279, 281, 282, 313.
Flemish Pirates, 30.
Flogging of Sailors, 326.
Flora, 57, 375—380.
Fly-boat, seizure of a, 32, 274.
Flying Horse, the, 30.
Fogs, 61.
Foreign Goods and Merchandise, 174.
Fort, Aulney's, 16, 19, 20, 22, 30—35, 186—187.
  Baron Castin's, 16, 19, 20, 22, 30—35, 186—187.
  Castine, 158, 191—192.
  George, 37, 40, 49, 158, 159, 161—162, 188—189, 205.
  Knox, 205.
  Madison, 158, 191—192.
  Pentagoet, 16, 19, 20, 22, 30—35, 186—187, 254, 256, 258, 266, 272, 280.
  Point, 34, 46, 218.
  Porter, 158, 191—192.
  Pownal, 35, 65, 218.
  Preble, 158, 191—192.
  The—at Thomaston, 157.
  The French, 16, 19, 20, 22, 30—35, 186—187, 311, 325.
  The United States, 158, 191, 192.
Fort Point Ferry Company, 179.
Freemasons, 89—90, 224, 225, 226, 227, 230.
French Documents, 250—254, 256—260, 260—266, 268—286.
  the, 14—19, 30—35, 155, 186—187, 311.
  Settlements, the abandonment, 35.
Frenchman's Farm, 325.
  Pond, 325.
Furs, trade in, 16, 33, 170, 279.
Galatea, the, 45.
Gazette of Maine, the, 92.
Genealogical Table, 198.
General and Social History of Castine, 85—110.
General Putnam, the Ship, 38.
  Washington, the Sloop, 100.

Geology of the Territory of Penobscot, &c., 57.
Ghost, a Drummer's, 324.
Gold Coin, a, 195.
Good Templars, the, 91.
Graduations from High School, 154.
Grants to Proprietors, terms of, 64.
Green Dragon, the, 92.
Greyhound, the, 45.
Guard House, 254, 256.
Hainey's Plantation, 43, 192, 202, 301.
Hamden, the Ship, 38, 45, 302, 304.
Hamourahiganiaques, the, 275.
Hancock Agricultural Society, 91.
　　　County, 104.
　　　Debating Club, 91.
　　　Fire Company, 100—102.
　　　Fire Engine, 100.
　　　Guards, 102, 163—166, 363, 364.
　　　Lodge, 88, 89—90.
　　　The Steamboat, 178, 180.
　　　The Vessel, 159.
Hardscrabble, 132, 185.
Hatch's Point, 43, 190.
Hazard, the Brig, 38, 304, 326.
Hearse, the 81, 82.
Hector, the Ship, 38, 304.
Height of the Peninsula, 42.
Henry's Point, 43, 192.
Heroism, Act of, 228.
Hero of Castine, the, 161.
Hiram, capture of the, 95—98.
Hooke House, the, 193—194.
Hope, the, 17.
Hornet, the Sloop, 231.
House Warmings, 87.
Hutchings' Narrative of the Siege, &c., 322—328.
Hunter, the Ship, 38, 45, 302, 304.
Illumination of Town, 87.
Importance of Pentagoet, 37.
Independence Day, 87.
Indians, the, 13, 16, 31, 33, 34, 263—265, 268, 270—273, 275—280, 282—284, 286.
Inhabitants, 19, 20, 47, 48, 67, 75, 142, 158, 159, 182, 242, 243.
Inflammation of the Lungs, 103.
Inns, 88, 91—92.
Insanity, 103.
Insects, 59
Installations, &c., 117, 119, 122, 128, 129.
Instructions to Grandfontaine, 1670, 250—254.
　　　Menneval, 272.
　　　Penobscot Committee, 66—67.
Insurance, 174.
Intemperance, 82, 87.
Inventory of Property, 181—182.
Islands, 14, 43, 45, 46, 48, 56, 185, 192, 263, 269, 324.
Isle Perceè, Castin forbidden to go to the, 269.
Itinerant Preachers, 112, 120.

Jane, the, 266.
Jarvis House, the, 92.
J. M. Tilden, the Schooner, 99.
Journal of Weather, 59—61, 61—63.
J. P. Whitney, the Ship, 232.
Keefe, Mrs., trial of, 108.
La Heve, 254.
Lakeman House, the, 91.
Landing Place of the Americans, 41, 42, 192.
　　　of the British, 328.
Lark, the Schooner, 94.
Latitude and Longitude, 55.
Lawrence Bay, 55.
Lawrence's Journal, 314—320.
　　　Orderly Book, 320—322.
Lawyers of Castine, &c., 212—217.
Lett, the Island of, 25.
Letters of Acceptance, 116, 121—122.
Letters from Colbert to Frontenac, 262, 263.
　　　from Perham to Wm. Williamson, 328—336.
　　　of Castin to Denonville, 1687, 268—270.
　　　of Denonville to the Minister, 1687, 270.
　　　of Denonville to the Minister, 1688, 274—275.
　　　of L'Auverjat to de la Chasse, 1728, 287—289.
　　　of Lovell to Saltonstall, 310—311.
Liberal Temperance Society, the, 91.
Light House, the, 179, 185.
List of Plants found in Castine and vicinity, 375—380.
　　　of Hancock Guards who went to the Aroostook, 363—364.
　　　of Soldiers in French and Indian War, 362.
　　　of Soldiers in War of Rebellion, 366—374.
　　　of Soldiers in the War of Revolution, 362.
　　　of Soldiers in the War of 1812, 363.
Liverpool Trader, the, 159, 229.
Lock-up, the, 84.
Londoner, the, 202.
Long Island, 45, 48.
Loyalists, the, 313.
Lucy, the, 159.
MacZachlar's Order, 337.
Madockawando, 14, 33, 275—276.
Magazine of Fort Pentagoet, 255, 257.
Mail and Mail carriers, 93—94, 241.
Maine—admitted to the Union, 81.
　　　Early Exploration of, 14.
　　　. Province (or District) of, 34.
　　　the Steamboat, 178.
Majabigaduce, 15, 313.
Majetaquados River, 353.
Mammalia, 58.
Mann House, the, 193, 325.
Manufacturers, 179—180.
Maps of the Coast, 36.
Marche-bagaduce, 15.

Mariners, 229—231.
Marriages, 23, 125.
Martinique, Island of, 31, 263.
Massachusetts—Commonwealth of, 18.
   33.
   General Court of, 33,
   37, 64, 65, 66.
   the Sloop, 35,
Matchebiguatus, 15.
Martinicus, Island of, 31.
Mayflower, the, 229.
Members of Congress from Castine,
   380.
   Governor's Council, 381.
Memoir concerning some wines, 266—
   267.
   of M. Talon, 258, 259, 259—260.
   Frontenac, 1674, 260—262.
   the Colony at Acadia, 273—
   274.
   upon the abduction of Castin,
   278.
Memoranda of things needed at Pesca-
   doué, 285.
Merchants, 172—175, 232, 238.
Methodist Society of Brooksville, 134.
Methodist Society of Castine, 130—132.
Methodist Society of Penobscot, 132.
Michigan, the Schooner, 90.
Militia at North Castine, 354, 355.
Military Celebrations, 87, 88, 167.
   Companies, 102, 155—168.
   History, 153—169.
   or Naval Officers, 17—21, 29,
   31, 32, 34—44, 225—227.
Mill, Aulney's, 18, 19, 325.
Minister's Lot, &c., 64, 72, 75, 118, 120,
   121.
Missionaries, 13, 33, 111, 112, 125.
Missouri, the Steam Frigate, 178.
Mollusks, 59.
Money at Interest, 182.
Monmouth, the Ship, 38, 301, 304.
Mortality, 102—104.
Mose-ka-chick, legend of, 16.
Mullett House, the, 193.
Municipal History of Brooksville, 239
   —241.
Municipal History of Castine, 73—84.
Municipal History of Penobscot, 64—
   72.
Munitions of War, 38, 158, 164, 165.
Murders, 99, 105—108.
Nancy, the Schooner, 178.
   the Sloop, 38.
Naskeag, 26.
Nations that have occupied Castine,
   155.
Natural Advantages of the territory,
   170.
   Scenery of the territory, 56,
   184—186.
Nautilus Island, 40—45, 56, 292, 294,
   326, 327.
Nautilus Island Battery, 192.
   the Sloop, 40, 43, 292, 298, 302,
   317, 323, 326.

Navigation, 178—179.
Necklace of Porcelain, 275.
Negew, 20, 249.
Negro Islands, 324.
New England, Governor of, 19.
   People, &c. of, 31.
New Ireland, 64—65.
New Plymouth, 250.
Newspapers, 92—93, 340.
Normal School, 146—148.
Northern Bay Pond, 185.
North, the Sloop, 40, 201, 292, 298, 299,
   302, 316, 323, 326.
Norumbegue, 14.
Note by the Minister, 266, 282.
Notification by the Inhabitants, 65, 201.
Nova Scotia, 20.
Oath of Allegiance, &c., 40, 329.
Old Houses, 193—194.
Oldtown, Town of, 14.
Oleron, Town of, 21, 25.
Oliver Spear, the Schooner, 159.
Oneida, sinking of the, 228.
Oranger, l' arrival of, 29.
Orcutt's Harbor, 56, 185.
Order of Judge at N. Y. to Thos.
   Sharp, 263.
Orders,—Military, 47, 156, 157, 159, 263,
   321, 322, 337.
   of P. O. Department, 160.
Ordinations—see Installations.
Ornamental Trees, 83.
Otter, the Ship, 45, 326.
   Rock, 326.
Oyster River, attack on 14.
Pallas, the 304.
Parishes, 115, 116.
Parish Meetings, 117.
Part First, 13.
   Second, 53.
   Third, 247—374.
Parish Records, 117, 118, 122—125, 126
   —134.
Penobscot Bay, 13, 14, 36, 55, 56, 61.
   Expedition, 328.
   Municipal History of 64—72.
   River 14, 16, 52, 55—56, 184,
   185, 229.
   Sailors in War of Rebellion,
   374.
   Soldiers in War of Rebellion,
   372—374.
   Steamboat Navigation Com-
   pany, 180.
   Taken by the Dutch, 260.
   Territory of, 311.
   Town of, 13, 38, 53, 55—57,
   64—75, 81, 91, 94, 99, 112,
   114, 116—118, 205, 206,
   211, 215, 224, 226, 243,
   244.
Pentagoet, 13—16, 18, 20, 26, 29, 31, 33,
   35, 73, 254—256—266.
   Attacked by Pirates, 260—
   262.
   Documents concerning, 250,
   253, 258—263, 265, 266.

Pentooskeag, 35.
Peruvian, the Sloop 157.
Petition to the President, 78.
Petitions, 46. 78, 114—115, 123—124, 140—141, 146, 166, 174.
Physicians, 104, 217—224.
Pierce's Pond, 185.
Pictu, the Schooner 157.
Pirates, 261.
Plan of Fort George, 188.
  "   Pentagoct, 187.
Plantation No. 3, 64—66, 76.
Plaster, a wonderful 221—222.
Platform near Fort Pentagöet, 255, 257.
Plymouth Colony, 16, 17, 33.
Poetical Quotations, 21, 23, 53, 77, 86—87, 105, 110, 118—119, 190, 236.
Polly, the Schooner 94.
Pomroy's vessel cut out by Little, 327.
Ponds, 55, 56, 185, 325.
Poor Farm, the 82.
Population, the 29, 32, 35, 65, 138, 181, 183, 242—244.
Port Rasoir, 276.
Postage, 93.
Postscript to Calef's Journal, 311—314.
Pountygouyet, 14.
Preamble to Const. of Soc. Lib. Ass. 90.
Presents to Madockawando, 276.
Price Current, 171, 177.
  of Beaver Skins, 170.
Priest, 13, 111, 112, 283.
Proclamation by McLean,&c., 304--307.
  by Lovell, 307---309.
Providence. the Sloop, 38, 304, 325, 326.
Provisions, 38, 47, 140, 171, 173, 174, 177.
Public Mourning, 88---89.
  Tomb, 83.
Puritans, the, 111.
Quarantine, 82, 104.
Quarries, the granite, 185, 242.
Queen Anne's War, 34.
Queen's Birthday, 87.
Radiates, 59.
Raisonnable, the, 45, 302.
Recruiting Office, 156.
Register of St. Jean Baptiste, 23, 286,
Relics, 194—197.
Religious matters, 68, 70, 111---134.
  services, 88, 89, 112, 117, 119, 125, 128, 132.
Remarks concerning Acadia, 275—276.
Removal of Courts, 69, 183.
Report of M. de Champigney, 278.
  M. Denonville, 264, 265.
  M. de Menneval, 272---273.
  M. Monseignat, 276---277.
Reports of Committees, &c., 67, 74-76, 113, 137, 143, 144, 151--153, 175.
  of Committee of Conference (Penobscot). 74---75.
  of Committee of Conference (Proprietors), 67--68.

Reports of Congress. Com. of Ways and Means, 174—176.
Representatives to Legislature, 381—382.
Reptiles, 59.
Resignations, &c., 119, 128, 129.
Resolve confirming grant to D. Marsh, &c., 338---341.
Resolve of town, &c., 66, 70, 76, 80---81, 112---113.
Revenge, the, 304.
Rheumatism, 103.
Rifleman, the Sloop, 353.
Right of Search, 77,
Rio de Gomez, the, 14.
  de las Gamas, the, 14.
  Grande, the, 14,
  Hermoso, the, 14.
  Santa Maria, the, 14.
Rising Virtue Lodge, 91.
Roads, the, 71, 75, 94, 184, 185, 239.
Robert Morris, the Ship, 232.
Rope-walk, the, 100, 177, 181.
Rose, the Frigate, 31.
Rozier, Cape, 16, 40, 56, 73, 135, 136, 139, 192, 198, 199 220, 242.
Roster of Artillery Company, 162.
  of Castine Light Infantry, 364—365.
  of Hancock Guards, 363—364.
Rover, the Sloop, 38.
Sachems, Indians, 14, 24, 30, 33.
Sagadahock, Governor of, 30.
St. Helena, the, 301, 325.
  James, the Ship, 232.
  Sebastian, the Ship, 254, 258.
Sally, the, 38, 178, 304.
Samuel Adams, the Ship, 232.
Samuel Noyes, the Schooner, 99.
Santillana, the, 325, 326.
Savages---See Indians.
Scalping of Indians, 34.
Schools, &c., 69, 71, 72, 75, 135---154.
  private, 146.
School---Agents, 137, 143.
  Appropriations, 136, 138, 139, 142, 143, 144, 240.
  Committee, 136, 137, 151, 153, 240.
  Diplomas, 153.
  Districts, 135---146, 149, 150.
  Fund, 137, 138.
  Houses, 135, 136, 139, 142, 145, 146, 148.
  Reports, 151—153.
  Statistics, 148---150.
  State Normal, 146, 148.
Screw Augur, 179.
Seal of Hancock Lodge, 90.
Scotch Pilot, a 17.
Sea-Men's Battery, 190.
Selectmen of Castine, 382-385.
Settlements, the abandoned, 35.
Settlers, the English, 16, 34, 35.
Sexton, duties of the, 121, 126.

Shells, 57.
Shipwrecks, 98—99.
Sidewalks, 83,
Siege of Penobscot, 37—47, 322—328.
Sky Rocket, the Ship 38, 46, 304.
Small Change, 48.
Small Pox, 104.
Smuggling, 174.
Snap Dragon, the privateer, 160.
Snow Storms, 60.
Social Library Ass., 83, 90.
Soil, the 57.
Sonconaquins, the 275.
Sons of Temperance, the, 91.
South Bay Meadow Dam Co., 180.
Specie, 48, 174, 194—195.
Spencer, the, 157.
Springbird, the Sloop, 38.
Stages, 94, 173.
State Guards, officers of Co. E., 369.
    Rights, doctrine of, 79.
    Senators, 381.
Steam Flour Mill, 180.
Stocks, the, 69.
Stores, 171, 172, 173.
Students from Bangor Seminary, 133.
Substance of a letter from Castin, 285.
Substance of letter from Subercase, 286.
Summary of Memoir upon Acadie, 271.
Summary of Memoir upon Canada, &c., 277--278.
Summary of letter from Castin, 270.
Summary of letter from Perrot, 265—266.
Summary of letter from Subercase, 286.
Summary of letter from Villieu, 281 —282.
Suppers, Public 86, 87.
Surrender of Pentagoet, 20, 254--256.
Survey, of town, 66.
Susup, trial of 106.
Sword, a white pine, 161.
Sylph, the Sloop, 157.
Synopsis of letter from Bonnaventure, 280--281.
Synopsis of letter from Palmer, 263—264.
Synopsis of letter from Villebon, 279 —280.
Tapley's Hill, 185.
Tarratines, the, 13, 30.
Teachers, 146--150.
Temperature, 60.
Temperance, 82, 84, 91, 103.
Tenedos, the Frigate, 157, 355.
Territorial divisions, 55--56, 311.
Theatre Royal, the, 86—87.
Tomb, a--presented to the Town, 83.
Topographical and Descriptive Chapter, 55--63.
Tories, 300, 303, 313, 325, 326, 328.
        treatment of the, by the Americans, 300, 303, 313.
Torture of Thomas Gyles, 32.
Town--Aid in 1861, 168.

Town—Bounties (1861, 1865), 168.
    Credits (1861, 1865), 168.
    Directories, 385—388.
    House, 72, 83, 143, 144, 240.
    Library, 83. 84, 90.
    Meetings, 66—84, 112—116, 135 —137, 239, 240.
Townships, 311—312.
Trade, 170—174.
Trading House. 16, 17.
Traditions, 15, 16, 109—110.
Trask's Rock, 41, 42, 192.
Treaties, 19, 20, 33, 251—252.
Treaty of Breda, 251—252.
Trees in bloom, &c., 63.
Trials, Criminal, 105, 108.
Trinitarian Church, 127—130.
Typhoid Fever, 103.
Tyrannicide, the Sloop, 38, 304.
Uniforms, finding of some, 324.
Union House, the, 92.
Unitarian Meeting House, the, 193.
        Society, the, 120—126.
Universalist   "   "   120—126.
Valuation of Town, 181—182.
Vegetables, early, 63.
Vengeance, the Ship, 38, 304.
Vessels captured, 26, 32, 45, 48, 94—98, 327.
Virginia, the, 45.
Visit of Governor Andros, 31.
    "   "   Pownal, 34—35.
Voters, law in regard to, 73.
Wadsworth Bay, 51, 191.
Walker's Pond, 185.
Walks and Drives, 184—186.
War between England and France, 20, 362.
    Aroostook, 163--165, 363--364.
    of 1812, 79, 80, 157--161, 173--176, 363.
    Rebellion, 84, 167—169.
    Revolution, 34—52, 201, 202, 204, 362.
    Queen Anne's, 34.
Warnings from Town, 69, 74.
Warren, the Frigate, 38, 295, 301, 304.
Washington, mourning for, 88.
Washingtonian Society, 91.
Water Street, 76.
Wealth, the Sloop, 178.
Wealth, Journal of, 59—63.
Welcome to Isaac Parker, 86.
Wescotts's Battery, 190, 325.
West Point Battery, 191.
Whaleboats sent to Boston, 43.
Whiting House, the, 193.
Wildcats, Bounty for, 80.
Windmill, the, 76, 189, 190.
Winds, prevailing, 61.
Wines, cargo of, 30, 31.
Winslow Farm, 19, 325.
Winthrop, the, 44.
Yankee Doodle, 303.
Yankee Doodle upset, 193.

WS - #0026 - 290120 - C0 - 229/152/22 - PB - 9781333682194